More praise for *Epic*

"*Epic Encounters* is a vitally important book because it warns against easy explanations of U.S. foreign policy." *Diplomatic History*

"Indeed epic, providing a wide-range and sophisticated analysis of the 'cultural logic' behind America's expansionist foreign policy." *Journal of American History*

"An excellent study of the influence and uses of American perceptions of the Middle East." *Middle East Journal*

"Subtle, skillful, and enormously informative." *Journal of American Studies*

"The fact that the arguments of *Epic Encounters* are far-reaching does not take away from their brilliance: McAlister's method is immensely adaptable, and the resulting histories are anything but monolithic." *Postcolonial Studies*

"Pathbreaking. . . . Essential reading for . . . understanding the multi-faceted role of the Middle East in American—and world—affairs." *American Jewish History*

"A must read. . . . McAlister clarifies the foundations of many crises." *Palestine Solidarity Review*

"An important addition to the literature on U.S. policy in the Middle East in the post–WW II period." *Choice*

"A model for those interested in the interconnections of culture and foreign policy in an era of globalization. An engrossing read." Amy Kaplan, author of *The Anarchy of Empire in the Making of U.S. Culture*

"Melani McAlister develops a 'post-orientalist' approach to U.S. culture, foreign policy, and identity. *Epic Encounters* is a blockbuster of a book." Robert Vitalis, author of *When Capitalists Collide: Business Conflict and the End of Empire in Egypt*

Epic Encounters

AMERICAN CROSSROADS

EDITED BY EARL LEWIS, GEORGE LIPSITZ,
PEGGY PASCOE, GEORGE SÁNCHEZ, AND DANA TAKAGI

Epic Encounters

Culture, Media, and U.S. Interests
in the Middle East since 1945

Updated Edition, with a Post-9/11 Chapter

MELANI McALISTER

University of California Press
BERKELEY   LOS ANGELES   LONDON

University of California Press
Berkeley and Los Angeles, California

University of California Press, Ltd.
London, England

©2001, 2005 by The Regents of the University of California

Library of Congress Cataloging-in-Publication Data

McAlister, Melani, 1962–
    Epic encounters : culture, media, and U.S. interests in the Middle East
since 1945 / Melani McAlister.—Updated ed., with a post 9/11 chapter.
        p.   cm.
    Includes bibliographical references and index.
    ISBN 0-520-24499-0 (pbk. : alk. paper)
        1. Middle East—Foreign relations—United States. 2. United States—
Foreign relations—Middle East. 3. Middle East—Foreign public opinion,
American. 4. Mass media and public opinion—United States. 5. United
States—Civilization—1945–   6. Public opinion—United States. I. Title.

DS63.2.U5M37 2005
327.56073'09'045—dc22   2004059882

Printed in the United States of America

11   10   09   08   07   06   05
10   9   8   7   6   5   4   3   2   1

The paper used in this publication meets the minimum requirements of
ANSI/NISO Z39.48-1992 (R 1997) (*Permanence of Paper*).

To my families—
the one I was born to, and the one that friends
and love have made.

And to Carl, who is friend and family and more.

Contents

Illustrations

Preface to the 2005 Edition

The first edition of *Epic Encounters* was published in September 2001. That coincidence of timing meant that it was inevitably read in light of the painful questions raised by the terrorist attacks on New York and Washington. The book's concerns—with U.S. cultural representations of the Middle East, U.S. foreign policy, the role of religion in politics, and the politics of race, among others—brought it into a broad conversation in the United States and elsewhere about history, culture, and September 11. I believe the particular contribution of this study was its analysis of the ways in which popular culture and foreign policy have intersected over the last fifty years, as diverse groups of Americans have fashioned for themselves a series of political and cultural understandings of the Middle East. Popular culture, public debates, the news media, and various social and religious movements forged a web of meanings that have often facilitated—and sometimes challenged—the expansion of U.S. power in the Middle East, even as they worked to construct a self-image for Americans of themselves as citizens of a benevolent world power.

There were, of course, many questions that the first edition of *Epic Encounters* did not address. It did not discuss Osama bin Laden, although he had been behind several attacks on U.S. installations in the 1990s. Nor did it analyze the history of U.S. involvement in Central Asia, which was outside its geographic focus. The book also could not answer, except indirectly, the question "Why do they hate us?" since this study was, and remains, an Americanist account of the construction of U.S. interests. I consider those interests to be both political and cultural, or rather, to be the product of the intersection of the two, which are intimately and inevitably intertwined. As I hope the book also shows, the construction of U.S. "interests" is not an uncontested process. There has never been a univocal

"American" response to the Middle East. Even when it seems as if one set of cultural norms or political voices dominates the landscape, there are critical alternatives, from both the right and the left, from different racial groups, and from a variety of religious perspectives.

When the first edition was published, scholarship on culture and U.S. foreign policy—on the culture of American power—was still in its infancy. Edward Said's *Orientalism* had been the touchstone for those of us who hoped to bring his subtle attention to the cultural politics of European empire to bear on U.S. history. Several generations of scholars and political activists around the world are in Said's debt, and with his death in the fall of 2003, we lost an intellectual voice of unprecedented integrity and insight. In the wake of *Orientalism*, several groundbreaking books within U.S. and postcolonial studies (by Ali Behdad, Amy Kaplan, Lisa Lowe, Emily Rosenberg, Gail Bederman, and others) appeared, but each still needed to make the argument, sometimes laboriously, that cultural products mattered to understanding the U.S. role in the world, and that cultural analysis could make a contribution to that understanding.

Since the mid-1990s, however, scholars from several different disciplines have heeded Amy Kaplan's call, which I discuss in the introduction to this book, to move beyond the traditional domestic focus of American Studies and the limits of political history within foreign policy studies, and to bring the cultural analysis of empire into the heart of U.S. studies. This more recent work includes fine books from within the field of American Studies by Laura Briggs, Matthew Jacobson, Christina Klein, Mary Renda, Shelley Streeby, and Mari Yoshihara, among others. At the same time, scholars trained in the history of U.S. foreign policy, including Christopher Jespersen, Kristin Hoganson, Michael Hunt, Akira Iriye, Andrew Rotter, and Penny von Eschen, to name only a few, have begun to turn their attention to the role of cultural images and popular culture in diplomatic history. These analyses have argued in different ways that the boundaries between the national and international spheres, between culture and politics, between state actors and transnational flows, and between cultural analysis and policy history are far more porous than previous academic divisions of labor have recognized.

In addition, an increased consciousness of the realities of globalization has provided the occasion for work that crosses the boundaries of nationally based studies to undertake genuinely transnational analyses. Although *Epic Encounters* takes U.S. culture and policy as its topic, it benefits enormously from work that insists that the boundaries of thought, culture, and identity do not stop at national borders. For me, the influence of the work of Paul Gilroy is preeminent here, but many others have reframed crucial questions about the borders of scholarly analysis, including Anthony Appadurai, Michael Denning, George Lipsitz, Mary Layoun, and Michael Hardt and Antonio Negri.

This updated edition of *Epic Encounters* includes a new chapter, "9/11 and After: Snapshots on the Road to Empire," which explores the complex weave of cultural and political narratives in the U.S. public sphere since September 11. My hope is that this chapter will show that the process of making meanings of the events of September 11 has required cultural work, and that no one response was inevitable, even as a range of political actors and cultural institutions converged in the process of making the war on terrorism into "common sense."

Any attempt to reckon with the world after September 11 is necessarily constrained by the force of current events: we are looking backward at something that is still rushing ahead. As a college teacher, however, I am cognizant of the fact that, by 2006, most of my freshmen students will have been thirteen years old on the day that begins this new chapter. My goal is to write a history that will help them better understand what are likely to be the defining political events of their lives.

I cannot claim that the analysis in the new chapter has the full benefit of scholarly distance, to the degree that such a thing can ever be achieved. While I have been as honest and as careful as I can in my assessment of what has happened in the few short years since the terrorist attacks on New York and Washington, I am aware that any study of recent and deeply traumatic events like terrorism and war will be profoundly marked by those wounds.

As this goes to press, struggles over the meaning of the memory of September 11—and the possibility of forgetting the suffering of others—are both very much alive. The third anniversary of September 11 has just been commemorated. Where the twin towers once stood in New York, the memorial to the victims is under construction. In Afghanistan, people have been freed from the repressive rule of the Taliban only to find themselves, everywhere outside of Kabul, ruled by local leaders only marginally less strict in their interpretations of Islam, and even less able to provide security to the populace, than the former government.

In Iraq, the United States has handed over power to an Iraqi government that is only officially sovereign. The U.S. occupation has not ended, and is not likely to end for some time. Violence has continued to escalate, and there and elsewhere in the world, terrorism remains a threat and a reality. Throughout the Middle East, anti-Americanism is at an all-time high, among even those people who might once have been at least ambivalent about U.S. intentions and actions. With the failures in Iraq, the question of what role the United States will play in the Middle East and elsewhere is uncertain. Certainly the ambitious and deadly dreams of the Bush administration have now been exposed as a costly imperial gamble. What price we will all pay is yet not fully reckoned.

Washington, D.C.
November 2004

Preface to the First Edition

In the summer of 1974, at the age of twelve, I left home for a weeklong stint at a Baptist summer camp for girls. Camp Mundo Vista was situated in a beautiful wooded area near Asheboro, North Carolina. Having grown up as a Southern Baptist in a small town nearby, I was enthusiastic about the camp routines: daily Bible study; games and contests, including Bible drills in the time-honored tradition; plus swimming, crafts, and campfires. Our camp counselors were sincere young women from area colleges. We girls were completely infatuated with them. At night, they taught us to sing the upbeat, modernized hymns that were the hallmark of Christian youth activities in the 1970s. At the time, we had no sense that we were part of a larger cultural movement, as what would become the New Christian Right began to emerge from a peculiar combination of fundamentalist energy and the Jesus People's attention to cultural relevance.

I loved Mundo Vista. I loved the sincere, devout, affectionate female world we made there. But what I remember best about that summer happened on the last day. We were holding final vespers in the outdoor chapel, early in the morning. The counselors had decided to end our week at camp with a parade of nations; some girls would march around the chapel area carrying the flags of many countries, then they would line up in pyramid formation along the stepped rows of the chapel. With the light coming over the trees, the flag carriers filed in and took their places as the rest of us sang hymns. When the formation was completed, I looked up at the place of honor at the top of the pyramid. To my surprise, I saw not one, but two, national flags. There was, as I had expected, the American flag. And beside it, another. Confused, I asked one of my counselors what that blue and white flag was, up there on equal footing with the familiar Stars and Stripes. She responded in a reverential tone that nonetheless seemed to state the obvious. That's the flag of Israel, she said. At that time, I didn't even know where Israel was, but from that moment on, I knew that it mattered and that, for Christians, it represented some aspect of our faith that the American flag alone could not signify.

Several years later, in my senior year of high school, I had a very different experience, but one that also involved an authority figure, my own enthusiasms, and a nation in the Middle East. It was sometime in the spring of 1980, several months after Islamic militants had taken American hostages at the U.S. embassy in Iran. I was not a particularly political teenager, but I had been captivated by the dramatic story of the hostages in the embassy as it played out on the nightly news. As the crisis wore on, I remember the increasing frustration, the genuine bafflement people felt: Iran was very far away; Islam was a mystery; and yet every night on the news we saw Iranians unleashing extraordinary, seemingly unmotivated anger toward Americans. Shortly after the embassy takeover, I took the first overtly political action of my life. Along with a few other friends, I began wearing a white armband to commemorate and support the hostages.

This expression of sympathy with the hostages was not a controversial act in my conservative small town. Almost no one, I imagine, would have disagreed with its intent. But those of us who did it signaled a certain kind of earnestness; we marked ourselves as sincere and civic-minded. Sometime during this armband-wearing period, our biology teacher took time out from class one day to give a short lecture on his views of how the United States should resolve the hostage crisis. "Simply tell the Iranians that they have twenty-four hours to release the hostages," he began. "If they don't, drop one nuclear bomb on one of their cities. Then give them another twenty-four hours; then drop another bomb." Pretty soon, he was sure, those hostages would be out of there. This hawkish little lecture in diplomacy was clearly addressed to those of us who wore white armbands; having signaled our concern, but not necessarily our militancy, we were invited to join in a solution that combined both. I remember feeling distressed. I was upset about the hostages and deeply interested in their fate, and I certainly didn't have a solution to the Iran crisis. But I knew, though I could barely articulate it, that bombing Iranian cities was not what I'd had in mind.

In each of these moments, a web of emotional investments, particular histories, and political assumptions intersected to establish the Middle East on my youthful cognitive map. In learning about the flag of Israel or the hostages in Iran, I assimilated not just bare facts but facts inevitably infused with cultural values. Finding out about the Middle East meant learning—at the same time and in ways that cannot be fully untangled—how to respond to it, emotionally and politically, and specifically as an American. In both these instances, my knowledge developed from particular interests, and those interests in turn emerged from a web of cultural, political, religious, and economic realities that I did not control, and often was not even cognizant of. Although my ideas about the Middle East have changed considerably, I remain a product of the formative power of those encounters.

At one level, neither of the two occasions I have described from my own life can fairly be described as "representative" of a larger American relationship with the Middle East. The particular history of a Southern Baptist girl in 1974, for example, would have been quite different than that of an elderly Jewish man in Chicago, though each of us might have been thinking about Israel. And the meanings of Iran in 1979 might vary considerably if one were an African American soldier training for a hostage rescue mission or a young Iranian student working in his dorm at a Midwestern college, while two other drunk students stood outside the door shouting anti-Iranian slogans.[1] Still, both these occasions in my life were exemplary in one sense: they indicated the complex forces at work in how people learn about the world that is not immediately around them.

This, then, is a book about the cultural politics of encounter. It focuses not on the literal, face-to-face meetings that happen in travel or at borders but on the ways in which people in the United States have encountered representations of the Middle East that helped to make it meaningful to them. Myriad types of representations—from news reports to films to popular novels—have influenced the understandings that Americans have had of their own "interests" in the region. Culture matters in these understandings because cultural productions played a significant role in making the Middle East meaningful to Americans, particularly after 1945, when the United States dramatically expanded its political, economic, and military power in the region. This book examines the links between cultural artifacts, national and religious identities, and U.S. foreign policy in the Middle East. In particular, it explores two factors, the presence of oil and the religious claims to the region, that have made the Middle East central to U.S. nationalist and expansionist discourses.

The book looks beyond the history of Jewish-American and Arab-American affiliations with the Middle East to explore the meanings of the region for audiences not generally assumed to have an obvious affinity with its inhabitants. In fact, American engagements went far beyond those particular connections. Popular, general-audience representations of the Middle East frequently mobilized its historical and religious significance to serve as narratives of American national identity. And these narratives were consistently concerned with issues of racial and gender differences within the nation. Representations of the Middle East simultaneously figured the United States in relation to its "outside" (in terms of international power relations) and in relation to its "inside" (the diverse and hierarchical construction of identities within the national borders). At the same time, conceptions of the Middle East have also been employed by communities and groups that are not the "general" audience (often presumed to be white) for popular culture or news accounts. In particular, some African Americans have been interested in the Middle East, less for reasons of "national interest" than for the ways in which its religious and cultural heritage might be used to assemble and understand black identity itself. Thus, representations of the Middle East have been and continue to be a site of struggle over both the nature of U.S. world power and the domestic politics of race, religion, and gender.

In exploring the cultural politics of U.S. interests in the Middle East, I have two primary interests of my own. The first is both historical and political: in the years since the Iran crisis, my early experiences have been translated into an intellectual commitment to analyze the terms under which the United States has constituted itself as a global superpower in the postwar era. The second is methodological, and yet also political: with few exceptions, the study of American opinion about the Middle East either has been narrowly framed through the analysis of various opinion surveys or has used a mass communications model to study negative stereotypes. In the process, scholarship has often assumed one of two stances—either American interests are determined by a rational choice model, in which policymakers and the public interact to determine the objective needs of the nation; or "interests" are determined by a manipulative ruling class that injects the population with stereotypes and propaganda in order to obtain its assent to official policies. A more subtle investigation will counter both these views, by suggesting that "interests" and "consent" are constructed in highly complex ways, and that multilayered investments in the Middle East have been mobilized by very different people living in the United States. In pursuing that track, I want to highlight the significance of cultural production in the making of interests. The politics of culture is important, not because politics is *only* culture (or because culture is *only* politics), but because where the two meet, political meanings are often made.

Marx once famously argued that people *do* make history, but not in circumstances of their own making.[2] While I do not believe that analysis alone can dismantle the relations of power whose history I partially explore here, I am convinced that, without that analysis, we are likely to misread the ways in which power works. Those of us who are struggling to imagine a different world need to understand much more about the circumstances not of our own making. The cultural history of interest is one place to begin.

Introduction
Middle East Interests

Every image of the past that is not recognized by the present as
one of its own concerns threatens to disappear irretrievably.
    —Walter Benjamin, "Theses on the Philosophy of History"

This is a book about the cultural and political encounters that have made the Middle East matter to Americans. It chronicles how, in the years between World War II and the turn of the twenty-first century, Americans engaged the Middle East, both literally and metaphorically, through its history as a sacred space and its continuing reality as a place of secular political conflict. Thus people in the United States encountered the Middle East through war, but also on television shows; as part of the struggle over oil, but also in debates over ancient history; in discussions of religion, and also in constructions of race. This study, therefore, aims to expand the idea of "encounters" to include those that happen across wide geographic spaces, among people who will never meet except through the medium of culture. And like so many encounters that cross social or spatial divides, those chronicled here were often ambivalent and confusing: they were fraught with tension and ripe with possibility.

Two factors, the presence of oil and the claim to religious origins, have been particularly important to these encounters. Oil has often seemed the most obvious of these two—an irreducible material interest. And for decades, beginning in the 1940s and intensifying after the oil crises of the 1970s, narratives of a U.S. "national interest in oil" were present in everything from presidential statements to car advertisements. By the time of the 1990–1991 Gulf War, when the United States led a multinational coalition to support Saudi Arabia and Kuwait against Iraq, oil was presumed, both by those who supported and those who opposed the war, to be a primary American interest and a motivation for U.S. policy.

Claims to the Middle East as a site of religious origin have wielded a similar power, if in a different register. Because Judaism, Islam, and Christianity each take the "Holy Land" as their site of origin, religious narratives helped forge the connection that allowed many people in the United States to see themselves as intimately involved with the Middle East, as having a legitimate cultural investment that was sometimes a profound political interest as well.

Yet to speak of oil or religious origins is not so much to explain the relationship as it is to open a question. The Middle East has loomed large as a U.S. interest, especially since 1945, when the United States became a global superpower and the Middle East became one of the most contested regions in the world. But neither the investment in oil nor the meaning of religious history was preordained; each emerged from a complex layering of cultural, religious, and social practices. Representations of the Middle East—of both the ancient religious sites and the modern nations—helped to make the area and its people meaningful within the cultural and political context in the United States. In other words, the Middle East was not immediately available as an American interest; instead, it had to be made "interesting." *Epic Encounters* examines the role of cultural products, from films to museum exhibits to television news, in establishing the parameters of U.S. national interests in the region. Cultural practices have been central to that project, and claims about oil and origins were the twin pillars of its logic.

With the Arab-Israeli conflict providing a constant context, official American policy toward the Middle East in the last fifty years has vacillated between two poles: distance, othering, and containment define the first; affiliation, appropriation, and co-optation constitute the second. In some moments and from some perspectives, particular nations in the region have appeared as partners and allies in the extension of U.S. power. Indeed, during the first decades after World War II, American encounters were most often posited as affiliations, and U.S. interests were framed in terms supportive of the region's anticolonial movements. At the same time, U.S. policymakers posited as an alternative to colonialism a "benevolent" American partnership, which included nearly unlimited U.S. access to Middle Eastern oil.

As policies and politics hardened in both the United States and the Middle East in the 1970s and 1980s, however, attention focused on the Middle East as a military and/or cultural threat requiring containment. Antiterrorism and the "oil threat" emerged as primary concerns in the media and in U.S. policy. Then, with the fall of the Soviet Union and the defeat of Iraq in the 1990–1991 Gulf War, the older theme of U.S. benevolent partnership reemerged, this time in the context of President H. W. Bush's New World Order. Of course, the poles of containment and co-optation often existed simultaneously, sometimes contesting each other, sometimes simply as two aspects of one policy.

If we want to understand the consistent involvement that Americans have had with the Middle East, however, we will need to go beyond, without discarding, this official story. In practice, Americans' encounters with the Middle East have included everything from pilgrimage to captivity to war, and they have been defined by emotions ranging from admiration to fear to disdain. To understand *these* multifaceted relationships, we must consider the politics of representation: that is, the negotiation of political and moral values, as well as the development of an often uneven and contested public understanding of history and its significance. I argue that cultural products such as films or novels contributed to thinking about both values and history in two ways. First, they helped to make the Middle East an acceptable area for the exercise of American power. Second, they played a role in representing the Middle East as a stage for the production of American identities—national, racial, and religious. The two aspects were interdependent, as the construction of identities and the staging of U.S. "interests" in the Middle East have often gone hand in hand.

While the idea of a U.S. national interest in oil has made the Middle East central to constructions of expansionist nationalism, the sense of religious connection (Muslim, Jewish, or Christian) has sometimes worked in the opposite direction, as a basis for racial solidarities or transnational affiliations. Ancient histories and biblical tales have influenced how people viewed contemporary Middle East politics, in part because events of the religious past have been, in Walter Benjamin's terms, "recognized by the present as one of its own concerns." Narratives of the Middle East's distinctive historical and moral significance have voiced convictions about community, identity, and faith. The fact that the Middle East was the site of religious origin stories has made it, perhaps more than anywhere else in the world, a powerful site of affiliation not only for Jews or Arabs but also for others—African American Muslims, fundamentalist Christians, and amateur Egyptologists, among them—who have claimed the spaces and histories of the Middle East as their own.

Religious, racial, and national narratives frame identity in distinct ways. The stories they tell and the loyalties they require often overlap, but just as often they are in profound, sometimes violent, conflict. This study examines both the official and the unofficial versions of the U.S. encounter with the Middle East. It explores the cultural logic that supported U.S. policies in the region, from the remarkable intersection of biblical epic films and cold war security doctrine in the 1950s to the news media and popular culture accounts that made Israel an icon of effective power after Vietnam. It also traces mobilizations of the Middle East that challenged or offered alternatives to that dominant logic, including African Americans' construction of an Islamic-influenced cultural radicalism in the 1960s, debates over the legacy of ancient Egypt in the 1970s, and Christian conservatives' focus on Israel as a major site for fundamentalist narratives of Armageddon.

I intend *Epic Encounters* to be a contribution to placing U.S. history and culture firmly within the overall history of colonial and postcolonial power. The analysis here aims to address what Amy Kaplan has defined as three major absences in scholarship on the United States: "the absence of culture from the history of U.S. imperialism; the absence of empire from the study of American culture; and the absence of the United States from the postcolonial study of imperialism."[1] To place the history of U.S. global power at the heart of the study of U.S. cultures, and to give culture a central place in an analysis of the production and reproduction of U.S. power, is to resist many of the categories that have separated the "domestic" from the "international." Identities, cultures, and conflicts have often refused to be contained within the borders of the nation-state; in the case of the extraordinary growth of U.S. hegemony in the last fifty years, the nation-state itself has expanded its influence and its reach so profoundly as to belie any attempts to understand "Americanness" outside of that expansion. This study highlights the fact that American global reach has significantly transformed the meanings of the nation itself; in the postwar period, the realities of U.S. power have structured the process of defining a rich variety of American—and "un-American"—identities.

MORAL GEOGRAPHIES AND THE CULTURAL FIELD

The postwar significance of the Middle East for Americans coalesced as part of the process of constructing a cognitive map suitable for the new "American Century." This mapping involved the development of what Michael Shapiro has called "moral geographies": cultural and political practices that work together to mark not only states but also regions, cultural groupings, and ethnic or racial territories. Moral geographies shape human understandings of the world ethically and politically as well as cognitively; they consist of "a set of silent ethical assertions" that mark connection and separation.[2] Different moral geographies can coexist and even compete; each represents a different type of imaginative affiliation linked to certain ideas about significant spaces.

In the following chapters, I trace the cultural history of the moral geographies that Americans have used to understand the Middle East. The book explores how Americans have claimed their "interests" in the Middle East, from Suez to Iran to the Persian Gulf, with the understanding that those interests have included not only oil or political influence but also religious affiliation, cultural power, and racial identity. I argue that the Middle East has been both strategically important and metaphorically central in the construction of U.S. global power. Yet the development of U.S. foreign policy in the postwar period was also intimately intertwined with the construction of a larger set of values and meanings that were not limited to, invented by, or entirely under the control of policymakers. Moral geographies of the Middle East have also provided alternatives to official policy, framing transnational affiliations and claims to racial or religious authority that challenged the cultural logic of American power. Moral geographies, in other words, are deeply historical and highly contested products, forged at the nexus of state power, cultural productions, and sedimented presumption.

In examining these diverse histories, I have operated from certain more general understandings of the connections between culture and politics. In particular, the arguments in the chapters that follow depend on two fundamental premises: first, that foreign policy has a significant cultural component; second, that understanding the political import of culture requires that we position cultural texts *in* history, as active producers of meaning, rather than assuming that they merely "reflect" or "reproduce" some preexisting social reality.

The first premise is simply that foreign policy itself is a meaning-making activity, and one that has helped to frame our ideas of nationhood and national interest. Foreign policy statements and government actions become part of a larger discourse through their relation to other kinds of representations, including news and television accounts of current events, but also novels, films, museum exhibits, and advertising. To examine these very different types of materials in relationship to one another is not to suggest that they are all the same thing, or that they work the same way. Obviously, the practice of foreign policymakers, be it the establishment of diplomatic contacts with a former guerrilla leader or an order to send troops into a foreign territory, works from a set of assumptions and constraints that differs from that of filmmakers or television news producers. But foreign policy is a semiotic activity, not only because it is articulated and transmitted through texts but also because the policies themselves construct meanings. By defending borders, making alliances, and establishing connections, foreign policy becomes a site for defining the nation and its interests.

In fact, the conduct of foreign policy plays a central role in the construction of nationalism, though foreign policy is only a part of that process. As Benedict Anderson has argued, "nation-ness is the most universally legitimate value in the political life of our time."[3] On Anderson's account, nationalism is a cultural development; nations are "imagined communities" rather than natural entities, and as such they depend on cultural articulation and construction. The cultural and political mapping of salient space plays an important role in constructing the political legitimacy of the nation as the site of political subjectivity and identity.[4] This mapping occurs in many sites, from the weather maps on the nightly news to the daily newspapers' lists of the nation's best-selling novels. The nation-state is modernity's most powerful moral geography. Today, in the postmodern era of globalization, the nation-state may be undergoing a fundamental challenge, as the following chapters discuss. Global capital, virtual communities, and mobile populations threaten both the nation's political legitimacy and its status as an identity container. Postmodernity has produced it own powerful geographic imaginations, in which territory, community, and political affiliations are being reconfigured. As of yet, however, nationalism remains a crucial part of world politics: people battle to achieve or maintain their nations, as in Palestine or among the Kurds in Iraq; to forge new ones out of disintegrating empires, as in Russia or the Balkans; or to maintain the power of their own nation against others, as in the Gulf War.

Foreign policy is one of the ways in which nations speak for themselves; it defines not only the boundaries of the nation but also its character, its interests, its allies, and its enemies. The affiliations and disaffiliations that the discourse of foreign policy seeks to construct are never permanent, however. They are always unstable and subject to change. Alliances shift or "national interests" alter, expanding or contracting in an unstable global environment. The nation finds itself threatened by the specter of doubt or dissent within, and by the very real possibility of challenge by those outside its boundaries. In fact, this sense of danger and instability in foreign policy discourse is central to its success. As David Campbell has argued: "Ironically, . . . the inability of the state project of [ensuring] security to succeed is the guarantor of the state's continued success as a compelling identity. The constant articulation of danger through foreign policy is thus not a threat to the state's identity or existence; it is its condition of possibility."[5] The continuing sense of threat provides support for the power of the state, but it also provides the groundwork for securing "the nation" as a cultural and social entity. The "imagined community" of the nation finds continuing rearticulation in the rhetoric of danger.

The second premise of this study is that culture is an active part of constructing the narratives that help policy make sense in a given moment. The historical and political significance of cultural texts lies in the fact that they are integral aspects of both history and politics. The task of any study of culture, then, is to reconstruct the larger world in which a given cultural form was made meaningful. This means, first and foremost, that a cultural product, be it a novel or a painting or a film, cannot be understood solely through "immanent" analyses that stay within the text itself. An examination of the formal qualities or narrative strategy of a single text, be it Amy Tan's *The Joy Luck Club* or Sylvester Stallone's *Rambo*, is often the first step toward understanding how culture works, but it is *only* a first step, if one wants to explain how and why that product was meaningful in its time. Textual analysis, standing alone, tends toward what the French sociologist Pierre Bourdieu calls a "derealization" of cultural works: "Stripped of everything which attached them to the most concrete debates of their time ... they are impoverished and transformed in the direction of intellectualism or an empty humanism."[6] Bourdieu also argues, however, that many cultural critics make the opposite error: determined to connect "culture" to "society," they assume that "society" exists somewhere outside of "art," which is then presumed to "reflect" society, in some direct or indirect way. Bourdieu calls this presumption "the short circuit effect," and warns against attempts to interpret a cultural text as a straightforward expression of an outside reality, be it the author's biography (Amy Tan writes about Chinese mothers because of her childhood experience with her Chinese mother) or the world of politics (*Rambo* as an expression of men's fear of feminism).[7] Such "external" analyses are inevitably limited, in that they assume a direct one-to-one correlation between an artistic product and the interests or situation of the artist (whether the artist is viewed in terms of her individual biography or as a "representative" of some larger social group). Such "imputations of spiritual inheritance" fail to acknowledge the specific rules and conditions of what Bourdieu calls "the field." In the case of the cultural field, those conditions would include the meanings of "art" in a given moment, how different types of art relate to each other, the rules for what counts as "good" or even "profitable" in the world of culture, and the economic situation of cultural producers.

The cultural field exists in continuous relationship with the other fields in the larger social system, and this relationship is far more complicated than direct reflection. If we want to argue that cultural products are politically significant—and they often are—we simply cannot make the assumption, implicitly or explicitly, that movie producers or struggling novelists are producing (or reproducing) the ideologies needed by the ruling political elite, which is itself often quite divided. Instead, we have to "explain the coincidence" that brings specific cultural products into conversation with specific political discourses.[8] Even if a movie explicitly attempts to justify a political position (as the 1956 version of *The Ten Commandments* tried to do), the impact of its statement depends on the overall situation, including artistic questions, such as how seriously the film is reviewed; the issue of whether or not audiences interpret the film as a political statement (which is then related to the history of film viewing and the status of the particular film genre, among other things); and the larger political question of whether the statement being made speaks in harmony with, or in opposition to, other important political positions at the time. The apparent "statement" of a text, then, is not the same as its historically constituted meaning.

A central thesis of this book is that cultural productions help make meanings by their historical association with other types of meaning-making activity, from the actions of state policymakers to the marketing of Bible prophecy. This suggests that we might ask less about "what texts mean"— with the implication that there is a hidden or allegorical code to their secret meaning—and more about how the texts participate in a field, and then in a set of fields, and thus in a social and political world. By focusing on the intertextuality, the ecumenicalism, and the common logic of diverse representations, I indicate the ways in which the production of a discourse about the Middle East comes to be understood as authoritative, as "common sense." This production of knowledge occurs not through the conspiracy or conscious collaboration of individuals but through the internal logics of cultural practices, intersecting with the entirely interested activity of social agents. Instead of focusing on the problem of negative stereotypes of people in the Middle East (and there have been many) or on the role of the media in directing public opinion, this model focuses on the cultural work that happens at the messy intersections. We can begin to see how certain meanings can become naturalized by repetition, as well as the ways that different sets of texts, with their own interests and affiliations, come to overlap, to reinforce and revise one another toward an end that is neither entirely planned nor entirely coincidental. If the end product is the successful construction of a discourse of expansionist nationalism, what we examine here is not a conspiracy, nor a functionalist set of representations in the service of power, but a process of convergence, in which historical events, overlapping representations, and diverse vested interests come together in a powerful and productive, if historically contingent, accord.

ORIENTALISM AND BEYOND

Since the publication of Edward Said's groundbreaking analysis in 1978, the term "Orientalism" has become shorthand for exoticizing and racist representations of "the East." Orientalism is a certain type of lens; through it, Europeans and Americans have "seen" an Orient that is the stuff of children's books and popular movies: a world of harems and magic lamps, mystery and decadence, irrationality and backwardness. Said's *Orientalism* provided a detailed analysis of the history of such images, as well as a language for understanding how the cognitive mapping of spaces (East versus West) and the stereotyping of peoples are both intimately connected with the processes of economics, politics, and state power.[9] Since its publication, *Orientalism* has served as the inspiration and the model for a flowering of academic and political analyses of colonial and postcolonial power. The scholarship that has productively used Said's framework is so extensive that a comprehensive list is impossible; it includes a broad range of studies of European or American encounters with Asia, the Middle East, and Africa.[10] Precisely because it has been and continues to be so valuable, scholars who want to suggest other models, as I do, must first account for the limits of the Orientalist framework.

In Said's classic formulation, Orientalism is a large and multifaceted discourse, a "textual relation," that became central to European self-representation in the eighteenth and nineteenth centuries. Focusing on representations of the Middle East, Said argues that Orientalism distributed a certain kind of geopolitical awareness—"the world is made up of two unequal halves, Occident and Orient"—through various aesthetic, scholarly, and historical texts.[11] Orientalism operates on a binary logic: Orient versus Occident, Europeans versus Others, Us versus Them. These binaries parallel and draw heavily upon the logic of gender construction: the Oriental is "feminized," thus constructed as mysterious, infinitely sexual and tied to the body, irrational, and inclined toward despotism; the European is "masculinized," and posited as civilized, restrained, rational, and capable of democratic self-rule. Orientalism, Said suggests, is preeminently a "citational" discourse, in which authors or artists draw heavily on previous representations, using travel accounts or paintings as if they were their own experiences (some haven't even gone to the "Orient" at all). In this oddly self-enclosed network of authorities, citing other Western writers or an earlier generation of images is the primary proof of "authenticity" and accuracy.

Orientalism provided one primary grid through which Europeans in the eighteenth and nineteenth centuries made sense of their imperial project. During the heyday of European power, imperialist representations were part and parcel of an enormously effective practice of world rule. In 1914, at the high point of classical imperialism, Europe held most of the world outside the Americas as colonies, protectorates, dominions, dependencies, and commonwealths.[12] The moral logic of imperialism required that Europeans form what Etienne Balibar has described as an "imperialist superiority complex," through which the project of imperialist expansion was able to transform itself, in the minds of its practitioners, "from a mere enterprise of conquest into an enterprise of universal domination, the founding of a 'civilization.' "[13]

Orientalism was politically important because it had an extraordinary identity-forging power at the moment that modern identities were coming into being. The Orientalist concept of the "East" played a significant role in constructing European identity, in defining an "us" that was opposed to "them," and in constructing the "modern" and rational self as opposed to the primitive and irrational Orient. For example, anti-Islamic representations were frequent, even (or especially) among experts on Islam, who often presented Islam as an "imposter" religion that bred both fanaticism and corruption. Islam was the "bad" alternative to Christianity, just as the "Orient" was the backward and decadent (if also strangely appealing) half of the East-West binary.[14] For Said, Orientalist scholarship, art, and travel narratives were intimately entangled with the military, economic, and political strategies of European states. By offering Europeans the certainty that they already knew what there was to know of the East, representations became practices: they laid the foundation for imperial rule.

Recognizing the usefulness of Said's intervention, scholars in recent years have also challenged and revised important aspects of his argument. Several have pointed out that Orientalism in colonialist Britain and France was never as internally unified or as stable as Said argues. Instead, it existed as "an uneven matrix" that was taken up differently in different moments.[15] In addition, critics have argued, Said seems to suggest that the best alternative to Orientalism is simple humanism. If only Europeans had been able to see Arabs in terms of their "ordinary human reality," history might have been very different. This vision of an unadorned human encounter ignores our inevitable imbrication in the political and moral assumptions of our historical moment. There are no "empty humans" who can face each other outside of history or cultural values.[16]

In addition to these general concerns, other problems arise when the Orientalism paradigm is brought to bear on the study of U.S., as opposed to European, encounters with the Middle East.[17] As I discuss in detail later, nineteenth- and early twentieth-century popular culture and political narratives frequently did mobilize the Orientalist fascination with exoticism, sexuality, and decadence. Like their European precedents, American cultural texts often seemed to take a mix-and-match approach to representing the "East," making of China and Saudi Arabia and India and Morocco a single world deemed "Oriental." At other times, however, the Middle East emerged as a distinct entity, separated out from the logic of a generalized "East." Quite often, too, different nations in the Middle East were distinguished from each other: not only Israel as opposed to the Arab states but also Egypt versus Saudi Arabia, or Jordan as distinct from Libya. The bulk of this book, in fact, tells the story of *post*-Orientalist representation in the United States, that is, the period after World War II when American power worked very hard to fracture the old European logic and to install new frameworks.

Two factors in particular have complicated Orientalism in the United States. First, the Orientalist paradigm fundamentally depends on the presumption that the "us" of the West is, or is perceived to be, a homogeneous entity. Said argues that Orientalist discourse represented the European subject as (racially, ethnically, and culturally) unified, and thus clearly distinct from the peoples of the East. However, U.S. representations of the Middle East, especially those since 1945, have been consistently obsessed with the problem of domestic diversity. Narratives of nationality are perhaps always more concerned with internal difference than Said acknowledges,[18] but in the United States in particular, racial distinctions within the nation were a structuring concern. As I discuss later, the racial status of Middle East immigrants has been part of the dynamic, but only a relatively small part. More often, the politics of black-white relations have influenced the meaning given to different parts of the Middle East—be it Israel or Mecca or Egypt. African Americans, both civil rights activists and black nationalists, have claimed certain histories as their own, and these claims have challenged, complicated, and conspired with dominant discourses that have represented the region as a resource for American nationalism and a site for the expansion of U.S. power. Thus in the postwar period, the us-them dichotomies of Orientalism have been fractured by the reality of a multiracial nation, even if that reality was recognized only in its disavowal. In other words, there was never a simple, racial "us" in America, even when, as was generally the case, whiteness was privileged in discourses of Americanness.

A second problem is *Orientalism*'s neat mapping of the "West" as masculine and the "East" as feminine. In many ways, Said's argument that the East was linked to femaleness (and thus to irrationality, sexuality, and lack of capacity for democracy) makes sense. For more than two decades, political theorists and women's historians have carefully dissected the division of public and private spheres, analyzing the ways in which industrializing nations began to separate out certain spaces designated as "private"—those signified by home and hearth—and then to gender those spaces "female." Women's association with the private world in the eighteenth and nineteenth centuries was supposed to provide a haven of tranquillity for men, an escape from their stresses in the industrializing, competitive, market-driven "public." But it also worked to ensure women's unequal access to citizenship, voting, and political life.[19] Similarly, Said and others have suggested that the representations of "Orientals" as feminized (sensual, domestic, nonrational) and the West as masculinized (rational, intellectual, and public) served to legitimate the exclusion of colonized peoples from democratic rights. In this model, citizenship and nationality were necessarily represented as white and male.

Important as such analyses are, however, they do not adequately account for the ways in which "the feminine" has been mobilized to represent nationality, citizenship, and the public. Certainly in the postwar United States, the "universal" subject of the nation-state is *not* imagined simply as male, and citizenship is not simply a matter of *public* life. Instead, the discourse of Americanness has insisted on the centrality of properly ordered private life—inevitably understood as the heterosexual couple and the family—to the public legitimacy of the nation. Women are central figures in this project of representing the nation through the figure of a family. And like the nation itself in foreign policy discourse, the family is imagined as continuously imperiled, under threat from within and without. Thus the "private" world of the marriage, home, and family is necessary to constructing the "inside" of the national community; that "inside" is then mobilized to represent the nation itself in its public mode.[20]

The complexities of race and gender also highlight the fact that, too often, scholars and activists have used the term "Orientalism" to characterize everything from *Madame Butterfly* to television news accounts of the Viet Cong. Yet not all stereotypes, even those of Asians or Arabs, are Orientalist; they might be racist, imperialist, and exoticizing without engaging in the particular logic of Orientalism: binary, feminizing, and citational. When "Orientalism" is used to describe every Western image of every part of the Eastern half of the world, the definition has become too flexible for its own good. Despite these theoretical and historical limitations to the Orientalism framework, however, it remains a useful and evocative characterization of a certain European and American "way of seeing."[21] Rather than endlessly fracturing the definition of Orientalism, or throwing it out altogether, I believe we need to be careful to distinguish when Orientalism *is* at work, and when it is not. If Orientalism does not adequately explain all the diverse ways that Americans came to represent the Middle East, it nonetheless does describe one important version of that encounter. If it was never the *only* manifestation of public fascination with the region, it also never disappeared as a way of comprehending and ultimately domesticating the Middle East for American consumption. Putting Orientalism in its place, then, becomes part of the analytical and historical task at hand.

THE MIDDLE EAST AS "HOLY LAND"

To understand the post-Orientalist logic of the years since World War II, we need to examine in more detail the distinctly Orientalist representations that dominated U.S. encounters with the Middle East in the nineteenth and early twentieth centuries. For most of the nineteenth century, Americans' primary interest in the Middle East was the "Holy Land." Although nineteenth-century maps marked all land to the east of Europe as the "Orient," most people nonetheless distinguished the Near East from areas farther east, such as China and Japan. The Near East, particularly the land of Palestine (which had been ruled by the Ottoman Empire since 1517), was understood as inferior and backward, but also as old, exotic, and connected to the West through Jewish and Christian history.[22]

American travelers began to visit Palestine in earnest in the 1830s, and for those with means travel became quite common after the Civil War. Under the Ottoman Turks, the area was relatively sparsely populated (forty thousand in 1890, when the population of New York City was approximately 3 million), primarily by Muslim Arabs but with some small number of Eastern Christians and Jews. Most American visitors went to Palestine for religious reasons. By visiting the places mentioned in the Bible, they intended to see for themselves the proofs of the authenticity of Christian narratives, and to get a better picture of the life and ministry of Jesus.[23] The biblical scholars who began writing and publishing in the 1830s shared the same presumption: in the face of revisionist "higher criticism" of the Bible and challenges to its historical accuracy, the exploration and study of the lands and historical geography of Palestine and other biblical sites would unearth proofs of the Bible's literal truths.[24]

The vast majority of American tourists were Protestant Christians, who saw themselves as having a particularly meaningful connection to the region on the strength of their religious beliefs. This claim to the Holy Land was inseparable from the popular self-perception that Americans were not only the literal inheritors of God's favor but also better versed in the Bible, and thus more intimately connected with its ancient geographies, than Europeans. Historians have noted the extraordinary inculcation of topographical knowledge via church Bible studies in the nineteenth century. The Methodist Episcopal Church, for example, encouraged young students to take up fantasy existence in the Holy Land and to write letters home to their families from their imaginary tours. For visitors, then, the Holy Land was often linked to nostalgia for childhood and the Bible lessons learned at home. As one Episcopal bishop wrote of his 1874 trip to Palestine:

> This is the first country where I have felt at home.... As I try to
> clear away the mists, bring forward the distant, and make present
> what seems prehistoric, I find myself at my mother's side and my
> early childhood renewed. Now I see why this strange country
> seems natural. Its customs, sights, sounds, and localities were those
> I lived among in that early time, as shown to me by pictures,
> explained by word, and funded as part of my undying property.[25]

Most travelers also believed that the contemporary residents of Palestine would provide a living illustration of biblical customs, since they presumed that the Arabs would have changed little in the nineteen centuries since the time of Jesus.[26] Facing their Arab contemporaries, they posited them as people untouched by time, living in a continuing "prehistory." Rather than assuming that one moment in time might include many different ways of life, they characterized geographic and cultural difference across space as a historical difference across time. Anne McClintock has described this presumption as the imperial trope of "anachronistic space"—that is, space imagined as "prehistoric, atavistic, and irrational, inherently out of place in the historical time of modernity."[27] Within this representation of a contemporary place as an example of the "living past" was imbedded the assumption that in time the forces of "modernity"—meaning Europeans and Americans—would inevitably sweep it aside. Thus even though Americans had a specific interest in the Holy Land that differed from that of Europeans, they produced images of it that were decidedly Orientalist in character, exhibiting the same kind of exoticism and fascination with decadence as Europeans did, and presuming that white Christians were in possession of a rationality, historical consciousness, and purposiveness that was denied to the Oriental.

The audience for reports and descriptions of the Holy Land seemed insatiable. Travelogues from Holy Land trips were extremely popular in the United States from the 1830s onward. By the 1850s, literally hundreds of travelers were publishing accounts of their trips, and a surprising number of these were frequently reprinted. William Cowper Prime's *Tent Life in the Holy Land* (1857) was one widely read and conventionally pious version; the painter Bayard Taylor's popular 1855 narrative was decidedly more secular. The missionary William Thomson's *The Land and the Book* (1858) became a best-seller and eventually a classic that remained in print well into the twentieth century. Sold by traveling salesmen and given away at church contests, these reports told of the enthusiasms experienced by emotional travelers on seeing Jerusalem and recounted colorful (and sometimes hostile) encounters with the natives of the area. Many expressed shock at what they described as the "filthy" and degenerate state of the local population, who, after all, were supposed to be serving as exemplars of biblical customs. Combining adventure narratives and religious education, the guides transcended the divide between Protestant piety and nineteenth-century popular culture.[28]

Both the sanctimoniousness and the racism of the travel guides made them easy targets for the young journalist Samuel Clemens. Embarking on his own trip in 1866, Clemens reported on his tour in a series of letters for a California newspaper; these were then edited and published as Mark Twain's first commercially successful book, *Innocents Abroad; or, The New Pilgrims' Progress* (1869). Clemens frequently contrasted his own sardonic reactions to the more conventional pieties of his predecessors. Noticing that he felt no particular desire to weep when he first saw Jerusalem, for example, Clemens compared himself to travel writer William Cowper Prime: "[Prime] went through this peaceful land with one hand forever on his revolver, and the other on his pocket-handkerchief. Always, when he was not on the point of crying over a holy place, he was on the point of killing an Arab."[29]

Some Protestant Christians concerned themselves with the Holy Land less because of its place in history than because of its future in biblical prophecy. Beginning in the 1870s, American evangelist Dwight Moody traveled across the United States preaching his version of "premillennialist dispensationalism," a method of biblical interpretation based on the belief that God had divided time into distinct periods and that each period, or dispensation, had its own characteristics, scriptural exhortations, and distinct method of salvation. Many of Moody's views were codified and popularized in the 1909 Scofield Reference Bible, which became the standard version for many evangelicals.[30] The Holy Land was central to this system, since dispensationalism asserted that God had a distinct plan for the Jews at the end of time; this plan included the literal restoration of Jews to the land of Palestine and the rebuilding of the ancient Temple in Jerusalem. Moody taught that Christ's return was imminent and encouraged his audiences to read the "signs of the times." Moody's teachings challenged the emergence of both Social Gospel perfectionism and liberal modernism by arguing for a return to the Bible, insisting that the millennial era would be inaugurated by God, not by the good works of humankind. Moody became the best-known leader of an evangelical revival that swept the nation in the late nineteenth century; he went on to found the Moody Bible Institute, which became one of the most important training grounds for evangelical pastors and trained laypersons.[31] In their fascination with the Holy Land as the once and future site of God's action in history, these early twentieth-century evangelicals were to become the spiritual inspiration for the fundamental-ist turn to Israel nearly a century later, in the 1970s and 1980s.

Nineteenth-century Christians of all stripes were also captivated by the physical layout of Palestine. Art historian John Davis has described the re-markable proliferation of Holy Land spectacles after 1840, as changing modes of artistic production provided new ways for audiences to capture the experience of travel, and thus to share in the religious and moral de-velopment thought to accompany a journey abroad. In the 1840s and 1850s, audiences flocked to view the large-scale painted panoramas that toured the country. Panoramas significantly extended the viewing experience over that offered by single canvases by giving an all-around view from a particular spot, say a hill overlooking Jerusalem. They thus positioned the spectator—in Mary Louise Pratt's phrase—as "monarch of all I survey."[32] While land-scapes of the American West were popular subjects for panorama, "realis-tic" views of the terrain and sights of the Holy Land predominated. In the 1850s John Banvard added a new dimension, by slowly unscrolling his giant canvas (between twenty-five and forty-eight feet tall) to give the illusion of movement. Already famous for his "three-mile-long" painting of the Mis-sissippi, Banvard created a Holy Land canvas that walked the audience through most of Palestine. Visitors were usually invited to buy pamphlets that described the views in detail. Banvard then presented the panorama as a performance, narrating the scenes as he slowly scrolled the panorama, and spectators became virtual tourists on a pilgrimage to the major religious sights of the Holy Land.[33]

The Holy Land panoramas were just one dimension of an emerging nineteenth-century fascination with vision and spectacle. Although obser-vation and cataloging had certainly been an aspect of modernity and the scientific revolution since the seventeenth century, a more specific interest in viewing and exhibition came to infuse European and American culture in the 1800s. Timothy Mitchell has described the surprise registered by Egyptian visitors to Paris in the 1890s when they encountered this Euro-pean obsession with "rendering things up to be viewed." Whether one was visiting world's fairs or scientific expositions, walking down the busy city streets, or entering the new entertainments that dotted every corner, Eu-rope and America seemed to be places where one was "continually pressed into service as a spectator," invited to see the innumerable exhibitions and displays that represented the rest of the world for Europeans and Ameri-cans. More important, this spectatorial fascination encouraged Europeans and Americans to view the world itself as an extended exhibition.[34] In this universe, reality was never secured until it could be positioned as an object to be viewed. Only after some part of the world or some group of people could be constructed as an exhibit—and preferably also represented in a visual medium (painting or photography) and through description in a novel or travel narrative—could that place or experience be understood, ordered, and organized. This, Mitchell argues, led Europeans to a great historical confidence based in "the certainty of representation" and to an attitude toward the reality they viewed that he describes, with understatement, as a particular "political decidedness."[35]

This confidence in the view emerged paradoxically, however. By the 1820s, scientists were already beginning to explore the unstable structure of human visual capacities—the afterimage, the nature of light and its relationship to the retina, the capacity to simulate the appearance of movement through the rapid display of still images. All these phenomena began to suggest that vision itself was not entirely an objective reflection of an outside world, but that the observer, in the concreteness of his or her body, played a role in producing a subjective, autonomous experience of what was seen. The increasing scientific studies of vision suggested that it was a contingent representation (dependent on the particular structure of the retina, the specific capacities of the brain to interpret information) rather than a simple mimetic function.[36] In the 1830s and 1840s, audiences in Europe and the United States became fascinated with visual illusions, with photographic tricks, with images of movement. In the latter half of the nineteenth century, as exhibits, photography, and other types of visual images (including, eventually, the cinema) came to carry particular status as authentications of reality, of truth, they did so in tandem with the excited realization that the equation of seeing with truth was also fundamentally unstable. Jonathan Craig argues that certain types of representation were invested with the task of accuracy and authority precisely because they provided a "mirage of a transparent set of relations [between observer and observed] that modernity had already overthrown."[37] Spectacle, views, and exhibitions seemed to respond not only to the desire for particular information (about the West or about Jerusalem) but to the larger and particularly modern cultural fascination with the problem of when, and how, "seeing" might—or might not—be the same as "believing."[38]

It was in this context that both photographs and three-dimensional stereoscopic images were pressed into service by those who advocated "universal Holy Land visual literacy." By the end of the nineteenth century, the Holy Land images were the most popular subject for the more than five million stereographs produced in the United States. Marketed to Sunday schools, door-to-door, and at public events like the Philadelphia Centennial Fair, Holy

Land images "made their way into the homes and schools of hundreds of thousands of Americans."[39] Stereoscopes played with the issue of unstable perception, since they provided an illusion of three-dimensionality from two-dimensional photos. But they also promised accurate representation and religious knowledge. The illusion was a route to truth.

Perhaps the most telling example of Americans' desire to immerse themselves in Holy Land imagery was the construction of a small-scale walk-through model of the Holy Land by the Chautauqua Assembly in New York State. The first version of "Palestine Park" was begun in 1874, at the founding of the community that would become nineteenth-century America's most important center of Bible and nature teaching. The park was expanded over the next several years, eventually developing into a 350-foot-long three-dimensional map, complete with cast-metal cities, a small river Jordan, and Chautauqua Lake as the Mediterranean. The park, which soon became known (and copied) all over the country, served as a teaching instrument for children, as well as a site for adults to dress in costume and re-create both biblical and "Oriental" tableaux.[40]

All of these popular amusements combined "spectacle" with "scholarly-ness" to stage Holy Land viewings as ennobling for the viewer. They saturated the culture, combining Orientalist themes of exoticism with the complex nexus of adoration and appropriation that most Protestant Americans felt for the land they claimed as spiritual heritage. By the end of the Civil War, when tourism began to escalate dramatically, travelers were beginning to view their own experiences in terms of those they had seen or read about—and finding themselves disappointed. One Unitarian minister complained that he was frustrated by the small, unimposing size of Jerusalem; he particularly regretted that none of the popular images of the city had been taken from the direction of his approach.[41]

The disjuncture between expectation and experience was sometimes itself a proof of the superiority of Christianity, since the failures of the local population to live up to the biblically inspired romantic hopes of Americans was generally explained as evidence of a general "regression and decrepitude" that were connected both to the "weakness and vices of the Ottoman rule" and to "elements of the Mussulman character."[42] Still, the disappointments of face-to-face encounters did not diminish interest in Holy Land exotica. And as the nineteenth century wore on, the detailed representation of "biblical" spaces was enriched by several best-selling novels with Holy Land settings, particularly *Ben-Hur* (first published in 1880), *Sign of the Cross* (1896), and *Quo Vadis* (1895). *Ben-Hur* was such a sensation that it became the first fiction to be carried by the Sears and Roebuck

Figure 1. Line drawing from the lavishly illustrated 1904 edition of Lew Wallace's *Ben-Hur*. The novel was a best-seller from the time of its appearance in the 1880s until the 1920s.

catalog, which purchased a special edition of one million copies and soon sold out. The novel was also made into a well-known stage play.[43] These popular novels were often visual texts as well; the 1900 edition of *Ben-Hur*, for example, also included full-page photos and drawings of many of the major attractions of the area, including scenery, pottery, jewelry, and animals, as well as "typical" native inhabitants.[44] All the fiction texts flowered on a well-tilled field, since for almost five decades, various modes of representation, including travelogues, paintings, panoramas, stereographs, and the Palestine Park, had framed U.S. perceptions of the region through acts of religious, especially Protestant, appropriation. The stories of a biblical past were mapped onto a geographic fetish that constructed a moral position; by viewing and knowing the "Holy Land," Protestant observers fashioned for themselves a spectacular piety.

SHOPPING THE ORIENT

As the nineteenth century drew to a close, the "Orient" joined the "Holy Land" as an American concern. For most of the century, white Americans had been focused on continental expansion to the West and Southwest; they had paid relatively little attention to colonizing other parts of the world and therefore had not developed the Europeans' interest in information about their far-flung empires. In the 1890s, however, two factors coalesced to heighten U.S. interest in lands abroad and in the "East" in particular. First was the anxiety about the saturation of white settlement in the American West. Many Americans, like the young historian Frederick Jackson Turner, believed that American democracy had developed out of the economic equality that frontier expansion had made possible and the personal independence that it had made necessary. With "the close of the frontier" and the rapidly expanding populations of U.S. cities, white Americans were increasingly anxious about what would happen without new territories to settle.

The second factor was concern about the economic limits of the nation, which emerged with new urgency in the 1890s. The U.S. economy was just beginning to reach the point where industrialization and increases in mechanization meant that productive capacity might conceivably outstrip consumer demand. (By 1900, the United States would lead the world in the production of manufactured goods.) During a major economic depression from 1893 to 1897, labor strife was intense, frequent, and often violent, as workers and owners battled—quite literally—over wages, working hours, and safety. In this context of "overproduction," depression, and labor struggles, capitalists' search for new markets, particularly the famous "China market," became a near obsession, not only for business owners focused on their profits but also in U.S. political life more generally.[45]

Yet the age of imperialism was ending. There were, as Joseph Conrad's hero Marlowe complained, fewer and fewer blank spaces on the map of the world.[46] Although the question of whether the United States would aim for noncontiguous imperial expansion was not yet settled, the sense of territorial and economic limits was profound. One scholar has pointed out that it was precisely in the 1890s that both Europeans and Americans became fascinated with the occult. Looking for new worlds to conquer, he suggests, late Victorians turned otherworldly.[47]

It was also in this period that the "Orient" became a highly visible symbol in the emerging structures of a consumer culture. If economic production meant that there were more goods to sell, and the limits of imperialism made conquering new markets less certain, then increases in the average consumption per person would, in time, become a favored answer to the overproduction dilemma. The new urban department stores took it upon themselves to ease their customers into a modern world of increased commodity consumption. These stores were also, not incidentally, early leaders in using images of the Orient to sell consumer goods. Facing a world of nineteenth-century producer-citizens, who had long considered shopping itself to be suspect, department store designers sought to lower people's resistance to purchasing, and advertising sought to trigger buying on impulse, aiming for the emotions rather than rational thought and calculation. Store displays highlighted the link between shopping and sensuousness or sexuality, both of which were associated with the Orient. Harem scenes, Japanese gardens, Persian carpets and fabric, stores decorated as mosques or desert oases: the Orient was everywhere in these consumer stagings. European Orientalist representations had long associated the East with colorful dress and decor, with sexuality and luxury, with indulgence and irresponsibility—all qualities to be encouraged in consumers. In 1903, Siegel-Cooper's in New York produced a six-week-long "Carnival of Nations" climaxing in "Oriental Week," which included a show that offered theatrical representations of a Turkish harem, a parade of dancing girls, a genie of the lamp, and Cleopatra of the Nile.[48] A few years later, in 1912, Wanamakers staged a giant "Garden of Allah" fashion show in New York, based on themes from a very popular novel of the same title by British writer Robert Hitchens.

In fact, the *Garden of Allah* themes quickly became a phenomenon in themselves. At the time of its publication in 1904, the book had been a failure in England, but the melodramatic story of an Englishwoman who finds sexual adventure "in the desert," yet who learns her lesson in the end, sold extremely well in the United States. Soon, two silent films were made from the book (in 1916 and 1927; there was a later sound version in 1936). *Garden of Allah* was also adapted for the theater; the performance was a "giant spectacle" complete with an onstage sandstorm and live animals. Garden of Allah restaurants and hotels popped up all over the country; advertisements and magazine covers featured drawings inspired by the book and the play. Department stores staged performances and displays based on the theme. Wanamakers, for example, produced a fashion extravaganza featuring "Algerian" fashions, actual Arab models, and a string orchestra playing "oriental" music. The show attracted thousands of women, many of whom were either left standing or refused entrance altogether.[49]

As one cultural historian has suggested, the appeal of Orientalist themes went well beyond simply promoting the loosening that was a part of the emerging consumer society. Exotic Eastern and Near Eastern motifs were popular in the period before World War I in cultural sites that had nothing to do with selling dry goods. Orientalism was the cultural logic through which American culture symbolized a break from nineteenth-century Protestant piety and marked the nation's entry into "modernity."[50] At turn-of-the-century Coney Island, for example, the dancer "Little Egypt" was a popular attraction.[51] Silent films such as *The Arab* (1915), *Intolerance* (1916), *Cleopatra* (1917), *Salome* (1918), *An Arabian Knight* (1920), *The Sheik* (1921), *A Son of the Sahara* (1924), *Son of the Sheik* (1926), and *A Son of the Desert* (1928) also registered the Orientalism common in the larger culture.[52] But shopping in particular became linked to the exotic pleasures of the Orient, which allowed the new discourse of commodity culture to simultaneously praise the practice of indulgence and disavow it, by linking it to foreignness. In this moral geography, the East speaks of something missing in the world of the American work ethic; it is what one longs for; it is the iconography of sexual desire and the possibility of purchasing the feelings that go with that desire—reverie, release, sensual pleasure—through the goods associated with it. And the department store, like the Orient itself, was grasped as an exhibition, a spectacle, even a dream.

Commodity Orientalism was associated with the post-Victorian norms that in the early twentieth century produced a multilayered rhetoric of "emancipation" linking the New Woman, companionate marriage, modernity, and consumerism. In this, the spectacle of Orientalist consumption was very different than that of the Holy Land documents that promised knowledge and piety through visual representation. The new Orientalist display was part of a larger challenge to the Protestant producer ethic that had begun to break down the "separate spheres" for women and men by

Figure 2. In *The Garden of Allah* (MGM, 1927), a young New Woman (Alice Terry) goes to Algeria, where she discovers adventure in the desert and falls in love with an escaped Trappist monk, played by Ivan Petrovich. Courtesy of the Museum of Modern Art Film Stills Archive.

bringing women increasingly into the public and the marketplace. This transformation did not emerge without a great deal of ambivalence. In silent films, for example, the New Woman, with her supposed independence, sexual aggressiveness, and newly acquired vote, was at once admirable *and* threatening. In many of these films, the "Orient" was associated with women's fantasies and women's sexual power in particular. As Gaylyn Studlar has argued, the figure of the "vamp" epitomized this link: a powerful, Orientalized woman who was mysterious and alluring but also dangerous. The quintessential vamp was Theda Bara, the Jewish actress who in the late 1910s starred in both *Cleopatra* and *Salome,* and whose publicity materials often insisted that her name was an anagram for "Arab Death." Associating the sexually voracious woman with the sexual disorder of the East, Hollywood's production of the "vamp" suggested the threat of the despotic woman. Some commentators made clear that they considered the threat quite real: worried that men were on the verge of capitulating to the de-

Figure 3.   Advertising poster for *The Sheik* (1921), starring Rudolph Valentino. The film was one of a wide range of Orientalist cultural productions in the early twentieth century. Courtesy of Paramount Pictures. *The Sheik* copyright © 2000 by Paramount Pictures. All rights reserved.

mands of women, one 1922 marriage manual railed against the "menace" of "excessive sexuality or the Woman Vampire."[53]

The popularity of Rudolf Valentino, however, and in particular the iconic status of his two "Oriental" films, *The Sheik* (1921) and *Son of the Sheik* (1926), suggest that his numerous female fans engaged the issues of sexuality, the Orient, and consumer culture on rather different terms. Edith Hull's novel *The Sheik* (1919) had been an international best-seller; as in the *Garden of Allah*, its heroine is a young Englishwoman who goes to the desert to seek adventure. There, she meets a handsome but barbarian Arab sheik, who rapes her (in the film, only the threat of rape is suggested) but whom she also falls in love with. At the end of the tale, the olive-skinned "Arab" is revealed to be an Englishman, son of a noble father and a Spanish mother; with this knowledge, the spunky New Woman heroine marries him.

In this liminality of Arab/not Arab, Valentino's sheik was similar to Lawrence of Arabia, the British military officer who became renowned on both sides of the Atlantic for his exploits fighting alongside the Arabs against the Ottomans during World War I. In the United States, Lawrence's story was most famously presented by Lowell Thomas, an American journalist who covered the war and had joined Lawrence for part of his time in battle in the Middle East. Thomas returned home in 1919, intending to launch a lecture tour recounting his experiences in France, the Balkans, Germany, and the Middle East. It quickly became apparent, however, that only the Middle East lectures drew large audiences, so Thomas focused his topic and renamed his performance "With Allenby in Palestine and Lawrence in Arabia." Illustrated with films, colored lantern slides, and special lighting effects and accompanied by music, the lecture tour was a multimedia production that drew on the traditions of both Chautauqua and vaudeville. In it, Thomas depicted Lawrence, who spoke Arabic and frequently wore Arab dress, as a romantic adventurer and a military hero. The show began with some success in New York, then went to London, and later all over the world, eventually playing to four million people. Over the next few years, Lawrence's story became virtually its own industry: a hagiographic biography by Thomas in 1924 became an international best-seller; Robert Graves's more sober account, *Lawrence and the Arabian Adventure*, was published in 1927. Lawrence published his own reflections, *Seven Pillars of Wisdom*, in a small subscribers' edition in 1926; the book was then repackaged in an abridged edition, *Revolt in the Desert*, which immediately sold one hundred thousand copies.[54]

Valentino's sheik films almost certainly drew upon the transatlantic popularity of the Lawrence legend. But unlike Lawrence, who was presented as a war hero and a model of manly behavior for schoolboys, Valentino was a "woman-made man," whose masculine appeal lay almost entirely in his sexual allure. Marketing for *The Sheik* played up the titillation quotient of the Arabian setting, assuring audiences that the movie was "in the full torrent of the Oriental tradition" and that "when an Arab sees a woman he wants, he takes her."[55] Despite a barrage of criticism suggesting that the film played into the "masochistic appeal" of seeing a "fair girl in the strong hands of a ruthless desert tyrant," *The Sheik* catapulted Valentino into stardom. Filmed in close-up, with the backlighting and soft focus usually reserved for female stars, his body uncovered and displayed, Valentino became a spectacle, providing the occasion for unprecedented expressions of female desire.[56]

As a star figure, Valentino was ethnically marked. An Italian immigrant who played a series of exotic "others," Spanish, Russian, and, of course, Arab, his popularity with women elicited a defensive response on the part of some observers that was often explicitly nativist and racialist. Miriam

THE RIDE TO AKABA
May 9 – July 6 : 1917

Figure 4. This map of the Middle East as a strategic military battleground in World War I was the frontispiece for Robert Graves's enthusiastic portrait, *Lawrence and the Arabian Adventure*, 1927.

Hansen has described the ways in which Valentino himself became marked by the racial connotations of the films he starred in. In the early 1920s, when anti-immigrant nativism was particularly hostile to Italians and Jews, insinuations of a color continuum linked the "olive-skinned idol" with Arabs or Orientals, and ultimately with African Americans. These associations suggest something of the complex racial status of "Arabs," who were presumed to live elsewhere, as opposed to the immigrants, like Valentino, who represented a racial threat within. The various sex and marriage scenarios in which Valentino starred thus flirted with miscegenation, even as they were able to avoid actually depicting something so presumably shocking to its audience. In the backlash against Valentino—no less significant for its sometimes playful and ironic tone—men claimed to be baffled by white women's interest in the ethnically tainted star. One cartoon in a fan magazine showed an audience watching *The Sheik:* the women were enraptured while the men looked disinterested and disdainful. The caption read: "The Nordic sneered at Valentino while his women-folk thrilled to this jungle python of a lover."[57] In this gender-specific logic, "Orientalism" was, for both men and women, a significant trope that connected exoticism, sexuality (especially female sexuality), consumption, and—through all this—the lure and danger of decadence. The Orient, like the Holy Land, was linked to spectacle, though the meaning of spectacle itself had changed, from its nineteenth-century associations with religious and scientific knowledge to the turn-of-the-century links to femininity, consumerism, and loosened sexuality.

Representations of ancient Egypt soon became a site where those two trajectories merged. Throughout the 1800s, ancient Egypt had been a source of great fascination in the United States. In the 1820s and 1830s, the Egyptian revival in architecture made its mark on a large number of American buildings, particularly cemeteries and prisons.[58] Anthropologists studied ancient Egypt for what it might reveal about the origins of civilization, and their findings were taken up as part of a much larger debate about race and slavery in the antebellum period. (I discuss this scholarship and its impact in chapter 3.) Egyptology itself became an object of popular interest, and by midcentury, around the country amateur Egyptologists were giving public lectures illustrated with mummies, funerary objects, and pictures of the Sphinx and the Pyramids brought back from digs in Luxor or Aswan.[59]

At the end of the century, as film scholar Antonia Lant has shown, there developed a significant iconographic link between the popularity of "things Egyptian" and the development of early cinema. Egypt, both ancient and modern, was fascinating in part because it was widely considered to be a "transitional place"—at the intersection of Africa, the Middle East, and points beyond. Ancient Egyptian artifacts also highlighted a rather different transition, that from life into death, and suggested the possibility of immortality. Similarly, public discussions of early cinema often represented film viewing as an "in-between state," not quite dreaming, not quite waking. Perhaps even more important, cinema represented itself as a way of preserving what had disappeared, a type of mummification that could even bring the dead back to life for future generations. "Egypt became a mode of expressing the new experience of film," Lant argues. "Even before the arrival of cinema, writers on Egypt associated that culture with magic, preservation, and silent, visual power—all qualities that anticipate the character of cinema."[60] Egypt's associations brought to cinema the two seemingly contradictory functions of the Middle East as spectacle: the promise of the preservation and advancement of knowledge fused with the exotic reveries of a dream.

In 1922, a new element emerged when archaeologists discovered the intact tomb of the ancient Egyptian pharaoh Tutankhamun. The artifacts from the tomb constituted what many contemporaries considered the greatest find in the history of archaeology. As the treasures were uncovered during the winter of 1922–1923, newspapers from around the world carried daily reports on the dig's progress. The artistic style of the tomb objects became a cultural phenomenon, affecting furniture design, architecture (again), and especially fashion. The long, lean look of the silhouettes on the tomb paintings was promoted in conjunction with the "modern," slender look of the New Woman; simple, geometric shapes and the use of a few striking colors were the hallmarks of the "Egyptian-influenced" fashions that dominated women's styles in the mid-1920s. Even the signature flapper haircut—a short, clean bob—was said to have been derived from tomb paintings. Over the course of the 1920s, one journalist has argued, "Egyptian influences were totally assimilated into the new 'modern style' they helped create."[61]

A year after the Tut discovery, in 1923, Cecil B. DeMille released the silent film *The Ten Commandments*. Although the bulk of the movie centered around a modern story of two brothers, it was the prologue, set in ancient Egypt, that received the most media attention. Foreshadowing the gushing hype that would accompany DeMille's 1950s epic films (including the 1956 version of *The Ten Commandments*), newspapers and industry magazines eagerly reported on the enormous expenditures required to film the magisterial scenes of the Hebrew Exodus: the twenty-five hundred inhabitants of a tent city and three thousand animals, including horses, camels, burros, poultry, and dogs. Rather than using the close-ups and closely edited sequences that were already becoming characteristic of Holly-wood, DeMille filmed the prologue as a succession of extreme long shots, which gave the appearance of a didactic series of tableaux for the edification of spectators. What emerged was, in the words of one film scholar, some-thing akin to "anti-modernist civic pageantry."[62] In this case, as with the Holy Land views of the previous century, spectacle was staged for the pur-pose of "truth." But, again, the Orientalist promise of sensation and exoti-cism was also close to the surface, since the Egypt of the Exodus was also, in 1923, the Egypt that had spawned Tut fashions and Isis haircuts.

EXPANDING INTERESTS

Orientalism in its various forms highlighted the iconographic status of for-eign lands in the production of new domestic consumers. But the turn of the century was also a period in which "foreign lands" themselves became objects of direct political and economic investments, as American compa-nies and the U.S. state began to extend their interests beyond the North American continent. In 1898, direct U.S. political involvements expanded dramatically, first with the annexation of Hawaii (1898) and then with the Spanish-American War (also 1898), which resulted in the conquest of the Philippines, the annexation of Puerto Rico and Guam, and the formation of a "protectorate" in Cuba.[63]

It was precisely at this moment, however, that imperialism became a matter of widespread public debate in the United States. After the Spanish-American War had led to the occupation of Cuba and the Philippines, the United States found itself in a long, bloody war against the Filipino guer-rillas who had first fought for their independence against Spain and now continued the battle against a new occupying power. In the United States, Americans hotly debated the question of "imperialism," and the terms of that debate would have a lasting influence on the domestic understanding of the nature of American global power.

Pro-imperialists used several key arguments. Some seemed to support U.S. occupation for reasons of simple racial hatred. American military lead-ers and soldiers, many of them veterans of the recent Indian wars, reported themselves anxious to get involved in "the nigger fighting business." As one young man wrote home to his family in 1899, "I am in my glory when I can sight my gun on some dark skin and pull the trigger."[64] Others used a more familiar economic rationale—"Trade follows the flag," they pro-claimed. Still others aimed for moral suasion, insisting that the Filipinos, "our little brown brothers," deserved the twin benefits of Christianity (i.e.,

Protestantism, since most Filipinos were already Catholic) and American civilization. The civilizing argument was linked to the work of American Christian missionaries who, believing that all people were candidates for salvation, had determined to carry out the "evangelization of the world in one generation."[65] In many cases, then, imperialist rhetoric came directly from the assumption that all peoples were capable of civilization and should thus have the cultural opportunity of "benevolent" Americanization.[66]

Opposition to imperialism also included diverse arguments. Some leading citizens, including Mark Twain, the philosopher William James, and W. E. B. Du Bois, expressed a straightforward support for democratic self-rule. Many others opposed imperialism from the overtly racist fear that U.S. rule in the Philippines would require absorbing more nonwhite peoples into the nation.[67] For them, the desire to incorporate the potential economic benefits of an empire, in terms of both markets and labor, was in tension with the political imperative to maintain a racially exclusive narrative of national identity.[68] In this case, the anti-imperialist position was *not* an argument against U.S. economic hegemony or against the more general kind of political power that would allow the United States to have extensive political influence overseas; instead, it was a pragmatic position about the best way to wield U.S. power.

Ultimately, the bloodiness of the Filipino resistance led to a general disillusionment with direct colonial rule. In practice, U.S. globalizing interests at the turn of the twentieth century did not require such direct control of new territories. The United States had already conquered a great deal of territory beyond the original British colonies under the rubric of Manifest Destiny. That, along with its own history of anticolonialism, would allow the United States to begin to frame its global goals as something other than, and very different from, the old-style imperialism.

In the years before World War II, U.S. state policy and U.S. businesses converged to promote the economic influence of U.S.-based corporations as an alternative to conquest. Under this framework, which historian Emily Rosenberg has described as "liberal developmentalism," Americans assumed that all nations could and should replicate the U.S. model of economic, political, and cultural "development." A major impetus behind government support for business expansion lay in business concerns about the problem of overproduction and the need for new consumers, but U.S. policymakers and exporters also believed that by making mass products (sewing machines, condensed milk, cameras) available cheaply, they would help increase living standards in Latin America, Asia, or Africa, while also improving the U.S. strategic position and making money for American businesses. In 1912, President Taft called the strategy "dollar diplomacy."[69]

Dollar diplomacy did not mean that the U.S. government did not act politically and militarily: the United States intervened in Latin America more than a dozen times between 1910 and 1930 when U.S. businesses were threatened by nationalist uprisings. But the most powerful and effective promotion of the United States happened through the export of American-made goods. In the world of exports, U.S.-based corporations came to represent "America" abroad, and, conversely, "America" came to be signified by its commodities, particularly its cultural commodities. Of all these, none was more important than Hollywood movies.

After World War I, the U.S. film industry emerged as the most powerful in the world. During the heyday of the silent film, foreign box office receipts were an important part of almost every Hollywood production: by 1925, U.S.-made films accounted for 95 percent of those shown in Britain, 70 percent of those in France, and 80 percent of those in South America.[70] Although the movie industry was not yet as large a part of the U.S. economy as it would become after World War II, movie exports were highly valued, on the assumption that movies not only sold themselves but also sold desire for the products and lifestyles they displayed. "Trade follows the film," expansionists proclaimed, highlighting with satisfaction the American strategy of commercial expansion rather than territorial control. In 1925, an article in the *Saturday Evening Post* announced with satisfaction, "The sun never sets on the British Empire and the American motion picture."[71]

Even the coming of sound in the late 1920s did not destroy the leadership of the American movie industry; the U.S. share of the French, German, and British markets dropped less than 15 percent between 1927 and 1931. During World War II, the European audience declined precipitously, of course, and Germany banned the importation of any American movies in areas under its control. But after the war, the United States succeeded in breaking down some of the protections previously instituted in Europe and increasing U.S. film exports, sometimes even linking film deals with aid under the Marshall Plan. In the Middle East, Latin America, and Asia, Hollywood continued to supply from 60 to 90 percent of all movies. By the 1950s, international exhibition receipts often represented more than half of the ultimate film gross.[72] Hollywood was thus part of a project of expansion in two ways: in its Orientalist mode, it was a site of representing the world abroad to U.S. audiences; as an industry, it was also deeply invested in cultivating foreign audiences for an American product. Nowhere is the dual nature of U.S. "interests" more clear than in this two-way flow of Hollywood.

After World War II, U.S. involvements abroad expanded dramatically. Because the United States had been relatively untouched by the war, American-based businesses, which had already been a considerable economic force, became the powerhouses of the increasingly globalizing economy. Economic power, including U.S. foreign aid, also often translated into U.S. government influence, while military power, also built from the economic boom, frequently helped to make that influence into hegemony. At the very least, the third world became a site of contest between the United States and the Soviet Union, both of which now exhibited the "great historical confidence" once attributed to Europe. Nowhere was this more true than in the Middle East, where U.S. political and economic involvements expanded rapidly in the postwar period. The following chapters trace the logics that helped to make that expansion seem meaningful and even necessary to many Americans. Here I want to simply mention four of the overarching concerns that have helped to shape U.S. involvements in the region since 1945.

The first concern with the Middle East has been military and strategic. Official U.S. policy toward the Middle East has generally focused on material advantage and political alliances, though this has often been articulated in moral terms. Policymakers in the postwar period consistently defined several primary issues, but until 1989, by far the preeminent of these was the cold war contest with the Soviet Union. This contest had a moral component—"saving countries from communism." But in the Middle East as elsewhere, it also had a clear economic and strategic aspect—the cold war played out as a struggle for influence and economic relationships with the formerly colonized nations emerging into independence. The Middle East was crucial to this struggle, due in part to the geographic centrality of the region: it sits astride communication lines and travel routes connecting Europe, Africa, and Asia; it also abuts the southern border of the Soviet Union (and, with the disintegration of the former Soviet Union, Russia). The United States' strategy in the region developed out of a sense that the Soviet Union should not and could not be allowed to dominate the region (or to control its oil supplies). At the same time, U.S. policymakers were well aware of the fact that the Middle East was a primary site of the former colonial empires of Britain and France: as the United States began to compete for dominance in the postwar era, it would do so as a counter to European, as well as Soviet, influence.

The second concern has been less of a policy interest than a more general sense of religious attachment—a feeling of involvement and "rights" that revisits the earlier fascination with the "Holy Land," but in new and expanded ways. Christianity, Judaism, and Islam all take the Middle East as their point of origin, and adherents of those religions living in the United States have placed great importance on claiming—and narrating—the history and meaning of ancient Middle Eastern events for contemporary life. Thus, while Jews and Arab Muslims are among those presumed to have a "natural" interest in the Middle East, this is only part of the story. (Those associations, too, have complicated histories. It would be quite wrong to assume, for example, that American Jews have only one view of the meaning of Israel for Jews; the debates about Israel have been passionate and sometimes divisive. Part, but certainly not all, of that history has been explored in recent scholarship.)[73] In addition, and more centrally for this study, religion is important for many others who have made cultural and political claims to the region, from African American Muslims to white fundamentalist Christians. As one way of mapping identities and affiliations, religious narratives have not infrequently been mobilized in the service of nationalist and expansionist politics. But the major monotheistic religions have also constructed complex "transnational" affinities of spiritual community, which have served as a resource for articulating diverse identities and interests that have sometimes challenged those defined by U.S. policymakers.

The third major concern for Americans has been U.S. support for Israel. Whatever the moral and political arguments about the founding of Israel in 1948, there is no question that the presence of the new state transformed the Middle East. The Arab-Israeli conflict has become a long-term structuring factor in the politics of the region. Israel and Arab nations have fought five wars in the last fifty years; one of those (in 1973) brought the United States and the Soviet Union to full nuclear alert. For the United States, the commitment to Israel has changed over time. American aid to Israel increased dramatically, for example, after the 1967 war. But U.S. policymakers have consistently indicated both strong support for the existence of Israel (articulated in moral terms, in part as a response to the European Holocaust) and a commitment to a multifaceted alliance with Israel that includes military, political, and economic components.

Finally, U.S. policy has focused on oil.[74] The consumer economies of the United States, Europe, and eventually Japan needed oil to power their machines, heat their homes, and drive their cars. Access to that oil, at favorable prices, became a preeminent postwar foreign policy goal. That goal emerged from the particular history of U.S. oil policy. Before the 1920s, American domestic oil production more than met domestic needs. But in the years after World War I, U.S. government geological surveys began to predict (erroneously) the imminent exhaustion of domestic reserves. Securing access to foreign oil supplies soon became a priority for U.S. policymakers.[75] Although Britain and France dominated most of the Middle East, U.S. companies managed to establish joint cartels with several European companies. By the end of the 1930s, U.S. giants had already gained control of a sizable share (42 percent) of known Middle Eastern oil reserves.[76] In 1945, one State Department report could proclaim that Saudi Arabia, an area of traditional British influence, was "in a fair way to becoming an American frontier."[77]

At the end of World War II, the postwar paradigm was already in place: American-based oil companies would, as much as possible, obtain access to oil and other strategic raw materials through concessions negotiated in conjunction with the main colonial power in the region, Britain. These economic arrangements were often secured with the assistance of the U.S. government and backed up with the promise of political and even military intervention on behalf of the corporations, their local allies, or both. In the immediate postwar period, for example, the United States intervened numerous times in the Middle East to support pro-Western governments, prevent the rise of "radical" nationalist regimes, or "guarantee the oil supply." In 1953, the newly formed Central Intelligence Agency (CIA) secured the northern border of the new "American frontier" by helping to overthrow Mohammed Mossadegh, the elected but nationalist-minded leader of Iran, when he tried to nationalize Iranian oil.[78] As with other globalizing industries, including film, U.S.-based oil corporations presented themselves as operating in the national interest, and U.S. state power seemed to agree.

At the same time, U.S. policymakers used the expanding commerce to strengthen political and military ties with national leaders in the Middle East. With the worldwide decline of British and French imperialism, those leaders would be beholden to their own national constituencies, and the task of wooing decolonizing nations, from Egypt to Saudi Arabia to Iraq, became a strategic preoccupation. As the nations of the Middle East emerged to independence in the 1950s, however, nationalist leaders like Gamal Abdel Nasser in Egypt, Prime Minister Khaled al-Azm in Syria, and Mohammed Mossadegh in Iran often spoke of steering a course of independence between the United States and the Soviet Union. The United States did not hesitate to occasionally respond to the "threat" of nonalignment with military or covert action. For example, CIA operatives intervened in Syria in 1957, covertly supporting a military coup against a pro-communist government and overtly massing troops on the Syrian border. In 1958, fourteen thousand U.S. troops intervened in the civil war in Lebanon.[79] As one analyst has pointed out, the 1950s were a decade of "turbulent and often spectacular confrontations between the United States and Europe and the emerging nationalist forces in the Middle East."[80] Still, the nonaligned movement allowed several Arab leaders to get economic aid and military support from one or the other of the superpowers, and thus, for a while at least, to maintain their own relative independence. As the cold war wore on, such middle grounds became increasingly difficult to sustain.

Control over oil became increasingly contentious in the 1960s, as the major oil companies struggled to maintain their dominant position. Increasingly, U.S. policy depended on the cultivation of local allies. By the 1970s, the Nixon Doctrine, which originally had been articulated as a call for the "Vietnamization" of U.S. commitments in Southeast Asia, was extended to call for funding and arming friendly governments in the Middle East, which would then serve as proxies for the protection of American interests. The pillars of this policy in the later 1970s were Iran, Saudi Arabia, and Israel.[81] As happened elsewhere in the world, these allies were touted as bastions of moderation, stability, and pro-Western sentiment in a sea of threat. When, in 1979, one of those pillars, Iran, "fell" to Islamic fundamentalists, the result was a U.S. foreign policy debacle of the first order. When, in 1990, another of those pillars, Saudi Arabia, was considered to be under threat of a potential Iraqi invasion, that assessment led to a war that involved almost every state in the region as either an ally or an enemy.

These four primary interests—strategic position, religious ties, support for Israel, and access to oil—often worked together, both in policymaking circles and in public discussion. But at times they competed, or had more or less relevance. The multifaceted history of U.S. cultural and political interests in the Middle East is the history of these contending forces; the confluence and the contradictions of those forces defined the contest over the nature and extent of postwar U.S. power in the region.

DEFINING THE MIDDLE EAST AND ITS PEOPLE

Developing U.S. political and economic investments in the Middle East after World War II were accompanied by an increased scholarly interest in the contemporary political forces shaping the region. The postwar paradigm of "area studies" was not necessarily born of the cold war; interest in the modern Middle East was clearly present earlier, at universities such as Princeton, which founded the first department of modern oriental studies in 1927 (as opposed to the traditional Orientalist focus on language, ancient history, and religion). But such scholarship was given new life by the cold war's sense of political urgency, and in the 1950s, prewar proposals for the "organic" and "synthetic" study of the social evolution of the Middle East began to receive government, foundation, and university funding. At the same time, a new generation of Arab scholars, many of whom trained in

Europe, began to produce their own political-historical studies, which in turn influenced scholarship in the United States. For various bureaucratic and intellectual reasons, however, Middle East studies did not become fully institutionalized until 1967, when the Middle East Studies Association (MESA) was founded.[82]

From the beginning, the study of the contemporary Middle East was bedeviled by definitional problems: What were the parameters of the "Middle East"? What made it distinct from other regions? Traditional Orientalist scholars, interested in the ancient texts and sites, could presume that Egypt, or the Hebrews, or Islam provided a unifying force. In the 1910s and 1920s, for example, archaeologists had focused on the contribution of the Middle East to the history of "Western civilization," which they argued had begun in the Fertile Crescent (Iraq and the Levant) and moved westward. But in the period after World War II, the founding of Israel combined with the growth of secularizing forces in the Arab world meant that "Islamic culture" was no longer an even minimally satisfying rubric. Some definitions of the Middle East attempted to make the Arabic language the defining force that linked the areas from North Africa to Saudi Arabia, but what about Israel and non-Arabic-speaking Iran and Turkey? Others traced the historic impact of Islam, or simply marked as the "middle" East the spaces between "sub-Saharan" Africa and Europe on the one hand and "Asia" on the other. But the internal differences among various countries in the region remained so significant as to nearly fracture any attempt at systematic definition: the diversity of cultures and peoples in Morocco or Egypt, for example, separated them from the more homogeneous culture in Saudi Arabia; or, to take another example, the different schools of Islam that predominated in Iraq (Sunni) and Iran (Shia) meant those neighbors had distinct, sometimes contending, theological influences, as well as very different histories of public religious life. The attempt to tell a "total story" of culture and society that would tie together the diversity of the region was itself something of an imperializing ambition, and Middle East studies, like some other area studies programs, often ended up overly concerned with the attempt to construct a content for itself.[83]

For scholars in Middle East studies in the United States, the publication of Said's *Orientalism* in 1978 also raised fundamental questions about the constitution of the field and the politically invested nature of knowledge about the region. Said had suggested that Middle East studies was part of "the knitted-together strength" of a long discourse of Arab and Muslim inferiority that had not been limited to Europe.[84] The final chapter of *Orientalism* made clear that, in Said's view, the United States in the postwar period had simply taken over the Orientalist mantle from the former European powers. These criticisms of scholarly practice as, in essence, anti-Islamic, intersected with the more overt political fissures in the field, which was as divided by the Arab-Israeli conflict as the region itself. The resulting intellectual impasse, combined with the definitional quagmire, meant that the field itself was in perpetual crisis.[85]

Defining the race and culture categorizations for Middle Eastern immigrants to the United States proved equally confounding. The first generation of Arab immigrants, who had arrived in the United States between 1890 and the beginning of World War I, were generally Christians from Lebanon and Syria. They were a relatively small population: in the first decade of the century, Syrian immigrants were twenty-fifth out of thirty-nine immigrant nationalities, and their numbers were only 7 percent as large as the number of Jewish immigrants in the same period. Syrian and other Arab immigrants were all but halted by the 1924 immigration laws that established national quotas based on the 1890 population.[86]

The racial status of Arabs was often unclear. Some observers posited Syrians as a distinct race; the Associated Charities of Boston, for example, reported in 1899 that "next to the Chinese, who can never in any real sense be American, [the Syrians] are the most foreign of foreigners."[87] Yet in 1919, the average income of Syrians was three times that of the U.S. population as a whole. And in popular Orientalist films and novels, Arabs were generally distinguished from Africans, who were presented as inferior to the exotic peoples of the "East."

For Arabs and other immigrants, however, racial status was not simply a matter of cultural "common sense"; it was a legal question with serious consequences. Until 1952, U.S. law, building on the Naturalization Act of 1790, allowed naturalized U.S. citizenship only to "free white persons and persons of African nativity or descent."[88] In the 1910s, the question of the racial categorization of Syrians or other Middle Easterners went before U.S. courts on numerous occasions, often with conflicting results. Like other rulings on the race of Armenians or Indians or Asians, those that dealt with Arabs used a mishmash of criteria to determine racial classification: race might be determined by the "look" of the claimant, the geographic location of his or her home, or the complex ethnological and scientific arguments of the period that claimed to explain the biological and/or historical basis of race.[89] In the Massachusetts case of *In re Halladjian* (1909), for example, the judge's decision on the "whiteness" of Armenians was accompanied by the observation that "the average man on the street ... would find no difficulty in assigning to the yellow race a Turk or Syrian with as much ease as he would bestow that designation on a Chinaman or Korean." A year later, however, in *In re Mudarri*, the court maintained that Syrians should be classified as Caucasian and commented that "this court has long admitted Syrians to citizenship."[90] But in 1913, a South Carolina court decided that Faras Shadid, who had a skin color "about that of walnut," was not white. Nonetheless, two years later, the Fourth Circuit Court of Appeals (*Dow v. United States*) reversed a South Carolina court's decision that Syrians were ineligible for citizenship, arguing that Blumenbach's classification of the races in 1781 had defined the inhabitants of certain portions of Asia, including Syria, as "white persons."[91] A Massachusetts court decision of 1944 reached a similar conclusion, declaring that one Mohamed Mohriez, who had been born in "Arabia," was eligible for citizenship. Arabs, the judge reasoned, "belong to that division of the white race speaking Semitic languages. ... Both the learned and unlearned would compare the Arabs with the Jews toward whose naturalization every American Congress since the first has been avowedly sympathetic."[92] This legal definition seemed to fit with emerging popular perceptions, in which Arab immigrants were considered to be particularly assimilated in American society. In the 1940s, for example, Salom Rizk was chosen by *Reader's Digest* to lecture across the United States as the quintessential American immigrant.[93]

The second wave of Arab immigration came after the 1948 Arab-Israeli war, when Palestinian refugees scattered across the world. The new immigrants differed in important ways from the first generation: they were predominantly Muslim, from one-third to one-half were Palestinians, and they were far more likely to retain cultural and national ties to the land of their birth. Still small in number by the standards of U.S. immigration, these new arrivals began a process that would not be completed until the end of the immigration quota system in 1965: Arabs in the United States moved from being largely Christian, assimilated, and middle-class to become a population divided by nationality, religion, education, and class. After 1965, Detroit became a major center for Arab newcomers. Already a relatively large number of Arab immigrants had made Detroit their home since the turn of the century: 555 "Syrians" worked at the Ford motor factory in 1916. The numbers slowly increased via the family chain migration that is common with many immigrant communities. With the loosening of immigration laws in the 1960s, Arab-speaking immigrants became the fastest-growing ethnic community in the area, and Detroit became the city in which Arabs and Arab-Americans are most visible as a group.[94]

The fact that Arab immigration has been historically so small, however (and, outside of Detroit, largely invisible), meant that these immigrants were not a significant factor in how the Middle East has been represented to Americans. Unlike, say, the depictions of Chinese, which frequently have been influenced by the immigrant status of the Chinese in America (and vice versa), Arabs played a largely symbolic role in American culture until the 1980s. As I discuss in chapter 6, even at the end of the 1990s, the presence of Arab immigrants had only begun to be recognized in the dominant culture and, even there, largely through a concern over "domestic" terrorism.

Moreover, immigration of other non-Arab groups from the Middle East was, before 1965, minuscule. Iranians, whom I discuss in chapter 5, were first recognized as a community by other Americans during the Iranian hostage crisis in 1979–1980, though they have also since become a distinct subcultural force in a few cities, particularly Los Angeles.[95] At the turn of the century Jews also immigrated to the United States in large numbers, but not generally from the Middle East. The southern and eastern European Jews who arrived after 1890 were legally considered "white" (and thus capable of naturalization as citizens), although they were nonetheless singled out in popular political parlance as a distinct "race."[96] Anti-Semitism was often virulent; it was a decisive factor in the 1924 law that set immigration quotas by national origin. The relationship between the descendants of the European Jewish immigrants and the contemporary Middle East is extraordinarily complex. Although the majority of American Jews have never lived in Israel, most now feel strong emotional ties to that country. Yet the relationship of American Jews to Israel has been the subject of decades of passionate debate in the Jewish community, and the valence of that relationship has altered many times. While I do touch upon some aspects of this debate, it is not a focus of this study. For most people in the United States, the Middle East became meaningful as an area of U.S. interest in ways that did *not* take into account the fact of either an Arab immigrant community or an American Jewish connection. When the numbers and visibility of Arab and Muslim immigrants increased in the 1980s, the new demographic consciousness did begin to alter the cultural representations of the Middle East. For the most part, however, the Middle East was "outside"; when it was claimed, it was often as history and heritage, but almost never as "home."

CONTESTED ENCOUNTERS

This study analyzes the importance of representations of the Middle East in the construction of postwar U.S. nationalism and the contest over the meanings of "Americanness." The chapters that follow trace some of the multiple encounters that mapped the Middle East for Americans. They do not, of course, tell all of the possible stories about those encounters. In particular, they do not focus on the connections that many people generally assume to be predominant in U.S.–Middle East relations: Jewish hopes for Israel, Arab investments in Palestine or the rest of the Arab world, or Iranian connections to Iran. These stories have been told elsewhere. Instead, each chapter aims to trace something of the unexpected convergences that have made the Middle East matter to Americans who might otherwise have ignored it.

Overall, I argue that, after World War II, political and cultural conditions in the United States produced a post-Orientalist model of representing the Middle East for American audiences. These new representational dynamics were not always in the service of U.S. state power; in certain cases they explicitly contested the presumptions of official U.S. policies. But even the official rhetoric of nationalist expansionism worked to establish the United States as different from the old colonial powers, and it did so in part by fracturing the East-West binary on which traditional Orientalism had depended. If U.S. appropriations and representations of the Middle East did *not* follow a simple Orientalist paradigm, that was because the project of separating the United States from European imperialism, or distinguishing the Middle East from the rest of the Orient, functioned strategically. In the logic of the last fifty years, one alternative to European power/knowledge over the Orient was American power in the modern Middle East.

Chapter 1 examines the discourse of "benevolent supremacy" that developed in the first decade after World War II, when U.S. interests were framed in terms of supplanting the former colonial powers by supporting the region's anticolonial movements. The chapter focuses on the trope of exodus from slavery as it appears both in biblical epic films like *The Ten Commandments* and in foreign policy documents of the 1950s. These texts, I argue, drew upon and revised the civil rights connotations of the exodus narrative. Working through a gendered logic that figured "slavery" in sexual terms—as a problem for (white) women in relation to despotic men— the films offered right-ordered marriage and the "freely chosen subordination" of women as the solution. They then cast that subordination as a model for the relationship between the United States and the decolonizing nations of the Middle East, constructing U.S. power as a "benevolent supremacy" that would replace older models of direct colonial rule.

Chapter 2 examines the Middle East as a signifier in the construction of African American political and religious identities between 1955 and 1972. Drawing on the writings and speeches of Martin Luther King Jr., James Baldwin, Elijah Muhammad, Malcolm X, and Amiri Baraka, among others, this chapter traces competing constructions of salient ancient histories and contemporary affiliations between African Americans and the Middle East: on the one hand, the Christian-influenced civil rights movement's evocation of the ancient Hebrews and the modern-day Israelis; on the other, Black Muslim constructions of affinities with both Islam and contemporary Arab anticolonialism. Both groups challenged the nationalist expansionism of official policy, even as they reproduced some of that policy's key assumptions. The chapter concludes with a close reading of Ishmael Reed's *Mumbo Jumbo*, which aimed to usurp the dominance of both Christian and Islamic influence, in part by turning to the ancient Egyptians as a source of religious and historical identification.

The 1970s were a period of transition and contest, as the legacy of Vietnam and the impact of the 1973 oil embargo came to frame U.S. encounters with the Arab states and Israel. Liberals and conservatives held competing models of the United States' role in the world. Mainstream liberals envisioned a multipolar world that took into account the economic power of the oil-rich Middle East. This model, in which the United States would function as a kind of supreme manager rather than an enforcer, competed with conservative paradigms of the United States as a hegemonic power in the region, ready to reassert the military toughness of the cold war era in a more global environment. Chapters 3 and 4 explore two very different cultural and political conjunctures in which these competing models found expression—one associated with Egypt and one with Israel. Chapter 3 analyzes the American tour of the *Treasures of Tutankhamun* exhibit in 1977–1979 in the context of the oil crises of the previous five years. Through a detailed reading of the exhibit itself, as well as the news accounts and popular culture embrace of Tut, I argue that the Tut representations were incorporated into a dominant rhetoric of imperial stewardship over the resources of the Middle East. The chapter goes on to examine a related debate about the racial and cultural status of the ancient Egyptians (were they black or white?), which soon became intertwined with narratives of contemporary international politics. Tut became an extraordinary nexus, where responses to the 1973 oil crisis, recognition of the new realities of Arab wealth, and debates over racial identities in the United States intersected and sometimes collided.

The managerial model that infused the official Tut representations was challenged by conservatives and other cultural commentators, whose rhetoric of military reassertion coalesced in the iconography that surrounded Israel in the 1970s. Chapter 4 highlights the ways in which Israel came to be revered for its prowess on the battlefield and its antiterrorist activities. I survey sources that range from Christian apocalyptic literature to television news coverage of terrorism to suggest that Israel became *less* a symbol of religious and cultural affiliation for Americans (as it had been in many ways in the years immediately following the Holocaust and the founding of the state) and more an emblem for a conservative argument about the legacies of Vietnam. In that logic, Israel, unlike the United States, seemed to many to be a nation that was not afraid to fight—and win.

In 1979–1980, this new cultural concern with antiterrorist toughness solidified in U.S. responses to the Iranian hostage crisis. Chapter 5 traces media and popular cultural representations of the capture of U.S. hostages at the American embassy in Tehran, along with the related policy discourse of antiterrorism. The language of threat and containment permeated policy texts and popular culture, helping to construct the United States as an "aggrieved space" distinguished by its (feminine) suffering. The hardening of anti-Islamic sentiment in the 1980s contrasted sharply with the Black Muslim narratives of the 1960s; the new logic presented the region less as a site for affiliation and appropriation than as a source of external and internal threat to Americans.

With the fall of the Soviet Union and the defeat of Iraq in the 1990–1991 Gulf War, older themes of U.S. benevolent partnership reappeared, this time in the framework of President George Bush's New World Order. Chapter 6 argues that the representations of the Gulf War were intimately intertwined with the problem of representing the nation in the context of increased immigration and a revitalized consciousness about racial diversity. By figuring the military as a diverse microcosm of U.S. society, Gulf War discourse linked domestic concerns over multiculturalism to a rhetoric of military and political expansion. What I describe as "military multiculturalism" was enabled by the unquestioned world predominance of the U.S. military, but it was dependent on an understanding of the Middle East as "outside" any meaningful definition of Americanness. When Arab immigrants to the United States became visible within that discourse, their presence threatened to shatter its fundamental assumptions.

In each of these chapters, I suggest that the politics of identity in the United States was intimately interwoven with the changing cultural logic of U.S. foreign policy. The Middle East was not a static interest, but a mobile sign—it played a role in staging American world power, and the struggles over the meanings of Middle East history and the control over Middle East resources profoundly affected American self-fashionings.

1   "Benevolent Supremacy"

The Biblical Epic at the Dawn of
the American Century, 1947–1960

No modern nation possesses a given "ethnic" basis....The
fundamental problem is therefore to produce the people. More
exactly, it is to make the people produce itself continually as a
national community. Or again, it is to produce the effect of unity
by virtue of which the people will appear, in everyone's eyes, "a
people," that is, as the basis and origin of political power.
                              —Etienne Balibar, "The Nation Form"

No earthly power can be supreme in the universe....From a
practical standpoint, however, let us note that an ascendancy of
right could become, to all temporal intents and purposes, a practical
supremacy in world affairs. With such a sovereignty in being,
humanity could look forward confidently to an evolution toward
eternal standards of perfection. In contrast, with evil forces in
ascendancy in world affairs, there would be an ever increasing
menace to the continued existence of mankind on earth.
                    —Charles Hilliard, *The Cross, the Sword, and the Dollar*

When Cecil B. DeMille's *The Ten Commandments* opened in New York in
November 1956, the critical consensus was that the director had created a
middle-brow, melodramatic, and highly suspect account of the biblical story
of Moses. *Newsweek* described the film as forced and "heavy-handed,"
while the reviewer for *Time* called *The Ten Commandments* "perhaps the
most vulgar movie ever made," lambasting the acting, the casting, the sets,
and even the effects.[1] Bosley Crowther of the *New York Times* was less caus-
tic but still decidedly lukewarm about the film, commenting dryly that "this
is unquestionably a picture to which one must bring something more than
a wish for mere entertainment in order to get a full effect from it."
Crowther suggested that DeMille's film would find its audience mostly
among religious viewers: "For those to whom its fundamentalism will be
entirely credible, it should be altogether thrilling and perhaps even spiritually profound."[2]

The rising tide of religious feeling in the United States in the 1950s, apparent in such trends as the rise in church attendance and the increasing

number of people who claimed to believe in God, did seem to explain something about the box office success of a film like *The Ten Commandments*. In the year before the film's release, William Herberg's *Protestant, Catholic, Jew* had noted the new piety but argued that religion had lost its theological foundation, becoming instead a "civic religion of the American Way of Life."[3] Ads for *The Ten Commandments* carried blurbs from religious leaders, including an endorsement from the Cardinal of New York, as well as a rabbi and two ministers, a Southern Baptist and a Methodist. At a luncheon for religious leaders in Manhattan just after the opening, DeMille piously explained, "I came here to ask you to use this picture, as I hope and pray that God himself will use it, for the good of the world."[4] *The Ten Commandments* was framed as a religious experience, but one that also told the Jewish/Christian story of Moses in a contemporary dialect, as a tale of sexual temptation, moral virtue, and the triumph of community.

Despite the critical consensus against it, DeMille's version of the Exodus story earned $18.5 million in gross domestic rentals in 1957, the first full year of its release. (By way of comparison, Elvis Presley's film debut, *Love Me Tender*, earned only $4.5 million that year.) The film's success was not surprising; *The Ten Commandments* was simply the biggest and most popular of the cycle of religious epics that swept the nation in the first half of the decade. For six of the twelve years from 1950 to 1962, a religious historical epic was the year's number one box office moneymaker. For the first four years of the decade (1950–1953), an epic with biblical themes was first or second every year.[5]

The popularity of religious films was not, however, based on simple piety. DeMille himself refused to characterize *The Ten Commandments* as just a retelling of the biblical story of the Hebrew Exodus from Egypt—and even less as "mere entertainment." Instead, he framed the religious narrative in terms of contemporary politics. In the prologue to the film, DeMille made a personal appearance on-screen in which he spoke directly to the audience, offering a modern interpretative lens for his historical film: "The theme of this picture is whether men should be ruled by God's law, or by the whims of a dictator like Ramses. Are men the property of the state, or are they free souls under God? This same struggle is still going on today." DeMille suggested that his film explained two visions of social organization. In one view—atheistic and statist –"men" were "the property of the state." In the other, people existed as "free souls under God." DeMille clearly invited his audience to equate the religiously coded individualism of the latter with the United States.[6] The prologue thus offered *The Ten Commandments'* anti-slavery theme as something more than the recounting of the Hebrew slaves' escape from Egypt; it was also a comment on the contemporary struggle by Americans against what DeMille had in other venues referred to as "Red Fascism"—totalitarianism exercised by either the Left or the Right.[7] This identification of communism and fascism as subspecies of "totalitarianism," equally opposed to "democracy" or "Americanism," was one of the most powerful rhetorical strategies of the cold war, one that resonated across the political spectrum.[8] DeMille's mobilization of that rhetoric encouraged his audience (and some subsequent critics) to read the film as a straightforward cold war allegory.

But contemporary events also suggested another connection: the premiere of *The Ten Commandments* in the fall of 1956 coincided almost exactly with the Suez crisis in the Middle East, in which modern Israelis and modern Egyptians faced off in a dramatic conflict. In response to the nationalization of the Suez Canal by Egyptian President Gamal Abdel Nasser, the combined forces of Israel, France, and Britain had launched an attack, arguing for the need to protect international shipping. As the crisis escalated, the *New York Times* noted the "profound" coincidence and suggested that, in fact, the modern conflict between Egypt and Israel "has its preamble in the Book of Exodus."[9] The Suez crisis and *The Ten Commandments* thus provided for each other a mutually constituting interpretative lens.

Yet although culture and politics both spoke of the Middle East, they seemed, at least at first, to come to different conclusions about the Israeli-Egyptian conflict. DeMille's film offered a view that was clearly favorable to the Hebrews in their struggle against their Egyptian masters. But when the United States intervened in the Suez crisis, it was on behalf of Egypt's Nasser. Refusing to back the European powers, the Eisenhower administration put severe economic pressure to bear on Britain to stop the invasion. Expressing U.S. officials' frustration with the course of events, Secretary of State John Foster Dulles complained, "What the British and French have done is nothing but the straight, old-fashioned variety of colonialism of the most obvious sort."[10]

Despite the apparent contradiction between a movie that castigated an ancient Egyptian pharaoh and a U.S. policy that seemed to support a modern Egyptian leader, this chapter suggests that, in fact, both *The Ten Commandments* and the foreign policy positions of the United States during Suez were part of a larger discourse about the nature of U.S. power in the Middle East in the postwar period. Focusing on three of the most popular films of the 1950s, *The Ten Commandments* (1956), *Quo Vadis* (1952), and *Ben-Hur* (1959), I argue that the biblical epics made representations of the religious history of the Middle East central to a discourse of U.S. "benevolent supremacy" in world affairs. Examining both the rhetoric of "epicness" that surrounded the films and the ubiquitous trope of exodus from slavery within them, I suggest that the biblical epics should be read not simply as antitotalitarian narratives but as anticolonial ones, situated at the moment when the United States took over from the European colonial nations the role of a preeminent world power.

The biblical films themselves were not univocal or isolated texts, nor were they simple allegorical reflections of an already-stable ideology. The meanings the films had in American culture in the 1950s depended on their intersections with other texts, on the interpenetration of different cultural and political sites. These conjunctures were the source of the films' considerable power. In particular, the narrative of the Hebrew Exodus had a long history of interpretation and invocation, which the biblical epics drew upon and significantly revised.[11] The refigured associations of the exodus trope played a part in narrating ideas about the United States' role in the decolonizing world. Those associations, those meanings, did not develop in isolation, but through a multifaceted set of representations that included not only films but also political activism, news accounts, and foreign policy (its texts and its activities).

My analysis of the discourse of "benevolent supremacy" begins by examining the rhetoric and political logic of National Security Council document 68 (NSC-68), which established many of the parameters of postwar U.S. security policy. Written in 1950, in the context of other policy positions and political crises, NSC-68 made a comprehensive argument that the United States was locked in a worldwide struggle over fundamental moral issues. Much as George Kennan's famous argument for containment in the journal *Foreign Affairs* had done three years earlier, the secret policy document of the National Security Council expanded the scope of the cold war to include not just the Soviet Union but any third world nations, including those in the strategically important Middle East, that might be influenced by the Soviet Union's "way of life." The chapter goes on to analyze the specific ways in which the biblical epic cycle contributed to the production of a discourse of U.S. power that framed it as inevitably global in its scope, benevolent in its intent, and benign in its effect. In particular, I examine the politics of the exodus narrative, which the epics consistently retold in terms of international relations, while nonetheless drawing upon and revising other possible meanings that were circulating in the public sphere in the United States—primarily the liberation rhetoric of the emerging civil rights movement. Both the epics and NSC-68 mobilized, and then transformed, the logic of liberation from racial slavery to support a political construct of U.S.-dominated liberty. In so doing, they used a complex and pernicious language of gender to suggest that American world power would produce a well-ordered international family.

THE MOMENT OF NSC-68

In the years immediately following World War II, the dominant question for the former Allies was the nature of the emerging global world order. With the defeat of Nazism, the underlying tensions between the Soviet Union and the Western nations emerged full force. For the Europeans, communism in Europe and decolonization movements in their empires presented themselves as the two great challenges of the era. The United States shared these concerns but from a rather different perspective. Anticommunism united Europe and the United States, but anticolonialism offered U.S. policymakers a unique opportunity to challenge European power. Emerging national independence movements argued against the continuation of European colonialism after a war that supposedly had been fought to free the world from tyranny. The Soviet Union often enthusiastically supported anticolonial movements, knowing that the independence of the decolonizing nations would come at the cost of European empires. The genius of U.S. foreign policy in the late 1940s and early 1950s was its ability to bridge the gap between European and third world nationalist views, to develop a better appreciation of the potential of third world nationalism and anticolonialism than the old colonial powers did, and to respond in a way that set the United States apart. Drawing on the anti-British and anticolonial rhetoric that formed the heart of American national origin stories, U.S. policymakers and pundits suggested that an American-dominated international order would best guarantee the expansion of democracy and secure the liberty of all nations. In 1951, Charles Hilliard's right-wing tract coined the phrase "benevolent supremacy" to describe this approach, but the essentials of his argument traversed the political spectrum.[12]

In 1941, Henry Luce, publisher of *Life* and *Time*, had written an enormously influential editorial, "The American Century," in which he argued that the United States was destined to be "the Good Samaritan" and "the powerhouse of the ideals of Freedom and Justice" in the postwar world. Assigning the United States the idealistic responsibility of feeding the world and organizing the peace in the wake of the disaster in Europe, Luce also argued that the United States had the "right to go with our ships and ocean-going airplanes, however we wish, when we wish, and as we wish."[13] Luce's vision was remarkable not only for its hubris but also for the way in which it seemed to express the common sense of a large sector of the U.S. elite. Although his views were challenged by some liberals and leftists, notably Henry Wallace, Luce's optimistic belief in the universality and benevolence of American values found great resonance in the immediate postwar years.[14]

The same year that Luce published his manifesto, President Roosevelt and Prime Minister Churchill announced the Atlantic Charter, which declared that both Britain and the United States would "respect the rights of all peoples to choose the form of government under which they will live." Although Churchill insisted that the language of the charter was intended to refer only to Europe, to those countries "now under Nazi yoke," some colonial governors were immediately worried about its implications, and Churchill had to offer a clarification in the House of Commons.[15]

At the end of the war, in this environment of increasing claims and rising tensions, the United States and the Soviet Union faced off over several major conflicts in Europe, including the division of Germany and the fates of Poland and Czechoslovakia. Taking a dim view of Soviet intentions and inclined toward broad assessment of Soviet capabilities, American policymakers were also concerned about what they viewed as the potential for Soviet expansion in the Middle East.[16] In early 1946, the head of the State Department's Division of Near Eastern Affairs circulated a memo, "The Present Situation in the Middle East—A Danger to World Peace," which suggested that the end of the war had removed the barriers to Soviet expansion in the West (i.e., Germany) and in the East (i.e., Japan). "Judging from recent events in the Near East," the official argued, "Russia now appears to be concentrating upon the removal of a third barrier in the South."[17] The location of the Middle East at the Soviet southern rim made the region important as a strategic asset; strong and friendly governments there could help block Soviet expansion while also securing U.S. influence. In the zero-sum game that was quickly developing, it was assumed that all nations would be allies of one superpower or the other. At the same time, U.S. officials, faced with what they believed to be an imminent domestic oil shortage, made the Middle East and its oil supplies a preeminent concern, calling secure access to oil "one of the great interests of the whole country."[18] Secretly, American concerns and interests in the region found expression in a series of Pentagon plans for the conduct of nuclear war against the Soviet Union. Written during the middle to late 1940s and early 1950s, these blueprints routinely assumed that the first and often motivating step in war would be a Soviet attempt to gain control of Middle Eastern oil fields and the Suez Canal. The presumed weakness of the British Empire and its dependence on U.S. power were central to the worldview of these plans, as was the assumption of the perfidy of the Soviet Union and the importance and vulnerability of the Arab states.[19]

As cold war attitudes began to harden in official Washington, policy-makers' worries about the Soviet Union in the Middle East came to seem prescient. In the early months of 1946, a crisis brewed in Iran. During World War II, Britain and the Soviets had jointly occupied Iran, with an agreement to withdraw their troops after the war. But a debate over whether the Soviet Union could gain access to oil concessions in northern Iran, parallel to those granted to British and American interests in southern Iran, led the Soviets to delay withdrawing their troops in the apparent hope of forcing more favorable economic agreements. The crisis highlighted the importance of access to oil for both superpowers, but U.S. officials argued that American interests in Iran included not only securing oil concessions for American companies but also blocking Soviet expansion and preventing threats to other Middle Eastern reserves, particularly those in Saudi Arabia. In the spring of 1946, under severe U.S. and international pressure, the Soviets came to a quick agreement with Iran on the troop withdrawal and oil exploration agreements.[20] (Seven years later, in 1953, the United States would once again act in Iran, when the CIA supported a royalist coup against a nationalist-minded and democratically elected leader who had nationalized the nation's oil.)[21]

From the State Department perspective, the United States' goal was to support leaders in the Middle East who would keep their countries from falling under either British or Soviet influence. A year after the Iran crisis, U.S. officials had a historic opportunity to promote that aim, with President Harry Truman's dramatic announcement of the Truman Doctrine. In a speech before Congress in March 1947, the president told the nation that Great Britain could no longer carry out its international commitments to aid either the conservative Greek government, which was fighting Communist-led forces, or the Turkish military, which was coming under Soviet pressure. Therefore, he said, the United States must take up the task. Moreover, Truman announced, the United States must be willing to support, in virtually any area of the world, "free peoples who are resisting subjugation by armed minorities or outside pressures." Both Greece and Turkey were handled by the Division of Near Eastern Affairs in the State Department, and both countries were considered part of the crucial Middle East gateway that might open the way to Soviet domination of the oil fields and potentially allow Soviet penetration into Europe and/or Asia. The Middle East had long been a stronghold of the British Empire, and after the breakup of the Ottoman Empire at the end of World War I, Britain had further strengthened its position in the region. Now the United States would be taking over key aspects of that role, as the military protector of friendly governments and thus as a major player in the area.

The Truman Doctrine looked well beyond the local conflict, however, impressively expanding the terrain of the cold war into a worldwide struggle between "alternative ways of life" and offering a generalized justification for U.S. interventions in the third world, not only the Middle East. Truman offered to "assist free peoples to work out their destinies in their own way" on the understanding that "totalitarian regimes imposed upon free peoples, by direct or indirect aggression, undermine the foundations of international peace and hence the security of the United States." Truman established a new standard of broadly defined and global American "interests" under the rubric of supporting the independence of "free peoples" fighting subjugation.[22] Truman's speech was designed to "electrify the American people" into supporting a substantial increase in aid to Greece and Turkey, and ultimately taking over British "responsibilities" for ensuring the survival of pro-Western governments around the world.

Even within the Truman administration, there was opposition to this new, expansive framework. Commerce secretary and New Deal stalwart Henry Wallace had earlier countered Luce's manifesto with his own call for "The People's Century." In 1946, he expressed his frustration with the emerging conception of a bipolar world order and denounced "any ideas of 'the American Century' or 'the Anglo-Saxon Century' ... any recrudescence of imperialism even under enlightened Anglo-Saxon atomic bomb auspices."[23] Once the Truman Doctrine was announced, opinion still was not settled about the nature of U.S. power: after decades of depression and war, there was a distinct isolationist strain in American political life when it came to foreign affairs. Conservative Republicans, as well as New Deal liberals like Wallace, had serious doubts about a Pax Americana. But increasingly opinion consolidated in the Truman administration, hardening about the nature of the Soviet Union and the necessity not only for U.S. leadership but also for U.S. supremacy.

The worldview articulated in the Truman Doctrine found its most sustained and perhaps its most influential expression in what was to become known as NSC-68. Drafted in 1950, primarily by Paul Nitze, then chief of the Policy Planning Staff of the State Department, NSC-68 was a report to President Truman on national security policy. The paper was classified as top secret until 1975, so it was read only by high-level policymakers. But those policymakers were exactly its intended audience. The document was designed, in the words of Secretary of State Dean Acheson, to "bludgeon the mass mind of 'top government' so that not only could the President make a decision but that the decision could be carried out."[24] NSC-68 soon also became a blueprint for articulating those policies to the lower level bureaucracy and the public. Despite its top secret classification, its basic outlines were broadly known, and its fundamental assumptions were articulated again and again by policymakers throughout the decade. As one historian has described it, NSC-68 was "the most famous unread paper of its era."[25]

The language and logic of NSC-68 framed the cold war conflict in the starkest of terms and made clear that the stakes were the allegiances and values of the rest of the world. It exaggerated the Soviet threat, arguing that the Soviets had the military capability "immediately to undertake and carry out" an attack that would simultaneously overrun Western Europe, launch air attacks against the British Isles, attack the U.S. mainland and Canada with atomic weapons, stop a major counterattack by Western forces, and go on to drive toward the Middle East, while still having enough left over for diversionary tactics in other areas.[26] The overall goal of the argument was to marshal support for engaging in a worldwide struggle against communism and thus for increasing the U.S. military budget threefold. As Acheson later described it, NSC-68 consciously simplified the complex political situation: niceties and nuance gave way to "bluntness, almost brutality, in carrying home a point.... [P]oints to be understandable had to be clear. If we made our points clearer than truth, we did not differ from most other educators and could hardly do otherwise."[27]

NSC-68 is a long, complex document, one that has merited considerable attention and interpretation by historians and social scientists.[28] I focus here on one aspect of the paper, one that was especially relevant to its intersections with the cultural texts of the biblical epics: the construction of the cold war as a global contest of wills and of values, in which slavery, sexuality, and sin are central to the political struggle for ascendancy in the postwar order.

NSC-68 divides the world geographically into two centers of power, the United States and the Soviet Union. This division is paralleled by a division between the "free society" and the "slave state." "There is a basic conflict," the text argues, "between the idea of freedom under a government of laws, and the idea of slavery under the grim oligarchy of the Kremlin."[29] The slave state is the inevitable result of a Soviet ideology. The Soviet Union is "animated by a new fanatic faith, antithetical to our own, and seeks to impose its absolute authority over the rest of the world" (25). Forty-five years after the fact, the discourse that linked communism and slavery has become so familiar that it is almost naturalized; even those who question the equation can be numbed to the striking originality of the move. But a reading of the full text of NSC-68 leaves no doubt regarding the rhetorical power of the gesture that equated the Soviet Union with slavery, slavery with the "degradation" and "submission" of the individual to the state, and submission with the "perversion" of true religious faith:

> For the breath of freedom cannot be tolerated in a society which
> has come under the domination of an individual or group of indi-
> viduals with a will to absolute power. Where the despot holds
> absolute power—the absolute power of an absolutely powerful
> will—all other wills must be subjugated in an act of willing
> submission, a degradation willed by the individual upon himself
> under the compulsion of a perverted faith. (28)

Under the influence of a Nietzschean superman or a powerful ideology, individuals would be influenced to accept, even welcome, their own enslavement.

In the context of American history, the rhetoric of opposition to slavery has clear racial connotations; within the binary logic of NSC-68, the United States is constructed as a nation that has put an end to racial slavery and will stand against the reinstitution of slavery in any (totalitarian) form. But as quickly as the racial connotations of slavery are evoked, they are refigured: slavery becomes the *willing* subjugation of the will of the individual to another; it is linked to "degradation," "compulsion," and perversion. The "perverted faith" of the slave state leads men to "will" themselves to other men. Despots dominate the slaves by the power of their superior will. The slave is a slave because *he* submits; as a subservient male, his submission has the markers of both a gender and a (homo)sexual transgression.[30]

NSC-68 argues that the perverted faith of the slave state is being preached to the peoples of the former imperial colonies. There is a real danger that the ex-colonials will submit. Even if there were no Soviet Union, the development of new independent states would mean unpredictable changes: "We would face the fact that in a shrinking world the absence of order among nations is becoming less and less tolerable." The question emerges, then, "whether the world will long tolerate this tension without moving toward some kind of order, on somebody's terms" (52). This changing world, NSC-68 suggests, requires the stabilization that an American-dominated order would provide.

Without it, the Soviet Union might easily control the new nations. The alternative to Soviet global power, the paper suggests, is a public "demonstration" of the superiority of freedom to slavery:

> The assault on free institutions is world-wide now, and in the context of the present polarization of power a defeat of free institutions anywhere in the world is a defeat everywhere....[W]e must work with our allies and the former subject peoples to seek to create a world society based on the principle of consent....The idea of slavery can only be overcome by the timely and persistent demonstration of the superiority of the idea of freedom. (27–32)

In that context, the "will" of Americans must be strengthened. If the United States fails to confront the Soviet Union, it will be cultivating the same kind of weakness that submitted to the rise of communism in Eastern Europe and allowed the end of colonial empires. Proper assertion is the answer: "Our fundamental purpose is more likely to be defeated from lack of the will to maintain it, than from any mistakes we may make or assaults we may undergo because of asserting that will" (54). It is within this discourse that the struggle over values takes on a world-historical dimension: the combination of racial, gender, and sexual transgressions of the "slave state" requires that communism be met, wherever it appears, by the demonstration of a superior will. Thus consent and submission, faith and the perversion of faith, slavery and freedom became the intertwined terms by which policymakers framed U.S. world power.

In response to the impact of NSC-68 within the government, a group called the Committee on the Present Danger organized a political campaign to promote its conclusions to the public. This committee was a group of "worthy citizens" who, after studying the secret document, could then go to the public and say: "We are advised, and you can accept what we say." In speeches and interviews, their task was to convince the nation of the need not only to increase military spending substantially but also to make a commitment to intervening where necessary to create an "order" that would be favorable to the United States. The Committee on the Present Danger continued to function until 1953, when its members considered themselves to have done their job. They disbanded, certain that there was widespread government and public support for permanent increases in military spending, rearmament and aid to Europe, and anticommunist ideology.[31]

Many policymakers and unofficial leaders believed, given the history of isolationism and postwar exhaustion, that the public needed to be educated and prodded. Yet already by the late 1940s, there was also an emerging assumption in the public sphere generally that decolonization and independence were inevitable for most of Britain's and France's colonial possessions and that the United States would be heir to a new world order. The U.S. press mirrored policymakers in expounding on the decline of the British Empire and wondering about its implications. In mass newspapers and magazines, this concern unfolded within the long-standing fascination with British royalty and power—a fascination that mixed both wonder and contempt. Between 1951 and 1953, for example, the British royalty graced the cover of *Newsweek* eight times.[32] (In that same period, the McCarthy hearings were reported in a cover story only once.) These articles often interspersed royalty lore with a frank discussion of the decline of British world power. By this point, Britain had faced or was facing revolts or independence movements in India/Pakistan, Burma, Ceylon (Sri Lanka), Kenya, and Palestine; the French were under siege in Vietnam, Laos, and Cambodia and were seeing the beginning of serious opposition in Algeria. In January 1950, *Newsweek* mused on this reality in an article that linked the recent travels of Foreign Secretary Ernest Bevin to the likely future of heiress apparent Princess Elizabeth. Bevin's task, *Newsweek* pointed out, was "to preside over the dissolution of the British Empire," an empire held "by a Britain no longer able to pay the price of admiralty." When she ascended to the throne, Elizabeth would inherit "an empire that has evolved out of all recognition."[33]

Three years later, *Newsweek* published a long cover story which reported that Elizabeth, now queen, and her husband, Philip, were making their first official Commonwealth tour in a much-changed world. The magazine's ambivalence about the British and their empire was obvious. On the one hand, the article detailed Elizabeth's trip, enthusiastically describing the number of miles traveled and the extent and cost of preparations. A world map of the queen's route was illustrated with stick figures of the various dark-skinned natives of Jamaica, Australia, the Fiji Islands, and Africa. Surely these subjects were still loyal, *Newsweek* mused, and "the sight of the royal couple would make millions in [the queen's] outermost realms feel less lonely and more securely bound to the crown." On the other hand, the article pointed out that this was not the same kind of empire that her grandfather King George V had ruled: India was now a republic, Pakistan was preparing to follow, and nationalist tensions were apparent everywhere in Africa. The cover of the magazine made the point explicit in a nice double entendre; a full-page photo of the royal couple was captioned in large letters: "Elizabeth and Philip: At the Edge of Empire."[34]

Although Hilliard's term "benevolent supremacy" was not widely used, the phrase underscored a sense that American power would have a different basis than that of either Europe or the Soviet Union. "There need be no time or effort lost by a benevolent community in answering criticism such as 'imperialism,'" Hilliard assured his readers in 1951. "The attraction of kindred elements into an ever increasing area of benevolent sovereignty should be … the announced and enthusiastically sought objective of the forces of good will throughout this earthly globe."[35] At the policy level, such sentiments linked U.S. economic and military strength to a program that was anticommunist, anticolonial, and supportive of free markets. The political centerpiece of this program was a series of regional alliances and bilateral partnerships. Of course, U.S. anticolonialism, however much it might be expressed in rhetoric, was generally tempered by the more compelling thrust of the cold war, as evidenced by U.S. support for France in the mid-1950s, including direct backing of French colonialism in Indochina and economic aid that helped undergird the French war against Algerians fighting for independence. But the overall aim was generally to shore up the political and economic stability of European allies while displacing or moderating their influence in areas of military or economic importance to the United States.

The special significance of the Middle East within the discourse of benevolent supremacy derived from the importance of oil resources to the West (and to the East) and from the region's geographic position—bordering the Soviet Union, Europe, and the Mediterranean. During the 1950s, this interest was expressed publicly through the formation of the Central Treaty Organization (1955), through five major acts or threats of military intervention, and through military and economic assistance programs involving Saudi Arabia, Turkey, Israel, and Greece.[36] The Middle East was not the only area of concern; it did, however, serve as a central staging ground for an assertion of U.S. postwar dominance in relation to both the European allies and the formerly colonized and decolonizing nations.

The Middle East was important to the discourse of benevolent supremacy for another reason as well: the production of meanings *about* the Middle East had a more general import for the construction of U.S. international power in the postwar era. In popular culture, representations of the region drew on biblical stories, religiously inflected moral lessons, and ancient history as the foundation for building multifaceted associative meanings for contemporary politics and international relations. The biblical epic films were significant in this regard, not just for what they said about the Middle East but also for what they made the Middle East say about the world.

THE "HISTORY" OF EPICS

The biblical epics of the 1950s were not presented only on the theater screen; they also were made available to viewing audiences through a range of extrafilmic discourses. The epics were profoundly multitextual representations. Framed by reviews and discussed in innumerable newspaper and magazine articles, they were events in themselves.[37] The potential audience was made aware that the religious epics offered *more:* a bigger screen, longer movies, and the opportunity to enjoy realistic and historically accurate depictions of ever-wider vistas and ever-expanding terrains. Like the Holy Land images of the nineteenth century, epic films promised historical and religious knowledge, combined with the promise of "views" and spectacle. As NSC-68 had expanded the sphere of vital U.S. interests to a global scale, the extrafilmic discourse of epicness and authenticity that surrounded the biblical films established the vast terrain of "history," "biblical times," and "religion" as the province of the knowledgeable viewer.

Until recently, scholarship on the biblical epics has been remarkably sparse.[38] Those film scholars and historians who have attended to the genre have often seen the religious content as entirely superficial, dismissing the epics as "surge and splendor" costume dramas whose function was to compete with the arrival of television by offering expensive visual spectacle and sexualized display.[39] A few critics have followed DeMille's lead in reading the films as simple cold war allegories, as reflections of an already-stable ideology rather than as productive texts in their own right. Alan Nadel, for example, has argued for reading *The Ten Commandments* in terms of both the policy of containment and American foreign policy in the Middle East, but his analysis depends on a fairly literal-minded allegorical interpretation, as when he argues that the world of the Egyptians has three chief sites of conflict, "each corresponding to a socioeconomic class in postwar America."[40] This suggests a kind of conscious, careful ideological intent that few films actually exhibit.

More promising has been discussion of the cultural work of historical films in general. Vivian Sobchack has argued that historical epics are as much about *historicity* as they are about any particular historical event. "The Hollywood historical epic," she writes, "is as central to our understanding of what we mean by the 'historical' and 'History' as any work of academic scholarship."[41] Indeed, when DeMille released his first biblical epic of the sound era, *Samson and Delilah* (1940), his director of research, Henry Noerdelinger, launched a forty-city tour to speak about the film's historical background. The film was endorsed by the International Council of Christian Education, but it was also said to be making a more secular splash: harkening back to the days of Orientalist department store shows, a *Newsweek* cover story reported that designers were featuring tie-ins of women's clothes influenced by *Samson and Delilah's* Minoan period costumes.[42]

The studios and the media went to extraordinary lengths to establish biblical epics as History on a grand scale. The producers of *The Ten Commandments*, for example, highlighted the supposedly unusual amount of preproduction research that was behind it, and many of the interviews and articles in the popular press reproduced this assertion. The *New York Times* repeated studio claims that "historical research alone cost hundreds of thousands of dollars and involved material from some 1,800 reference books and myriad documents on several continents." *Time* similarly reported that De-Mille spent "three years and $300,000 in research."[43]

In addition, DeMille and Noerdelinger published a rather remarkable volume called *Moses and Egypt*, which documented all the sources used as background for the film. The book described the life and times of Moses and the historical story of the Exodus as told in the accounts of the "ancient historians." Citing both Christian and Jewish religious scholars as its main sources, the book served as an unusual and rather anxious authentification for the film, both historical and religious. DeMille's introduction to *Moses and Egypt* also made explicit his claim to historical authority. By documenting the basis for his decisions about what to show and how to show it in the film, DeMille insisted that his role as director required, and was based on, his command of historical materials and information. He quoted at some length a letter written to him by a "prominent professor," who enthused: "The challenge you must meet...is even greater than that faced by the historian.... [You] must solve every problem, no matter how small or detailed...; you cannot say, along with the historian, 'I do not know.' "[44] This positioning of the films *as* history, then, suggested not only the moral significance of film histories but also the authority of the director-cum-historian.

In virtually every instance, the media's claims for historical knowledge were linked to an even more enthusiastic rhetoric of "bigness" and effectiveness, which then enabled the grand authority that the epics required. In part, this derived from the particular association that the biblical epic had with the introduction of widescreen formats in the early 1950s. Although widescreen techniques were used for a range of films, including Westerns and adventure tales, the biblical epic quickly came to be defined as a widescreen genre.[45] Several of the biblical films, including DeMille's *Samson and Delilah* in 1949 and *Quo Vadis* in 1952, were made before the onset of widescreen, but after the introduction of CinemaScope in 1953, every one of the biblical epics was produced in one or another widescreen format. Perhaps not surprisingly, the first CinemaScope production was the biblical epic *The Robe*. The film's premiere at the Roxy Theater in New York City in September 1953 included sixty-five hundred "invited guests" and more than six thousand onlookers who gathered outside the theater to celebrity watch.[46] The film, based on a best-selling novel, was extremely popular, breaking opening-week box office records, grossing more than $20 million in 1953, and inviting comparisons to the most popular movie made to date, *Gone with the Wind*. The public fervor in both the industry and the popular press combined excitement over the film's technical feats with the already common discourse of biblical/historical authority and the reverent reporting of film costs and gross. The combination seemed to invite hyperbole, as well as some sarcasm, as when *Hollywood Reporter* columnist Mike Connolly commented: "*The Robe* just has to be the greatest grosser of all time. It might even outsell the Bible."[47] In fact, no reviewer of any of the biblical epics could resist discussing the "bigness" of the films, and the tie-in articles in *Life* and *Look* almost always began with lists of the number of extras and the costs incurred, along with a detailing of the lavishness of the sets and an assurance of the impressive number of years the film had been in the making.[48]

The extrafilmic claims for "epicness" reached perhaps their highest pitch with *The Ten Commandments*, as reviews and articles piled superlative upon superlative: the film was "gigantic," "grandiose," "impressive," "the most colossal of all."[49] *Life* profiled DeMille and the movie in frankly aggrandizing terms, announcing to readers that on the set in Egypt, DeMille had "found things proceeding on the grand scale to which he was accustomed." After expanding upon the number of cast members, the multitude of animals mobilized, and the large size of the set, the article compared DeMille to the pharaoh himself: "Imbued with the biblical spirit, he had set the tone of his whole approach months before when addressing his writers to the task before them. 'So let it be written, gentlemen!' he had said. 'So let it be done!' It was now being done."[50] Even reviewers who reviled the film spoke of it in terms of its epic scale, as when *Time* described it as not simply bad but "perhaps the most vulgar movie ever made"—and then went on to point out that DeMille constructed the biggest movie set in history.[51]

That the making of biblical epics was largely an American phenomenon was not an accident. In the United States, the will to "epicness" was combined with the resources needed to mount an epic enterprise of filmmaking and with the publicity and worldwide distribution networks that could make such an enterprise profitable. After World War II, Hollywood was in a posi-

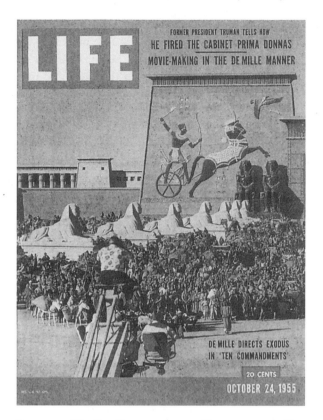

Figure 5. *The Ten Commandments* (Paramount, 1956)
on the cover of *Life* magazine in October 1955, a year before its release. Courtesy of *Life* magazine © Time Inc.

tion to capitalize on its already strong international distribution system
to establish its near-complete dominance in world cinema. Despite the economic significance of this global audience, however, the intertextual context
of the films positioned them and their audience as specifically American.
Christian Metz has argued that film spectators experience their "primary
identification" with the knowledge possessed by the camera as transcenden-
tal agency. The identification an audience feels with the characters on screen
is secondary, helpful but not required in positioning an audience as invested
in a story.[52] Metz's argument is useful in analyzing the historically specific
spectator position produced by the biblical epics. While there are generally
"positive" characters as protagonists in the epics, the presumed American audience for the films was invited to identify strongly not only with the agency
of the camera but also with the agency that produced the spectacle. Viewers

were implicitly included in this relationship of authority through their access to the knowledge that the filmmaker had accumulated and by their participation in the grandeur—the epicness—of the films' display. Although theoretically any spectator could identify with the agency of production, the extrafilmic discourse suggested that Hollywood (and thus America) was unique in its ability to command the resources and the organization required to stage an epic film.

An identification with the production process would also allow audience members to participate in the films' specific claims about history. And historical representations, be they textbooks or scholarly studies, have often been central to the construction of national identities. Nations require narrations, accounts of the particular history of "the people" who are supposed to constitute the national community.[53] The histories told in the epics were not, seemingly, *about* Americans, yet the films did signify the Americanness of their protagonists, as I discuss later. Beyond that the discourse of epicness suggested that audiences would gather an expansive historical knowledge that was also a form of nationally specific spectatorial power, much as the Truman Doctrine had suggested that benevolent supremacy would require Americans to learn about, and then to intervene in, a world they might be unfamiliar with. "Epicness" situated filmmaking as a form of American power—and film-*going* as a practical and accessible participation in that knowledgeable relation.

THE PEOPLE OF THE EPICS

Quo Vadis (1952) opens with an extreme long shot of a winding road in a wide green vista, with horses and men marching in the distance. The camera then cuts to a frontal medium shot of a soldier on a horse, and then to drummers and other soldiers walking down the dusty road. Some of the soldiers are whipping men whose arms and legs are in chains. A male voice narrates, with the sound of the whip as punctuation:

> Imperial Rome is the center of the empire, the undisputed master
> of the world. But with this power inevitably comes corruption: No
> man is sure of his life, the individual is at the mercy of the state,
> murder replaces justice. . . . Rulers of conquered nations surrender
> their helpless subjects to bondage. High and low alike become
> Roman slaves, Roman hostages. There is no escape from the whip
> and the sword. That any force on earth can shake the foundations
> of this pyramid of power and corruption, of human misery and
> slavery seems inconceivable . . .

But such a force *has* arisen, and it is the task of *Quo Vadis* to tell the story of early Christianity as the "new faith" that will challenge the old Roman Empire and point the way to a "great new civilization." *Ben-Hur* has a very similar plot, in which Roman misrule is challenged by the "troublesome people" of Judea, and the presence of Christ signals the coming of a new order. In *The Ten Commandments*, the setting is imperial Egypt rather than imperial Rome, but the despotism and slavery are equally the hallmarks of the corrupt Ramses and the Egyptian court, and Moses represents "the people" who will construct a new order.[54]

The ancient histories told by the biblical epics were almost universally stories of a particular type: a history of "the people"—to use the common term from the narrative voice-overs—either Hebrew or Christian or both, who are engaged in a valiant struggle against oppression and slavery. The plots inevitably expose the totalitarian nature of an older imperial form, be it Roman or Egyptian, and suggest that the old empire is in decline. The narrative then constructs an alternative, a Hebrew/Christian nationalism, individualistic in its emphases, which is politically, morally, and sexually superior to the old order it will displace. In each case, an implicitly democratic people challenge both empire and slavery, and legitimate faith confronts the false faiths of the old order. Through a powerful set of parallels, overlaps, and refigurations, the ancient Jewish and/or Christian histories of the films are infused with a particularly *national* signification, and thus recuperated as a usable past, suitable for imagining "America" at the moment of European decline.

The epics construct their moral and political logic through the organization of space. In *Ben-Hur*, for example, the protagonist, Judah Ben-Hur (Charlton Heston), moves through three types of space: imperial staging grounds, slave prisons, and nationalist havens. These moral geographies carry distinct social and political meanings. At the beginning of the film, Judah is a wealthy and well-respected leader in his home province of Judea, though as a Jew living under the yoke of the Roman Empire, his freedom and autonomy are limited. From the first shot of the film, the audience is cued to the oppressive weight of imperial space via repeated images of Roman might: lavish, colorful parades; incessant military marches; sumptuous meals. One of the advantages of the widescreen format was that it made possible the use of unprecedented panoramic views, which in turn allowed expansive representations of imperial pomp and circumstance. In general, the epics took full advantage of the opportunity, which then only encouraged critics to dismiss them as simply "costume dramas," with emphasis on the costumes. But representations of imperial space were, in fact, saturated with meaning. In *Ben-Hur* the empire is represented by the parades that Roman soldiers make through Jerusalem, the Roman baths where the military governor Messala and his officers relax, and Rome itself. These scenes are distinguished by white, harsh lighting, as well as by a preponderance of long shots and panoramic views. The colors are brilliant, and sometimes sumptuous, but never warm—primary colors, particularly reds and whites, predominate. Imperial space is not space the audience is invited *into*; its excess, its staging as spectacle and display, constructs the audience as a distanced observer.

The plot pits Judah against the representatives of Rome, primarily through his conflict with his old boyhood friend Messala, who grew up in Judea but has since gone to Rome and risen in the ranks. When Messala returns to the province, he is a Roman military leader and thus an oppressor; his mistake is believing that Judah will be his collaborator. When Judah refuses to aid him, Messala uses a pretext to arrest Judah's mother and sister, and to condemn Judah to become a slave in the galleys of a Roman ship.

The ship is a slave space; on it, Judah is simply one of hundreds of condemned men rowing the ship, known simply by his number, 41. The scenes of Judah's captivity highlight the crowded, sweating bodies. The camera moves awkwardly in and out of the ship galley, peering into the half-lit, shadowy pit or, aimed upward, taking in the harshly lit deck of the ship through the galley's bars. Like the Roman prison where Judah's mother and sister are kept, the slave space literally lies *under* the sites of Roman authority, inevitably linked to it as the dark side of unjust power.

The third type of space offers an alternative order to the imperial-slave nexus. It is best described as "nationalist" space; it represents the democratic character of the anti-imperial opposition, as well as promise and hope of freedom for the Jews who struggle against Rome. Judah Ben-Hur's home before the Romans destroy it is one such space. Shot in soft lighting, with the sets designed in warm colors and the characters dressed in simple, flowing garments, it marks democracy as an aesthetic. The home of the sheik who helps Judah prepare his revenge against Messala is similar: the glowing bronze and rich reds—very unlike the harsh reds of Rome—make it a welcoming place, where the characters are shot in medium close-up, and the conversation is gentle and playful.

The contrast between these various spaces and the moral orders associated with them is particularly striking when they collide. Early on in the film, for example, the new Roman governor of Judea parades through the streets of Jerusalem. The Romans' march through the narrow streets is pompous and intimidating. The soldiers, in their grays, whites, and reds, are surrounded by dust and filmed in a white daylight. The cutaways from the

Figure 6.   Judah Ben-Hur (Charlton Heston) enjoys a meal in the home of Sheik Ilderim (Hugh Griffith) in *Ben-Hur* (MGM, 1959). Their companionship constructs one of *Ben-Hur*'s inviting, nationalist spaces. Courtesy of the Museum of Modern Art Film Stills Archive.

parade to the Jews who watch from the sidelines provide a vivid contrast: the medium shots and close-ups show two or three faces at a time, lit by warm yellows. The Jews are dressed in simple browns or cream; their homely garb is unpretentious and serviceable, but appealing.

The Ten Commandments employs very similar strategies. Also starring Charlton Heston, as Moses, the plot focuses on Moses' growing awareness that he is not, and cannot be, part of the ruling Egyptian dynasty. He discovers that he is a Hebrew, gives up his pursuit of the Egyptian beauty Nefertiri (Ann Baxter), and goes to the desert to find his true calling. Once Moses leaves the Egyptian court, the film organizes a consistent contrast between the Hebrews and the Egyptians that is coded both by color and by lighting. During the Exodus scene, for example, the mass movement of the Hebrews is represented by panoramic shots of the crowd, but these are intercut with vignettes featuring two or three people, often children, who enact "human" and humorous minidramas. (Three children struggle to get a mule to move; a baby girl follows a flock of geese; two children excitedly describe events to their blind grandfather.) The Hebrews wear warm browns and occasional muted blues or soft yellows. The Exodus montage is also marked by a remarkably consistent naming of individuals; as the camera scans the crowd, the Hebrews call to each other by name: Rebecca, Rachael, Benjamin, Naomi, Joshua. Through the use of names and frequent close-ups, the insertion of humorous vignettes, and the focus on children, the film privileges the Hebrew space of the Exodus as individualizing and welcoming.[55]

In contrast, the Egyptians chasing the Hebrews are represented almost exclusively through panoramic shots of masses of soldiers and horses, with only an occasional cut to the angry face of Ramses (Yul Brynner) as he leads them to their doom. The Egyptian soldiers are undifferentiated regiments of blues and whites and ugly browns; the extreme long shots mark imperial space as totalitarian, as a space without individuals. The pharaoh, despotic and domineering, has subjugated the soldiers to his will—they are slaves in a slave state.

The epics construct Hebrew/Christian nationalism as the political and morally superior successor to imperial rule and the slave state. Within the coded discourse of the films, the Hebrews and Christians function in complex ways to represent the "new empire" they will usher in. The claims for the moral stature of "the people" seems at one level to have simple cold war connotations. The plot and narration of the films suggest that the Romans and the Hebrews are totalitarians—dictators and slave masters who, in DeMille's terms, make "men the property of the state." The alternative to the slave state is the democratic space of human encounter. In the films in which "the people" are early Christians (as in *Quo Vadis* and *The Robe*), their association with Americans is suggested by the religiously tinged language of contemporary anticommunism, especially given the long history in American political culture of equating Christianity with Americanism.[56]

In fact, the Americanness of "the people" is suggested even when the story focuses on ancient Hebrews (as in *The Ten Commandments* and *Ben-Hur*). Of course, it is a classic move of much Christian theology to appropriate the Jewish tradition as "prehistory" of the Christian narrative, as the phrase "Old Testament" suggests. In this vein, Alan Nadel has argued that the Hebrews in *The Ten Commandments* are consistently marked less as Jews than as proto-Christians: the details of Moses' life are structured with strong parallels to the Gospel accounts of the life of Jesus; the scene of the first Passover is organized to replicate the traditional Christian iconographies of the Last Supper, with Moses at the center of a long table and others clustered around him.[57] *Ben-Hur* works through a similar logic. While Judah Ben-Hur is explicitly presented as a Jew (at least twice in the film, for example, we see a shot of Judah laying his head against a door where a Jewish symbol—first a Star of David, later a mezuzah—is visible next to him), his story is a Christian story. He lives at the time of Jesus; his path intersects with that of Jesus and his followers in myriad ways; and at the end of the film, Judah is led to follow the teachings of this "new rabbi" by Esther, his Jewish beloved (who is played by the Israeli actress Haya Harareet). Thus, the miraculous events of Judah's life are presented as testament to the truth of the Christian revision of Judaism. In making Christians of Jews, the plots seem to invite a reading that equates Hebrews/Christians with Americans and atheistic or idolatrous Romans/Egyptians with communists.

This equation of ancient Hebrews with Christianity and Americanness surely did its own kind of cultural work in the 1950s, when the issue of Jewish assimilation was of major concern, both to Jewish political organizations and to Hollywood. In the early postwar period, Hollywood had produced several "problem films" about anti-Semitism, all of which addressed the irrationality of hatred against Jews and presented their heroes as ideal American types. The epics and their Americanized heroes could well have functioned as part of the "whitening" of the racial status of Jews in the years after the Holocaust, precisely through their exclusions and brutalizations of ancient Jewish history.[58]

The Hebrew/Christian "people," however, signify something more multidimensional and complex than any straightforward allegorical reading would suggest. The decline-of-a-corrupt-empire theme within the films also invites an interpretation of "the people" as the formerly colonized peoples of the third world. The casting of the films would seem to encourage such a view: in almost all instances, the Hebrews/Christians are played by American actors, while the Romans/Egyptians are usually played by non-American, often British, actors. The differences in the accents and personal carriage of the actors are mobilized as signifiers of imperial versus democratic values, with the Romans/Egyptians standing in for the fading British Empire and the American actors playing the brave inhabitants of the new, decolonizing nations.[59] In Ben-Hur, for example, the relationship between Judah Ben-Hur, a Jew, and Sheik Ilderim, an Arab, is solidified by their shared refusal to acknowledge the right of Roman rule in Palestine. Throughout the film, the Romans consistently hurl insults at both Jews and Arabs, asserting their own superiority and announcing the gloriousness of the Roman Empire. The parallels to the failed British Mandate in Palestine (1916–1945) are remarkably close to the surface.

The founding of Israel in 1948 is clearly relevant to these stories. In Israel, Jewish nationalism had found a direct and contemporary expression. In the wake of the Holocaust, Israel was the one country, of all those forged out of the old British Empire, whose independence was most supported in the West. Truman's competition with the Soviet Union to be the first nation to offer recognition to the new state is just one example of the unique moral status Israel carried.[60] The epic cycle sometimes seemed to bring this connotation to the surface of the narrative. In *Soloman and Sheba* (1959), for example, the Moabite king boasts that he will drive the Hebrews "into the sea," while Solomon proudly announces that his country, so recently a barren desert, has been transformed: "It is a joy to make the desert bloom," he sighs.[61] Yet the films also did more; they drew upon, but also transformed, the associations that would have conflated the Hebrews of the narrative with the modern Israelis who had just so visibly formed their nation in Palestine.

The role of Sheik Ilderim in *Ben-Hur* is interesting precisely because his presence disallows any reading of the film as an exclusive statement of Jewish/Israeli nationalism. The sheik is one of the few "Arab" characters in a genre that is obsessed with the ancient Middle East as the site of an originating Hebrew-Christian nationalist tradition. It would be easy to interpret him as just a bumbling negative stereotype. Played in brownface by the Welsh-born actor Hugh Griffith, who won an Oscar for the role, the sheik is in some ways a cartoonish figure, generous but often silly, whose flamboyant behavior and rough manners are matched by his rather outlandish affection for his horses, whom he calls his "children" and his "beauties." A close reading of his role, however, quickly highlights the limitations of any ideological reading of these films based simply on an analysis of "negative stereotypes of the (Arab) other." The sheik is, after all, one of the heroes of the film. He is generally represented as a kindly character, albeit rather foolish and comic. Focusing only on the stereotypical aspects of this representation will tell us almost nothing about the important ideological work the character does within the film as a whole.

Sheik Ilderim is important because he is a central part of *Ben-Hur*'s anti-Roman contingent. He is presented in privileged terms within the film, aligned with the warm colors and human scale of the film's "nationalist space." The narrative places the sheik as Judah's strongest backer; he provides Judah's horses and gets him into the all-important chariot race where he will confront the Roman Messala. Near the end of the film, just before the chariot race is to begin, Sheik Ilderim suggests that the fight against Roman imperialism is a shared battle; placing a Star of David around Judah's neck, he urges him to win the race: "The Star of David—to shine out for your people and my people together, and blind the eyes of Rome!" Ben-Hur's victory against Messala is clearly a nationalist victory not just for

Jews but also for Arabs and (implicitly) for all those who stand with them against imperial rule—that is, for America as well.

The potential multivocality of such moments is not so much a textual problem as it is part of the genre's richness and power. In the context of the 1950s, it would not have seemed incongruous for Rome and ancient Egypt to simultaneously suggest the failures of the British Empire and the Soviet Union. In other texts, such as NSC-68, the equation of slaveholding, imperialism, and communism made common sense. Similarly, the collective identity of "the people" is able to signify both American cold war nationalism and the "formerly subject peoples" who have freed themselves from the "slavery" of empire. The Hebrew-Christian signifier elegantly links two signifieds: in the chain of substitutions and exchange within the texts, the trope of "the people" equates "Americans" and "subject peoples" as anticolonial signs.

THE GENDERED LOGICS OF THE SLAVE STATE

Liberation from bondage is a theme in almost all the epics; in each case tyranny makes "the people" slaves, or prisoners, or persecuted. In *The Ten Commandments,* Hebrews are held as slaves by the Egyptians. A 1955 film directed by Howard Hawks, *Land of the Pharaohs,* is set in an earlier period, but it narrates the enslavement of the (light-skinned) Kushites by the Pharaoh and their eventual exodus. In *Ben-Hur,* not only is Judah himself condemned to be a slave, but all the peoples of Judea are prisoners of Roman tyranny. In *Quo Vadis* and *The Robe,* Rome is persecuting and imprisoning Christians and enslaving other peoples. Overall, the essential misrule embodied by both Romans and Egyptians is marked by three, related "facts": they hold large numbers of slaves; the leadership is corrupt and despotic; and they treat women as sexual property. Taken as a genre, the religious epics link slaveholding, totalitarianism, and sexual despotism.

The problem of slavery in the films had multiple resonances not only for foreign policy but also in relation to politics and identity within the United States. As we have seen, the language of NSC-68 suggested slavery as a sexual and gender perversion—a failure of manliness that led men to be slaves to other men. The films solicited and refigured those allusions through a rhetoric of anticolonial liberation that also drew heavily on the simultaneous circulation of the racialized meanings of the exodus trope within the emerging civil rights movement. Thus the racial connotations were multifaceted: while the Hebrew stories did point toward the positioning of Jews within U.S. racial discourse, almost all the films also suggested, through the exodus trope, the contested status of African Americans. In fact, the interpenetration of the "foreign" and "domestic" meanings of the anti-slavery narrative makes clear that the construction of U.S. international authority depended on the reformulation of domestic constructs of race and gender. At the same time, this flow also worked in reverse: race and gender constructs *within* the United States became meaningful in part through the construction of U.S. nationalism and international power.

The exodus story had a long history in black thought well before the rise of the civil rights movement in the late 1940s. It was central, for example, to mainstream black churches during most of the nineteenth and early twentieth century, as part of the language through which the political hope of worldly liberation for African Americans was both articulated and contained. Black Christianity saw African American history as a retelling of the Hebrew story, as a potential site for the reentry of God into history for the liberation of a people. Thus the church, on the one hand, consolidated black identity and articulated the notion of a *right* to liberation; on the other, it promised that liberation would come from the hand of God, and it focused on personal faith rather than social transformation.[62] Traditional African American spirituals often retold the biblical story—"Go Down Moses" is only the most well-known example—and several important literary productions, such as James Weldon Johnson's poem "Let My People Go" (1927) built on and reinterpreted those spirituals.[63]

In his study of black-Jewish relations, Jonathan Kaufman describes the exodus metaphor as a primary link between black and Jewish history. In the eighteenth and nineteenth centuries, he argues, "the story of the Jews enslaved in Egypt became the first protest story, Negro spirituals the first protest songs."[64] The narrative of the ancient Hebrews and their struggle for freedom was thus mapped onto American terrain: the Ohio River as the Jordan, the South as Egypt, the North as the promised land. This mapping of biblical stories onto lived geography was not unique to African Americans, of course; the story of Exodus had been translated into "spatial history" and moral geographies by diverse communities, including the Anglo-Saxons, the Puritans, and Israeli Jews.[65]

As the civil rights struggle began to heat up in the 1940s and 1950s, African American activism made itself highly visible as a political force: in 1941, for example, A. Phillip Randolph threatened to bring one hundred thousand people to a Negro March on Washington unless Roosevelt ended segregation in the defense industries.[66] In 1947, the Congress of Racial Equality (CORE) sponsored a bus ride through the South to test the Supreme Court ruling that Negro passengers on interstate routes could not be forced to sit at the back of the bus. At the federal level, several important policies were beginning to be altered. In 1948, Truman issued an executive order ending segregation in the armed forces. In June 1950, the Supreme Court outlawed racial segregation in graduate schools.[67] The better-known markers of the rise of the civil rights movement happened slightly later: the *Brown v. Topeka* decision was handed down in 1954; fourteen-year-old Emmett Till was murdered in Mississippi in 1955; the Montgomery bus boycott began in late 1955 and continued through 1956.[68]

Within this foment, the black ministers who later formed the backbone of the Southern Christian Leadership Conference (SCLC) made their interpretations of exodus into a powerful political rhetoric. The exodus narrative galvanized congregations and local black communities into action and allowed sympathetic whites to cast their support for racial justice in moral and religious terms. The link was articulated in the writings of major African American thinkers, as well as in a broader, more colloquial way in churches and meetings, in songs and in sermons. Joseph Lowery, one of the founders of SCLC, described the message as inherent in African American interpretations of the Bible: "And the gospel to [African Americans] was a liberating gospel, because when they read about God delivering Moses and the Children of Israel, they saw the parallel between the experience of the Israelites and the black experience. And they figured that God was gonna deliver them."[69] Michael Walzer's report of his visit to Montgomery, Alabama, in 1960 vividly recounts the emotional power of the story for the grassroots civil rights movement when at least some of the black churches began to take a role in political leadership:

> In a small Baptist church, I listened to the most extraordinary sermon I have ever heard—on the book of Exodus and the political struggle of southern blacks. There on the pulpit, the preacher... acted out the "going out" from Egypt and expounded on its contemporary analogues: he cringed under the lash, challenged the pharaoh, hesitated fearfully at the sea, accepted the covenant and the law at the foot of the mountain.[70]

Walzer's description reveals that the old metaphor took on a new and powerful urgency in this period of unrest and activism. Civil rights historians have offered similar assessments: what could sometimes serve as a call for divine intervention could, at other times, evoke the need for organized—

and very human—political action. A strong metaphoric affiliation linked the narrative of ancient Hebrew liberation from bondage and the purposeful imagining of liberation from discrimination in the United States.

That intimate connection between metaphor and social movement was particularly evident in the writings and speeches of Martin Luther King Jr., who spoke repeatedly of the liberation of black Americans in the language of biblical exodus. King developed a national reputation as a result of his role in the Montgomery bus boycott of 1955. His writings, essays, and speeches were widely disseminated after the events in Montgomery, and he made his reputation in part through the broad publication of his works. King's sense, stated over and over again, was that civil rights was part of an international movement, not just in terms of the obvious connection he felt to the Gandhian movement in India but also to a larger sense of a worldwide social force rising to fight oppression. He saw the rise of anticolonialism and the rise of civil rights not just as parallel sets of events but as a connected force, with the two movements influencing each other in direct ways.[71] The success of the new nationalisms, particularly in Africa and India, provided a living model for the kind of successful struggle that King envisioned in the United States. The exodus trope linked support for nationalism abroad with a vision of (nonnationalist) liberation and integration at home—everywhere, the enslaved people were rising up against pharaoh and demanding to be free. For King, decolonization on the world stage was part of the same "quest for freedom and human dignity" that inspired the nonviolent civil rights movement.[72]

In his last sermon, which he gave in Memphis the night before he was assassinated, on April 3, 1968, King reiterated the themes that he had consistently used for more than a dozen years in his work as a civil rights leader: "The masses of people are rising up," he said. "And wherever they are assembled today, whether they are in Johannesburg, South Africa; Nairobi, Kenya; Accra, Ghana; New York City; Atlanta, Georgia; Jackson, Mississippi; or Memphis, Tennessee—the cry is always the same—'We want to be free.'" Once again, King also connected the long struggle of African Americans with the sojourn of the Hebrews in Egypt:

> You know, whenever Pharaoh wanted to prolong the period of
> slavery in Egypt, he had a favorite, favorite formula for doing it.
> What was that? He kept the slaves fighting among themselves. But
> whenever slaves get together, something happens in Pharaoh's
> court, and he cannot hold the slaves in slavery. When the slaves get
> together, that's the beginning of getting out of slavery. Now, let us
> maintain unity.

In the words that have come to represent King's finest hour, he ended the speech by linking his leadership to that of Moses, who took the Israelites to their promised land but could not enter: "I just want to do God's will. And he's allowed me to go up to the mountain. And I've looked over. And I've seen the promised land. I may not get there with you. But I want you to know tonight, that we, as a people, will get to the promised land."[73] The promised land, as King envisioned it, was not only for African Americans but also for the "masses of people"—those whom, in other speeches, he referred to as the "colored people of the world." "The struggle for human dignity," he frequently said, "is not an isolated event."[74]

Among African American intellectuals and activists in the 1940s and 1950s, there was widespread support for anticolonial movements, though the specific character of this support varied widely. In recent years, several important histories have explored postwar black perspectives on world affairs. Anticolonialism, Penny von Eschen has argued, "was critical in shaping black American politics and the meanings of racial identities and solidarities."[75] Some black radicals, such as W. E. B. Du Bois and Paul Robeson, offered critiques that linked both colonialism and U.S. support for oppressive regimes to American racial practices at home. But others, such as Edith Sampson or Walter White, traveled abroad as representatives of the United States and tempered their criticism of domestic racial politics, while supporting the cold war paradigm of U.S. policy.[76] I discuss the parameters of African American anticolonialism in more detail in chapter 2; here I merely want to suggest its visibility and viability and to highlight the presence of a certain kind of rhetorical logic that made the exodus trope an important link between racial politics at home and abroad.

With the end of World War II, it became clear that the "domestic" discourse of civil rights was now being self-consciously articulated on a world stage. In the late 1940s and early 1950s, the organized activities of the civil rights movement received a good deal of attention in the foreign press, as did some well-publicized cases of violence and discrimination against African Americans: threats and violence against returning servicemen, attacks on blacks who attempted to vote in the South, and lynchings.[77] In 1949, when a group of American citizens went on an international tour as part of "America's Town Meeting of the Air," they faced repeated questions about racial politics. "In country after country we heard the same theme song," one of the participants said. "It wasn't so much that communism would bring greater satisfaction to the people. It was that in the U.S.A, which boasted of its freedom and many advantages, how was it there was discrimination against the Negroes, that lynchings still occurred."[78] The gains of the civil rights movement in the 1950s were fueled by the developing sense, among most white liberals and some conservatives, that segregation at home was viewed as incompatible with U.S. "leadership" and alliance building in the decolonizing world.

The extensive coverage of U.S. racial injustice in the foreign press provided ample ground for worries that the failure of civil rights would lead to failures of U.S. foreign policy. Official concern was pronounced, so much so that a Justice Department brief filed in the *Brown v. Board of Education* case in 1954 announced anxiously that "it is in the context of the present world struggle between freedom and tyranny that the problem of racial discrimination must be viewed."[79] When the *Brown* decision was handed down, the *Washington Post* echoed the sentiment: "It is not too much to speak of the Court's decision as a new birth of freedom.... America is rid of an incubus which impeded and embarrassed it in all its relations with the world. Abroad as well as at home, this decision will engender a renewal of faith in democratic institutions and ideals."[80] The *Washington Post's* language for speaking about a civil rights victory—a "new birth of freedom" and the "renewal of faith"—once again linked domestic racial issues to the victory of "democratic institutions" in a worldwide contest. As NSC-68 had indicated, the "idea of slavery" must be overcome by a "demonstration of the superiority of the idea of freedom"—a demonstration that must begin at home if it was to be effective abroad.

A few years later, in 1960, the African American writer James Baldwin looked back on the link between anticolonialism and civil rights as one heavy with irony. Baldwin believed, and was sure that most of his contemporaries believed, that the *Brown v. Board of Education* decision was simply an exercise in realpolitik:

> Most of the Negroes I know do not believe that this immense
> concession would ever have been made if it had not been for the
> competition of the Cold War, and the fact that Africa was clearly
> liberating herself and therefore had, for political reasons, to be
> wooed by the descendants of her former masters. Had it been a
> matter of love or justice, the 1954 decision would surely have
> occurred sooner; were it not for the realities of power in this
> difficult era, it might very well not have occurred yet.[81]

From the Justice Department to James Baldwin, the simultaneous concern with African American liberation and the politics of decolonization forged a complex rhetoric that was also a double-edged sword.

The biblical epics operated within and as part of these powerful racial figurations of the antislavery theme, which linked the language of civil rights to a narrative—either credulous or critical—about U.S. international leadership. *The Ten Commandments* is the most obvious example: the Hebrews are clearly constructed as a despised race in Egyptian society, whose characteristic symbols (the Hebrew robe found with Moses) are a mark of shame and a sure indication of inferior (slave) status. The slavery of the Hebrews is established as an issue of national and racial identity, and Moses must acknowledge his Hebrew heritage and give up his Egyptian privilege to discover for himself "why a Hebrew—or any man—should be a slave!" The parallels between Hebrews and blacks are also sometimes made explicit within the film text, as when Moses' Egyptian mother, Bithia, joins him and his family just before the Exodus. Bithia brings her Nubian slaves with her for the flight out of Egypt, and they become participant-observers of the first Passover meal.

Other films in the genre participate in a similar construction of the enslaved and tyrannized. Early in *Ben-Hur*, when Judah comes to visit Messala for the first time, Judah is announced by a Roman officer who refers, disgustedly, to the "Jew at the door." In *Quo Vadis*, those who are persecuted include both the various people conquered and enslaved by Rome and the small but growing community of Christians, presented as a motley crew of Jews, Greeks, Lygians, and a few Romans, challenging the empire with their new faith. In every case, "the people" are either a persecuted minority or a "minoritized" majority, whose complex web of racial, national, and ideological identifications puts them at the mercy of totalitarian power. To this degree, the films establish their implied liberalism vis-à-vis the 1950s discourse on race; the logic of exodus/resistance in the film plot is that no minority should be oppressed.

In fact, this energetic support for the oppressed and their struggles opens up the possibility of a spectator positioned for "excessive" nationalist identification. Although Judah Ben-Hur, for example, says repeatedly that he does not condone violence, the audience is offered the blood sport of Judah's chariot race with Messala as a potent revenge fantasy. While the final segment of the film tries to undo the enthusiasms of the race by having Judah discover forgiveness through his experience of watching Jesus crucified, it cannot compete in visual or emotional power with the confrontation between Judah and Rome. Similarly, the spectator is invited to enjoy the spectacle of the plagues that Moses visits on the Egyptians and to support the logic that suggests that if the Pharaoh will not "let my people go," then immediate liberation, via the wrath of God and man, is an appro-

Figure 7. Nefertiri (Anne Baxter) refuses to give her love to Ramses (Yul Brynner) in *The Ten Commandments* (Paramount Pictures, 1956). Courtesy of the
Museum of Modern Art Film Stills Archive.

priate response. Both films encourage audiences to identify with the protagonists and/or the agency of the director as particularly American, but
they also risk donating their support to a critique of *any* hegemonic power,
including an American one. Taken as a whole, the epic genre appears to offer
an implicit and somewhat anxious acknowledgment of this possibility, in
part through the constant reassurance that the nonviolent liberalism of a
"new faith" is the chosen path of a truly democratic people.

More important, the films stage the desire for liberation, only to then
contain it through a strategic deployment of gender. In virtually all the
films, the "racial" slavery of "the people" is paralleled by, and made available through, representations of the problem of the *sexual* slavery of individual characters. Like NSC-68, the biblical epics evoke the domestic racial
associations of the exodus story only to redeploy the antislavery narrative
as a metaphor for the struggle of the individual against (sexual) submission. In *The Ten Commandments*, a series of doublings and parallels figure
slavery in decidedly sexual terms: the Egyptians are consistently marked as
tyrannical in sex as well as in politics. Yul Brynner's Ramses, for example,
is titillatingly cruel as the future husband and master of the Egyptian

princess Nefertiri. When Nefertiri, betrothed to Ramses for reasons of state, defiantly tells him that she will never love him, Brynner as Ramses raises one eyebrow and responds sardonically: "Does that matter? You will be my wife. You will come to me whenever I call you, and I will enjoy that very much. Whether you enjoy it or not is your own affair." Similarly, another character, the evil overseer Dathan, forcibly takes the young slave Lilia as his concubine. Even Moses is at risk; he will fail his people if he becomes a "slave" to his desire for Nefertiri.

Quo Vadis engages in a similar kind of doubling—a refiguration of the political problem of despotism and slavery onto the individual sexual fate of characters. Quo Vadis establishes a connection between slavery and rape through the character of Lygia (Deborah Kerr), a beautiful young Christian woman who was once a "hostage of Rome" and who has since been freed. Lygia attracts the interest of the Roman soldier Marcus Vinicius (Robert Taylor), the handsome protagonist who is nonetheless presented initially as arrogant and shallow, interested only in telling battle stories of his exploits in the Roman army and in bedding as many women as possible. Marcus's desire for Lygia, and her refusal to acquiesce to the status of sexual property, becomes the organizing plot of the film. In one early scene, Marcus, insisting that Lygia has too many ideas in her head, grabs her, tells her that he wishes she were a slave, and states that he would have offered a "king's ransom" for her. Lygia responds furiously: "What a way for a conqueror to win a woman, to buy her like an unresisting beast!"

Lygia is a "Lygian," whose people were victims of Roman imperialism, but her nationalist and anti-Roman loyalties are quickly refigured as sexual independence. By the end of the film, Marcus has asked Lygia to marry him, and Lygia, who has consistently resisted any attempt to take her loyalty, now freely chooses to become Marcus's wife. Throughout the film Lygia has vociferously pronounced against Roman war-making and Roman slavery, but she finds the solution to her objections in Marcus's willingness to engage in the rules and rituals of Christian marriage. In the logic of the film, the Roman system of taking women as sexual slaves is the mark of Roman tyranny; consensual heterosexual marriage is the normative practice of the oppressed.

Within the marriage plot of the epics, slaveholding is a kind of sexual dysfunction, a "perverted faith." For the hero, the tendency toward taking sexual slaves is best overcome by marriage to a strong-willed but ultimately—and voluntarily—subordinate woman. The ideal woman in the epics is one who refuses to be treated like (sexual) property. In The Ten Commandments, the audience is cued that Moses will ultimately marry the

Figure 8. In *Quo Vadis* (MGM, 1954), Lygia (Deborah Kerr) will not be taken as a slave by Marcus (Robert Taylor) but will freely choose her wifely subordination once he asks her to marry him. Courtesy of the Museum of Modern Art Film Stills Archive.

young woman Sephra when she announces that she will not dance with her sisters before Moses and the men of her desert tribe: "I am not going to be displayed like a caravan's wares—before Moses, or any other man." Sephra, like Lygia in *Quo Vadis* or Esther in *Ben-Hur*, is nonetheless established within the film as subordinate to her husband; she quickly takes up the role of enabler and supporter and, despite her diegetic refusal to be displayed, is frequently depicted by the portrait shots that mark female "to-be-looked-at-ness."[82]

This particular figuration of the spunky, independent woman who nonetheless chooses to take up her subservient position in marriage was a familiar device in the 1950s, when anxiety over women's sexual subjectivity and the status of marriage was rampant in intellectual discourse and in middle-class popular literature.[83] The biblical epics stage a complicated series of parallels and displacements that *evoke* the racial connotations of slavery only to (partially) dispose of them via normative marriage. The films posit slavery as the problem, and appropriate, consensual sexuality in the form of freely chosen subordination in marriage as the solution.

The transference of social conflict onto the "individual" and "private" sphere of sexuality uses the public-private split to refigure the political connotations of the antislavery rhetoric within the films. Of course, it is nearly impossible, in general, to maintain a fire wall between the terrain designated as public and that called private. From talk show television to the state laws governing marriage, private lives have long been public concerns. The reverse is also true: politics infuses our private world, from the racial and gender discourses that position us as individuals to the ability of the state to educate us, tax us, and take us to war. Fictional texts have frequently participated in this interpenetration; the resolution of political problems through appropriate marriage is a well-established strategy of bourgeois narrative.[84] In the epics, too, marriage is not simply a displacement of the "public" onto the "private" or a simple dichotomy of public man/private woman. While the mobilization of gendered sexuality *seems* to be a privatization of politics, it also works to make the right ordering of private life into a political statement. Sexual conflict takes on significant, but reconstituted, political salience, reinvigorating the marital terrain with more general political meanings.

The reconstructed narrative of anti-(sexual) slavery uses the codes of gender to gesture toward a model of "benevolent supremacy" in world politics as well as in marriage. Spunky wives serve within these narratives as the audience for and complement to the political activities of the male hero. As Amy Kaplan has suggested in her analysis of the romantic adventure novels of the 1890s, female heroines play a crucial role as observers and validators of the action. In Kaplan's reading, the feminine does not occupy the space of the silent, occluded "other"; instead, the feminine gaze serves as a "window or lens focused on masculine exploits abroad."[85] The connection between turn-of-the-century imperialist fictions and those of the 1950s is in fact quite direct: both *Quo Vadis* and *Ben-Hur* were best-selling novels in the 1890s. In the biblical epic films, the camera itself positions the female heroine in precisely the role Kaplan describes, as the receptive female audience for whom masculine activities are performed. For example, Judah's fiancée, Esther, framed in portrait shot, watches Ben-Hur promise to seek revenge on the Romans. Similarly, Sephra watches Moses come down from the mountain after he has seen God and Lygia watches Marcus at his triumphal march through the city. In each case, the female activity of looking represents the viewpoint, and the authority, of the camera. Gender thus functions in a more complex way than just to suggest female subordination. It does that, but the masculine political activities also require loving feminine approval, staging an encounter between "masculine" violence and "feminine" marriage that authorizes *both*.

The significance of these gendered constructs for imagining relations between national groups is apparent if we return to the character of Sheik Ilderim in *Ben-Hur*. The sheik plays the central role usually reserved for women: he is Judah Ben-Hur's spectator or, in Kaplan's terms, the beloved "for whom primitive violence is performed."[86] The sheik and Esther have similar relationships to Judah. In one scene, Esther is shown joyously watching Judah's kindness to her old father; in the next, the sheik is shown happily watching Judah talk to his beloved team of horses, which Judah will ride to victory in the chariot race. In both cases, Esther and the sheik are observers who delight in Judah's acts of kindness to those they love. The sheik is linked to Esther not only through his similar role in the plot but also formally, through a series of parallel shots. About midway through the film, Judah is reunited with Esther after his long years in the Roman galleys. The reunion between Judah and Esther is framed by two meetings with Sheik Ilderim, and the intense conversation between the two lovers is filmed from exactly the same camera angle as those between Judah and the sheik, about thirty degrees to the front of Heston's right shoulder, showing him in quarter profile and his companion in three-quarter profile. The sheik is also linked to Esther through his doubling of the role of support and companion to Judah. During the climactic race, it is the sheik and his companions (not Esther) who provide the diegetic audience for Ben-Hur's triumph. As Judah (the Hebrew-Christian-American) faces Messala (the Roman-British-Soviet military commander) in a final confrontation, the action of the chariots is interspersed with frequent cutaways to the sheik and friends, always in medium shots or close-ups, watching and cheering as Judah drives the horses. (There are also cutaways to the Roman governor, usually in long shot, looking forlorn and angry.) The Arab sheik, like the wife figure he parallels, takes up a feminized position of freely chosen subordination—a relation of consent, not slavery—to the Americanized hero of *Ben-Hur* and the new order he ushers in.

This complex array of parallels, refigurations, and coding allows the biblical epics to construct a narrative that links slavery, sexual deviance, marriage, and empire. In *Quo Vadis*, two major plot lines intersect and complement each other: the chase/romance between Marcus and Lygia parallels the political intrigues in the court of the Roman emperor Nero. At one point, the comparison is all but explicit, as a scene in which Marcus threatens Lygia with rape is intercut with short scenes of Nero plotting the burning of Rome. In addition, Lygia's Christianity not only is a signifier of her moral and sexual purity but also provides an explicit alternative to Roman imperialism. Lygia consistently urges Marcus toward a model of "a gentler and more powerful way" of gaining the allegiance of Rome's subjects; her invocations to less imperial violence against conquered peoples double and refigure her refusal to be "taken." Near the end of the film, Lygia's friend and mentor, the evangelist Paul, tells Marcus that if he wants to be an acceptable partner to Lygia, he must meet the requirements of Christianity. At the same time, Paul makes it clear that Christianity offers not only a "new god" but also a strategy for international relations:

MARCUS
VINICIUS: Tell me what I should do.

PAUL: Well, you own slaves, do you not?

MV: Hundreds. Good ones too. Why?

PAUL: Jesus wishes no man to be in bondage. You should set them free.

MV: But they're mine! I own them.

PAUL: But you can't buy human beings, Marcus. Faith in Christ is based on love; he asked all people to love one another.

MV: You want me to love the whole human race? You want me to love Partheons, Egyptians, Persians, and all the rest who want to put a blade through my ribs?

PAUL: Has it occurred to you to put down your sword and renounce war against these people? Has it occurred to you that you might conquer them with love?

Love is not the alternative to conquest but the alternative model *of* conquest. The freely chosen subordination of the good wife suggests the value of a "conquest of love" in reformulated imperial relations. The wife who refuses slavery but chooses her subordinate position vis-à-vis the hero, like the feminized sheik, provides a model of the proper (new) relation between the leaders of "the people" and the people themselves. Within the films, racial slavery is made meaningful as sexual slavery; or, to put it differently, gender and sexuality become the terrain on which the problem of slavery is presented and resolved in the narrative. Marriage is staged as an analogy for a refigured imperialism, a new kind of benevolent supremacy in world affairs that links the new, nonimperial rulers with the peoples of the Middle East via a relationship of consensual and unequal union.

THE MIDDLE EAST AND BENEVOLENT SUPREMACY

The Suez crisis of 1956 offered a dramatic example of the ability and willingness of the United States to set terms for a revamped relationship with the newly decolonizing world.[87] It also made apparent the strategic importance of the region to the United States, which had previously seemed to grant primacy to Britain. For several years, as President Eisenhower later wrote, "no region in the world received as much of my close attention and that of my colleagues as did the Middle East."[88] In Egypt, Nasser had come to power in 1952, in a bloodless coup that deposed King Farouk, the final link to British rule.[89] Although Egypt had become formally independent from Britain in 1923, it had retained a "special relationship" that included British control over the Egyptian army until 1948. For many years after Egypt's nominal independence, Britain considered it a crucial part of the British empire, and the Middle East a strategic center of British influence. One of Nasser's main goals as president was to raise money to finance the building of the Aswan High Dam. In July 1956, the United States had abruptly and ignobly backed out of a promise to finance the project; a few weeks later, Nasser nationalized the Suez Canal, claiming the right to revenues from the canal for Egyptian development.

On October 29, 1956, in response to the nationalization and to Egypt's refusal to allow Israeli shipping through the canal, Israel made a "surprise" attack on Egypt's Sinai Peninsula, pushing toward Suez. Israel was working in secret collaboration with Britain and France, both of which publicly threatened to intervene, insisting that their purpose was to protect continued navigation through the canal, which they claimed was endangered by Egypt's nationalization. When Nasser refused an ultimatum to withdraw his troops from the canal, the British and French began a massive bombardment of the Egyptian coast in preparation for a planned invasion of Egypt and a takeover of the canal.

The U.S. reaction was swift and decisive. Making evident the fact that the United States would and could dominate "the West" as it established relations with the newly decolonizing world, President Eisenhower refused to support Britain and France in a major confrontation with the Middle East's most prominent nationalist leader. When Britain's actions caused a run on the pound, the United States refused to provide additional money from the International Monetary Fund. In addition, Eisenhower threatened to stop shipments of American oil to Britain. With Britain also facing a cutoff in Middle East oil (Egypt had blockaded the canal immediately after the invasion, and Syria had stopped the pipelines running from Iraq), the U.S.

threat was pivotal.[90] Less than eighteen hours after the invasion began, the fighting halted. On November 15, United Nations forces arrived to patrol the cease-fire.

Contemporary commentators and historians alike have seen the forceful and unexpected American response as decisive in saving Nasser from the combined armies of Britain, France, and Israel. The U.S. administration had no real love for Nasser, and over the next two decades, relations with Egypt would vary considerably. In the 1960s, for example, the United States was the main source of food aid for Egypt; from 1960 to 1965, the United States provided $300 million in grain shipments through the Food for Peace program.[91] But Eisenhower and Secretary of State John Foster Dulles also agreed with the leaders of Britain and France that Nasser needed to be weakened, that he had opened the Middle East to Soviet influence, and that he had become too independent and arrogant.[92] In particular, all three powers were concerned about Soviet influence and worried that Nasser's brand of Arab nationalism, if it spread, might threaten Western access to the cheap and abundant supplies of Middle East oil.

It was the question of appropriate means that divided the United States and its European allies. Eisenhower wanted to weaken Nasser while avoiding military actions that might not play well on the third world stage. Eisenhower and his administration saw the emerging nationalism in the Middle East as a bellwether for changes in the rest of the world. At a National Security Council meeting on November 1, 1956 (two days after the start of the Israeli crossing of the Sinai), Secretary of State Dulles argued, "It is nothing less than tragic that at this very time, when we are on the point of winning an immense and long-hoped-for victory over Soviet colonialism in Eastern Europe, we should be forced to choose between following in the footsteps of Anglo-French colonialism in Asia and Africa or splitting our course away from their course." Eisenhower put the point succinctly: "My emphatic belief is that these powers are going downhill with the kind of policy that they are engaged at the moment in carrying out. How can we possibly support Britain and France if in doing so we were to lose the whole Arab world?"[93]

The United States' shielding of Nasser was part of the production of a new discourse of power in the Middle East—one simultaneously mindful of rising Soviet power, anticolonial insurgency, and European (particularly British) imperial decline. American actions at Suez were yet another site for the construction of new and "benevolent" global authority. Two months after the crisis was over, the president announced the Eisenhower Doctrine, a proposal for economic and military assistance to nations in the Middle

East, which was linked to an assertion that "the armed forces of the United States [could be used] to secure and protect the territorial integrity and political independence of such nations . . . against overt armed aggression from any nation controlled by International Communism."[94] This framework would, in a general way, structure U.S. relations with the Middle East for at least two decades. The policy of making alliances with decolonizing Arab states would not preclude strong ties with Israel, particularly after the 1967 war.[95] The operative terms were the American refusal of empire, the right of "free peoples" to choose their destinies, and the consensual partnership between U.S. power and a subordinated third world nationalism.

These political events, intersecting with the concurrent rhetoric of policy texts like NSC-68 and the logic of biblical epic films in Hollywood, became part of a larger set of meanings that can be understood only by looking at their "knitted-togetherness," at the ways in which world events and cultural texts constructed meanings for each other.[96] If, for example, one saw the biblical epics films in another context—say, in television reruns—they would likely have rather different resonances. In the 1950s, however, every representation of the power of "democratic institutions and ideals" could be understood as another proof of what NSC-68 had called "the superiority of the idea of freedom" over the "idea of slavery." Taken as a genre, the biblical epics encouraged an opposition to slavery and thus united with the antislavery and antisegregation discourse of the contemporaneous civil rights movement. At the same time, the racial liberalism of the antislavery theme was represented in and through a discourse of normative (consensual) heterosexuality and marriage. The films' formal and thematic tropes used marriage and gender to refigure the domestic racial connotations of antislavery into a statement of the moral authority of Americanized leadership. Taken in relationship to the other meanings being made by policymakers and media accounts, the epics constructed a narrative of "benevolent supremacy" that used marriage as its model.

The diverse and overlapping sites for the production of "benevolent supremacy" were precisely what gave the discourse its richness and flexibility—and its salience. In the statements of foreign policy officials, in popular culture, in newspaper and magazine articles, and in the highly visible staging of U.S. foreign policy, the discourse was powerful precisely because it was multifaceted and variously located. Within that logic, an implicit support for civil rights was *necessarily* linked with unequivocal support for American supremacy abroad. What was at stake was the question of how to manage power relations in the postwar world; the result was a broadly diffused construction of the United States as a "world leader" that refused to behave like a colonial power. Within this frame, not only must the support expressed for civil rights by mainstream liberals in the 1950s be understood in the contexts of the cold war and U.S. expansionism, but both U.S. global power and domestic racial liberalism must be understood as linked through a gendered logic that used marriage as the trope for newly structured relations, both "inside" and "outside" the nation. By bringing together racial liberalism, the re-inscription of women's subordination in marriage, ideologies of Judeo-Christian heritage, and the struggle for supremacy in the third world, the discourse of benevolent supremacy used representations of the Middle East to construct a vision of U.S. national power fit for the dawn of the American Century.

2 The Middle East in African American Cultural Politics, 1955–1972

raise up christ nigger
Christ was black
krishna was black shango was black ...

> Shango budda black
> hermes rasis black
> moses krishna
> black ...
and we are the same, all the blackness from one black allah ...
—Amiri Baraka, "It's Nation Time"

"I'm not an American; I'm a black man."
—Muhammad Ali

Just after the Suez crisis had ended, in December 1956, Martin Luther King Jr. spoke in Montgomery, Alabama, on "Facing the Challenge of a New Age." Looking at events in the decolonizing world, King argued that the "old order was passing away," and that the "colored people" of the world were moving toward freedom by establishing their own governments and their own educational systems. Drawing on the exodus trope that was his hallmark, King pointed out that these new nations had "broken loose from the Egypt of colonialism and imperialism." African Americans would benefit, he argued, from "the new order of freedom and justice" that was coming into being. King's rhetoric was familiar, but the situation had changed: now he was speaking against the backdrop of Suez, when Egypt had been invaded by two colonial powers in alliance with Israel. At that moment, Nasser had consolidated his position as an international symbol of anticolonial nationalism. It was Nasser, not the Israelites, who had stood up against the "old order." So King was careful to distinguish pharaonic Egypt—the metaphoric "Egypt of colonialism and imperialism"—from the contemporary state, whose "nationalistic longings" were part of the "new order being born."[1]

A few months later, the African American intellectual W. E. B. Du Bois, an ardent anticolonialist and a longtime supporter of Israel, responded to the Israeli invasion of Egypt at Suez with a poem that positioned Israel ambiguously within a rhetoric of liberation. To the degree that it referred back to the slavery and Exodus of the Hebrews, the poem positioned Israel sympathetically. Du Bois's long history of support for Zionism enabled him to acknowledge Israel's fears of "pharaoh." But Suez, he said, had turned the tables and placed Israel in the role of oppressor of the modern inheritors of slavery:

> Young Israel raised a mighty cry
> "Shall Pharaoh ride anew?"
> But Nasser grimly pointed West,
> "They mixed this witches' brew!"
> ... Israel as the West betrays
> Its murdered, mocked, and damned,
> Becomes the shock troops of two knaves
> Who steal the Negros' land.
> Beware, white world, that great black hand
> Which Nasser's power waves
> Grasps hard the concentrated hate
> Of myriad million slaves.[2]

Du Bois refused to posit Nasser as the ruler of a metaphorical "Egypt of colonialism and imperialism." Instead, Nasser points toward the West, where the "witches' brew" of the Suez invasion has made Israel into a pawn for colonial power. In its collaboration with Britain and France, Israel has betrayed the suffering of the Jews—its own "murdered, mocked, and damned." For Du Bois, Nasser's authority lay in his role as racial spokesperson; the "great black hand" of his power came from the fact that both "blackness" and "slavery" united colonized peoples. Invading Egypt thus put Israel, which Du Bois had earlier described as "bringing a new civilization into an old land," on the wrong side of the "concentrated hate" of the colonized.

In the 1950s and 1960s, the conflict between Israel and its Arab neighbors took on a new salience in African American cultural politics. In part, the energized significance of the Middle East had to do with decolonization. African American intellectuals and activists had supported and been inspired by anticolonial movements for years, not only those in Africa, but also in India, Asia, and—increasingly after World War II—the Middle East, where several nations, including Egypt, Syria, Iraq, and Algeria, played a prominent role in the emerging nonaligned movement.

The significance of the Middle East was also connected to important changes in religious practice and religious culture among African Americans in the postwar period, particularly the shifting politics of black Christianity and the emergence of the Nation of Islam as a visible force. Religious narratives connected African Americans, by history and analogy, to various (and sometimes competing) constructions of events in the Middle East, both ancient and modern. Black Christians often narrated that connection as a spiritual tie to the slavery and suffering of the Hebrews. They also claimed the geography of the Middle East as a Christian space: for black Christians in the mid–twentieth century no less than for white travelers in the nineteenth, the river Jordan and the Nile valley, the city of Jerusalem and the valley of Canaan were intimately familiar and emotionally resonant. But like Christianity, Islam also claimed the Middle East as a "holy land," looking to major religious sites in and around Jerusalem, as well as Mecca and Medina in Saudi Arabia.

The centrality of the Middle East to Islamic histories and to many Muslim rituals encouraged the increasing visibility of Arab cultures and Arab politics in African American communities after 1955. For the Nation of Islam, Arab and Islamic history, along with the history and mythology of ancient Egypt, provided the origin stories for a diasporic "black man's" culture. With the rise of the Black Arts movement and black cultural nationalism, Islam became a cultural symbol for many people who were not converts. By the early 1960s, one did not need to have entered a Muslim temple or read a Nation of Islam newspaper to know that black Islam had moved far beyond the sectarian curiosity it had been just ten years earlier. In this period, many African Americans began to do something that almost no one else in the United States, besides Arab Americans, had ever done: they claimed a positive sense of alliance to both Arab culture and the forces of Arab nationalism. Thus, between 1955 and 1972, a potent combination of religious affiliation, anticolonial politics, and black nationalist radicalism turned claims upon the Middle East into a rich resource within African American communities. For both Christians and Muslims, religious culture made salient not only ancient histories but also contemporary political events in the region, particularly the conflict between Israel and the Palestinian Arabs for control over territory.

In recent years, scholars have become much more conscious of the role that transnational contacts and cultural productions play in discourses of community—national, racial, and religious. Cultural theorist Paul Gilroy has described this process as the interconnection of "routes and roots"; that is, the ways in which transnational cultural contact (travel across borders and barriers) has provided the framework for spatial imaginations and historical narratives that transcend narrow nationalisms.[3] The tendency has been to see the transnational elements of black culture in the United States as focused exclusively on identifications with Africa. However, in complex ways African American intellectuals, writers, and artists have looked not only to Africa but also to other areas, and particularly to the Middle East, as site and source for explorations of blackness and the recovery and reconstruction of black history.

By attending to this cultural and religious history, our understanding of *political* events can become more nuanced and complex. For example, we begin to see the ways in which the anticolonial radicalism of a new generation of African Americans was linked to the reconstruction of the moral geographies associated with religious communities. A proper understanding of the cultural and political histories of African Americans requires us to look beyond the well-documented influence of the Judeo-Christian tradition. In particular, this chapter suggests that African American investments in, and interpretations of, the Arab-Israeli conflict developed, at least in part, out of the religious and cultural alternatives to black Christianity that became influential in the 1960s. By 1967, these connections had a significant impact in several arenas: African American understandings of U.S. foreign policy in the Middle East, particularly the 1967 Arab-Israeli war; black-Jewish relations in the United States; and the contest between civil rights and black nationalism as models for African American liberation.

"THAT MARVELLOUS MOVEMENT"

By the middle of the twentieth century, the biblical language of exodus had provided a profound metaphorical link between black and Jewish history for many decades. As we have seen, the story of the biblical Exodus was actively invoked as part of the civil rights struggle from the 1940s on. The alliance between African Americans and Jews in the early civil rights movement was almost certainly strengthened not only by the active Jewish participation in the activities of the movement but also by this sense of deep, historical connection. James Baldwin suggested exactly that link when, writing in *Commentary* in 1948, he explained, "At this point, the Negro identifies himself almost wholly with the Jew. The more devout Negro considers that he *is* a Jew, in bondage to a hard taskmaster and waiting for a Moses to lead him out of Egypt." The Old Testament, Baldwin went on, had suggested the possibility that hard times might be a sign of God's grace.

"The covenant God made in the beginning with Abraham and which was to extend to his children and to these latter-day exiles also: as Israel was chosen, so are they."[4]

Before the 1950s, however, the most ardent and articulate statements of links between African American political aspirations and those of Jews in the Middle East came not from Christian churches or biblical allegories but from early black nationalists, who, in the late nineteenth and early twentieth centuries, supported black repatriation to Africa.[5] These thinkers saw in the still nascent Zionist movement a harbinger of, and model for, their own aspirations. Martin Delany, often hailed as the progenitor of black nationalism in the United States, turned to the model of Zionism in his 1852 emigrationist polemic, *The Condition, Elevation, Emigration and Destiny of the Colored People of the United States Politically Considered*. The Jews, Delany wrote, are scattered throughout Europe and elsewhere,

> looking forward in high hopes of seeing the day when they may return to their former national position of self-government and independence let that be in whatever part of the habitable world it may.... Such then is the condition of various classes in Europe; yes, nations.... And however unfavourable their condition, there is none more so than that of the coloured people of the United States.[6]

Similarly, Edward Wilmot Blyden, perhaps the most important black nationalist thinker of the nineteenth century, was fascinated with "that marvellous movement called Zionism." In 1850, Blyden immigrated to Liberia, where he became active both in state institutions and in the development of Pan-African ideology. In 1898, he published a pamphlet called *The Jewish Question*, in which he not only supported the right of Jews to a state in Palestine but also asserted a strong emotional link between his race and the Jewish people. The booklet, as he described it, was a "record of the views held by an African of the work and destiny of a people with whom his own race is closely allied both by Divine declaration and by a history almost identical of sorrow and oppression."[7]

In the early twentieth century, and especially in the years following the 1917 Balfour Declaration (in which Britain promised to support a "national home for the Jewish people" in Palestine), the two most influential black nationalist thinkers in the United States—Du Bois and Marcus Garvey—actively supported plans for a Jewish state.[8] Du Bois consistently reported on the issue during his tenure as editor of the National Association for the Advancement of Colored People (NAACP) journal the *Crisis*, as well as in his monthly magazine for children, *The Brownie's Book*.[9] And in 1920,

Marcus Garvey also linked his back-to-Africa movement with Zionism: "A new spirit, a new courage, has come to us simultaneously as it came to other people of the world. It came to us the same time it came to the Jew. When the Jews said, 'We shall have Palestine!' the same sentiment came to us when we said, 'We shall have Africa.'"[10] For Garvey, as for Delany and Blyden, the rhetoric of the exodus pointed to the *literal* necessity for emigration; unlike their Christian counterparts, they denied that the biblical story could be mapped onto the domestic space of the nation and refused the argument that African Americans could be liberated by incorporation as American citizens.

The establishment of the state of Israel in 1948 was celebrated in the U.S. news media and widely seen as a historic recognition of and (partial) atonement for the European Holocaust.[11] Many African Americans, even those who were not interested in their own literal immigration to Africa, responded with special enthusiasm to the idea of liberation and a homeland for Jews. In 1947, Walter White, the executive director of the NAACP, had played a crucial role in lobbying African nations to vote for the UN resolution partitioning Palestine into Jewish and Arab areas. And African American activist Ralph Bunche, the UN secretary for peacekeeping, was active in negotiating the end to the Arab-Israeli war in 1948 on terms generally considered favorable to Israel.[12] In 1948, the NAACP passed a resolution stating that "the valiant struggle of the people of Israel for independence serves as an inspiration to all persecuted people throughout the world."[13] Within this frame, Israel—as one of the "new nations" seeking freedom and national rights—represented a powerful model made all the more powerful by the biblical story of exile and return, and by the ways in which this rhetoric had played a central role in the successful transformation of the Zionist movement into the Israeli state.[14]

But this general support for Israel was also complicated by the role of Arab states in the nonaligned movement. Historian Penny Von Eschen has argued that by the late 1940s, black anticolonialism generally had moved away from the broader critique of imperialism that was dominant in the late 1930s and early 1940s toward foreign policy views that accepted both the primacy of anticommunism and the positive benefits of U.S. hegemony.[15] Even Martin Luther King Jr., who was a strong supporter of anticolonial movements throughout the 1950s and 1960s, sometimes engaged in the kind of instrumentalist logic that echoed that of white liberals and some mainstream black leaders. The United States would be worthy of "world respect and emulation" and maintain its "prestige as leader of the free world," King argued, only if it addressed the problem of race and color prejudice.[16] In passages like these, King's rhetoric skirted the edge of the imperial racial liberalism that was the foundation of the mainstream discourse of benevolent supremacy. Within that logic, social justice at home, or even small steps in the direction of racial progress, would be mobilized within cold war anticolonial discourse as proof of the moral right of the United States to stand as "leader of the free world."

By the mid-1950s, however, the emergence of the nonaligned movement was once again opening up space for an anticolonial critique that was not merely a replication of U.S. policy. Along with figures like Castro, Kwame Nkrumah of Ghana, and Jawaharal Nehru of India, Egypt's Nasser represented an emotionally explosive convergence of anticolonial defiance and a global racial consciousness.[17] Nasser was one of the most visible and outspoken leaders of the nonaligned movement's clarion call, the 1955 Asian-African Conference at Bandung, Indonesia, where twenty-nine nations from Africa, Asia, and the Middle East gathered to speak out against the pressure placed on them to join the cold war alliances. The Bandung conference inspired great enthusiasm from the African American press, which hailed it as "a clear challenge to white supremacy" and "a turning point in world history" that made clear that "the majority of the world's people think there is an alternative to following blindly the lead of either Russia or the United States."[18] The writer Richard Wright went to Bandung. There, he reported, "a racial consciousness, evoked by the attitudes and practices of the West, had slowly blended with a defensive religious feeling ... a racial and religious system of identification manifesting itself in an emotional nationalism which was now leaping state boundaries and melting and merging, one into the other."[19] Bandung provided the opportunity for formerly colonized nations to assert their independence, to speak out against racism and colonialism, and to criticize the specific foreign policies of the United States and the Soviet Union.

As the leader of Egypt, Nasser also represented a particular connection between black and Arab anticolonialism: just as Egypt was geographically positioned at the intersection of the Middle East and Africa, in the years after Bandung, Nasser positioned himself as a leader in connecting African and Asian anticolonial movements. "We have a unique and rare personality in the person of Gamal Abdel Nasser," one street corner orator in Harlem observed. "He made it scientifically clear that Africans, the Arabs, and the Muslims have one common enemy, European imperialism."[20] In 1957, Nasser hosted the follow-up event to Bandung, the Afro-Asian People's Solidarity Conference in Cairo, where, according to some scholars, he took over the position of leadership that previously had been assumed by

India's Prime Minister Nehru.[21] Nasser's successful weathering of the Suez invasion made him a hero in the decolonizing nations, as well as among many African Americans. An avowed Arab nationalist, Nasser nonetheless came to represent black and African defiance. And though the Suez crisis did not receive as much coverage as Bandung had in the black press (which at the time was focused on the Montgomery bus boycott and other developments in the emergent civil rights movement), many black intellectuals, including King and Du Bois, criticized what they viewed as a frankly imperialist action by France, Britain, and Israel. Observers would later look back on Suez as something of a turning point in African American perceptions of the Middle East—the moment in which Arab anticolonialism came home to black Americans.[22] It was the beginning of a larger transformation, which by the late 1960s would bring black Islam, Arab nationalism, and African American radicalism into a powerful historical alliance.

THE NATION AND ITS LIMITS

In the early to mid-1960s, the Nation of Islam brought its interpretation of Islam to prominence in the African American community and defined Islam as the religion of black American militancy. Two events, separated by just over a year, in two very different spheres of cultural activity, marked the rapid rise of Muslim visibility and the association of Islam with anticolonial critique. Two prominent African American men, Cassius Clay, an athlete, and LeRoi Jones, a poet and a playwright, took highly visible and conscious steps away from their old identities and affiliations and began instead to articulate a black consciousness and politics based on the teachings of Islam.

On February 25, 1964, the twenty-three-year old fighter Cassius Clay defeated Sonny Liston and took the world heavyweight boxing title, the most lucrative prize in professional sports. On the day after his triumph, Clay, who had already become one of the most well-known and controversial figures in the boxing world, announced at a press conference that he was a Muslim.[23] Until that day, Clay had been known as a playful, rather apolitical youngster with a fondness for pink Cadillacs, extravagant bragging, and comic poetry. But in the months before the fight, rumors of his association with the Nation of Islam (NOI) had circulated widely, and he had been seen frequently in the company of Malcolm X, whom he had invited to his training camp in Miami.[24] A few weeks after the fight, Elijah Muhammad, the leader of the Nation of Islam, bestowed on Clay his Muslim name: Muhammad Ali. Clay's victory and subsequent announcement were widely reported, and his association with the NOI generally was viewed with skepticism or anger. In the spring of 1964, when Malcolm X left the Nation, Ali stayed and quickly became the most famous Black Muslim in the country and one of the Nation of Islam's most prominent spokespersons. Just a few months later, Ali embarked on a tour of Africa and the Middle East; when he returned, he announced to the press: "I'm not an American; I'm a black man."[25]

In 1966, Ali's status as a political figure took a new direction when he refused induction into the U.S. Army, saying, "I'm a member of the Black Muslims, and we don't go to no wars unless they're declared by Allah himself. I don't have no personal quarrel with those Viet Congs."[26] That refusal—that risky stand on behalf of the politics of his religious belief—transformed Ali's image: vilified in the mainstream media, he became one of the most visible and influential antiwar figures in the country. He was, in the words of poet Sonia Sanchez, "a cultural resource for everyone in that time," a man whose protest against Vietnam became an emblem of the far-reaching influence of the black nationalist critique of American nationalism and U.S. foreign policy.[27]

In 1965, a little over a year after Muhammad Ali's highly public conversion, LeRoi Jones left his literary circles in Greenwich Village to move uptown to Harlem, where he founded the Black Arts Repertory Theatre/School (BARTS). In Harlem, Jones turned his back on his earlier ties with Beat poetry, and even on his more recent success with plays on race relations. (In 1964, *The Dutchman* had won an OBIE, the off-Broadway theater awards presented by the *Village Voice*.)[28] He turned instead toward the task of building a community theater and developing the themes and writing styles that would launch the Black Arts movement. During his time at BARTS, Jones wrote *A Black Mass*, a one-act play that presented in dramatic form the Nation of Islam's central myth, the story of Yacub, the evil scientist who "invented" white people. Then, in 1968, Jones also changed his name, to Ameer (later to Amiri) Baraka. He studied Sunni Islam, under the tutelage of Hajj Heesham Jaaber, who had been affiliated with Malcolm X near the end of Malcolm's life.[29] By then, Baraka, whom his contemporaries considered to be "the most promising black writer" in the nation, was also the best-known representative of the Black Arts movement, a champion of black cultural nationalism, a significant theorist of the reemergence of committed art, and an articulate critic of U.S. imperialism. In the 1970s, he would turn away from Islam and toward Maoism.[30] But from at least 1964 until 1973, Baraka and others saw Islam as an authentically black religion that would be central to the requisite development of an alternative black culture and a liberated spirituality. Islam, Baraka believed, offered "what

Figure 9. Muhammad Ali on the streets of New York in 1968, after being stripped of his boxing title for draft evasion. Photo: Brian Hamill, Archive Photos.

the Black man needs ... a reconstruction ... a total way of life that he can involve himself with that is post-American, in a sense."[31] African American Islam in general and the Nation of Islam in particular offered a religious affiliation that was also political and cultural. For African Americans disaffected with the Christian church—those frustrated by the commitment of black Christians to brotherhood with whites or angered by the continuing violence by white Christians against nonviolent civil rights activists—Islam offered an alternative, a basis for a black nationalist consciousness that was separate from the civil rights goals of integration into a white-dominated and oppressive nation. Its moral geographies were also different from dominant constructions of "Americanness" or the official mappings of U.S. foreign policy. And despite the fact that what emerged in the 1950s and 1960s has often been called (even by its adherents) "black nationalism," the community it envisioned provided an alternative to—and in some sense a fundamental critique of—the nation-state. African American Muslims could claim a symbolic countercitizenship, an identity that challenged black incorporation into the dominant discourse of Judeo-Christian Americanness.

The Nation's emergence as a significant social and political force in black communities in the late 1950s followed a period of disarray and declining membership in the 1940s. When Malcolm X was released from Norfolk prison in 1952, he played a major role in the organization's expansion, establishing temples in cities all over the country. By December 1959, the Nation had fifty temples in twenty-two states; the number of members in the organization is difficult to estimate, but by 1962 it was probably in the range of fifty to one hundred thousand, with many more supporters. In 1962, *Muhammad Speaks,* the principal NOI newspaper, founded by Malcolm X, had the largest circulation of any black paper in the country.[32]

The Nation of Islam was an avowedly "black nationalist" organization, but its vision of black nationalism cannot be fully understood separate from either its explicitly religious content or its insistently transnational dimensions. The religious and the transnational aspects are, in fact, intimately related: although the Nation of Islam was *unorthodox* Islam, Elijah Muhammad had, since the 1930s, consistently affirmed the significance of its connection to other Muslim communities around the globe, particularly those in the Middle East. The Nation challenged the assumption that African Americans were simply or primarily a subset of all Americans; its political imaginary never posited black nationalism as a self-contained subnationalism, even when Elijah Muhammad or Malcolm X made claims for the right to control specific tracts of land within the United States. Instead, the NOI built on the fact that Islam was a major world religion with a strong transnational orientation. Muslim governments and Muslim communities often forged ties across borders, politically and culturally, as well as religiously. Drawing on this global vision, the Nation developed a model of community that linked African Americans both to Africa and to "Asia" (by Asia, Elijah Muhammad seemed to mean primarily what is usually called the Middle East).[33]

By the time it began to reach a larger audience in the 1950s, the Nation of Islam's vision drew on the several decades of black anticolonialist activity that had envisioned African Americans as part of a Pan-African diaspora. At the same time, the Nation's theological politics departed from that earlier activism's primary focus on Africa, opting for a more expansive transnationalism that included much of the nonwhite world (Latin America is something of an exception). Like the Pan-Africanist intellectual and cultural movements of the 1930s and 1940s, however, the Nation of Islam described the connections between African Americans and colonized peoples through a language of naturalized race. Elijah Muhammad simply claimed both Africa and the Middle East as black heritage, insisting that the Arabian Peninsula and the Nile valley were the historic home of what he called the "Afro-Asiatic black man" now living in America.

The Nation also tapped into a larger set of concerns as Christianity began to be challenged within the black community as inadequate to the spiritual and political needs of African Americans. In what was perhaps his most famous essay, "Letter from a Region in My Mind," published in the *New Yorker* in 1962, James Baldwin explored his own Christian heritage, the failures of the church, and the concomitant appeal of the NOI, which had recently begun to gain broad public attention. For Baldwin, the appeal of Islam lay precisely in its challenge to Christianity's Eurocentric heritage and links with imperialism:

> The Christian church itself—again, as distinguished from some of
> its ministers—sanctified and rejoiced in the conquests of the flag,
> and encouraged, if it did not formulate, the belief that conquest,
> and the resulting relative well-being of the Western population,
> was proof of the favor of God. God had come a long way from the
> desert—but then so had Allah, though in a very different
> direction. God, going north, and rising on the wings of power, had
> become white, and Allah, out of power, had become—for all practi-
> cal purposes anyway—black.[34]

If the Christian Bible had provided, for King and earlier for Baldwin himself, metaphors to articulate the hope of liberation, Christianity was also increasingly becoming identified with the European powers that evoked it to justify their international expansion. The African American Christianity that aligned itself with the Hebrews was being challenged on the world stage: by the fact that colonial and neocolonial powers used their Christianity to justify their imperialism, by the fact that the Israelis had themselves become a significant regional power, and by the violence and entrenchment of the southern whites who were fighting to prevent civil rights gains within the national borders. As Baldwin indicated, some African Americans felt increasingly impatient with the civil rights model of "beloved community"; for these men and women, that community was implicated by its association with a white-identified Christianity that rose "on the wings of power" abroad and taught accommodation with power at home.

The significance of this religiously influenced political refashioning was profound. In the NOI temples being rapidly established in urban areas in the late 1950s and early 1960s, ministers brought a message of worldwide black Islam to thousands of African American converts.[35] The Nation taught that Islam was the "natural religion of the black man," which had been stripped from the Africans who were sold into slavery and taught their masters' Christianity. Lectures in the temples usually, and often harshly, indicted the traditional Christianity of the African American church and argued that African Americans should recognize their true heritage as the descendants of the Muslim prophet Muhammad. Arabic, the Nation taught, was the original language of black people not only because many of the Africans who were taken into slavery and carried to the New World spoke Arabic but also because "the so-called Negroes" in America were descendants of the original Arabic-speaking peoples to whom Islam was revealed.[36] As the religious service began, the minister welcomed his parishioners with the Arabic greeting: "As-salaam-alaikum" (peace be with you), and the members responded, "wa-Alaikum wa salaam" (and also with you). At the Islamic schools set up by the Nation, Arabic lessons were an integral part of the curriculum: Arabic language instruction was said to begin at the age of three.[37]

The Nation's theology included an alternative genealogy for black Americans—understood to be descendants of the original inhabitants of Asia in general and Mecca in particular. As Elijah Muhammad wrote in his 1965 treatise, *Message to the Blackman in America:* "It is Allah's (God's) will and purpose that we shall know ourselves.... He has declared that we are descendants of the Asian black nation and the tribe of Shabazz... the first to discover the best part of our planet to live on. The rich Nile Valley of Egypt and the present seat of the Holy City, Mecca, Arabia."[38] The "Asian black nation" suggested a rich cultural inheritance that echoed the Asian-African alliance established at Bandung.

This alternative genealogy was also organized around gender, as exemplified in the segregation of men and women at Nation of Islam services. Elijah Muhammad linked the control of women's bodies (and his opposition to birth control) to the preservation of the "black man's" heritage through the production of new children. "The woman is man's field to produce his nation," Muhammad wrote. "You protect your vegetable crops from worms and thieves. Is not your woman more valuable than that crop of corn, that crop of cotton, that crop of cabbage, potatoes, beans, tomatoes? ... Yet you are not careful about your women. You don't love them."[39] Women's bodies were the literal site through which the nation would be produced, but also the metaphorical land that the "black man" would cultivate as his own. Elijah Muhammad taught "respect" for women but also the necessity of controlling them: "There is no nation on earth that has less respect for and as little control of their women as the so-called Negroes here in America."[40] The NOI doctrines on gender relations implicitly contrasted Islam with the Christian-influenced civil rights movement, in which women were active participants and men were often engaged in a nonviolent resistance that some African Americans viewed as feminizing. At the same time, it also connected to the mainstream liberal sociology of the period, which claimed that the pathology of black men was produced by the matriarchal power of black women.[41] Elijah Muhammad's insistence on women as precious resources that must be controlled promised a remasculinization of the black struggle and a clarification of gendered spaces within the nation.

Nation of Islam teaching revised, without discarding, important aspects of Christian symbolism that were salient in the black community.[42] At one level, the NOI directly attacked Christianity as a white religion and insisted that all black people were by nature Muslims. Nation of Islam meetings often included a display, drawn on a blackboard, featuring two flags: on one side of the board, a U.S. flag with a cross beside it, and underneath it the caption "Slavery, Suffering, and Death." On the other side, a flag bearing the Islamic Crescent, and underneath it the words "Islam: Freedom, Justice, and Equality." Beneath both was the question "Which one will survive the War of Armageddon?"[43] Elijah Muhammad's message to African Americans focused on pride and transformation; he argued that the Christianity of their slave masters had functioned to continue their spiritual enslavement. At another level, however, Muhammad's theology built directly upon the stories of the Bible, succeeding them with additional revelations that he argued would provide the key for understanding the old teachings in the way they were intended, rather than through the perversions of white Christianity. In this way, as Malcolm X once suggested, Islam was the true inheritor of an "old time religion" that was also a source of militancy:

> There is nothing in our book, the Koran, that teaches us to suffer peacefully. Our religion teaches us to be intelligent. Be peaceful, be courteous, obey the law, respect everyone; but if someone puts his hand on you, send him to the cemetery. That's a good religion. In fact, that's that old time religion. That's the one that Ma and Pa used to talk about: an eye for an eye, and a tooth for a tooth, and a head for a head, and a life for a life. That's a good religion. And nobody resents that kind of religion being taught but a wolf, who intends to make you his meal.[44]

Claiming the mantle of Old Testament justice and opposing New Testament forgiveness, this teaching used the Hebrew Scriptures to justify a racial, political, and moral geography that pitted (black) Islam against (white) Christianity in a worldwide and historic struggle.

The Nation of Islam's vision of a worldwide Islamic alliance confronting white Christianity challenged the black Christian sanctification of ancient Israel and offered an alternative sacred geography with Mecca as its center. Significantly, Elijah Muhammad taught that the stories told in the Old Testament were prophecies rather than histories, and that, as prophecy, they spoke of the contemporary experiences of African Americans rather than the historical experiences of the ancient Hebrews. "Before the coming of Allah (God), we being blind, deaf, and dumb, had mistaken the true meanings of these parables as referring to the Jews. Now, thanks to Almighty God, Allah ... has made us to understand these Bible parables are referring to us, the so-called Negroes and our slave masters."[45] Within this paradigm, Jews were not those whose ancient history was the prototype for contemporary liberation, as was the case for King and other civil rights leaders, but those whose putative status as "the chosen people" usurped the position of the black people in relation to God. This scriptural interpretation did a complex cultural work for the Nation: obviously, it carried the kernels of the NOI's anti-Semitism, which would become more pronounced over the coming decades. And surely this metaphorical removal of Jews from the stories of the Old Testament had particular salience in terms of the domestic tensions that were already rife in urban areas between African Americans and Jews.[46] But the specifically religious content also worked affirmatively as well, by mobilizing, appropriating, and refashioning an honored tradition to claim as one's own, as earlier Christianity had done with Judaism, or as the Romans did with Greek mythology.

This mixture of denigration and affirmative appropriation was also apparent in the Nation's attitude toward modern-day Israel. Like earlier black nationalist movements, the NOI saw in the success of Zionism an example and motivation for black nationalism. Malcolm X often referred to Israel respectfully in his speeches and interviews, even as he argued for the rightness of the Palestinian cause, as in this remarkably ambiguous passage from his *Autobiography:*

> If Hitler *had* conquered the world, as he meant to—that is a shuddery thought for every Jew alive today. The Jew will never forget that lesson.... [T]he British acquiesced and helped them to wrest Palestine away from the Arabs, the rightful owners, and then the Jews set up Israel, their own country—the one thing that every race of man in the world respects, and understands.[47]

This grudging respect did not translate into emotional identification with Zionism's success, as it did within much black Christian discourse, but it did further establish the complex meanings the Middle East held for the Nation of Islam and its members. If, as nationalists, they respected and even hoped to emulate Jewish nationalism, they nonetheless saw the Arab struggle with Israel as a parallel to the Nation of Islam's struggle for national self-determination in the United States, where the Nation claimed the right to "separate" from the rest of the United States by taking control of three or four states in the South for black people. Both the Arab (largely Muslim) population in Israel/Palestine and the black ("originally Muslim") population in the United States were in a contest over land; control over that land was essential to nationalism and political rights. In a 1960 speech, Malcolm X insisted on the naturalness of the alliance: "The Arabs, as a colored people, should and must make more effort to reach the millions of colored people in America who are related to the Arabs by blood. These millions of colored peoples would be completely in sympathy with the Arab cause!"[48]

In keeping with this sympathy, Malcolm X exhibited a detailed attention to international relations. Inspired and influenced by events in the third world, and even by the very notion of a "third world," which provided a sociopolitical language for the alliance of nonwhite nations, Malcolm X often talked about the 1955 Bandung conference as one example of the affiliation of nonwhite peoples against colonialism.[49] After being appointed minister of the Harlem mosque in 1954, he established active contacts with many Arab and African leaders at the United Nations, who, in turn, seemed to view the members of the Nation as fellow travelers—though their practice of Islam was highly unorthodox, they were potentially valuable allies in the fight against imperialism.[50]

Of the many connections the Nation established, those with Egypt were particularly important. The focus on Egypt developed for several reasons. First, like most black nationalists, NOI leaders believed emphatically that Egypt was a black nation and that the greatness of ancient Egyptian civilization was proof of the historical greatness of black culture (see chapter 3). Second, Egypt was (and is) largely a Muslim nation; therefore, it embodied the link between ancient black greatness and contemporary Islam. Finally, there was Nasser himself, who in the wake of Bandung and Suez had come to represent black and Arab defiance. Not surprisingly, in 1956 the various NOI publications had endorsed the Egyptian seizure of the Suez Canal and strongly opposed the actions of France, Britain, and Israel.[51]

The Nation of Islam identified with colonized nations politically, from the standpoint of a "colored" nation oppressed by whites. But the NOI also drew very specifically on cultural and religious identifications with Arab nations, which were understood to be also racial and historical. A year after Suez, in December 1957, Malcolm X organized a meeting on colonial and neocolonial issues that included representatives from the governments of Egypt, the Sudan, Ghana, Iraq, and Morocco. From that meeting, Elijah Muhammad sent a cable to Nasser, who was hosting the Afro-Asian People's Solidarity Conference in Cairo. Muhammad, describing himself as the "Spiritual Head of the Nation of Islam in the West," used the cable as an occasion to address Nasser and the other national leaders as brothers, as coreligionists, and as peers:

> As-Salaam-Alikum. Your long-lost Muslim brothers here in America pray that Allah's divine presence will be felt at this historic African-Asian Conference, and give unity to our efforts for peace and brotherhood.
>   Freedom, justice, and equality for all Africans and Asians is of far-reaching importance, not only to you of the East, but also to over 17,000,000 of your long-lost brothers of African-Asian descent here in the West.... May our sincere desire for universal peace which is being manifested at this great conference by all Africans and Asians, bring about the unity and brotherhood among all our people which we all so eagerly desire.[52]

The cable, and Nasser's friendly reply, circulated widely within the Nation. These contacts later facilitated Malcolm X's trip to Egypt in 1959, where he laid the groundwork for Elijah Muhammad's visit to Mecca in 1960.[53]

The Nation of Islam made explicit the link between a shared heritage and shared origin: a myth of commonality remapped the dominant imaginative geography that separated the Middle East from Africa by uniting Africa and northwestern Asia (the Middle East) into one geographic space deemed "black Asiatic-African." The vision of one black culture meant that blackness was no longer simply a synonym for Africans and people of recent African descent, but a *literal* linking together of large groups of non-Europeans—the "Asians and Africans" connected, in Malcolm X's words, by history and "by blood."

Elijah Muhammad's genealogical and political views circulated widely in the early 1960s, both within and beyond the African American community. Mainstream media heavily reported the "Black Muslim" phenomenon, in multiple television specials and interviews (often with Malcolm X), paperback "reports," and newspaper and magazine articles.[54] The Nation of Islam was discussed extensively in public discourse surrounding *The Autobiography of Malcolm X*, which was published in 1965, just months after Malcolm X was assassinated.[55] The organization was also covered in magazines with primarily black audiences, including *Negro Digest, Sepia,* and *Jet.*[56] In addition, the Nation made a concentrated effort to construct its own, alternative public sphere based on a system of widely disseminated newspapers and large public meetings. From 1959 to 1961, the organization published five different newspapers and magazines; one of these, *Muhammad Speaks,* launched in May 1960, became extraordinarily successful, garnering a circulation of over six hundred thousand by 1961.[57] Nation members also produced plays and songs: Louis Farrakhan (known as Louis X in this period) produced two plays in the early 1960s, *Orgena* ("a Negro," spelled backward) and *The Trial,* both of which were performed for Muslim audiences at rallies and meetings. Farrakhan, who had been a Calypso singer before converting, also wrote and recorded several songs, including "White Man's Heaven Is Black Man's Hell" and "Look at My Chains!"[58]

As cultural source and resource, then, the Nation of Islam functioned through diverse sites. As a religious and political organization, it took culture and media seriously, but it also existed and had an impact in many spaces and locations that Elijah Muhammad did not directly control. The Nation thus had an impressive influence well beyond its membership. One site for the diffusion of an Islamic sensibility beyond the bounds of the organization was the remarkable infusion of NOI mythology into the cultural products of the emerging Black Arts movement, which then went on to influence the direction of black liberation politics as the 1960s drew to a close. The signs of the Nation were frequently incorporated into the artistic productions of a new generation of young writers, who made the symbols and myths of this African American Islamic sect part of the raw material for the production of a new, black, postnational culture.

ONE BLACK ALLAH

When LeRoi Jones left Greenwich Village to found Harlem's Black Arts Repertory Theatre/School in 1965, Malcolm X had just been killed. Young African American intellectuals and activists found themselves and their communities in shock and torn by heated debates over the split between Malcolm X and Elijah Muhammad, as well as by questions of who was responsible for the assassination. When *The Autobiography of Malcolm X* was released, it became an immediate best-seller, creating a sensation within the circles of young, increasingly radicalized men and women who had listened to Malcolm X's speeches and were now riveted by the story of his life.[59] It was in this context, coming to terms with the death of the country's most important spokesperson for black radicalism, that Jones/Baraka set out to create a community-based popular theater and to invent a form and language that would reach African American audiences with a message of black (post)nationalism. As Baraka later wrote, he and his colleagues wanted "an art that would reach the people, that would take them higher, ready them for war and victory, as popular as the Impressions or the Miracles or Marvin Gaye. That was our vision and its image kept us stepping, heads high and backs straight."[60]

Although BARTS was short-lived (it collapsed within a year), its founding was an inspiration to a new generation of poets and playwrights. Black theater and poetry soon burst onto the national scene—a flowering of African American cultural production unlike anything since the Harlem Renaissance. African American poets and writers began to produce prolifically, and they quickly found venues for their work as several new publishing houses devoted specifically to black literature were born, including Dudley Randall's Broadside Press, Chicago's Third World Press, and Washington's Drum and Spear Press. In addition, new or revamped literary magazines and academic journals chronicled the scene, including *Umbra*, *Black Scholar*, *Journal of Black Poetry*, *The Liberator*, *Black Books Bulletin*, *Black Theater*, and, most important, *Negro Digest/Black World*.[61] Baraka himself was also a model; his transformation from highly literary poet into a radical artist committed to straightforward poetic language and generally short, accessible plays inspired the young writers who were publishing and performing in his wake (and quite consciously in his debt): Ed Bullins, Sonia Sanchez, Marvin X, Ben Caldwell, and Nikki Giovanni, among others.

Perhaps the most striking aspect was the development of a radical, independent theater movement. Within a year of the founding of BARTS, small community theater groups were being formed around the country in Detroit, New Orleans, San Francisco, Chicago, Washington, D.C., and Los Angeles. The new community theaters produced plays and held poetry readings not only in traditional theaters but also in schools, at local meetings, and in the streets.[62] In April 1966, *Negro Digest* produced its first of several annual issues on the black theater; later that year, a San Francisco–based group, which included Baraka (who was then a visiting professor at San Francisco State College), performed at the annual convention of CORE.[63] By 1967, the new black theater was being widely discussed as a major development in the arts of the decade, so much so that when Harold Cruse published *The Crisis of the Black Intellectual,* he ended the book with two chapters on African Americans and the theater, analyzing the significance of BARTS and declaring that "there can be a cultural method of revolutionizing the society in which the theater functions as an institution." A year later, the nation's most important drama journal, *The Drama Review* (*TDR*), published a special issue on black theater.[64]

Poetry and plays were the favored genres of the Black Arts movement, despite the fact that both had, up until this point, appealed to a very narrow audience. These forms were, in Pierre Bourdieu's terms, subfields of highly restricted production, and they usually carried the cultural capital (and the distance from popular culture) that came with their elite position.[65] But the short poem and the one-act play are often more accessible to new or nontraditional writers, precisely because they are short, and Black Arts movement artists tried with some success to broaden the audience for both genres. Writing in a self-consciously vernacular language, in free verse and street talk, and distributing work in small pamphlets and magazines, in paperback anthologies, and in public performance, young artists aimed for a style and a format that were accessible and relevant to people who might otherwise be uninterested in or intimidated by "art." Like earlier avant-garde movements, they wanted to eradicate the separation of "art" from "life."[66] Ed Bullins, a playwright who began writing during this period and who went on to become one of the most prolific and most frequently produced playwrights of the late 1960s and early 1970s, argued (as did many in the movement) that black theater and poetry were effectively transforming both genres and audiences:

> Black literature has been available for years, but it has been circulating in a closed circle.... It hasn't been getting down to the people. But now in the theatre, we can go right into the black community and have a literature for the people... for the great masses of Black people. I think this is the reason that more Black plays are being written and seen, and the reason that more Black theatres are springing up. Through the efforts of certain Black artists, people are beginning to realize the importance of Black theatre.[67]

The genuine popularity and broad reach of these new works is only part of the story, however. No matter how many performances they gave in local venues, or how many inexpensive editions they distributed, these poets and playwrights never had the kind of direct reach enjoyed by major political or religious groups, including the Nation of Islam itself. Nonetheless, they could have a significant impact precisely because of the prestige that art, even popularized art, carried: the status it gave within the African American community, as well as the notoriety that the new artists were gaining in the mainstream, white-dominated media. The mix was potent—cultural capital combined with a new, populist approach and a broader audience. It gave art and artists a highly visible role in the African American community overall, and among younger radicals in particular, and it allowed for the dissemination and generalization of radical political and cultural perspectives. By 1966 the influence of Black Arts was strong enough that the new chair of the Student Nonviolent Coordinating Committee (SNCC), Stokely Carmichael, expressed concern that poetry writing (and, by extension, poetry reading) was threatening to overtake other kinds of political work. In a speech reprinted in the Chicago SNCC newsletter, he complained: "We have to say, 'Don't play jive and start writing poems after Malcolm is shot.' We have to move from the point where the man left off and stop writing poems."[68]

The Black Arts movement defined political struggle *as* cultural struggle; this cultural struggle, in turn, required a new spirituality. In literary circles, Islamic symbolism and mythology were incorporated into the self-conscious construction of a new black aesthetic and a revolutionary black culture. As literary critic Addison Gayle put it, "The historic practice of bowing to other men's gods and definitions has produced a crisis of the highest magnitude, and brought us, culturally, to the limits of racial armageddon."[69] The aim was to establish a basis for political nationalism through the production of a set of cultural and spiritual values "in tune with black people." Artists and theorists of the movement called upon those seeking black power to understand the significance of culture. "The socio-political must be a righteous extension of the cultural," Baraka argued. "A cultural base, a black base, is the completeness the black power movement must have. We must understand that we are *Replacing* a dying [white] culture, and we must be prepared to do this, and be absolutely conscious of what we are replacing it with."[70] The attempt to construct a new black culture was deeply intertwined with the search for religious alternatives to mainstream Christianity, a search that included not only Islam but also renewed interest in the signs and symbols of pre-Islamic and traditional African religions (such as the Yoruba religion) as well as the study of ancient Egypt. Baraka and others often mixed these influences together in an eclectic, sometimes deliberately mystical, mix.

Baraka's short play *A Black Mass* exemplifies the cross-fertilization and appropriation that linked Islam and the Black Arts movement in the self-conscious production of a black mythology. The play told the story of how white people had come to be born in an originally black world. It explained the current plight of black people, reversing the traditional associations of Eurocentric Christianity by making "whiteness" the category associated with evil and thus in need of explanation.[71] The play was a revision and a condensation of Elijah Muhammad's story, "Yakub's History," which explained the creation of white people from earth's original black inhabitants as the product of generations of genetic breeding.[72] Baraka wrote *A Black Mass* in 1965 while he was at BARTS, and it was first performed in Newark, New Jersey, in May 1966.[73]

When Baraka wrote *A Black Mass*, he was not a member of the Nation of Islam and did not even identify as a Muslim, though he would affiliate with orthodox Sunni Islam a few years later. Baraka would later mix Islam with his support of Kawaida, Ron Karenga's syncretic doctrine based on traditional African religions.[74] His fascination with the story of Yakub, however, and his general interest in the myths of the Nation of Islam were not idiosyncratic. Thus, although *A Black Mass* was not produced as often as some of Baraka's more explicit social commentary, Black Arts critics admired it. The editor and essayist Larry Neal, who was also Baraka's friend and colleague, described it as Baraka's "most important play" because "it is informed by a mythology that is wholly the creation of the Afro-American sensibility." Another commentator writing in *Negro Digest* called it "Jones' most accomplished play to date."[75] The play was an early, explicit statement of the ways in which, even after the death of Malcolm X and even with suspicions about Elijah Muhammad's role in the murder, the beliefs of the NOI were often presented *as* black culture, influencing and infusing a new black sensibility even for those who were not NOI adherents. In this sense, *A Black Mass* was both symptomatic and anticipatory of what would happen in the sphere of black cultural production over the next few years.

In *A Black Mass*, the character of Yakub, now called Jacoub, is introduced as one of three "Black Magicians" who together symbolize the black origin of all religions: according to the stage directions, they wear a skullcap, a fez, and an African *fila*.[76] The play's title alludes to the necessity of black revisions of religious ritual, and the play itself is designed to revise and rewrite white-centered origin myths. Not incidentally, it also defines and explains the theological problem of evil as represented in white people.

Baraka turns the Nation's myth into a reinterpretation of the Faust story and a simultaneous meditation on the role and function of art. As with Faust, Jacoub's individualism and egotism are his undoing, but his failings also signal the destruction of a community. Baraka's version of the story also draws on the Frankenstein tale; he conflates the six hundred years of Elijah Muhammad's "history" into a single, terrible moment of the creation of a monster.[77] Jacoub is a complex figure; his desire to "find out everything" makes him in some ways more attractive and accessible than his fellow magicians, who insist that "we already know everything" and that

Figure 10.   Jacoub creates whiteness in a performance of Amiri Baraka's *A Black Mass*. Courtesy of Photographs and Prints Division, Schomberg Center for Research in Black Culture, the New York Public Library, Astor, Lenox and Tilden Foundations.

creation or innovation is impossible and dangerous (24). But the play's condemnation of Jacoub is apparent not only in the fact that he is trying to create "whiteness" (surely the moral weight of that choice needed no further amplification for the primarily black audience to which the play was addressed) but also in his insistence that "creation is its own end" (24); this art-for-art's-sake view was precisely the aesthetic philosophy that Baraka and other leaders of the early Black Arts movement were determined to challenge and, if possible, eradicate.[78] The point was underscored by the fact that the play relied heavily on music composed and played by the avant-garde jazz artist Sun-Ra, since Baraka and other Black Arts movement theorists argued that black music should be the model for the new black literary culture.[79]

At the opening of the play, Jacoub is determined to pursue knowledge narcissistically, to create for the sake of creating, even though his creations are evil. The other two magicians, Nasafi and Tanzil, are trying to counter the pernicious effects of Jacoub's first invention, time, which they describe as a "white madness"(22). Unmoved by their pleas that he stop his "fool's game," Jacoub is determined to make his own creature—"a super-natural being. A being who will not respond to the world of humanity" (27). Castigated by the other magicians, Jacoub nonetheless proceeds with his experiment; as he does so, the natural world is disturbed by raging seas and thundering skies that have a Lear-like portentousness. Three women run in from outside, upset and frightened. They wail and moan, serving as a chorus and as representatives of "the people" who will be destroyed by Jacoub's creation. Despite the fear of the women, the objections of his fellow magicians, and the portents outside, Jacoub pours his solutions together: there is an explosion, out of which leaps a cold white creature in a lizard-devil mask, which Baraka's stage directions describe as covered in red capes and with a deathly white face. The women and the other magicians are horrified by the creature—one calls it "a mirror of twisted evil." Jacoub is undeterred as the creature vomits and screams, "slobberlaughing" its way through the audience (30). Jacoub insists that he can teach the beast to talk, but it has only two words, incessantly repeated: "Me!" and "White" (30–32).

The beast immediately tries to attack the women. It soon bites one of them, Tilia, who is quickly transformed into another monster, white-blotched and slobbering. With this "bite-caress" of the woman, Baraka adds Dracula to his stock of popular culture referents and in so doing brings sexuality to the forefront: the depraved and dangerous (and decidedly unsexy) red-caped beast infects the women first, using its lust to spread its "white madness."[80] At the end of the play, Tilia and the beast become hideous Adam and Eve substitutes. The two of them attack and kill the other women and the magicians, including Jacoub. With his dying breath, Jacoub condemns the two "white beasts" to the caves of the north. These two creatures will reproduce and eventually create the white race that comes to dominate and enslave the rest of the world.

If the play allegorically represents the rape of black women by white men, it also constructs "Woman" as the first and most susceptible base for the spread of "whiteness," reproducing the tendency of many nationalist ideologies to make women's bodies the sites of both nationalist reproduction and potential cultural impurity. As Phillip Brian Harper points out, this consistent association of proper blackness with proper masculinity in the Black Arts movement also meant that racial identification was figured in terms of a potent heterosexuality, whereby "judgements of insufficient racial identification [were] to be figured specifically in terms of a failed manhood for which homosexuality, as always, was the primary signifier."[81] *A Black Mass* describes white people as the spawn of monsters, a crime against the natural order, but distorted (black) reproduction is the unspoken yet crucial undercurrent.[82]

Throughout the play, Baraka uses a broad range of allusions to both high literature and popular culture—from Shakespeare to Dracula, Faust to Frankenstein. Werner Sollors has described Baraka's work as a "quest for a populist modernism," and indeed, one can see a strong modernist strain in the persistent high culture references (offered without a hint of irony) and the deep seriousness with which Baraka confronts questions of knowledge, of belief, and of good and evil. But we might also consider this play an early example of postmodernism, in that it goes beyond simply incorporating references to popular culture (which modernists, such as James Joyce, were quite prone to do), to a more postmodern appropriation of the structure and feel of popular culture genres.[83] Yet unlike much postmodernist writing, Baraka's mix of references is decidedly *un*playful, designed to undergird rather than undermine the story's status as origin myth. Baraka uses popular culture not to gesture toward a fully postmodern embrace of pastiche and ahistoricity but rather to present a profound sense of the significance and meaning of history for the black community.

This political commitment is nowhere more evident than at the end of *A Black Mass*, when a final voice-over issues a call to racial struggle, now framed in mythical and theological terms: "And so Brothers and Sisters, these beasts are still loose in the world. Still they spit their hideous cries. There are beasts in our world, Brothers and Sisters. . . . Let us find them and slay them. . . . Let us declare Holy War. The Jihad. Or we cannot deserve to live. Izm-el-Azam. Izm-el-Azam. Izm-el-Azam. Izm-el-Azam" (39). The call for jihad (Arabic for "righteous struggle" or "holy war") becomes a religious and moral response to the problem of evil, the answer of the present to the history presented in the play.

The influence of Islam and Islamic symbolism went well beyond Baraka's work; it was highly visible in the Black Arts movement in general, acknowledged, and often supported, even by those who did not share its religious presumptions. Members of both the Nation of Islam and orthodox African American Sunni Muslim groups were active in political and cultural organizations all over the country. Baraka's own interest in Islam continued to manifest itself in poetry and essays for the rest of the decade.[84] By the time Baraka and Larry Neal published the field-defining anthology *Black Fire* in 1968, and Ed Bullins edited the collection *New Plays for the Black Theatre* a year later, they were codifying (and canonizing) a body of work, produced and written in the previous several years, in which the influence of Islam was highly visible. Many of the plays and essays were either direct translations of NOI ideology (such as Salimu's "Growing into Blackness," which instructs young women on the proper Islamic way to support their men) or simply presumed a working familiarity with Islam on the part of the audience. Similarly, work by young poets was infused with Islamic references, which were often simultaneous testament to the influence of Malcolm X and/or Baraka: Gaston Neal's "Personal Jihad" is one example; another is the long poem, "malcolm" by Welton Smith, which speaks of "the sound of Mecca / inside you" and concludes with detailed references to the Yakub myth in "The Beast Section." The prominence of Muslim-derived names is also significant in both collections; many poems and plays are by writers who have changed their names to, among others, Yusef Iman, Yusef Rahman, Ahmed Legraham Alhamisi, Salimu, and Marvin X.[85] When Baraka published his own collection of plays in 1968, he introduced it with a poem that claimed the political power of the literary renaissance:

> this is an introduction to a book of plays
> i am prophesying the death of white people in this land
> i am prophesying the triumph of black life in this land,
>   and over all the world
> we are building publishing houses, and newspapers, and
>   armies, and factories
> we will change the world before your eyes,
>   *izm-el-azam,*
>   yes, say it,
>   say it
>   sweet nigger
>   i believe in black allah
>   governor of creation
>   Lord of the Worlds
>   *As Salaam Alikum*[86]

Looking at the cultural products and newspaper accounts of the period, it is clear that the Nation of Islam provided one significant touchstone for a larger project—that of re-visioning history and geography in order to construct a moral and spiritual basis for contemporary affiliations and identities. As Larry Neal described it: "The Old Spirituality is generalized. It seeks to recognize Universal Humanity. The New Spirituality is specific. It begins by seeing the world from the concise point of view of the colonized."[87] In *A Black Mass*, Baraka offered an Islamic-influenced narrative *as* empowering myth, *as* a culture specific to black people. Even though the vast majority of Black Arts writers and readers were not Muslims, this myth and culture became part of the language and geography of black cultural identity. For a new generation, culture then became the basis for constructing an alternative nation; and this (post)nation—with its own sense of spirituality and its own political vision—was the underlying utopian gesture of black nationalist thought and literature. Within this project, Islamic affiliations often functioned as both site and source for those black identities, linking African Americans to the Arab and Muslim Middle East in ways both literal and metaphoric.

COMMUNITIES IN CONFLICT

The cultural and religious influence of Islam would play an important role in African American responses to the 1967 Arab-Israeli war, and those responses in turn highlighted the increasing political tensions between African Americans and American Jews. The 1967 war marked the first major armed conflict in eleven years between Israel and Arab states, and its outcome made Palestinians (the "refugees" from the founding of Israel in 1948) into a highly visible component of the conflict. In the United States, as well as the Middle East, the war was also a turning point, one that expressed old animosities and exposed new power relations.

In May 1967, the ongoing tensions between Israel, Egypt, and Syria escalated dramatically. Egyptian president Nasser, involved in a war of words with conservative Arab regimes over the direction of Arab politics, had recently been criticized by Jordan and Syria for hypocrisy and cowardice in continuing to allow UN troops to be stationed on the Egyptian side of the border with Israel. The troops had been positioned in the Sinai in 1957 to guard the peace after the Suez crisis, but Israel had refused to allow them on its side of the border. Nasser, stung by the accusations of weakness and attempting to regain his prestige as the region's preeminent nationalist leader, moved his own troops into the Sinai in May 1967 and asked the UN troops to withdraw. Several days later, Nasser provocatively closed the Strait of Tiran to Israeli shipping. As American and European diplomats scrambled to cobble together a multilateral diplomatic and/or military response (the United States was particularly concerned to act carefully in light of the increasing controversies over its war in Vietnam), Israel insisted on the right of navigation through the international waters of the strait and declared the closure an act of war. On June 5, with tensions escalating on all sides, Israel launched an air attack that virtually destroyed both the Egyptian and Syrian air forces on the ground. Immediately, Jordan also entered the battle, attacking Israel with artillery and airpower. In just six days, the war was over, with Israel the clear victor. As a result of the conflict, the Israelis conquered several territories that had been previously controlled by Arab countries: the Gaza Strip (Egypt), East Jerusalem and the West Bank (Jordan), and the Golan Heights (Syria).[88]

For American Jews, the war had an extraordinary, transformative effect. In May, as Egypt's and Israel's armies prepared for war, as Nasser threatened immediate and total victory, and as the United States and the Soviet Union came to an agreement to stay out of the conflict, many American Jews feared that the Jews of Israel were about to be destroyed—"driven into the sea." Once the fighting began, on June 5, many attended, hour by hour, to the progress of the war. As one historian described it in 1968, people in New York were glued to their televisions or radios, to the point of carrying portables with them in the street. "At home we compulsively watched television," wrote one contemporary observer. "[I]n our cars we kept the radio on.... We had no mind for anything else."[89]

The impact of the war on Jewish identity in the United States was striking: Jewishness became more important, and identification with Israel became a more important aspect of Jewishness. Ten years earlier, in 1957, Nathan Glazer had commented that "the two greatest events in modern Jewish history, the murder of six million Jews by Hitler and the creation of the Jewish state in Palestine, have had remarkably slight effects on the inner life of American Jewry."[90] In 1967, faced with what they believed to be a potential second Holocaust in Israel, many American Jews began to pay much more attention to both. Young people rushed to Jewish agencies to volunteer to go to Israel to help; on the home front local communities all over the country raised more than $90 million in a week for the United Jewish Appeal's Israel Emergency Fund.[91] Arthur Hertzberg, writing in *Commentary* in August 1967, explained:

> The immediate reaction of American Jewry to the crisis was far more intense and widespread than anyone could have foreseen. Many Jews would never have believed that grave danger to Israel could dominate their thoughts and emotions to the exclusion of everything else; many were surprised by the depth of their anger at those of their friends who carried on as usual, untouched by fear for Israeli survival and the instinctive involvement they themselves felt.[92]

The crisis, he said, had evoked "a sense of belonging to the worldwide Jewish people, of which Israel is the center."[93] The joyful triumph experienced by many Jews at the end of the war led to a different sense of themselves. As the *New Republic* would put it, looking back on the occasion of the twentieth anniversary of the war, "The Six-Day War meant the restoration of Jewish power to the stage of world history."[94]

The immediate response to the Six-Day War was far more muted among most non-Jews, though decidedly on the side of Israel. But the younger black liberation movement, now moving in an increasingly radical direction, had a very different reaction. Already, young black activists were building on the cultural politics articulated by leaders like Malcolm X and Baraka. They were also influenced by the writings of the anticolonialist and Marxist Frantz Fanon, whose analyses of the colonial situation in Algeria became increasingly influential in the United States. Like Egypt, Algeria was a nation that combined Muslim, Arab, and African influences; it was also in the early 1960s still fighting a long and bloody struggle for independence from France, which was obtained in 1962. In *The Wretched of the Earth* (1961), Fanon emphasized the political importance of cultural identity for the colonized; he also suggested that violence could be a "cleansing force" for those who had been made to feel inferior by oppression.[95] In 1967, Black Panther founder Eldridge Cleaver reviewed *The Wretched of the Earth*, which he described as a "classic study of the psychology of oppressed peoples...now known among the militants of the black liberation movement in America as 'the Bible.' "[96] The young African American activists carrying around worn copies of Fanon's work drew pointed parallels to the ongoing struggles for decolonization and third world independence that went much further than the moral and political affiliations of the 1940s and 1950s. Black Americans, they argued, were an internal colony within the United States, alienated politically, culturally, and psychically from the dominant, white culture. These are "the last days of the American empire," Baraka wrote in 1964, and for African Americans to love America would be to become "equally culpable for the evil done to the rest of the world."[97]

Such ideas became especially important in SNCC, which, though it originally had been allied with the SCLC and the Christian-based civil rights organizations, had become increasingly identified with the internal colonization model for understanding African American oppression. In May 1967, the organization made its internationalist approach apparent by declaring itself a "human rights organization," establishing an International Affairs Commission, applying for nongovernmental organization (NGO) status at the United Nations, and announcing that it would "encourage and support the liberation struggles against colonialism, racism, and economic exploitation" around the world.[98] This internationalist approach was not an innovation or a radical departure; it built on both the anticolonial activism of earlier generations of black Americans and the more recent cultural and political influence of Islam and African-based religions. But SNCC's stance was seen—as it was intended to be seen—as a clear indication that the organization was making a decisive break with the mainstream civil rights organizations and their model of liberation in one country.

It was in this context that in the summer of 1967 the SNCC newsletter printed an article about the Arab-Israeli war. In June, just after the war erupted, the Central Committee had requested that SNCC's research and communications staff investigate the background to the conflict. A few weeks later, the organization's newsletter carried an article that described the war and the postwar Israeli occupation of the West Bank and Gaza in a decidedly pro-Arab fashion. The list of facts about "the Palestine problem" was highly critical of Israel (and not just the recent war): "Did you know that the Zionists conquered Arab homes through terror, force, and massacres? Did you know ... that the U.S. government has worked along with Zionist groups to support Israel so that America may have a toehold in that strategic Middle East location, thereby helping white America to control and exploit the rich Arab nations?"[99] The article was accompanied by two cartoons and two photographs that many people considered anti-Semitic. One of the cartoons depicted Nasser and Muhammad Ali, each with a noose around his neck. Holding the rope was a hand with a Star of David and dollar signs; an arm labeled "Third World Liberation Movements" was poised to cut the rope. One of the photos showed Israeli soldiers with guns pointed at Arabs who were lined up against a wall, and the caption read: "This Is Gaza, West Bank, Not Dachau, Germany."[100]

The newsletter and the statements supporting it were widely denounced in the mainstream press and the Jewish community. The executive director of the American Jewish Congress, for example, called the article an example of "shocking and vicious anti-Semitism." SNCC historian Clayborne Carson has argued that the piece was "unauthorized" and based on the opinions of one individual (the staff writer had been influenced by the Nation of Islam and had Palestinian friends in college). But, as Carson also points out, SNCC's Central Committee had surely expected a pro-Palestinian conclusion to the investigation it had requested, and it generally supported the conclusions that emerged.[101]

Carson believes that SNCC's decision to take up the Arab-Israeli war was part of a general trend toward taking "gratuitous statements on foreign policy issues"; by 1967, he concludes, support for third world liberation struggles was the only ideological glue that could hold the fracturing organization together.[102] Others mark the SNCC leaflet as an indicative moment, the "coming out" of a whole generation of young blacks who were increasingly arguing against the presence of whites in the black liberation movement and turning away from the black-white civil rights coalition that had included so many Jewish activists. Black radicals, in this view, were "using Israel as the benchmark for their repudiation of their civil rights past."[103] Certainly it was the case that, because the 1967 Arab-Israeli war had galvanized Jewish identity in the United States, criticism of Israel became a highly charged issue for Jews precisely at the moment that SNCC was making its public statements.

In general, these assessments have built on the assumption that, up to 1967, all available narratives of black liberation had placed African Americans in a de facto and unproblematic alliance with Israel—an alliance that would have continued had it not been for some individual or collective failure to sustain the domestic relationship forged between African Americans and American Jews in the civil rights movement. The fact that mainstream civil rights leaders quickly condemned the SNCC article and made statements in support of Israel seems at first to confirm this argument: the leaders of the old civil rights coalition, influenced by the black Christian narratives of exodus and the model of Zionism for black liberation, and perhaps appreciative of the role that Jews had played in the movement, felt an emotional and political commitment to Israel.[104]

But this division over the Arab-Israeli conflict also points to another story, that of the religious and cultural influence of Islam in the black community and its intersections with the increasing visibility of decolonization movements worldwide. Placing SNCC's response to the 1967 Arab-Israeli war in the context of black Islam and its role in the radicalization of African American culture and politics helps us reframe the questions we ask about that moment and about the history of black-Jewish and black-Arab relations overall. This alternative analysis avoids the common mistake of conflating of black-Jewish relations within the United States (and the concomitant issues of racism and anti-Semitism) with the meanings and significance of the Middle East for African Americans. While it is clear that the two issues—domestic relationships, on the one hand, and representations of Israel and the Arab Middle East, on the other—are related, too often the assumption has been that African American views of the Middle East *must* reflect black-Jewish relations in the United States and *must* be, to the degree that these views are critical of Israel or express affiliation with Arabs, an expression of black anti-Semitism.[105]

Anti-Semitism was present in the black community and the Black Arts movement, sometimes virulently. And it is not sufficient to say, as James

Baldwin once did, that blacks were anti-Semitic because they were anti-white.[106] In the case of Baraka (and in many of the pronouncements of the NOI), there was a profound difference (qualitative and quantitative) in the ways that white ethnicities were targeted. For example, in one well-known poem, "Black Art," Baraka called for poems that would fight the white power structure, commenting—in the violent rhetoric that was often typical of him—that ideal poems would "knockoff ... dope selling wops" and suggesting that cops should be killed and have their "tongues pulled out and sent to Ireland." But as Baraka himself later admitted, he held a specific animosity for Jews, as was apparent in the different intensity and viciousness of his call in the same poem for "dagger poems" to stab the "slimy bellies of the owner-jews" and poems that crack "steel knuckles in a jewlady's mouth."[107]

Certainly, anti-Jewish feeling had a bearing on the ways in which some people (black and white) formed their understandings of the Arab-Israeli conflict: there were instances at the time of the 1967 war—and there have been others since—of people who began by talking about the Arab-Israeli issue and ended by criticizing Jewish store owners or political leaders in the United States for matters unrelated to foreign policy.[108] (Of course, the tendency to conflate criticism of Israeli actions with a criticism of Jews is not limited to African Americans.) However, these anti-Semitic expressions simply do not explain the pro-Arab feelings of many African Americans in this period, since it would have been quite possible for them to be both anti-Jewish and anti-Arab. The pull toward Arab culture was something far more than an outgrowth of anti-Semitism.

I suggest that African American investments in the Arab-Israeli conflict had a significant history beyond the domestic tensions of black-Jewish relations, a history that developed *within* the black community as part of a search for religious and cultural alternatives to Christianity. This search was simultaneously a part of an ongoing process of redefining "blackness" in the United States. The struggle to define a black culture was never separable from the process of constructing transnational definitions of blackness—definitions that connected African Americans to people of color and anti-colonialism all over the world, including, quite centrally, the Middle East.

BEYOND ISLAM

As black nationalism gained prominence in the late 1960s, some writers and thinkers in the Black Arts movement began to offer challenges to the cultural politics of Christianity *and* Islam, expressing a desire to transcend both. Islam had always been only one of several religious resources available in this period, though a particularly prominent one. Groups like Ron Karenga's US Organization drew on an eclectic mix of various African traditions, updated and revised. Baraka himself supplemented his Islam with Yoruba symbols and beliefs; he also began, in the period after 1967, to add ancient Egyptian motifs. In an essay written from jail during the 1967 uprising in Newark, New Jersey, Baraka mixed Islamic prayers, Egyptian hieroglyphics, and references to traditional African gods in a mystical syncretism that figured Islam as the progeny of the original black culture in ancient Egypt: "O Allah O Shango (rulers of our ancient cities) O Osiris," he wrote, "we will be closer to you from now on."[109] Arguments that ancient Egypt was part of a black African heritage had been present for a long time in the black community (see chapter 3), but it was only in the later 1960s that some African Americans turned to Egypt not just as proof of a black African past but as a model for contemporary spirituality and culture.

The unofficial leader of this new vanguard was the young writer Ishmael Reed, whose first novel *The Free-Lance Pallbearers*, published in 1967, was widely and positively reviewed in both the mainstream press and the little magazines that defined and debated the new black aesthetic. One of the best-known and most admired writers of the Black Arts movement, Reed was nonetheless an articulate critic of what he considered to be the overly prescriptive orientations of Black Arts theorists like Baraka, as well as critics like Houston Baker and Addison Gayle.[110] In several novels, in his collected poems, and in interviews and essays, Reed presented himself as an iconoclast, both formally and spiritually. Committed to the cultural politics of black liberation, he agreed that black political struggle needed a black cultural politics. But he insisted on a different genealogy for African Americans, one that challenged the connection to a black Islam and instead constructed a historical, religious, and cultural matrix that privileged Caribbean voodoo (in the United States, hoodoo) as the authentic African American religion.[111] He linked these traditional religions directly back to the myths and gods of ancient Egypt, which he saw as a model for a liberated black sensibility distinctly separate from the values of the later Islamic conquest. This pantheistic moral geography was most highly developed in Reed's extraordinary 1972 novel, *Mumbo Jumbo*.

Mumbo Jumbo is a collage of textual forms; it mixes drawings, photographs, quotes from historical sources, and "reproductions" of fictional signs or handbills into a highly stylized narrative. The main plot, set in the United States in the 1920s, revolves around the travels of "Jes Grew," an infection making its way across America. One of the narrators refers to Jes Grew as an anti-plague, because, instead of killing, it enlivens those it infects. Jes Grew encourages dancing, sexual adventurousness, and a lack of respect for established authority. The novel's detective hero is PaPa LaBas, a practitioner of what Reed calls "HooDoo" at his Mumbo Jumbo Kathedral in Harlem, who is trying to solve the mystery of Jes Grew's origins even as he also tries to prevent it from being destroyed. Papa LaBas's antagonists are the members of the Wallflower Order, an ancient conspiracy that controls most centers of power and is trying to destroy Jes Grew. Like Baraka, who suggested that time itself was a "white madness," Reed implies that black culture is the site of a tradition that refuses the dubious benefits of "progress." PaPa LaBas and the Wallflower Order are reenacting an ancient battle that pits the forces of sensuality, pantheism, and HooDoo on the one side against the forces of conquest, rationality, and arid morality on the other.

We can see this at the level of both form and content. The novel culminates in a long monologue by PaPa LaBas about ancient Egypt[112] (161–191), in which he tells the story of Set and Osiris. Osiris is identified as the ancestor of a movement that, traveling from Egypt to the rest of Africa and then to Haiti, became the foundation of Jes Grew. Set, on the other hand, probably invented taxes. The conflict between Osiris and Set, in which Set emerges victorious, is a story of the betrayal of the forces of sensuality, creativity, and dance by the forces of rigidity, bureaucracy, and domination. PaPa LaBas narrates ancient Egypt as the site and source of modern African American spirituality. LaBas himself, as a practitioner of HooDoo, is the character in the novel who maintains the old ways; he is the link to Africa, to the pre-Islamic traditions that developed, in the Caribbean, into the practice of voodoo. LaBas's final monologue, which constitutes nearly one-third of the novel, revises and redeploys the myth of Osiris to figure Egypt, Haiti, and African Americans in a transnational alliance. Reed places racial formation in the United States in an international frame; anticolonialism throughout the world and black cultural nationalism in the United States are linked by their shared status as keepers of Jes Grew.

Reed's fascination with voodoo situates *Mumbo Jumbo* as part of the broader African American critique of Christianity in the 1960s and 1970s. The Wallflower Order of the novel is backed by the "Knights Templar," a medieval secret society that dates from the Crusades. The Christian Knights exemplify the tendency of Western culture to attempt to conquer all it touches: "They are a kind of Tac Squad for Western Civilization," Reed writes, bent on destroying the rest of the world's cultures (56).

If Reed's polemics against Christianity are undisguised, his handling of Islam is barely more nuanced. Islam is figured in the novel through the character of Abdul Hamid, a puritanical though well-intentioned Black

Muslim, who is smart but hypocritical. Although Hamid is theoretically respectful of black people, his narrow visions of God's law lead to Jes Grew's destruction. Islam, like Christianity, is an "Atonist" (monotheistic) religion, and Islam is guilty of some of the same kind of repression of sexuality that distinguished the Puritans. "Sounds as if you've picked up the old Plymouth Rock bug and are calling it Mecca," PaPa LaBas tells Abdul (36). And elsewhere: "You are no different than the Christians you imitate. Atonists Christians and Muslims don't tolerate those who refuse to accept their modes.... They are very similar, 1 having derived from the other. Muhammad seems to have wanted to impress Christian critics with his knowledge of the Bible" (34–35). Ultimately, it is Abdul who burns "the text" that is the object of PaPa LaBas's search.

In contrast to Christianity and Islam, Reed defends the richness of Egyptian culture and sees Egypt as a black African heritage that provides the site for an alternative vision of black identity as sexual, playful, intuitive, creative, and polytheistic. This spiritual alternative is thus also a sexual alternative: Christianity and Islam fail precisely in their shutting down of sex, play, and dance. Reed's model of spiritual/sexual liberation via Egyptian HooDoo is severely compromised, however, by its dependence on female submission and a rigorous heterosexual imperative. Reed represents women as sexual and energetic, as owners of their own bodies and subjects in their own right. He nonetheless also figures female sexuality as willingly receptive and passive. In the story of Set and Osiris, for example, Osiris's lover, the Egyptian goddess Isis, is said to blush because she knows that Osiris will soon "give her his 'rod of authority' " (166). While Reed's novel presents itself as a radical re-visioning of the beauty of sexual play, its revisions are also reinscriptions: the black women who Elijah Muhammad argued must be plowed and controlled in order to build the nation are, in Reed's alternative order, the bodies on which sexual freedom is transmuted into masculine virility.

Most literary readings of *Mumbo Jumbo* have emphasized its stylistic and formal innovations, the ways in which Reed disrupts the conventions of both the Western canon and the tradition of African American writing to create an early postmodernist text. Henry Louis Gates has argued that Reed's novel "signifies" on—appropriates and revises—the realist tradition of Richard Wright and Ralph Ellison by elevating indeterminacy and the play of language. In Gates's reading, Reed's postmodernism uses a narrative structure of doubling: the contemporary detective story of investigation is paired with the story of what happened in the ancient past to create a self-reflecting text that refuses closure and remarks on the nature of writing itself.[113]

In fact, Reed's text is even more complicated than Gates suggests. It uses the layering of time and the disruption of narrative to participate in a highly polemic kind of cultural work, offering a more playful, and in Reed's view more radical, mythology for African Americans at a moment when religious claims were central to the project of revisioning black culture. *Mumbo Jumbo* is actually set in three, not just two, separate narrative moments. First is the time of the ancient Egyptian past, site of the original conflict between the pantheist Osiris and monotheist Set. This narrative prefigures the conflict in the second, "contemporary time" of the novel, the 1920s, when PaPa LaBas and Jes Grew confront the Wallflower Order; the story of infection and investigation takes place in this second narrative time. The third time of the narrative is the 1970s. It is always implicitly and occasionally explicitly juxtaposed as yet another moment of cultural and ideological conflict between the forces of Jes Grew creativity and those of dominant morality. Reed establishes these three narrative times as allegorical transpositions of each other—versions of the same conflict are reenacted in each period, first between Osiris and Set in ancient Egypt, then between Jes Grew and the Wallflower Order in the 1920s, and implicitly between the black avant-garde and the upholders of tradition in the 1970s. But Reed also suggests that these narrative times exist simultaneously and contaminate each other, each moment existing in a kind of continuous awareness of and interdependence with the others.

About halfway through the novel, for example, the publisher Hinckle Von Vampton meets the young African American poet Nathan Brown in 1920s New York and tries to convince the poet to join the staff of Von Vampton's white-funded magazine, the *Benign Monster*. Reed's narration of their brief encounter links past and future into the narrative present in a difficult layering that refuses simple chronology: "That's why you would be such an addition to our staff, the publisher of the *Benign Monster insists* to this poet whose biographer *has written* '[his problem] *was* that of reconciling a Christian upbringing with a pagan inclination.'"(117, italics mine). Reed thus mixes the present time of the narration in the 1920s— the publisher *insists*—with the present perfect tense of a future, that is, the 1970s, in which a biographer *has written* a biography, and the biography says what the poet's problem *was*, in the simple past tense. This narration of the past from the view of the 1970s is stitched back into the present tense of the 1920s story, in one sentence that leaves all the seams showing. If postmodernism is defined in part by its commitment to pastiche, to an ahistorical mixing of historical styles and references, then the willfully *unseamless* stitching together of different temporalities is here exemplary of postmodernism's challenge to "historicity." Reed thus presents us with a very different sense of the status of myth than did Baraka's work, one that insists that history itself is meaningful only through a playful appropriation. Baraka's use of popular culture references was part of his commitment to a broad accessibility that was nonetheless a matter of high seriousness; Reed's distinctly inaccessible novel uses a highly literary style to insist on the importance of getting the joke.

The novel's temporal disruptions are paralleled and reinforced by Reed's remarkable disruption of the "look and feel" of the novel form itself. *Mumbo Jumbo*'s loosely novelistic mode is consistently interrupted by photographs, drawings, and charts that reflect or ironically comment on the novel's multiple narratives. During PaPa LaBas's final monologue about Set's victory over Osiris's forces of liberation, for example, the text is consistently interspersed with rather incongruous photos and charts. One of the first is a chart that shows "US Bombing Tonnage in Three Wars"—World War II, Korea, and Vietnam. The chart—so unexpected in the context of the Egyptian myth that it is strikingly funny—seems to link Set to the United States by ironic disjunction (163).

Both Benedict Anderson and Fredric Jameson have argued, in different ways, that the novel as a form has intimate connections to the production of nationalism and imperialism. For Anderson, the realist novel's switch between plot lines posited a community of people who exist simultaneously, moving forward collectively through time, despite the fact that they may never meet—thus providing "a precise analogue of the idea of the nation."[114] Jameson has made a rather different case, arguing that the temporal disjunctions and spare style of the modernist novel can be traced to the structuring absence of the empire within imperial cultures, to the *impossibility* of adequately acknowledging or representing imperialism—at least for imperialists.[115] To the degree that the novel as a form, in either its modernist or its realist modes, has been identified with the cultures of European and American nationalism and imperialism, the insistent and playful disruption of the novel's narrative with the literal insertion of other types of texts is an important alternative practice. The extranarrative images in *Mumbo Jumbo* offer a counter to the kind of closure that Reed identified with the various literary traditions he had inherited. (Here there is a distinction between what Reed does and the more common tactic of *verbally*, rather than visually, incorporating various types of narratives into the main story, as with someone like Dos Passos. It is also different from the formal echoes of nonnarrative forms one sees in Toni Morrison's jazz-influenced language.)

Reed disrupts the traditional novelistic geography that has narrated national identities, but he also subverts his own reinvention of a transnational identity as any kind of stable alternative. Late in the novel, the text is interrupted by a pair of very different pictures: one of a Christian gathering, probably in the 1920s, and the second of a group of young men, taken in the late 1960s or early 1970s, who have circled around what might be a stolen statue of a Native American Indian (184). The location of the photos invites a reading of them as commentary on the accompanying story of the "universal" origins of black culture, yet the juxtaposition of the two different images challenges any notion of "blackness" as one thing: it is both the respectable Christian family and the iconoclastic young men. The more recent photo also undercuts any image of life-giving forces as represented only by black cultures, since the young men are not only black but also white and Asian and Native American and Latino. Reed thus undercuts a reading of the Egyptian myth as a seamless story of essential, resistant blackness.

What Reed offers is not only a *historical* argument about the race of the ancient Egyptians but also an alternative theology and a refiguring of sacred cosmology; he makes a claim to the Egyptians not simply as ancestors but as polytheists. Reed's postmodern redefinition of moral geography figures ancient Egypt as the source for a cultural practice that is strongly identified with blackness but is not limited to African Americans. The cultural practices he privileges challenge the dominant, rational, and bureaucratic logic of the Wallflower Order and its colonialist spatial imaginary. His alternative, the HooDoo Aesthetic, links identity to cultural practice, to racial sensibility, and to the reinvocation of an ancient Egyptian/Caribbean past. It is this post-Islamic vision that will animate black cultural politics in the 1970s.

AND BEYOND THE BLACK ATLANTIC

In the early 1990s, Paul Gilroy published a paradigm-setting study of the circulation of cultures and peoples that constitute the "Black Atlantic." As part of a new approach to scholarship that highlights "border crossing," Gilroy's work (along with that of Lisa Lowe, George Lipsitz, and José Saldívar, among others) has provided an important model for analyzing transnationalism. These interventions have moved cultural studies and American studies well beyond the nationalist presuppositions that have explicitly and implicitly defined their previous practice.[116]

But Gilroy's analysis, extraordinary as it is, is also symptomatic in its exclusions. Two stand out. First, the useful reframing provided by the construct of the "black Atlantic" nonetheless replaces one geographic entity (the nation) with another (the Atlantic). The move reformulates, but does not overturn, the scholarly dependence on literal, spatial connections for understanding cultural constructs of identity. Second, while Gilroy acknowledges some black (and particularly African American) connections with regions other than the Atlantic, he still refuses to see black identifications with the Arab world as anything other than a failure to identify sufficiently with Jewish history. These two limitations are linked, in that both can be traced, at least in part, to lack of attention to Islam.

In the penultimate section of *The Black Atlantic*, revealingly titled "Children of Israel or Children of the Pharaohs," Gilroy makes a compelling argument against recent Afrocentric histories that insist on triumphalist accounts of unfettered black greatness from ancient Egypt onward. Gilroy argues, convincingly, for the importance of acknowledging African slavery (and thus loss and dispossession) as central to a transnational black history. Scholars of black culture must not forget the themes of suffering, escape, memory, and identity that transverse black history and unite certain strands of black and Jewish thought. By choosing to highlight slavery and the corresponding theme of diaspora, Gilroy's project of remembrance aims to illuminate the commonalities between black and Jewish history. It points out the ways in which both anti-Semitism and antiblack racism stand as indictments of the modern construction of race. This approach, he argues, can play a role in reasserting important political critiques of modernity, and of modernity's racial categories. In other words, to insist on remembering slavery as a central part of the black experience is also to refuse to forget the centrality of racism in the project of modernity. Rejecting the Afrocentric tendency to dehistoricize black history by focusing on an ancient period of rule, conquest, and triumphant kingdoms, in Egypt and elsewhere, Gilroy instead reminds us that a past marked by suffering and persecution, if properly remembered, may offer a special redemptive power to a people—"not for themselves alone but for humanity as a whole."[117]

Such remembrance is indeed crucial, both intellectually and politically. If it is to avoid its own kind of willful ahistoricism, however, this project will also need to account for two complicating factors. The first, which I have suggested in my discussion of Ishmael Reed and will take up in more detail in the next chapter, is the multifaceted role that appropriations of ancient Egypt have played in black cultural politics. While often a mainstay of simplistic, Afrocentric narratives of imagined racial purity, the claims to Egypt can also serve quite different ends, as in Reed's search for an impure and interrupted alternative to Wallflower morality.

The second factor is simply the reality that the meanings of Jewish history for African Americans have been transformed at different historical moments. The project of remembering suffering and slavery as a link between blacks and Jews also needs to account for the ways in which, within large segments of African American public life, Jews have come to be identified less by their suffering than by their power, both in Israel and in the United States. It must acknowledge how and why black culture in the United States turned toward other models, beyond the exodus/Zionist model, attending particularly to the complex religious affiliations that also linked African American identity with the Arab and Islamic Middle East. By taking Islam seriously, we can contribute to an understanding of religion in the twentieth-century United States that moves beyond Judaism and Christianity. That attention would then expand our analysis of transnationalism and would require us to think about identities on a truly global scale—the "roots and routes" of religious affiliations are not necessarily contiguous spaces.

Such a project also brings us back, in new ways, to one of the fundamental tensions in African American intellectual and cultural history since World War II: How are we to understand the relationships of African Americans to the project of U.S. nationalism and the realities of power in the nation-state? And how is that history bound up with the international relations of the nation as a whole? What does the role of the United States as the main power of the postwar world ("the chief neocolonialist power," in Larry Neal's phrase) mean for the notion of black or African American identity? What are the limits of seeing African American nationalisms as merely domestic matters?

Much of the discourse of civil rights viewed blackness as a subnational identity and saw the African American struggle as a striving for rights that would, if successful, transform the nation itself. At the same time, black nationalist writers sometimes tended to see blackness as a separate national identity, which in time would necessarily develop its own foreign policy, based on alliance with other peoples in a similar structural position as colonized people. But flowing through both of these visions has been another: that of blackness as a *trans*national identity, one that challenges the very notion of America as a nation by undermining the categories—of land, of culture, of politics—that underlay it. In many cases, this vision has also been a critique, as when literary critic Addison Gayle exhorted African American artists to turn their back on nationalist identities: "To be an American writer is to be an American, and for black people, there should no longer be any honor attached to either position."[118]

Thus African American cultural production in the era of black liberation challenged the very notion of *a* national identity in highly public and influential ways. That is one reason it matters. Not because transnational identities are magically unproblematic; the black cultural radicalism of the 1960s often framed black identity in terms that were ahistorical, masculinist, and anti-Semitic. This is its irony, its limit, and its loss. But the intervention was significant: a remapping of the world, an alternative moral geography (and a new imagined community) that did not begin and end with Africa. This religiously inspired transnationalism gained a broad currency. In a cultural field that ranged from poetry and plays to highly charged sports matches, from local community theaters to postmodern novels, religious and cultural claims to the Middle East, both ancient and modern, played a central role in re-figurations of black radicalism, challenging both the hegemony of black Christianity's religious values and the politics of integration associated with it. This alternative was far more than a policy critique; it was a fundamental challenge at the level of definitions. It was the search for an identity that would be, as both Baraka and Neal put it, "post-American"—something outside of, and in opposition to, the expanding role of the United States on the world stage. In a particular moment in the 1960s, this search challenged the ways in which ancient history and religious ideology had functioned in the discourse of benevolent supremacy. The African American claims to Islam and to Egypt were not dominant in this period, but they influenced the worldviews of a generation of black activists and would come to have a significant impact on debates about black culture and American power in the coming decade.

3 King Tut, Commodity Nationalism, and the Politics of Oil, 1973–1979

Whoever has emerged victorious participates to this day in the triumphal procession in which the present rulers step over those who are lying prostrate. According to traditional practice, the spoils are carried along in the procession. They are called cultural treasures, and a historical materialist views them with cautious detachment.
—Walter Benjamin, "Theses on the Philosophy of History"

If I'da known they would've lined up just to see 'im;
I'da saved up all my money, and bought me a museum!
—Steve Martin, "King Tut"

In April 1978, the comedian Steve Martin appeared on *Saturday Night Live* to perform for the first time his song "King Tut," which subsequently became a hit single, selling more than a million records. Martin's song was a parodic commentary on "Tutmania," the fascination with the ancient Egyptian king Tutankhamun that swept the United States from 1977 to 1979, when a collection of objects from Tutankhamun's tomb toured six American museums. *The Treasures of Tutankhamun* became the most popular museum show in U.S. history, and King Tut became a popular culture sensation, featured in television specials, coffee-table books, and memorabilia ranging from Tut statues to calendars to key rings. One company even sold a T-shirt for women that had a photo of Tut's gold mask on the front and the oddly defiant slogan underneath: "Keep your hands off my Tuts!"

Most commentators on *The Treasures of Tutankhamun* have focused on its role in forwarding the blockbuster approach to museum exhibition in the United States. The popularity of the exhibit has been understood, implicitly or explicitly, to be a function of the intrinsically fascinating character of ancient Egypt—of mummies, gold statues, and hieroglyphics. This account tells a different story: examining *The Treasures of Tutankhamun* as a diverse set of representations, it suggests that newspaper and television news stories, T-shirts and trinkets, books and magazine articles, museum catalogs, and the exhibit itself together created "Tut" as a significant cultural phenomenon. The Tut phenomenon was striking for two reasons: first, for the intimate relationship it forged between the high-culture world of museum exhibits and the popular traffic in celebrity icons, and second, for the way it became a site of struggle over both the nature of American world power and the domestic politics of race and gender.

The King Tut exhibit unfolded in the wake of a series of events that had culminated in the 1973 oil crisis—the 1967 Arab-Israeli war, the subsequent lower-intensity "war of attrition" between Egypt and Israel, a rising media fascination with Middle East terrorism, and the 1973 Arab-Israeli war (which brought both superpowers to full nuclear alert and the brink of a broader war). Official U.S. reaction to these events and media coverage of them figured the Middle East as a place of both great instability and increasing strategic value to the West—a place in which American "interests" were vital but by no means secure. Beginning in the late 1960s and especially after 1973, the United States intensified its efforts to stabilize the configuration of power in the Middle East and to consolidate its influence over the region. In the mid-1970s these efforts included the Camp David peace process and the development of client relationships with the Shah of Iran, Anwar Sadat of Egypt, and the Gulf monarchies. Nevertheless, nationalist and fundamentalist sentiment in the Middle East continued to challenge these ties between the United States and local elites, and threatened U.S. political and economic hegemony.

The 1973 oil crisis marked the beginning of what David Harvey has described as the end of the old Fordist economic system and the shift into a new regime of capital accumulation and entirely new systems of political and social regulation, both of which he links to the rise of a "postmodern" world.[1] Although this transition should be understood in terms of worldwide economic relations and a transnational transformation in meaning systems, it was mediated within the United States in profoundly nationalist terms, as a failure of U.S. political power to secure national access to economic resources, and as a problem of national will and authority. Postmodernism, then, can be understood as at once more complex and more narrowly focused than Jameson's "cultural logic of late capitalism"; in the mid-1970s, it was part of the reconstruction of a *national* identity forged as part of a reconstitution of international power relations.[2]

Within this logic, the King Tut exhibit participated in the mapping of the United States in relation to the Middle East by incorporating the ancient Egyptians into the construction of a contemporary region, whose borders were marked as permeable to American "interests." Within this logic, Tut was part of a reformulation of American nationalism in the late 1970s, at a time when national identities had been severely challenged by social movements at home and declining power abroad. At that particular historical moment, the Tut exhibit became an extraordinary nexus, where the aestheticization and canonization of art, the postmodern commodification of culture, the construction of American relations to the Middle East, and the politics of masculinity and racial identity within the United States were combined, contested, and revised.

MAKING ART AT THE MET

The Tut exhibit was a collection of "treasures" from the tomb of the "boy king" Tutankhamun, a minor Egyptian pharaoh who came to power in the fourteenth century B.C. Tutankhamun's previously unplundered tomb, discovered by the English archaeologist Howard Carter in 1922, had created a sensation when it was found, inspiring a craze for ancient Egypt that influenced fashion, art, and architecture in the 1920s. After the excavation, most of the objects from the tomb—the richly inlaid coffins, the elaborate furniture, the royal death mask of solid gold—became the property of Egypt's Cairo Museum. Fifty years later, *The Treasures of Tutankhamun* exhibit toured for almost three years in the United States, and more than seven million people saw the fifty-five objects in the show.[3] Publicity for the exhibit announced that the loan of the objects for the U.S. tour was a "gift from the people of Egypt," in honor of the American bicentennial.

In fact, the political and cultural investments in the Tut tour made it far more than a simple bicentennial "gift." The tour exemplified the significance of cultural exchange as an instrument in international relations, involving not only the export of U.S. cultural products but also the strategic mobilization and display of cultural imports.[4] Thomas Hoving, who was the director of New York's Metropolitan Museum of Art from 1967 to 1977, reported that he was originally unsuccessful in making a bid to Egypt for a loan of the Tut objects. Instead, he claimed, "the man who pulled off 'Tut' was Richard M. Nixon."[5] On Hoving's account, it was during a visit to Egypt in 1974 that President Nixon first asked Egypt's president, Anwar Sadat, to allow the King Tut treasures to visit the United States. Sadat had allowed fifty pieces from the tomb to tour the Soviet Union in 1973. Yet by 1974 he was beginning to move Egypt into the American camp; he had expelled two thousand Soviet military advisers in 1972, and he owed the survival of the Egyptian Third Army in the 1973 war with Israel to U.S. and Soviet cooperation. At Nixon's urging, Sadat ordered Egypt's Antiquities Service to cooperate in organizing a U.S. tour—one that would, at Nixon's insistence, include one more city than the Soviet tour and several more objects.

Figure 11.   The gold and jewel-encrusted death
mask of Tutankhamun, the most famous piece to
tour with *The Treasures of Tutankhamun* exhibit
in 1977–1979. Courtesy of Boltin Picture Library.

The U.S. government's investment in the Tut exhibit went even further.
The exhibit was funded by the government-supported National Endowment for the Humanities, along with the Exxon Corporation and a private
foundation, the Robert Wood Johnson Jr. Charitable Trust. In addition, Hoving reports that when the Met was having second thoughts about taking on
the responsibility of guaranteeing the safety of the priceless objects in the
exhibit, Douglas Dillon, the chair of the board of the museum, received a
telephone call from Henry Kissinger. Kissinger told Dillon that the show
was "a vital part of the Middle East peace process," and that if the Met did
not organize the exhibit, the federal government would be "disturbed." According to Hoving, Dillon took Kissinger's comment to mean that the Met
might permanently lose all federal grants.[6]

In this institutional relationship between the country's most powerful museum and the highest levels of the U.S. foreign policy apparatus, we see the ways in which the national public's cultural consumption was understood as a mode of ideological mobilization. Similarly, the fact that Exxon was a major funder for the exhibit points to the benefits U.S. oil companies reaped from their arts subsidies. However, the significance of the Tut exhibit lies less in its direct institutional affiliations with government agencies and American-based multinational oil companies than in its participation in a larger discourse of U.S. "imperial stewardship." Like "benevolent supremacy," the logic of imperial stewardship depended on combining universalist rhetoric with a presumption of American and Western superiority so profound that it remained unspoken. The "official" Tut narrative—as produced by museum curators, Egyptologists, and the mainstream press—aestheticized the Tut treasures, constructing them as "universal" art, something too ennobling and too precious (too "human") to belong to any one people (Arabs) or any one nation (Egypt). Instead, Tut was presented as part of the "common heritage of mankind"—a heritage that would be owned and operated by the United States.

For Hoving, the Tut exhibit was part of a larger project of transforming the relationship between art museums, long understood as elite bastions of high culture, and an increasingly alienated and media-saturated public. By 1977, the year before the Tut exhibit opened in New York, Hoving had led the Met through a widely publicized, and often criticized, series of expansions, acquisitions, and transformations aimed at making the museum more accessible.[7] In his memoirs, Hoving describes the changes, in typically immodest fashion, as "the most sweeping revolution in the history of art museums."[8] The underlying goal, as he articulates it, was to wipe out the scholasticism and elitism of the institution and to institute a new kind of direct relation between the art museum and the public: "The attitude should be one of *evangelism*. The museum should cry out: we will teach you about the great art of all civilizations. Speak directly to the art lovers in a way they can understand. Teach about quality, what's great, what's spine-tingling. Don't be ivory tower."[9]

As this kind of language makes clear, Hoving's "democratization" of the museum was profoundly dependent on the assumption that audiences needed to be educated into that democracy. That is, he was interested in expanding the reach and influence of art museums by teaching the public to see in a new way. Hoving claimed not to bore visitors with detailed accounts of the "historical significance" of a piece; he wanted instead to entice them with beauty, with a kind of immediate (but certainly not unmediated) apprehension of the artistic power of a work. Hoving was deeply committed to the belief that certain works of art were simply and unproblematically great; once the public had learned to appreciate that greatness, it would patronize the museum for the aesthetic, as opposed to the educational, historical, or moral, value of the experience. Hoving's thoroughgoing aestheticism extended to the Tut exhibit's initial conceptualization: he claims that when he went to Cairo to select the items from the museum's collection for the U.S. tour, he simply chose the objects that "looked great." The Met's Egyptian curator "tried to point out what was important or not from the Egyptological point of view, but I didn't listen. I knew what I wanted."[10]

This artistic frame stands in direct opposition to historical or anthropological narratives, in which museums use cultural artifacts to represent "a culture." To Hoving, the artifacts approach was anathema, and places like the Museum of Natural History were nothing more than "a place where great works of art became mere ethnological specimens."[11] Historical information about ancient Egypt was certainly included in the catalogs, books, and documentaries that accompanied the Tut exhibit, but it functioned as the context for a detailed appreciation of the quality and extraordinary value of the tomb's contents. Descriptions lovingly detailed the "delicate, superb craftsmanship," the "graceful" and "realistic" quality of the pieces, whose "style" and "perfection" were "incredible."[12] *New York Times* art critic Hilton Kramer praised the exhibit in similar terms, pointing out that "it is as an exhibition of art, not of history, that 'Tutankhamun' captivates the mind and bedazzles the senses."[13] The history was the frame for the art, rather than the art serving as illustration or evidence for the history.

If ancient Egyptian history might potentially distract from the notion of Tut's objects as great art, the history of the modern discovery of the tomb, on the other hand, validated Tut's artistic status. The exhibit itself was structured according to an archaeological plot, using Howard Carter's discovery of Tut's tomb to frame its presentation of the quality and value of the ancient Egyptian pieces. As visitors wound their way through the exhibit, they found themselves in galleries that reproduced the rooms of the tomb; the objects were numbered in the order in which they were excavated by Carter and his team. Beautifully lit glass cases were flanked by huge black-and-white photos of the original archaeological team as it opened cases and unpacked treasures. The audience, then, moved through the exhibit *as* Carter, sharing in the long and methodical search for the tomb site, the "final" season of digging, even the frustrations of trying to get work done when tourists and journalists were pouring into the tomb area and demanding to see the objects. As the Tut audience saw the photos, and read Carter's enthusiastic descriptions of his find, they shared in the drama of his discovery. As one reviewer effused, "The crowd's attention focuses on the same objects that Carter's small flame first revealed to him as it flickered off stone walls."[14] The audience was thus positioned by the exhibit simultaneously as the archaeologist/discoverer and as the connoisseur/appreciator of the universal heritage. The story was the dig, but the "find" was art, not artifact.

This structure of the exhibit-as-excavation was mirrored in the countless retellings of the Carter discovery story in the newspaper and magazine articles and the popular books that accompanied the Tut exhibit. Every aspect of the search, as reported by Carter in his memoirs, was repeated with the kind of strict precision and attention to detail usually reserved for scriptural exegesis. But the central story element that structured the narrative of the exhibit was undoubtedly the discovery itself. Carter's vivid evocation of his excitement, reproduced over and over again in the Tut literature, became the frame through which contemporary audiences were invited to view the tomb's treasures (and to participate in their recovery): "At first I could see nothing, . . . but presently, as my eyes grew accustomed to the light, details of the room within emerged slowly from the mist, strange animals, statues, and gold—everywhere the glint of gold."[15]

The tomb objects literally came into view through Carter's eyes; his sensuous descriptions presented the objects in the tomb as exquisitely crafted works of art, whose sheer beauty left him speechless. In this way, the universal heritage of art was retrieved and made available through the work of a Western archaeologist who was understood, as representative of the West, to be both discoverer and steward. The modern (Western) story provided the mark of the "historical"—the moment in which time becomes active and mobile—in the service of saving the ancient, the human, the eternal. The discovery of the Tut tomb was rendered significant not because of what it told Americans about the "other" but because of what it uncovered—what it rescued—in universal art.[16]

Although Howard Carter was generally venerated, he also came in for some criticism, precisely because of his role as the discoverer and keeper of the universal: his failures nearly destroyed the possibility for Western archaeologists to continue to lay claim to the treasures they excavated. Thomas Hoving's 1978 best-seller, *Tutankhamun: The Untold Story*, criticized Carter's arrogant belief that he really did "own" the Tut tomb. Carter's attitude created an adversarial relationship with the Egyptians and caused a significant nationalist backlash; in the end, he lost all rights to the Tut objects. Had Carter taken a more conciliatory approach, suggested Hoving, he might have been able to keep many of the objects, which he then would have been free to donate or sell to Western museums. To make his point, Hoving approvingly quoted a 1922 letter from four major Egyptologists to the head of Egyptian antiquities, which argued that the finds from Tutankhamun's tomb should *not* all revert to the Egyptian government. "That unique discovery, with its wealth of historical and archaeological facts," the Egyptologists wrote, "belongs not to Egypt alone but to the entire world." In American and European museums, the Tut objects would have been well taken care of by experts and well appreciated by Western audiences—an appropriate fate for their status as artistic masterpieces. Instead, they became the sole property of Egypt's Cairo Museum. Hoving reports that Carter's failure to recognize Egyptian nationalist feeling "alter[ed] forever the nature of archaeology, not only in Egypt but throughout the world."[17] Carter's conflicts highlighted a transformation in assumptions, which, if not entirely new in the early twentieth century, and still not entirely accepted at century's end, would nonetheless restructure the politics of culture: the spoils of archaeology were no longer the property of (Western) archaeologists—or their museum sponsors.

Hoving's narrative of archaeology's lost opportunity did important culture work in its own time. Working within the larger discourse of Tut as art, it linked the trope of archaeology-as-rescue to a profoundly nationalist and imperializing set of assumptions about the role of art collecting and art appreciation in the West. This was *not* the kind of imperialist condescension that assumed that colonized peoples have produced only "artifacts." Instead, art universalism, available intermittently at least since the rise of primitivism in the modern period, dramatically widened the category of art and cultivated a sophisticated taste that believed a Guatemalan stella is great art as surely as a European painting. This was a discourse of art that transformed cultural relativism into international art eclecticism, which then became integral to the making of a certain kind of American museum-going public. The incorporation of non-Western art into modernist assumptions of universal aesthetics was hardly new, and museums in the nineteenth century had already played some role in bringing the discourse of those aesthetics into the service of imperialism.[18] As museums exploded in popularity in the early 1970s, the museum public participated in defining the diverse cultural materials owned by the museums as "art," worthy of audience reverence and appreciation. The Tut exhibit expanded the appeal and reach of that aestheticization, not least through the commodification and mass marketing of Tut objects.[19] A subject position that was formerly available only to a certain very elite class fraction—that of the internationally savvy art appreciator—was now disseminated by the strategies of mass marketing the museum. The postmodern museum-going subject was sophisticated precisely *because* he or she was mass-mediated, able to appreciate "universal art" thanks to the "educational" power of a commodity culture, which markets Egyptian tomb objects in much the same way it markets Reeboks. The Tut phenomenon, I would argue, participated in the construction of an increasingly "democratized" subject position that was marked by the international and world historic scale of its art appreciation. However, these transformations remained very much within a capitalist and nationalist model: the great nations are not defined as those that *produce* the greatest art—they are those that *collect* it.

OIL AND THE UNIVERSAL HERITAGE

"Gold," Howard Carter had breathed in 1922, "everywhere the glint of gold." Fifty-five years later, nearly every discussion of the Tut exhibit included some remark on the large number of pure gold objects in the show. The *New York Times* suggested that the "materialism" of the exhibit was one of the likely reasons for the long lines that had suddenly begun forming outside of the formerly intimidating museum doors. Several other journals explicitly commented on the popular fascination with Tut's wealth, often to considerable satiric effect. The *New Yorker*'s "Talk of the Town" feature ran a short "interview" with Tut, figuring him as a slightly effete young artist who was firmly in control of his own commodification: "They say that there's a Tut madness, a Tut mania, that the show has been over-commercialized. Sure, we're peddling a few little items. But they're class knockoffs, man—beautifully reproduced, for the most part." The young Tut's fascination with gold was a sign of his sophistication and his implied difference from the awed (American) visitors to the exhibit: "It's about gold, man. Heavy metal, I mean. I'm quite comfortable with gold. I was into gold very early.... Gold doesn't *unnerve* me."[20] *Harper's* also meditated on the significance of the gold in "A King Tut Book of Etiquette," which advised potential visitors to the exhibit on how to behave once they finally reached the galleries: "If you have never heard of Tutankhamen, do not interrupt the tour to ask the lecturer why this show is being held in his honor. Tutankhamen is remembered because he managed to die at an early age and to keep his tomb sealed until gold hit record highs on the London exchange. This is the secret of immortality."[21]

This fascination with Tut's gold was often linked to lighthearted commentary on the commodification of the exhibit itself. Awe at the pricelessness of the gold treasures in the show intersected with a playful consciousness that Tut trinkets, such as statuettes and coffee mugs, were for sale at gift shops across the country. Rather than erasing any link between the ancient Egyptian past and the contemporary Middle East (as much anthropological discourse had done since the nineteenth century), the near obsession with Tut's gold functioned to articulate a connection between the two, to write the representation of Tut over the current situation. Tut as the signifier of extraordinary wealth resonated with a larger discourse that in the late 1970s was developing in response to the 1973–1974 OPEC oil embargo.

The oil embargo was instituted by the major Arab oil producers in retaliation for U.S. support for Israel in the 1973 October War. That war had begun with a surprise attack by Egypt and Syria against Israel; Jordan joined somewhat later. The aim was to regain territory that Arab states had lost in the 1967 war. The Arab armies initially made significant gains into Israeli occupied territories, and Israel suffered damaging losses of people and equipment, though it soon recouped and crossed into the Suez Canal. American policymakers supported Israel during the war by airlifting crucial equipment to the Israeli military. But the United States also joined with the Soviet Union in cosponsoring a UN cease-fire resolution that stopped Israel's counterattack before it could encircle and destroy Egypt's Third Army Corps. When the Soviet Union threatened to intervene unilaterally to enforce the cease-fire in order to protect Egypt, however, the United States responded by putting its forces on worldwide nuclear alert and preparing to send U.S. troops to the region. This reaction made clear that U.S. policymakers considered the Middle East an American sphere of influence, not to be left to the Soviet Union. But the initial successes of the Arab armies also suggested that the balance of power in the region was less tilted toward Israel than most people had imagined.[22]

That fact was brought home to Americans when the Organization of Petroleum Exporting Countries (OPEC), comprising mostly Arab oil producers, announced an embargo on oil shipments to Israel's allies, particularly the United States, Japan, and some European nations. By 1973, the United States consumed almost 70 percent of all oil produced in the world. Even though the United States had significant domestic production and could still buy oil on the world market, the embargo led to a rapid fourfold increase in the price of gasoline and to similar increases in heating oil. During the six months the embargo was in place, the United States experienced some gasoline shortages, and stories of long lines at the gas pumps and stressed-out motorists punctuated the evening news. President Nixon imposed a series of belt-tightening measures, including lowering highway speed limits and darkening monuments in Washington. He also asked that Americans voluntarily cut their driving, lower the heat in homes and offices, and reduce nonessential lighting.[23]

ZSCHIESCHE

I WANT YOU
TO LOWER
YOUR THERMOSTAT

Figure 12.   Energy conservation cartoon from
Time, 1973. Reprinted with special permission from
King Features Syndicate.

The response in the United States was a sense of crisis and anger. The sudden shortages and price increases threatened the cheap energy that had underwritten suburbanization and rising prosperity in the 1950s and 1960s. The oil crisis played a key role in successive economic recessions in the 1970s that cumulatively constituted the greatest economic downturn since the Great Depression of the 1930s.[24] Although many Americans suspected that oil companies were artificially inflating the crisis to increase their profits, a host of media accounts and editorials turned their anger on the Arab use of the "oil weapon." *Time* magazine described the Arabs' "new oil squeeze" by contrasting the cutbacks faced by "John Doe American" with the conspicuous wealth in Saudi Arabia: there, "Ferraris and Mercedes glistened in the showrooms, and the markets bulged with imported consumer goods."[25] Editorial cartoons suggested that Arabs were beady-eyed and greedy, with long hooked noses—remarkably paralleling the anti-Jewish discourse of earlier times. One cartoon, for example, showed a sheik whose long nose had become a gas nozzle. With an imperiousness born of more than two decades of postwar global hegemony, the writer of the accompanying article expressed outrage that the balance of power had shifted, that the industrialized nations "now bow down before [the Arab nations], ready to indulge any whim in the desperate hope that in response plentiful oil supplies might be forthcoming."[26] This was the beginning of what would soon become a staple of American popular cultural images: the greedy oil sheiks, with their hands on America's collective throat.

The period from 1974 to 1978 was in fact, in Daniel Yergin's words, "OPEC's imperium." Coming right after the U.S. defeat in Vietnam and the harsh economic downturn that accompanied it, this period marked the beginning of a long decline in U.S. dominance in world affairs. Diplomatic historian Thomas McCormick has argued that American policymakers and pundits responded to the transformation of the world political situation in two different ways. A conservative alliance argued that the maintenance of American hegemony required a recommitment to military strength that would protect U.S. economic interests and shield U.S. allies from the Soviet Union. These military hawks advocated the buildup of U.S. forces: it was in the mid-1970s that the military developed the Joint Rapid Deployment Task Force, later named the Central Command, in order to add greater speed and flexibility to possible U.S. military intervention in the Middle East. The United States could and must continue to play the role of global policeman, these conservatives argued, if it wanted to maintain the respect of European and third world nations while ensuring continued international economic expansion.

The other, more centrist view argued that American hegemony on the cold war model was over, and that the new "world order politics" called for the recognition of a multipolar world.[27] Of course, many African Americans and white radicals had been challenging the assumptions of superpower politics for years, but now the critique came from within the mainstream of the U.S. policy elite. These moderates—including most oil company executives—firmly believed that accommodation with the oil-producing nations was necessary. The adversarial relationship of the 1973 war had exacted a high cost, at least in terms of instability and a sense of dependence on the part of the Western nations. This dominant-center tendency thought that confronting OPEC (and particularly the Arab OPEC nations) would tend to fuel "radical nationalist" sentiments within Arab countries.[28] Those sentiments could lead the countries to take even more hard-line positions: they might nationalize the oil, or raise the prices to unbearable levels, or stop the flow of oil (the particular threat changed over time). The oil embargo had taught these centrists that world economic and political relations rested not on the display of military strength but on the ability to manage a new international order. According to political historian Jerry Sanders, they be-

Figure 13. In the mid-1970s, concern about the Arab control of oil was expressed in numerous cartoons and editorials, as in this drawing from the *New York Review of Books* in 1974. Courtesy of David Levine.

lieved that "such a new contract would better secure access to vital energy resources in the Third World than would any amount of sabre-rattling."[29] By 1976, when Jimmy Carter was elected president, this global managerialist view was dominant among policymakers, though it would very quickly be challenged, and overtaken, by a conservative resurgence.

In the years after 1973, policymakers, academics, and journalists filled countless pages with speculation on the problem of assuring continued U.S. access to oil in light of changed international conditions.[30] It was a commonplace that dependence on "foreign oil" was dangerous to the nation, and the oil companies and political leaders were often criticized in the press for obeisance.[31] Liberal and conservative pundits debated the best way to protect "our" access to oil. In the winter of 1978–1979, for example, Walter Levy published an article in *Foreign Affairs* that decried the complacency and shortsightedness of U.S. energy policy. Levy, one of the nation's best-known oil analysts, argued that the substantial decline in the real price of oil just after the embargo, between 1974 and 1978, had masked the continuing long-term problem of declining oil resources. Levy acknowledged that since the

end of the 1973 oil crisis, OPEC had been willing to produce adequate supplies of oil at "manageable prices." And the infusion of petrodollars into the
oil-producing countries had been recycled back into the West by the Arab
nations' prodigious spending on everything from arms to luxury cars. "The
American public's sense of urgency has thus tended to dissipate," he admitted. "At the moment . . . the oil crisis appears to be invisible."[32]

But for Levy, the "restraint" exercised by the OPEC countries in keeping prices down and production high was tenuous. Underlying the seemingly successful post–oil crisis transition to higher world oil prices was the
inevitable fact that the United States remained dependent on the economic
and political policies of foreign governments. Written just a few months before the fall of the Shah of Iran, which prompted a temporary constriction
of oil supplies and a price jump of 170 percent, Levy's clarion call was just
one example of many commentaries that decried the failure of U.S. policy
to deal adequately with either the problem of energy supply or the price of
dependence. The U.S. diplomatic response, initiated by Nixon and continued
by Carter, was to increase the integration of selected Middle East leaders
into the American fold, partly through diplomatic and economic ties, but
primarily through increased arms sales.[33] Arms sales to Iran and Saudi Arabia, in particular—the "two pillars" of the U.S. strategy of strengthening
Gulf state elites to ensure the protection of U.S. interests—soared in the
mid-1970s.

The terms of sharing this wealth had to be sufficiently generous to local
elites to forestall their disaffection and strengthen their regimes against nationalist pressures, while also protecting oil company profits and facilitating Western access to oil at easily affordable prices. It was this line of rea-
soning that underlay Walter Levy's 1980 argument, in a second article in
Foreign Affairs, that the economic stability of the West required that oil
prices be kept at a "manageable level." Oil, he argued, "must be conceived
in terms of a 'common heritage of mankind' that must serve both the wel-
fare of the producing countries and that of the importing countries."[34] Like
the construction of Tut as universal art, the construction of oil as the common heritage of mankind offered a blandly reassuring vision of the world
division of resources, managed by elites and loaned or traded among nations. From this perspective, Thomas Hoving's critique of Howard Carter's
"unreasonable" and "insensitive" approach to Egyptian sensibilities about
the tomb artifacts stood out clearly as a lesson: if one wants to maintain a
dominant position in the face of changing reality, reasonable accommodation is a far better approach than ill-considered confrontation.

The contradiction at the heart of the U.S. discourse on oil in the post-1973 period was that oil was conceived both as a "universal" resource and as an overpriced commodity that rightly belonged in American hands. It soon became a commonplace to point out that it was U.S. (and Western) technology that had made the enormous wealth of the Middle Eastern nations possible in the first place. Commentators also noted that it was the Western nations that *needed* (and thus appreciated) the oil. As with the development of pluralistic art appreciation in the West, it was "our" activity that gave "their" resources value. Without the industrialized world's appetite for OPEC products, it was said, the Arabs would still be poor desert sheiks, sitting on oil they did not know how to refine and could not make use of if they did.[35] Thus the logic of "common heritage of mankind" linked the appropriative art universalism of the mainstream Tut representations to the contemporary concern with maintaining U.S. access to Middle East oil on advantageous terms.

The fascination with Tut's gold highlighted tensions between the Tut objects as "priceless" universal art and as literal wealth. The extraordinary use of gold for everything from goblets to necklaces to decorative statues made the Tut exhibit literally as well as artistically priceless. The symbolism of gold linked a rarefied discourse of resource (art) management to a more prosaic concern with who (in nationalistic terms) would control the wealth the gold represented. Implicit connections were being drawn: between oil as a commodity on the world market and the world market price of gold that made Tut's treasures so priceless; between Tut's wealth and the new and conspicuous wealth of Arab oil producers; and between Tut's gold and the "black gold" of Middle Eastern oil. Thomas Hoving made the point succinctly: quoting Howard Carter, he informed his readers that the ancient pharaohs "were luxurious and display-loving Oriental monarchs."[36]

In the dominant construction of the Tut exhibit as "art," Tut could not be owned, only managed. As commodity, however, Tut became purchasable. The explosion of inexpensive Tut items, from desk calendars to coffee mugs, posited access to a symbol of riches in affordable terms. The Tut paraphernalia made it clear that Tut *could* be bought, and that if his treasures were a "common heritage of mankind," they were also just another one of the infinitely reproducible commodities of popular culture.

This gesture of the appropriation of wealth through its fake gold signifiers contained a good bit of self-irony. Nonetheless, it promised the possibility of taking back, and rather cheaply at that, some small piece of what seemed to have slipped away: that earlier sense that the "common heritage" was securely "ours." In the "Keep Your Hands Off My Tuts!" T-shirt, the question of ownership was staged in a gendered logic: the feminist-derived language of sexual self-possession echoed the question of national ownership, as Tut becomes the property of a spunky female who, like the women of the biblical epics, refuses to countenance unwanted advances on her (sexual) property. Tut became not only a universal heritage but also a prized national possession, the symbolic statement of commodity consumption as a nationalist discourse.

The commodity nationalism that appropriated Tut connected to the larger logic that fused Tut and oil into a narrative of national reassertion in the face of decline. King Tut and his treasures became interesting in the context of deep concern about the modern Middle East and its oil; both interests were narrated not only through the discourse of imperial stewardship and common heritage but also through a positioning of Tut and oil as commodities. In these interlocking constructs, imperial stewardship and commodity nationalism went hand in hand.

THE BLACKNESS OF EGYPT

The mobilization of Tut as part of a play for nationalist ownership did not persuade everyone. It was sharply contested by African American journalists and scholars, who refused to see the Tut treasures as "universal art" and thus countered the logic that read the Tut exhibit through a narrative of resource rescue. By insisting on the essential *Africanness* of Egypt, representations of Tut as black mapped the world in ways that challenged the reading of the tomb treasures as an allegory for oil. Claiming Tut as African rather than as "universal" (that is, white), these writers insisted that the history of Egypt must be relocated as part of the history of Africa, rather than only the Middle East. The implication was that the treasures of Egypt were part of the Egyptian and African context, *not* universal property to be apportioned out among those who had an interest in them. Like Ishmael Reed's evocation of Egypt, the African American claims to Tut posited an alternative history; but while Reed had challenged other Black Arts movement theorists, the black Tut proponents took mainstream media representations to task. Within these counterhegemonic narratives, the Tut treasures were marked as great precisely because they were the product of a black, African civilization that had something to teach the world by its particularity, not its universality. Using a logic that insisted on essential racial identities, African American writers and thinkers linked dominant representations of the Tut exhibit to what they saw as the racist bias of mainstream

Egyptology. They then reclaimed King Tut for "black history" rather than as the symbol of commodified "universal" art.

In February 1978, the Los Angeles City Council passed a resolution declaring Sunday, February 12, 1978, "King Tut Day." The declaration linked Black History Month to the opening of the Tut exhibit in Los Angeles. It pronounced Tut to be an exemplary black man, and proclaimed Tut Day as a celebration of black culture:

> Whereas, each of the rulers of the eighteenth dynasty . . . was either black, "negroid," or of black ancestry, and all would be classified as black if they were citizens of the United States today; and . . .
>
> Whereas it is particularly important to focus on positive black male images during black history month in order to instill self-esteem in and encourage self-discipline among young black males, who are often deprived of positive black images; Now, therefore, be it resolved that the Los Angeles City Council [declares King Tut Day] . . . for the increased cultural and historical heritage which has brought much awareness and enrichment to our community.[37]

The resolution was signed by Tom Bradley, the city's first African American mayor. The contemporary relevance of the Tut exhibit was made clear: Tut represented a historical heritage for African Americans; in particular, he presented a model of black masculinity for black youth. Although one of hundreds of commemorative resolutions that city councils all over the country routinely pass without much practical impact, the King Tut Day declaration also represented something of a high point: in Los Angeles, members of the African American community had declared Tut black, and had done so with all the apparatus of city officialdom behind them.

Several months later, just before the Tut exhibit arrived in New York, the Metropolitan Museum published a small booklet, "Tutankhamun and the African Heritage." In the foreword, Herbert Scott-Gibson explained that the purpose of the publication was to address concerns about the racial composition of ancient Egypt's population. Questions of race, he noted, "are, and have been, of concern to many people. In fact, for some, they are the most important questions that can be raised concerning that civilization." Examining the evidence of Egyptian tomb paintings and carvings, the booklet explained that the ancient Egyptians were never of a single physical type, and that individuals with "negroid" as well as "Asiatic" features held high places in Egyptian life. The question of what race the mass of Egyptians belonged to was difficult to answer, the booklet concluded, but "in general . . . the findings of such researches have characterized the Egyptian population as including

Negroes and individuals with negroid traits, but consisting mostly of individuals essentially europoid or caucasoid." On the other hand, the booklet argued, perhaps racial categorization was not really useful at all, since the boundaries between races were so fluid and lines between racial types so difficult to draw. Audiences seemed to be interested in race because of the modern use of the terms "black" and "white," but these were modern constructs fueled by present-day concerns. Serious scholars of ancient Egypt, the author implied, were not very concerned about racial categorization, and the ancient Egyptians themselves "may very well have cared far less about the answer than we do." Belying any pretensions to indifference to the issue, however, was the author's insistence that "scientists" generally considered the Egyptians to be more "caucasoid" than "negroid."[38] When the official catalog of the Tut exhibit was published, it summarized this stance almost unconsciously: describing a gold case with two images of the pharaoh, one in gold and one in black, it said, "Clearly the [black] color [of the face] has no ethnic significance, but its precise meaning is not easy to explain."[39]

For African Americans, the ideological stakes in these two different assessments of Tut's race were clear: as the nation turned to ancient Egypt, would African Americans see a chapter of a glorious past they could claim as their own? Or would they see yet another "proof" that great civilization was white? In the middle to late 1970s, parts of the black community became increasingly interested in the cultural reclamation of ancient Egypt. At a time when it appeared that the Black Art movement had all but disappeared as a site for cultural radicalism, and the African American political movements of the 1960s and early 1970s had been either absorbed into the mainstream, decimated by federal- and state-level police agencies, or devastated by internal dissent, a diffuse but influential black cultural nationalist alternative began to reach more broadly into the black community.[40] This emerging framework was less directly political than either the Nation of Islam or the Black Arts movement; it rarely claimed art as a weapon, but it did mobilize history as power. And it involved a mainstreaming of arguments that in the 1960s might have been the province of young radicals. Manifestations of cultural nationalism in the second half of the 1970s were apparent in everything from hairstyles to the increasing visibility of African American studies programs on college campuses, but it was in the popularization of interest in Egypt that a reformulated cultural radicalism found an expression at once historical, aesthetic, and political.

If ancient Egypt was reclaimed as a black civilization, then "civilization" could be claimed for blacks. And this was not just *a* civilization, but *the* foundation of "Western civilization." The enormously popular King Tut exhibit became one site for articulating an argument about the significance of ancient Egypt for black history and culture, and for bringing that argument into the mainstream of African American intellectual and political life. Thus, representations of King Tut became centrally implicated in the process of racial formation in the United States—the construction of *Tut*'s meanings were structured within the larger discourse about the domestic meanings of race.

Part of the continued currency of the claim that Africans had never managed to create "real culture" before European colonization depended, among other things, on the conscious exclusion of North Africa, including Egypt, from the "real" Africa—sub-Saharan Africa.[41] (It also depended, of course, on a highly selective definition of "civilization.") In this context, black popular magazines and newspapers as well as scholarly publications energetically countered what was viewed as the racial appropriation of Tut and ancient Egypt by white cultural and political elites. These articles were less concerned with proving to the black community that Tut was black (this they simply assumed) than with responding to the "whitening" of Tut in the official exhibition. In November 1977, the cover story of *Sepia* magazine raged against the "big Tut rip-off," calling it a "national insult to blacks."[42] In December 1978, WABC television in New York broadcast "Tutankhamun: A Different Perspective" as part of its weekly black-moderated series *Like It Is*. The show was organized as an interview with two proponents of the black Tut thesis.[43] At about the same time, the *New York Amsterdam News* ran a front-page article that complained about the breakdown of the only Harlem Ticketron machine on the day the Tut tickets went on sale, quoting frustrated ticket buyers who suggested that perhaps the breakdown was not a coincidence. Instead, the article implied, keeping black people out of the Tut show was very much in keeping with the exhibit's more general ideological exclusions: "Despite the hullabaloo over the gold treasures of King Tutankhamun ... there almost seems to be a conspiracy of silence about this fact—that this last pharaoh of the 18th Dynasty was Black."[44]

A few months after its cover article on the Tut exhibit, the *Amsterdam News* published a long editorial titled "Tutankhamen: Black Art Overlooked by White Eyes." The editorial writer, Sylvester Leaks, argued that the Tut treasures revealed truths of a black culture, "truths that heretofore were buried ... by the demented minds and racist lies of white historians." Leaks criticized Hilton Kramer's review of the Tut exhibit in the *New York Times*, arguing that Kramer deliberately underrated the Tut objects precisely because they represented the culture of Africa. Kramer's review had concluded that the Tut exhibit was valuable primarily as art rather than as history. But Kramer also argued that, as art, Tut was not even a particularly great exhibit; the Met's *Splendor of Dresden* show was of superior artistic quality. The *Amsterdam News* editorial suggested that Kramer's preference was profoundly Eurocentric: "Because it is Black/African, because Mr. Kramer is incapable of appreciating the true historical, cultural, art/religion aspect of 'Tut'—let alone understand it—he seeks to belittle its supreme importance by belittling it with the arrogance of ignorance. Although we see in the 'Treasures of Tutankhamen' the greatest art exhibit ever seen in our time, its real significance is cultural and historical." For Leaks, Tut was a preeminent example of the greatness of black history. Against Kramer's aesthetic evaluation, Leaks placed his own historical one. *The Treasures of Tutankhamun*, he argued, represented the lived religious and cultural beliefs of the Egyptians, "revealing to us the nature of our past, who we were, where we were. Hopefully, it will influence where we are going."[45]

The argument that Egypt was a black, or African, or Negro, nation had a long history in the African American community. Drawing on the writings and drawings of early European visitors to Egypt, African and African American thinkers argued that the original perception of the Egyptians as a black and/or African people had been deliberately revised during the course of the nineteenth century. Tutankhamun was just one example of an Egyptian ruler whose obvious blackness had been erased by mainstream media and the white-dominated discipline of Egyptology.[46]

When Howard Carter discovered the tomb of Tutankhamun in 1922, there was already a well-defined anthropological discourse about Egyptian racial origins dating back to the early nineteenth century. Studies of the ancient Egyptians had been central to nineteenth-century scientific racism: Samuel George Morton's *Crania Aegyptiaca* (1844), one of the urtexts of the scientific and anthropological classification and hierarchization of races, argued that the size and shape of Egyptian skulls placed them firmly within the "Caucasoid" (as opposed to the "Negro" or "mixed negroid") race (but beneath the other "types" in that family: Pelasgics and Jews). In the United States, the argument for the whiteness of the ancient Egyptians was considered to be an argument for the inferiority of Negroes, and it played a powerful role in the justification of slavery. In *Crania Aegyptiaca*, Morton had stated that "Negroes were numerous in Egypt, but their social position in ancient times was the same as it now is, that of servants and slaves."[47] Morton's arguments were cited and used extensively by his follower Josiah Nott, who traveled the South in the twenty years before the Civil War lecturing on slavery, black inferiority, and polygenesis, the theory that distinct races had existed since the beginning of humankind. In the 1850s, Nott collaborated with Egyptologist George Robbins Glidden, who had made a reputation for himself in his series of Egyptology lectures in the 1840s, to produce *Types of Mankind* (1854), which was an attempt to present scientific evidence for polygenesis. So it was that the American School of Anthropology, dominant until the rise of Darwinism, linked the whiteness of ancient Egypt's rulers to an argument about the separate creation of the races, which in turn was used as one of the widely cited "scientific" arguments in favor of slavery. Morton's arguments were later supported and elaborated by a whole range of archaeologists as the discipline came into its own in the late nineteenth century. Although the ancient Egyptians were sometimes admitted to be "mixed," Egyptologists tended to insist that the higher aspects of Egyptian civilization were the result of the influx of an "Asiatic" or Caucasoid race in the thirtieth century B.C.[48]

Thus in the 1920s, when King Tut first made his debut as the most important find in the history of archaeology, it was as the mummy of a white man—perhaps darker skinned than modern European whites because of exposure to the sun, but of "Caucasoid" stock. Egypt was understood to be both the most powerful civilization of the pre-Hellenic period and one of the foundations of Western civilization. Scholarly and popular narratives positioned Egyptian civilization, like the Greek and Roman civilizations that followed it, as the product of a superior stock of ancient peoples who, beginning perhaps in India, had slowly traveled west over the centuries, "following the sun." This stock had created each of the great civilizations of humankind, finally landing in Europe, and ultimately in America, to create the highest civilization known to history. The stakes in this theory were high, and the answers were clear: Egypt had been one of the early stops in the great westward march of white civilization.[49]

In black communities, reassessment of the racial status of the pharaohs (and thus the foundations of "Western civilization") had began even before the Tut excavation in 1922. By the late 1970s, when black writers and journalists focused on the whitewashing of Tut, they were working in a long intellectual tradition. Within this tradition, there were basically two kinds of arguments, with distinct but overlapping histories. The first was a generalist's appeal to the racial "look" of the Egyptians. The second was a more specialized argument that focused on the Nubian influence in dynastic Egypt.

The first argument was based on appeals to "common sense": when black Americans looked at Tut's mask, or at the tomb paintings on display in New York or London, they saw themselves reflected. In 1915, when W. E. B. Du Bois published *The Negro*, he had insisted that Egyptian monuments showed "distinctly Negro and mulatto faces" and claimed that Egyptology had been able to deny that the ancient Egyptians were "Negroes" only through a constant process of expanding the definition of "white" or "Caucasoid" and contracting the definition of Negro to exclude Egyptians. Although Du Bois noted that no truly scientific definition of race was possible, he also believed in the usefulness of the term "negro" to define the "darker part of the human family...a social group distinct in history, appearance, and to some extent in spiritual gift." Du Bois went on to argue that the Egyptian civilization was clearly not white but instead comprised a mixture of populations that approximated "what would be described in America as a light mulatto stock of Octoroons or Quadroons."[50]

Du Bois's argument and arguments like it had already made their way into the larger African American community by the 1920s. The Reverend Adam Clayton Powell Sr., pastor of the Abyssinian Baptist Church in New York City, described his opinion of the matter following a visit to Egypt and Jerusalem: "No colored man can go to Egypt and study the past and present achievements of its people without being proud that he is a colored man, for the Egyptians are undoubtedly Colored People.... All their statues have Negro features. Anyone who has seen the picture of the Sphinx knows that it resembles a genuine colored man."[51] In the 1940s, African American historian and pamphleteer Joel A. Rogers had also popularized the Egyptians-as-Negroes thesis in a set of self-published books and a series of newspaper columns and editorials, which were widely circulated in the black press. In *World's Great Men of Color*, which Rogers originally published in 1946, the "Celebrities before Christ" section is thickly populated with ancient Egyptians. Rogers based his argument on both ancestry (Hatshepsut and Thotmes III's grandmother was Ethiopian) and on physical depiction in sculpture (the book includes several photos of statues of pharaohs).[52] Thus Shirley Du Bois, W. E. B. Du Bois's wife, was operating within a well-established tradition when, writing in the *Black Scholar* in 1970, she insisted on the simple authority of the visual evidence of Tut's gold mask: "I traced the contour and shape of the face, with its high cheek-bones, full lips, wide nostrils and delicately hollowed cheeks beneath deep-set eyes, and I recognized the portrait of a sensitive young black man, who had died before his time."[53]

A second strand of argument, not entirely separable from the first, developed with the rise of decolonization and African nationalism in the 1950s. Drawing on a more technical discussion within anthropology and/or Egyptology, it was articulated and disseminated in its most detailed form by Cheikh Anta Diop, a native of Senegal widely described as the first African Egyptologist. Diop first made his argument in *Nations, negres et cultur*, published in Paris in 1955, which quickly achieved a following among African nationalists and French intellectuals. But Diop's work was not translated into English until 1974, when *The African Origin of Civilization: Myth or Reality?* was compiled from sections of two of his earlier works. In that same year, Diop also played a central role in organizing a UNESCO conference on the issues of race and Egypt; the conference made a highly visible statement in favor of the theory that Egypt was peopled by "Black Africans."[54] Diop built his case on a discussion of the similarities between modern African languages and ancient Egyptian, using them to trace possible ancient migration patterns out of central Africa into Egypt. He also drew on the findings of physical anthropology to argue that the physiognomy of the ancient Egyptians was "primarily Negroid."

Diop detailed nineteenth-century anthropologists' horror at the notion that ancient Egyptians might be considered black, and he paid special attention to the emergence of the dynastic race theory, which held that Egyptian high civilization was the product of an influx of Asian or Mediterranean migrants. A striking feature of Diop's work was its emphasis on the *race* of the Egyptians (as opposed to their cultural or historical ties to Africa) and its reliance on a notion of race as an essential, biologically fixed category. Race, he argued, is written on the body. Ultimately, his argument for the racial classification of the Egyptians depended as much on visual authentification as had Du Bois's or Rogers's claims. Speaking of the representations of ancient Egyptians on their monuments, he made a sweeping appeal to the "obviousness" of race: "From the common people to the Pharaoh, passing in review the dignitaries of the Court and the high officials, it is impossible to find—and still keep a straight face—a single representative of the white race or the Semitic race. It is impossible to find anyone there except Negroes of the same species as all indigenous Africans."[55] Diop also resorted to some rather dizzying contortions of logic to maintain his argument not only that ancient Egyptians were black but also that modern Egyptians (and modern "Blacks") share essentially the same "intellectual and affective dispositions." At one point, he argued both that the modern Egyptians are *not* appreciably different in skin color from their forebears and that they are, at the same time, noticeably lighter skinned than their genuinely black ancestors. The main point for Diop seemed to be that, no matter how much "crossbreeding" had taken place since ancient times, the racial essence of the Egyptians was unalterable. The "racial constants" of the early population had not been mitigated, he argued: "The color of the Egyptians has become lightened down through the years, like that of the West Indian Negroes, but the Egyptians have never stopped being Negroes."[56]

The racial essentialism in Diop's argument was all the more apparent when one considers that he did not seem to have considered "Arab," and he explicitly rejected "Semitic," as possible options for modern Egyptians. Whatever he or his audience took "Semitic" to mean—whether he meant to imply only "Jewish" or if the term included progenitors of those people known today as both Jewish and Arab—the assumption for Diop, as for Du Bois and others, was that the real debate was between "black" and "white" as the relevant options for racial classification. Of course, it was the case that already by the 1950s, Arab Americans had been established, in U.S. law at least, as "white." But popular racial classifications have never followed legal definitions in any exact way, and the public representations of modern Arabs had certainly not presented the exotic and menacing sheiks (or, in other public discussions, the "terrorists") as entirely "white." Instead, they were sometimes "Semitic," often "tribal," occasionally, as with Hoving, "Oriental," and almost always dark-skinned. Within the black community, the Nation of Islam had quite consciously appropriated Arabs as part of the definition of a multicontinent "black man," but that definition itself presented a world in which "blackness" included Arabness but did not replace it. Racial science had long since been discredited among scientists and physical anthropologists, but racial classification continued to have extraordinary salience in U.S. public life, including among African Americans. The fact that the ancient Egyptians were assumed to be either black or white replicated the major *political* divisions at the historical moment; in this sense, the discussion about physiognomy was really an argument about contemporary cultural claims.

In the 1970s, these debates found their way into the black press. Black intellectuals and journalists tended to see the struggle for Tut as a struggle for African American history and the reclamation of black identity. If this reclamation depended on an essentialist definition of race that ultimately reinscribed racial "difference" as a biological fact rather than as a social category, it also promised a story of black civilization that would offer a potent supplement, or sometimes a counternarrative, to the history of slavery and dispossession (and its concomitant associations with the "emasculation" of black men).[57] One commentary, referring to the extraordinarily popular television miniseries based on Alex Haley's family autobiography, made the comparison clear: "King Tut, as much as Kunta Kinte, is part of black America's roots!"[58]

This claim to ancient Egypt would eventually fuel the rise of Afrocentrism in the 1980s. The Afrocentric argument for Egypt would value the ancient Egyptians particularly for their geopolitical power and their military prowess; and as Paul Gilroy has argued, it had clear triumphalist, masculinist, and sometimes militarist overtones.[59] In its historical context, however, this narrative of Tut as part of a transnational and transhistoric black identity also challenged the dominant framing of Tut on several fronts. It turned to ancient Egypt for its contributions to black history rather than to universal art, thus countering both the appropriative logic of the museum and the associated narratives that incorporated Tut's gold into a discourse of imperial stewardship and commodity nationalism. If the Tut exhibit was particular and historical rather than universal and aesthetic, then the discursive link between Tut and international resource management was severed. If Tut was mapped as African rather than as Middle Eastern, it would be much harder to write the Tut treasures into the outcry over oil. The black claims for Tut as a racial heritage—a heritage written on the body and given meaning through black history—operated as a counter to the appropriation of the "universal" in the service of a narrative of resource rescue. The terms of this opposition posited Tut's blackness as tied to a specific cultural history that could not be appropriated by the dominant logic that framed Tut within commodity nationalism.

SELLING BLACKNESS, AMERICAN STYLE

Steve Martin introduced the "King Tut" song on April 22, 1978, when he hosted NBC's popular television series *Saturday Night Live*. The performance opened with Martin dressed in mock "Egyptian" regalia, directly addressing the camera. "I'd like to talk seriously just for a moment," he said, "about one of the greatest art exhibits ever to tour the United States...." Affecting a tone that was part documentary voice-over and part outraged talk-show host, Martin went on: "I think it's a national disgrace the way we've commercialized it, with trinkets and toys, T-shirts and posters.... So, while I was up in the woods recently, I wrote a song. I tried to use the ancient modalities and melodies.... I'd like to do it for you right now. Maybe we can *all* learn something."

Martin stepped back and began to sing as the curtain rose to reveal a band and backup singers, all dressed in "Egyptian" kitsch. Martin's song, a playful pastiche of musical styles and cultural references, presented itself both as a celebration of Tut's mass-culture popularity and as ironic anticommercialist commentary. Reflecting on Tut's treasures, the lyrics ruefully noted, "If I'da known they would've lined up just to see 'im; I'da saved up all my money, and bought me a museum!" The middle part of the song shifted tone, however, commenting sardonically on Tut's commodification: "He gave his life for tourism," Martin sang. And later, "They're *selling* you!" Yet in the overall context of the song, Martin's exaggerated concern for Tut's authenticity served to parody the "high art" discourse and anticommodification rhetoric of the art elites. His audiences appreciated the joke: in later performances of the King Tut song (as on his *Wild and Crazy Guy* album, released later that year), Martin had merely to ponderously intone the words "one of the greatest art exhibits of all time" to have his audience laughing in anticipation.

This slippage between protest against, and a longing to participate in, Tut's commodity status structured the performance. At the culmination of the song, a sarcophagus in the back of the set burst open to reveal a saxophone-playing mummy. The mummy's distinctive headdress mimicked the often-reproduced death mask from the Tut exhibit; he represented not just *any* mummy, but Tut himself. While the Tut/mummy played his sax solo, Martin danced to the back of the stage, where he picked up a food blender hidden behind some props and prepared it as an offering for the mummy. Tut, it turned out, had an insatiable desire for commodities, including small kitchen appliances. Tut's presence as a commercial sensation in the twentieth century linked him to commodity culture; like the department store Orientalism at the turn of the century, Tut's presence enabled the marketing of everyday consumer goods as exotica. Despite the song's playful protestations about commercialism, however, it was Tut's status as a commodity *himself*—circulating freely, available for purchase, use, and appropriation—that linked him to mass culture and invited Martin to see him as something more than a dead icon.

This staging of Tut's complex relation to the commodity form paralleled (and enabled) the song's slippery *racial* logic. During the course of the short performance (two minutes and ten seconds), Martin enacted a rapid transformation in his onstage persona, drawing heavily on racial markers. He began as self-consciously white, asking Tut in bewilderment, "How'd you get so funky?" But as Martin continued, he appeared more and more confident. In the next few verses, he managed to sample almost every mainstream black music style of the 1960s and 1970s. He sang several parts, incorporating both the high falsetto and the deep bass that were the trademark of Motown groups like the Temptations. Martin was backed by two young black women dancers, also in "Egyptian" dress, who switched back and forth between stylized poses (stiff-hand-in-front profiles that were obviously meant to recall tomb paintings) and exaggerated, hip-swinging

Figure 14. Steve Martin performs his wildly popular song "King Tut" on *Saturday Night Live* in 1978. Courtesy of NBC.

disco-Motown "backup" routines, while adding their voices to the chorus of "Tut, Tut, funky Tut; Tut, Tut, rockin' Tut." Throughout, the song described itself (and Tut) as "funky," "disco," and "boss." At several points Martin affected a "black" accent—as when he sang, "Tut, dancing by the Nile / Tut, the ladies love his style." By the time Martin called Tut his "favorite honkey," he did so from the position of a staged "black" voice, benevolently commenting on the surprising funkiness of his friend Tut.

The presence on stage of the Tut/mummy himself heightened the song's studied racial ambiguity. The man playing the role of the mummified Tut emerged from his sarcophagus with strangely affixed long curls as a headdress and wearing very obvious golden/brown face coloring. He then performed a brief sax solo, to the applause and cheers of the audience. This was Tut in blackface, but the black face also signified the "gold" of the commodity. Tut, Martin's "favorite honkey," had turned out to be a hip sax player with darkened skin, a funky Tut who pleased the "ladies," a "rockin' Tut" to whom one pays homage in a Motown-disco beat. In a very short time, Martin's song had thrown into question the racial meanings it seemed to establish: if Tut was white, he seemed to be approachable primarily through music and language coded as black. If he was black, he was not "naturally" so but had to be "blackened up." What the song posited as desirable about Tut was his funkiness, his saxophone-playing cool, and his racial indeterminacy, now made available through the reproduction and consumption of Tut in popular culture. Like Martin himself in this song, Tut seemed to confound the (stylistic) boundaries of race.

The Tut song helped to catapult Martin to the top echelon of American comedians, second only perhaps to Richard Pryor in the late 1970s. And though Martin never directly played black characters, he did develop a comic style that was deeply indebted to Pryor, who had single-handedly brought race-conscious and racially confrontational humor into the mainstream. As an African American, Pryor made his reputation on routines that focused on the differences between black and white culture; as a white man, Martin did much the same thing. For example, Martin's first feature film, *The Jerk* (1980), was built on the conceit that Martin was "born a poor black child," the adopted son of Mississippi sharecroppers. In Martin's family, he is the special child, and everybody else is too polite to mention that he is actually white. In one of the first scenes of the movie, Martin's mother makes him his "special meal" for his birthday—tuna fish on white bread, Twinkies™, and a diet soft drink. His brother thoughtfully wraps the sandwich "in cellophane, just like you like it." When the family sings the blues after dinner, Martin spastically and painfully tries to keep time with the music. *The Jerk* played with the notion that the cultural signifiers of whiteness are somehow genetic (white people can never keep rhythm, but they will have a *natural* desire for white-bread sandwiches wrapped in cellophane); at the same time, it worked to denaturalize race, precisely by making it more visible.

In his years appearing on *Saturday Night Live*, Martin helped to make it one of the preeminent sites for the self-conscious circulation, performance, and parodying of racial styles in the 1970s. In Martin's episode, the Tut skit was the last of several routines in which "blackness" signified hipness, cool, masculinity, and ultimately national identity—Americanness. The episode opened with the introduction of the Blues Brothers, the Dan Aykroyd–John Belushi duet that combined a loving parody of early blues singers with playful criticism of their commercialization. The Blues Brothers were also a commentary on the appropriation of black culture by the white mainstream: they were, in essence, white guys pretending to be black guys who were making fun of white guys who pretend to be black guys. In the same episode, the "wild and crazy" Czech brothers (Martin and Aykroyd) turned to *SNL*'s one black regular, Garrett Morris, for instructions in "American" techniques for catching "foxy chicks." The Czech brothers seemed to conflate their attempt to be "American" men with an attempt to be *black* American men—their exaggerated strut and their open-to-the-waist shirts suggested a reading of American culture through the film *Superfly* (1972).

The cultural style of *Saturday Night Live*, exemplified in blender-sacrifice and mock blues music, became a marker of both generational affiliation and class distinction in the 1970s. The postmodern taste of young professional managerial class (PMC) cultural consumers was exemplified in the ability of cultural texts like *Saturday Night Live* to straddle traditional divides between high and low culture—to hail a group of consumers who were both college-educated and mass-mediated. As Fred Pfeil has argued, the baby boomers were historically constituted not only by their class status but also by their experience as cultural consumers. The centrality of a youthful history of television watching, for example, constructed a shared language; members of the PMC marked their cultural self-recognition through the common stock of cultural references made available through the television shows of their childhood and adolescence.[60] Similarly, this generation defined itself by its participation in a thoroughly mass-mediated and often African American–influenced music culture, in part as a result of the mainstreaming of black popular music in the 1960s, from Motown to Jimi Hendrix.

There are, of course, many examples of white American culture drawing on and appropriating black culture (1920s dance styles, jazz, early rock, the Beats, etc.) as part of the construction of white (usually male) identity.[61] Kobena Mercer has argued that black culture was particularly important to the construction of white subjectivity in the 1960s, when consumption of black music and the adoption of black "style" served as expressions of white disaffiliation and disaffection: "The trope of the White Negro encodes an antagonistic subject position on the part of the white subject in relation to the normative codes of his own society."[62] In the 1970s, however, this taking up of the codes of blackness by whites was no longer mobilized in the construction of an essentially (if problematically) *antagonistic* relation to dominant culture. Instead, black cultural style became incorporated into a comfortable generational identity that defined itself through a certain cultural sensibility—an embrace of commodification, ahistoricity, irony, and the mobilization of cultural pastiche that only in retrospect would be described as postmodern.[63]

In this paradigm, identity was constituted through the purchase and display of style. This younger generation of white Negros began to see itself *as* black culture (or, more accurately, to see itself through its own appropriation of the signifiers of black culture). This could only happen once the signifiers of race began to be de-essentialized, to be removed from the body and to circulate like (and *as*) commodities. This postmodern deconstruction of the naturalization of race had an unequal impact: blackness, not whiteness, became the racial identity most available for commodification and appropriation.

The reformulation of white subjectivity used the codes of black marginality to construct a generational identity stripped of all but the most superficial markers of opposition or resistance. This black-inflected cultural style was also, at least implicitly, masculine. At a moment when traditional gender politics were under siege by the feminist and gay liberation movements, Martin's Tut was defined by his heterosexual virility: "Funky Tut" attracted "ladies" who "love[d] his style." Similarly, the detached cool of the Blues Brothers and the ineffectual sexual aggressiveness of the (Americanized) Czech brothers both pointed to a view of black culture as a resource for reconstituting white masculinity. Blackness became a set of codes and cultural behaviors that could be (at least potentially) owned and operated by white men.

At one level, the nationalist postmodernism of the Tut song may seem worlds away from the international resource management (imperial stewardship) narratives that surrounded the official Tut representations. Yet, like the high-art discourse of the official Tut narrative, the postmodern masculinity of the Tut song was implicated in the construction of a seductive form of commodity nationalism: this time, (black) style (rather than gold) was the commodity whose consumption defined the nation. In both cases, the signifiers of ancient Egypt were used to suggest something longed for, something that, in the proper context, could be possessed and circulated. The rhetorics of imperial stewardship and commodity nationalism linked Tut to the politics of oil, mapping Egypt as Middle Eastern and suggesting resource management as a framework for global relations. At the same time, some members of the black community attempted to mobilize the Tut exhibit as part of a logic of racial essentialism and a narrative of racial history that mapped Egypt as African. The politics of geography could not be more clear. And in each of these instances, people in the United States encountered the Middle East through narratives about history. Once again, however, the past was not simply the past; it was a marker for politics in the present.

4 The Good Fight
Israel after Vietnam, 1972–1980

Keep your eyes on the Middle East. If this is the time that we
believe it is, this area will become a constant source of tension for
all the world. The fear of another World War will be almost
completely centered in the troubles of this area. It will become so
severe that only Christ or the Antichrist can solve it. Of course the
world will choose the Antichrist.
> —Hal Lindsey, *The Late Great Planet Earth*

Do we lack power? ... Certainly not if power is measured in the
brute terms of economic, technological, and military capacity. By all
those standards, we are still the most powerful country in the world.
... The issue boils down in the end, then, to the question of will.
> —Norman Podhoretz, "Making the World
> Safe for Communism"

In the spring of 1967, as the war between Israel and the neighboring Arab
states was brewing, newspapers and television in the United States reported
on the progress of a very different conflict. In Vietnam, the U.S. military was
enmeshed in the second year of Operation Rolling Thunder, the bombing
campaign that dropped eight hundred tons of bombs a day on North Vietnam. Troop call-ups had increased, and the antiwar movement was conduct-
ing a ceaseless round of protest and confrontation with authorities. As the
war escalated, television news in particular brought it home, making Vietnam
"the living room war." A new generation of young reporters—David Hal-
berstam, Seymour Hersh, Peter Arnett, Morley Safer—were accompanying
U.S. troops nearly everywhere in the field. They filled the expanded evening
newscasts (which had been lengthened from fifteen to thirty minutes beginning in 1963) with dramatic, highly visual, and controversial reporting that
was virtually uncensored by U.S. military authorities. While most Americans
still described themselves as firmly in support of the war, doubts were spreading. That May, General Westmoreland, the commander of U.S. troops in Vietnam, was called home to appear before Congress, in a move that commentators assumed was intended to shore up political support for the war. Although

the general was received warmly by Congress, he did little to quell the public's doubts. *Newsweek* pointed out that, while Westmoreland had claimed to be explaining the situation in Vietnam, he had "never touched the fundamental questions causing all the concern in the first place.... Was the U.S. really prepared to fight a long war of attrition in Asia?"[1]

These questions echoed more general concerns, just beginning to emerge in mainstream debates, about the nature of U.S. power. As the Vietnam War dragged on, even some members of the foreign policy establishment began to wonder whether the United States was beginning to look more like an imperial power than an anticolonial one. Shortly after Westmoreland's appearance, no less an official than Secretary of Defense Robert McNamara made this rather remarkable observation: "The picture of the world's greatest superpower killing or seriously injuring a thousand noncombatants a week, while trying to pound a tiny backward country into submission on an issue whose merits are hotly debated is not a pretty one."[2] On the other hand, General Westmoreland and other military officials argued that the war could and would be won, even against an "unconventional" enemy, if only the United States followed a purposeful and sustained application of military force, backed by a willingness to sustain losses.[3] This debate over Vietnam policy would soon become a debate over Middle East policy as well, as U.S. officials and the American public faced the oil crises of the 1970s.

In May 1967, the escalating tensions between Egypt and Israel eclipsed public concern about Vietnam, at least for a while. In the Situation Room in the White House, the map of Vietnam was replaced with a map of the Middle East.[4] Then, in June, the Israelis surprised the world with their extraordinarily rapid victory over the forces of Egypt, Syria, and Jordan. Before war broke out, experts had suggested that the Arab forces were distinctly stronger and more battle-ready than they had been in either 1948 or 1956.[5] But doubts about the outcome were quickly put to rest; six days after the war began, Arab nationalists were humiliated, and Israel emerged as the preeminent military power in a region where the political and territorial map had been suddenly redrawn.

Whatever complicated feelings the 1967 war engendered among African Americans and American Jews, most news accounts focused simply on the drama of Israel's victory. Newspapers and TV news told of the rapid successes of the Israeli army, detailing the "stunning pre-dawn air-strikes," the "remarkable military triumph," and the "brilliant planning and execution of the Israeli attack."[6] Headlines such as "How Israel Won the War" highlighted the media's focus on the pragmatic details of the battle. Politically, Israel clearly had the vast majority of public support: in Washington, two hundred pro-Arab demonstrators (including some Black Muslims and members of the Student Nonviolent Coordinating Committee) faced more than twenty thousand pro-Israeli demonstrators.[7] Comparisons with U.S. actions in Vietnam were not lost upon observers. One columnist sarcastically proposed that the world should establish an agency to allocate wars so that they would not exhaust public attention by running simultaneously. A television comedian joked that the Israeli general Moshe Dayan should be hired to put a quick end to the fighting in Vietnam.[8] The conservative news magazine *U.S. News & World Report* made much the same point, quoting the observations of an unnamed U.S. military official: "The Israeli performance was proof of the only sound military strategy: When a country decides to go into a war, it goes in 'wham'—to win."[9]

Just over six months later, the illusion of any such rapid victory in Vietnam was shattered when North Vietnam and its allies launched the Tet Offensive. Eventually, U.S. and South Vietnamese troops repelled the attack decisively, but only after having fought Vietnamese communist forces in the courtyard of the American embassy in Saigon, with television cameras there to record every moment of the battle. For the American public, which had been told for years that the United States was winning—had almost won—the war, the fact that the communists had enough strength to launch such a daring campaign was in itself a shock. Thus at virtually the same moment that officials like Robert McNamara were bringing the antiwar movement's critique of the morality of U.S. power into the mainstream debate, serious questions emerged about the efficacy of that power. In other words, just as the United States began to look like an imperial power in the eyes of some of its citizens, it began to look like an imperial power in decline, unable or unwilling to shore up its own ambitions.

In the following decade, Israel came to be constituted as an icon in the post-Vietnam debate about the nature of U.S. world power. Just as the Arab oil embargo had figured prominently in arguments for a global managerialist model, Israel and its military played a key symbolic role for those who advocated the remilitarization of U.S. policy. As questions raged both about the morality of the U.S. war in Vietnam and about the role of the U.S. military more generally, Israel came to provide a political model for thinking about military power and a practical example of effectiveness in the use of that power.

For many American Jews and others, Israel had long stood as a very different kind of symbol: a reconstructed community built out of the ashes of the Holocaust. While not all Jews shared this sense of solidarity, most people who felt strong ties to Israel before 1967 did so because of their conviction that a precious haven was being created. In the 1970s, however, some

Americans came to invest emotionally and politically in Israel for very different reasons, and precisely through the more militarized image that emerged in the wake of Vietnam. This investment, which solidified the political ties between the United States and Israel, had a profound effect on foreign policy. Over the course of the decade, a dominant view emerged that it was at once morally just and in U.S. national interests to act not only *with* Israel but also *like* Israel on key international issues.

This new image of Israel was interconnected with domestic politics, but not in the way that many commentators have imagined. Both the Israeli lobby and American Jews have of course played an important role in framing U.S.-Israeli relations, but they did not—could not—construct U.S. cultural or political interests out of whole cloth. Israel played a rhetorical role in an argument about U.S. foreign policy and American identity. That argument itself was also connected to problems of gender: as feminism and women's political activism shook American culture to its core in the 1970s, the fascination with military power served to reassert a certain kind of masculinity. In the 1960s, black radicals had used Islam and Arab culture to assert their own masculinity against a civil rights movement perceived as too accommodating and overly feminized; in the 1970s, white evangelicals and political conservatives mobilized Israel as part of a challenge to the liberal and left-wing advances of feminism and the antiwar movement of the 1960s and early 1970s.

I trace the significance of the post-Vietnam figure of Israel through several locations. My analysis begins with an examination of representations of Israel in the late 1950s and early 1960s, focusing particularly on the novel and the film *Exodus*, both of which played a key role in bringing Israel into U.S. popular culture. I then detail the rising fascination with modern-day Israel in the subculture of conservative Christian fundamentalism. As the New Christian Right emerged and gained cultural recognition and political power over the course of the 1970s, its writers and preachers began to talk more and more about the role of the Middle East in the great end-time battles predicted in biblical prophecy. Israel was central to their scenario, and the fundamentalists' deep interest in the details of the contemporary Arab-Israeli conflict arose from an increased sense that the end times would be heralded by events in the Middle East. These religious concerns connected to a broader interest in Israel that developed as the battle against terrorism came to dominate U.S. headlines in the 1970s. I argue that Israel's response to terrorism was the source of a nearly endless public fascination, in large part because of how Israel figured into questions about declining U.S. military power. The meanings of Israel developed in conjunction with the concept of the "Vietnam Syndrome," the conservative reinterpretation that viewed the American defeat in Vietnam as a failure of political will.

Overall, I suggest that each of these dynamics, diverse as they were, included a dual focus on the importance of Israel as a moral exemplar and Israel as an admired military power. The chapter concludes by suggesting that this militarized image of Israel has not been sufficiently acknowledged as a factor in the New Right coalition that came together in the 1980 elections. As New Right revisionism came to dominate public understanding of what had happened in Vietnam, it had a new understanding of Israel as its subtext. Thus, several *different* discursive sites, each with its own institutional history and modes of representation, worked together in the 1970s to remake the dominant meanings of Israel in the United States. Over the course of the 1970s, Israel, or a certain image of Israel, came to function as a stage upon which the war in Vietnam was refought—and this time, won.

THE *EXODUS* PHENOMENON

In 1961, a film that told the story of the founding of Israel became one of the most popular movies in America.[10] Directed by Otto Preminger and starring Paul Newman as the young Israeli hero Ari Ben Canaan, *Exodus* was an adaptation of Leon Uris's best-selling novel of the same name. By the time the movie was released, the novel had already been on the best-seller list for eighty weeks, selling almost four million copies.[11] Over the next twenty years, the book would go through more than eighty paperback printings and sell another sixteen million copies. This book-and-film phenomenon presented Israel to a mass audience, most of which had, until then, paid relatively little attention to it. As one historian has suggested, in the late 1950s, most Americans still knew little about Zionism or Israel. After *Exodus* was published and the film released, its story became "the primary source of knowledge about Jews and Israel that most Americans had."[12] At the same time, many of the images and investments established in *Exodus* would eventually be transformed by the political and cultural narratives that emerged in the wake of the Vietnam War. The story *Exodus* told in 1960 was both a foreshadowing of what Israel was to come to mean to Americans and a document of a set of meanings that would soon be displaced.

Uris's book presented itself as a detailed historical account of the critical events that had unfolded in Europe and Palestine before, during, and after World War II: it tells of the Holocaust and the death camps; the postwar battles over Jewish immigration into Palestine; the rapidly escalating violence that raged between the British, Arabs, and Jews as Great Britain prepared to relinquish control of its colonial mandate in the region; the developing kibbutz movement; the war for territory; the founding of the state. *Exodus* is a highly political novel, structured by a complex web of war, romance, and redemption. Uris narrates his story through a biblical lens: the section headings are quotes from the Hebrew Scriptures, the Israeli characters constantly recall the promises of God to return them to their land, and even the Christian characters quote Bible verses and muse on the Jews' scriptural mandate.[13]

The plot of the film version of *Exodus* is simplified but maintains much of the multilayered structure of the book. It centers around Newman's Ari Ben Canaan, an underground leader fighting the British in Palestine, whose moral status as exemplar of the Israel-to-be is secured by his toughness and his deep personal integrity. Ari's foil and romantic interest is a Christian American nurse, Kitty Fremont (Eva Marie Saint). Kitty is initially confused and wary of the Jews in Palestine; as the film progresses, she is fascinated and occasionally repelled by the saga of Jewish sacrifice and commitment to which she is witness. Ari's skills place him at the center of several important historical events. First, he commands the ship *Exodus*, which successfully confronts the British and brings a large group of Holocaust survivors into Palestine despite immigration restrictions. Once in Palestine, he negotiates conflicts between the main Jewish guerrilla force, the Haganah, and the militant right-wing faction, the Irgun. He also leads a military unit in the 1948 Arab-Jewish civil war for control over territory. Just as important to Ari's character, and to the film's presentation of the Israel he exemplifies, he is a loving son who visits his father on the family farm and who commits himself to protect the kibbutz where his sister works, which was set up exclusively for children orphaned by Holocaust and war. By the end of the story, Ari has fallen in love with Kitty, but more important, Kitty has also fallen in love—with Ari, yes, but also with Israel.

Part conversion narrative, part romance, and part war movie, *Exodus* presents an enthusiastic portrait of Israel and the Jews who founded it. They are brave and valiant; they take up arms reluctantly, but they fight well; and they take care of their own. With the Holocaust as its back story, it is a loving tale of struggle, manliness, and state formation, of European and Palestinian Jews becoming Israelis, making (and earning) their state through their love of the land, their commitment to family, and their democratic ethos. Ari Ben Canaan is a great military leader who wants nothing more than to live simply on his family farm. He represents Israel as a nation that is sufficiently manly to go to war but sufficiently moral to regret war's necessity.

At the same time, both the film and the novel are decisively anti-Arab. The novel is simply vicious, littered with every imaginable stereotype—from Arabs who smell like goats to the once-beloved Arab friend who dares to desire a Jewish woman. The film version eschews most of the virulence that peppers the novel, but it adds an entire plot development in which Nazis arrive at a tiny village to advise the Arabs on how to deal with their "Jewish problem."

Like the novel, Preminger's film used a biblical frame. But as a film produced in 1960, *Exodus* signified its biblical affiliation not only by direct reference to the Hebrew Scriptures but also by reference to the religious epics that had dominated the box office in the 1950s. Like those films, *Exodus* was (mildly) criticized by reviewers for being "massive, overlong," and sometimes "irritating." Reviewers also, as with the biblical epics, reverently reported the money and time investments that were supposed to guarantee the film's historical authenticity: Preminger "spared no expense in reproducing historical events much as they occurred."[14] But there was also a crucial difference. Whereas the biblical epic films had Americanized (and deracialized) the Hebrew exodus narrative, *Exodus* attempted to Israelize Hollywood's typical signifiers of "Americanness."

Preminger's citations of the biblical genre are mostly stylistic: the distinctive, high-contrast lighting and a soaring, sentimental score. But there are several scenes that specifically recall the earlier movies, including a colorful, raucous crowd on the deck of the *Exodus* that harkens back to the joyful gathering-up scenes in *The Ten Commandments* and a dramatic final confrontation between Ari and his boyhood friend Taha that echoes the meeting between Judah Ben-Hur and his boyhood friend Messala in *Ben-Hur*.

This link between American tropes of national righteousness and the story of Israel's founding is reinforced by the movie's *other* homage to Hollywood genre films, the Western. In one scene, for example, Ari brings Kitty home to meet his parents. The camera pans a simple farm, where the father is feeding pigs and livestock; when Ari arrives, the old man calls excitedly to the mother, who hurries out the door wearing a dress and hairstyle that 1950s Hollywood used to signify western farm women. The scene is thus structurally and iconographically designed to recall the popular pioneer Westerns that were major features of the film and television landscape of the 1950s (from *Gunfight at the OK Corral*, written by Uris himself, to *Gunsmoke*). The link was not lost on observers, one of whom commented sardonically on the arrival of "the first Jewish Western."[15] In recounting the political events leading to the founding of Israel, *Exodus* uses stylistic citations that link it to the great historical genres of 1950s film. In other words, it mobilizes media references to other types of historical fiction in order to signify its own "historicalness."

Exodus itself soon came to function as popular history. Within a year of its release, Daniel Boorstein had complained in *The Image: A Guide to Pseudo-Events in America* that the film had become more real than the history it claimed to tell: "In 1960, a highly successful packaged tour was organized which traced the route of events in Leon Uris' novel *Exodus;* the next year El Al Israel Airlines announced a new sixteen-day tour which promised to cover the very places where Otto Preminger and his film crew had shot scenes for the movie version."[16]

In the years before *Exodus,* Israel had meant different things to different people in the United States, from the Christian interest in the Holy Land to those who hailed Israel as an exemplar of anticolonial (and pro-American) nationalism in the 1950s. African American intellectuals and activists had their own set of interests and investments in Israel, beginning before the founding of the state and continuing well into the 1960s. Among Jews, there was some debate about what Israel meant, especially among liberals and leftists; the socialist Bund, for example, had an often ambivalent relationship to Zionism, and in the years leading up to Israel's founding, a small group of Reform rabbis argued that Zionism's nationalist focus threatened Jewish assimilation in America and Europe and was undemocratic in Palestine.[17] Most American Jews, however, felt a profound emotional and political attachment to Israel, especially after the Holocaust. They viewed it as a nation where Jews would always be safe and as a site of democratic, even socialist, possibility. Later, in the 1960s and 1970s, Jewish feminists also began to express their solidarity with Israel, though this general support was often combined with strong criticism of specific Israeli policies, particularly in regard to the Palestinians. In fact, it was within the feminist movement that the African American writer Alice Walker developed her sense of the complex politics of Americans' emotional affiliation with Israel, and though she would express profound disagreement with both Israeli policies and what she saw as some Jewish feminists' uncritical support of Israel, she also gave voice to her own sense of moral affiliation with the founding of the state: "All I considered was the Holocaust, the inhuman fact that Jews were turned away by every country they sought to enter, that they had to live *somewhere* on the globe ... and I had seen the movie *Exodus,* with its haunting sound track: 'This land is mine, God gave this land to me.' "[18]

Exodus expressed those kinds of attachments through the personal and political dramas of its protagonists. It told details of the Holocaust that had been largely ignored, while refusing to present Jews only as victims. In *Exodus*, the Zionist story of Israel also became an American tale. Israel emerged in both the book and the film as an America-like refuge that had been hard fought and won (morally, politically, and militarily) from an often indifferent world. Certainly both the image of the Jewish pioneer and the trope of the tough Jewish David facing an Arab Goliath were well established in American culture before 1960. *Exodus* simply welded what had been rather scattered images into an epic tale of the founding of a new nation.[19]

At the same time, Uris's story marginalized the Israeli and Jewish Left: it dismissed the socialist kibbutzim, privileged traditional nuclear families over the radicalism of child-rearing alternatives, and reduced internal dissent in Israel to that between the mainstream Haganah and the right-wing Irgun. But this also was consistent with its Americanization of Israeli history; just as, in 1960, textbook histories of the United States tended to erase the indigenous history of the American Left, so Uris's narrative mainstreamed Israeli politics. In *Exodus*, the story of Israel was one of bravery, hard work, and individualism within a shared community: as the American frontier had been tamed, so the desert bloomed.

This presentation of Jewish life in Israel may have also influenced the positioning of Jewish identity within the United States. Before the 1950s, anti-Semitism had pervaded American social life, from the anti-Jewish violence perpetrated by the Ku Klux Klan, to popular culture stereotypes of Jews as greedy and dirty, to the segregation of Jews from white neighborhoods and limits on Jewish admission to certain universities.[20] Yet by 1960, Jews were no longer effectively marginalized, either economically or socially. Economically, almost half of all Jewish families in 1965 had incomes in the nation's top 25 percent, and the percentage of Jews in white-collar jobs was three times the national average.[21] Social anti-Semitism had also declined precipitously: in a national poll in 1960, 95 percent of respondents reported no objection to Jews living in their neighborhood. As Michael Rogin has argued, the rising tensions between blacks and Jews in the civil rights movement were one indication that Jews had been established, through a racialized class boundary, as a white ethnicity.[22]

But racialized images of Jews still haunted American culture and American Jewish life. Anti-Semitic stereotypes had long associated Jewish men with femininity, as well as aggressive sexual deviance. The Jewish family, like the African American family, frequently was represented in dominant culture as "inverted"; that is, as consisting of quiet, feminized Jewish men stuck in the private sphere of scholarship and religion, and aggressive women who ran the family and were active in the public spheres of market and work. Jewish women were caught between this image of themselves as domineering and even older representations of the oversexualized Jewess. Paul Breines's rich study *Tough Jews* argues that the images of gentle, bookish Jewish men were not simply external inventions; they had a basis both in the lived values of urban Jewish communities and in the Jewish literary renaissance of the 1950s that had idealized nineteenth-century and early twentieth-century eastern European Jewish culture. But this idealization of what Breines calls "gentle Jews" did not extend to everyone, and the public understanding of Jewish masculinity remained a contested issue.[23]

Exodus author Leon Uris was conscious of revising what he considered the predominant images of Jewish male weakness and hyperurbanism. In an interview conducted shortly after the novel appeared in 1958, he told a journalist: "We Jews are not what we have been portrayed to be. In truth, we have been fighters."[24] The construction of an alternative, more Americanized masculinity undoubtedly played a role in the continuing assimilation of American Jews, in part by reconstructing the image of the Jewish nuclear family in more male-dominated terms. In other words, the irony was that, in forging an identification with Israeli soldiers and their toughness, American Jews identified with an image of masculinity that placed them firmly in the mainstream of white American national(ist) images, from Teddy Roosevelt to John Wayne.[25]

This construction of Jews as white and properly gendered would matter outside the Jewish community, since Israel would come to matter profoundly to other "white" people, who in turn would identify with it as an ally and model. Of course, it is quite possible for white Americans to identify with people who are *not* marked as white—the entire history of "white Negro" affiliation makes that clear. Still, the repositioning of Jews in American racial logic and the positive framing of Israel were intertwined constructs; just as the Nation of Islam and other black nationalists were claiming Arabs as black and masculine, both Hollywood and Washington were representing Jews as white and masculine.

Still, for some time after the arrival of the *Exodus* phenomenon, modern-day Israel remained relatively peripheral to most public discourse in the United States. Certainly the Arab-Israeli conflict was in the news, on and off, after 1948, first during the Suez crisis in 1956, and then because of a few heated border conflicts between Israel and Egypt in the early 1960s. But beyond these events, there was little to follow up on the surge of interest that Uris had initiated. Of course, American policymakers continued to debate the United States' moral obligations and political interests in the face of the ongoing Arab-Israeli conflict. African American exodus narratives continued to wield significant power, and thus to forge ties with the state of Israel. These were exceptions, however, and beyond those investments, and those of the American Jewish and much smaller Arab American communities, Israel did not have a strong, emotionally charged meaning for most people in the United States. *Exodus* had captured the public imagination, but it did not yet represent a larger, sustained cultural investment. The 1967 war would change that dramatically.

PROPHECY AND ISRAEL

Three years after the Six-Day War, in 1970, a small religious publishing house released a thin book about biblical prophecy that would soon transform the cultural and religious landscape of the decade. The author, a relative unknown who had graduated from Dallas Theological Seminary and then toured the country as a lecturer for Campus Crusade for Christ, was Hal Lindsey. His exegesis of the relationship between the biblical prophecies of Armageddon and contemporary political events was titled *The Late Great Planet Earth* (*LGPE*); by the end of the decade, it had sold more than ten million copies, making it the best-selling book of the 1970s. (By 1998, estimates for total sales ranged between eighteen and twenty-eight million copies.)[26]

LGPE was an unusual book in a long tradition of Christian publishing. For decades, evangelical authors had analyzed the prophetic and apocalyptic books of the Hebrew Scriptures, particularly Daniel and Ezekiel, and of the Christian New Testament, particularly Revelation. An interest in prophecy was especially common among fundamentalists, who identified themselves as literal interpreters of the Bible. Like earlier authors, Lindsey viewed the biblical prophecies of the "last days" and the war of Armageddon in light of contemporary politics, focusing on the Middle East. *LGPE*'s fundamental argument was that certain key world events, which would signal the battle of Armageddon and the Second Coming of Christ, were beginning to happen in the 1970s, and that the nation of Israel (and its allies and enemies) would be central to those developments. As Bible analysis, Lindsey's book added little to the established framework of evangelical prophecy interpretation as outlined in scholarly texts and as taught in the nation's Bible colleges and seminaries. Indeed, some of his fellow students at Dallas Theological Seminary complained that Lindsey had simply repackaged his lecture notes.[27]

But if Lindsey's theories were derivative, his "repackaging" made impressive innovations at the level of style. *LGPE* was a very different sort of narrative than its predecessors, which were often academic, inbred books aimed at audiences of the already-converted. For example, the president of Dallas

Theological Seminary, John F. Walvoord, had published the evangelical standard, *Israel in Prophecy*, in 1962. A long, densely packed tome of close textual analysis, it presumed an audience both deeply familiar with the Scriptures and only loosely interested in the modern-day political happenings that were said to signal the coming apocalypse.[28] In contrast, Lindsey's breezy, upbeat style attempted to make the exegesis of complex biblical passages—and the accompanying discussion of contemporary politics—accessible and nonintimidating. Mobilizing the language of the sixties counterculture (or at least those popularized versions of the counterculture that had migrated into the mainstream), Lindsey tried to structure his discussion like an imagined rap session, sprinkling his prose with headlines like "Tell It Like It Will Be" (7), "Dead Men Do Tell Tales" (52), and "What Else Is New?" (86).

Lindsey's strategy was not unlike that of the Jesus movement, which in the late 1960s began to bring a reinvigorated energy to Christianity by constructing an alternative to mainline Protestantism. The Jesus People based their cultural style on selected aspects of the sixties counterculture, particularly the casual, unisex clothing and the interest in rock and folk music. With the political New Left in shreds after the battles of the late 1960s, the counterculture itself was increasingly separate from the anti-Vietnam radicalism that had fueled it. It was thus available, as a signifier, for a wide range of appropriations, including those by more conservative movements. *LGPE* presented itself as a layperson's, and particularly a young person's, guide: "We have been described as the 'searching generation,'" Lindsey wrote. "We need so many answers" (vii). Acknowledging that many young people were questioning the authority of political and social institutions, Lindsey offered a socially conservative vision in response: "In talking with thousands of persons, particularly college students, from every background and religious or irreligious upbringing, this writer found that many people want reassurance about the future" (7). This reassurance, *LGPE* said, was available from the Bible, which provided accurate prophecies of what was to come.

Although it aimed at a mass market of the young and the worried, *LGPE* initially made its reputation by selling to committed evangelicals. Released by a small Midwestern publishing house, Zondervan, it rode a rising tide of interest in religious and inspirational writings. These writings included a proliferation of books directed specifically at evangelicals, who by 1976 numbered almost eight million in the United States.[29] In the early 1970s, religious publishing had become the fastest-growing segment of the American publishing industry, even though books with religious themes rarely showed up on best-seller lists. Before the advent of universal product codes, the major lists (such as in the *New York Times*) were compiled by polling general-interest bookstore managers; since religious books were sold primarily through church conferences and small religious bookstores, they usually did not show up in the sampling polls. It was in this subcultural market that *LGPE* was first distributed; only later, after it had already sold half a million copies, did Bantam pick it up for release in a mass-market edition.[30] From then on, Lindsey's book was distributed at convenience and grocery stores, as well as in major bookstores, where it was often shelved alongside the "occult" and "New Age" paperbacks that were also selling at a brisk pace.[31]

Marketed to a mainstream audience as doomsday exotica, *LGPE* brought evangelical prophecy interpretation to bear on a detailed discussion of contemporary international politics. Unlike some analyses, which assumed that signs of the end times could be read primarily through the supposed moral degeneration of the United States, *LGPE* focused on events in the Middle East, Russia, and, to a lesser degree, Europe and China. Lindsey assumed that, however much his readers knew of scriptural texts, they were far less familiar with the outlines of Middle East politics; his response was to freely mix Scripture, historical background, and political advice. The "prophetic calendar" was moving forward, Lindsey insisted; the Second Coming of Christ was imminent and would take place in modern-day Israel. According to the Bible, three things had to happen before Christ would return: "First, the Jewish nation would be reborn in the land of Palestine. Secondly, the Jews would repossess Old Jerusalem and the sacred sites. Thirdly, they would rebuild their ancient temple of worship upon its historic site" (40). By 1970, two of those events had occurred, and both had involved a major Middle Eastern war. Arguing that the Bible predicted yet another conflict, *LGPE* included a map of the Middle East, marked with arrows indicating the expected invasion routes into Israel by the "Russian confederacy" from the north and the "Pan Arabic assault" from the south (144, 148).

Lindsey's detailed analysis of the world situation implied that white evangelicals needed to pay careful attention to politics—an unusual position in 1970. For the most part, white evangelical and fundamentalist churches had remained aloof from political life since the 1920s, when the Scopes Monkey Trial had subjected fundamentalist beliefs about evolution to public ridicule. Focusing on personal sin and inner salvation, fundamentalist doctrine had discouraged too much focus on "this world," as opposed to God's kingdom.[32] Black churches, on the other hand, which might well be called evangelical in doctrine, had been swept into political life during the civil rights movement, but had organized themselves more as big-tent Christians than specifically as evangelicals. The segregation of church life and the fact that both black and white evangelicals were concentrated in the South made race a particu-larly charged issue, since black Christians often squared off against evan-gelical whites over civil rights.

Most scholars have traced the increasing politicization of white evan-gelicals in the 1970s to their opposition to civil rights combined with concerns over a few other key domestic issues, particularly the changing educational environment (the Supreme Court ban on school prayer, new tax codes for religious schools, and curricular issues in the public schools) and the extensions of the liberal state. Many white fundamentalists and evangelicals also perceived a threat to their values in the antiwar and stu-dent movements. And they were profoundly affected by the public visibil-ity of feminist movements—from the famous Miss America pageant demonstration in 1968 to Congress's approval of the Equal Rights Amend-ment (ERA) in 1972 to the *Roe v. Wade* abortion rights decision in 1973. In their eyes, "women's lib" had become perhaps the most influential, and threatening, social movement to emerge out of the 1960s.[33]

These issues were undeniably important to fundamentalists, but the U.S. position in the world mattered to them as well. One tangible connection arose from the fact that evangelicals were disproportionately represented in the U.S. military. Southerners had for many years played a key role in the military leadership and were more likely to be among the midlevel officers in Vietnam. This southern overrepresentation in the military did not mean, of course, that any particular southern soldier was a fundamentalist. But by the early 1970s, both rank-and-file soldiers and military officers were de-claring their religious convictions, countering the traditional marginaliza-tion of religion in military culture. Bible studies, prayer groups, and Chris-tian breakfast meetings soon became routine at the Pentagon, as evangelical officers consciously increased their public visibility. At the same time, from the late 1960s on, fundamentalist preachers consistently and vocally sup-ported U.S. involvement in Vietnam.[34]

In 1970, however, the opening up of white evangelicals to politics was still in its infancy, and Lindsey's enthusiasm about the links between Bible prophecy and the details of the Arab-Israeli conflict was remarkable pre-cisely for its worldliness. The brew of political analysis and apocalyptic ur-gency proved potent, and after *LGPE*, evangelical intellectual life would never be the same. The book's unexpected popularity was at once a fore-shadowing and an exemplar of the emerging white evangelical politiciza-tion—a development that would consistently include a strong investment in modern Israel's military battles.

Lindsey's focus on Israel was not an innovation; it drew on a long history of passionate evangelical interest in the politics of Zionism. Certain basic doctrines had changed little since the late nineteenth century, including the commitment to biblical inerrancy and the premillennialist view that Christ must return before the thousand-year reign of peace predicted in the Bible could begin. Still drawing on the interpretations popularized in the 1909 Scofield Reference Bible, evangelicals held that the Bible's accuracy could be tested and confirmed by political developments, especially those concerning Israel. Fundamentalists who followed the Scofield framework were often referred to as premillennial dispensationalists: "premillennialists" because they believed that Christ would come before the promised millennium of peace, and "dispensationalists," based on their view that God had a specific plan for different peoples in different periods.[35]

Although many aspects of the time line of Christ's return and the ensuing millennium were (and are) hotly debated, certain doctrinal issues were commonly agreed upon. One important signal of the approach of the Second Coming of Christ would be the return of Jews to the Holy Land. As the end times approached, an Antichrist would arise, claiming to bring peace. At some point, believing Christians would be bodily lifted to heaven in an event premillennialists call the Rapture. After the Rapture, the Antichrist would oversee seven years of "tribulation"—economic distress, natural disasters, suffering, and the persecution of both Jews and newly converted Christians. Sometime during this period, Jews would rebuild the Jewish Temple in Jerusalem and begin the ancient rituals of temple sacrifice. At the end of seven years, Israel, threatened by a confederacy of most of the nations of the world, would face down her enemies at a final, terrible battle of Armageddon, during which Christ himself would return to do battle for Israel. After Christ's return, the millennial reign of one thousand years of peace would begin.[36]

This focus on Israel as an instrument in God's plan for human history had bolstered evangelicals' consistent support for Zionism in the early part of the century. An even greater enthusiasm was generated with the founding of Israel in 1948. While mainline Protestants had been divided on the issue of Israel (in the years just before and after the creation of the state, they debated the partition plan, the conduct of the 1948 war, the status of Jerusalem, and the situation of the Palestinian refugees), evangelicals and fundamentalists saw the establishment of a Jewish state in Palestine as a clear validation of prophecy and of God's action in history.[37] As William Culberson of the Moody Bible Institute wrote in 1960, Israel's rebirth was "the most striking of all the signs" of an imminent Rapture.[38]

If the founding of Israel was one sign, it was not the only one, and in the years after the initial excitement over the creation of Israel had worn off, the contemporary Middle East had appeared to be something of a backwater, even to evangelicals who had an interest in prophecy. Then, in 1967, the Israeli army's taking of Jerusalem galvanized evangelical observers. The war, the seemingly miraculous Israeli victory, and the transformation in the status of Jerusalem (a formerly divided city now entirely controlled by Israel) made contemporary Israeli-Arab politics look imminently and urgently relevant to evangelicals. L. Nelson Bell, the executive editor of *Christianity Today*, wrote in July 1967 that the Israeli takeover of Jerusalem "gives a student of the Bible a thrill and a renewed faith in the accuracy and validity of the Bible.... If we say, as the Arabs do, that Israel has no right to exist, we may prove blind to her peculiar destiny under the providence of God."[39] The "prophecy clock" had jumped forward, and statements about the prophetic significance of the war and its aftermath soon became an evangelical staple.

Thus while the mainstream media had focused on the logistics of Israeli victory in the 1967 war, and while Jews wrote of its effect on their emotional relation to Israel, Christian evangelicals interpreted the event as evidence of the quickening pace of God's action in human history. Lindsey argued that the 1967 war proved the final war of Armageddon would likely be triggered by the Arab-Israeli conflict. "It is [the Arabs'] ... fierce pride and smoldering hatred against Israel that will keep the Middle East a dangerous trouble spot" (76). For Jerry Falwell, then a young minister in Lynchburg, Virginia, the war also inspired the beginning of what would become a long-standing interest in Israel; he took his first of many trips to the Holy Land shortly thereafter.[40] And in 1970, Billy Graham, the nation's most well-known and most influential evangelist, released the feature-length film *His Land*. Featuring upbeat tunes by the young Christian singer Cliff Barrows, and criticized, even at the time, for its simplistic support of current Israeli policies, the film was the beginning of the multimedia presentation of evangelical interest in Israel.[41]

Four years after the war, a remarkable gathering of evangelicals consolidated the newly politicized interpretations of prophecy. In 1971 "The Jerusalem Conference on Biblical Prophecy," spearheaded by Carl Henry, the editor of *Christianity Today*, proved a stunning success, drawing fifteen hundred delegates from thirty-two nations.[42] The conference was welcomed by the Israeli government, which even provided the hall. Prime Minister David Ben-Gurion greeted the guests, who were entertained by the Jerusalem Symphony, Anita Bryant, and groups of Arab and Israeli schoolchildren. The speakers included prophecy luminaries from the United States and Europe, as well as two Arab Christians (no Muslims), one converted Jew, and one Israeli Jew.[43] Many of the speakers argued that Israel's control over Jerusalem was an indisputable sign that God's final dispensation for human history—when he would once again deal directly with his Chosen People, the Jews—was about to begin.[44] The speakers affirmed Israel's control over the newly occupied territories. One reminded the audience that God had promised Abraham all the territory from the "river of Egypt" (the Nile) to the great river of the Euphrates (in Iraq).[45] Biblical prophecies were coming true, the speakers said, but if evangelicals were to understand the events of the end times, they would need to know about worldly politics as well as Scripture. If, eventually, Jesus would descend from the heavens to fight for Israel, for now God seemed to be acting through the tanks and tactics of the Israeli military.

The rise of prophecy talk influenced the emerging arena of Christian mass media and popular culture. In the early 1970s, evangelical preachers began to make extensive use of television. Several changes in the previous decade had made the medium more attractive: in 1960, the Federal Communications Commission changed its regulations to allow stations to charge for the time they set aside for religious programming, and a number of UHF stations, usually independently owned, welcomed the chance to sell airtime in the slow Sunday morning period. By 1977, paid programs accounted for 92 percent of all religious airtime, as opposed to 53 percent in 1959. Since most mainline Protestant churches were not willing to solicit for donations on the air to pay for the shows, religious programming on television was soon dominated by smaller evangelical denominations or large independent churches. Jerry Falwell had begun broadcasting on local radio within a week of the founding of the Thomas Road Baptist Church in 1956; by 1967, he was producing the weekly *Old Time Gospel Hour;* in 1971, he was buying time on two hundred television stations around the country.[46] Audiences for Christian television shows grew noticeably in the 1970s: in April 1978, 28 percent of the public claimed to watch religious broadcasts, as opposed to only 12 percent in 1963. The introduction of the consumer VCR in 1975 also expanded the programs' visibility, since both films and television shows could now be remarketed on videocassette. By the end of the decade, evangelicals had moved outward from the "parallel institutions" that had long been part of their subculture, reaching new audiences while also increasing the media consumption of previous converts.[47]

The reach of evangelicals extended beyond the subculture of primarily southern and midwestern evangelical churches into the larger public. Although commitment to biblical inerrancy remained more common in the

South (as late as 1986, 40 percent of southerners described themselves as born-again Christians, as opposed to 19 percent of residents in the Northeast), the presence of evangelical believers increased, both numerically and in terms of geographic spread. In 1976, a Gallup poll found that fifty million people in the United States declared themselves to be "born-again." By the mid-1970s, public figures from across the spectrum had announced their conversions: Nixon aide and Watergate figure Charles Colson, rock star Eric Clapton, pornographer Larry Flynt, and former Black Panther Eldridge Cleaver all went public as born-again Christians.[48] Two weeks before Jimmy Carter was elected the first twentieth-century president to claim membership in an evangelical denomination, *Newsweek* magazine declared the Year of the Evangelical, commenting on "the most significant—and overlooked—religious phenomenon of the 1970s: the emergence of evangelical Christianity into a position of respect and power." The rise of evangelicalism and fundamentalism had, in the words of Richard Neuhaus, "kicked a tripwire alerting us to the much larger reality of unsecular America."[49]

Evangelicals made biblical prophecy a central part of their new visibility. In 1975, one popular evangelist, Jack Van Impe, who was already reaching a large audience via television, radio, cassettes, and books, presented a TV special, "The Middle East, World War III, and Christ's Return." Periodicals and newsletters also began to appear, with titles like *It's Happening Now* and *End Time Messenger*. The 1972 film *Thief in the Night*, the first part of a trilogy about the Rapture, was released on video and became a best-seller in Christian bookstores.[50] Lindsey himself would go on to write at least seven more books on biblical prophecy by the end of the decade, selling a combined total of more than twenty-one million books.[51] In 1977, *The Late Great Planet Earth* became a movie, with Orson Welles as the narrator. The film featured interviews with a rather extraordinary range of luminaries, including Israel's ambassador to the United Nations; peace activists; and a long procession of well-known ecologists, sociologists, and military experts. By 1978, even *Christianity Today*, the organ of mainstream evangelicals, was commenting sardonically on the rise of "doomsday chic."[52]

The Armageddon fascination in prophecy circles was only strengthened by political events in the Middle East. In 1973, the October war between several Arab states and Israel brought the United States to full nuclear alert. Soon after, headlines screamed about the Arab oil boycott that followed the war, and lines formed outside gas stations. As the crisis deepened, it was easy to argue that the Middle East was the world's most dangerous flash point, even without resort to Scripture. For evangelical writers and preachers, how-

The Good Fight / 173

ever, passages from the Bible highlighted the implications of a Middle East conflict whose consequences every American was feeling at the gas pump.

In 1974, the president of Dallas Theological Seminary, John F. Walvoord, followed up his earlier, scholarly study of prophecy by enlisting his son, John E., to coauthor a far more popular book, *Armageddon, Oil, and the Middle East Crisis,* provocatively subtitled *What the Bible says about the future of the Middle East and the end of Western civilization.* Illustrated with photos of Israeli troops in territories occupied in 1967 and long lines of cars outside U.S. gas stations, it described "the Oil Blackmail" of 1973 in terms that were very critical of both Arabs and U.S. oil policy. The maps and charts in the book were clear and detailed, explaining the European dependence on imported oil and tracing the history of major Arab-Israeli wars, including careful attention to military hardware and battle strategy. Listing the economic and political power that Arab nations accumulated in the wake of the 1973 war, the Walvoords argued that Americans would soon be faced with a difficult choice: the United States would give in to the Arab world in order to keep access to oil and the friendship of the industrialized nations, or it would support Israel and face the consequences. They had little doubt of the likely (and disastrous) outcome: "Inevitably, major concessions will have to be made at the expense of the power of the United States and of the security of the state of Israel."[53]

The Walvoords described a multipolar world, one in which U.S. military power was no longer sufficient to meet all threats, be they economic boycotts from the Arab states or determined guerrilla war in Vietnam. They predicted the United States would take the easy way out when faced with an issue of principle. The authors' "realism" about the nation's economic requirements was thus shot through with a moral horror that, in the post-Vietnam era, the United States would not fully support its allies if the cost was too high. The initial edition of *Armageddon, Oil, and the Middle East Crisis* sold 750,000 copies in the mid-1970s, but even these impressive sales almost certainly underestimate the intellectual impact within the evangelical community of a popular book by someone of John F. Walvoord's stature.[54]

For most prophecy writers, the return of Israel to all of its biblical heritage was a prerequisite to Christ's return. The Antichrist would then establish his headquarters in Jerusalem; most believed that he would initially present himself as a Middle East peacemaker. At some point during this period, Israel would find itself at war with the Soviet Union, at war with the Arabs, and then with most of the world. Several writers saw in the rise of Arab oil power a clear invitation for the predicted Soviet conflict with Israel. *The Coming Russian Invasion of Israel,* for example, explained that the

Soviet Union might have many secular reasons for such an attack, from grabbing Israel's mineral wealth to using the country as a base for spreading communism. "In the past twenty-five years," the authors explained, "Russia has increasingly become Israel's arch-enemy.... There has been an enormous outlay of men and material for war steadily flowing to the Arabs from the Soviets, and it amounts to one of the most fearsome military mobilizations in history."[55] Under the Nixon administration, détente with the Soviet Union had become U.S. policy, and arms control agreements were being negotiated at a rapid pace. In this context, evangelicals focused on the likelihood of a Soviet-Arab attack on Israel, rather than fear of an attack on the United States, as the moral armor of their anti-Sovietism.

Taken together, these materials built upon the presumed anti-Soviet and anti-Arab sentiments of their audience to shore up a pro-Israeli position. By 1984, Tim LaHaye's list of the reasons biblical Palestine was "the world's focal point in these last days" replicated the standard arguments in the much more militarized vein that had by then become common:

1. The Bible said so. ("Prophecy is history written in advance.")
2. Palestine is the center of the earth.
3. Oil! Oil! And more oil!
4. Israel is the third-strongest military force in the world.
5. Israel cannot be intimidated.[56]

The anti-Arab feelings generated by the oil boycott thus became an argument for strengthening the alliance with Israel. If Israel and the United States both had the Soviet Union and the Arabs as enemies, then Israel and the United States had that much more in common, if only the U.S. government would take the right stance.

As the evangelical movement became more outward looking in the 1970s and 1980s, many fundamentalists looked beyond Israel and the Soviet Union, increasing their missionary efforts abroad, particularly in Latin America. These international involvements did have an influence on Latin American politics and on cold war policy. But no part of the world held nearly the attraction that the Middle East and especially Israel had for evangelicals. In the words of John F. Walvoord, those other regions and their conflicts were not "prophetically significant."[57]

Evangelicals' very strong support for Israel and Israeli foreign policies in the wake of the 1967 and 1973 wars did not escape the attention of the Israeli government. Successive governments over the course of the 1970s clearly made a strategic decision to return the evangelicals' interest. The relationship had first emerged after Billy Graham's film *His Land* impressed Israeli officials with the potential base of support they might find among evangelicals. Israel's backing of the 1971 Jerusalem conference was an early manifestation of what would become its long courtship of conservative American Christians. As Paul Boyer has pointed out, the Israeli leadership privately "ridicul[ed] premillennialist readings of prophecy as those of a six-year-old child." But the Labor governments of the 1970s recognized the value of evangelicals as an important political bloc and dealt with them accordingly.[58]

In 1978, the right-wing Likud government came to power in Israel. By then, evangelicals had already proven themselves a political force in the United States. And, despite its support for Democrat Jimmy Carter in 1976, the community had strongly conservative inclinations. Conservative Christians in the United States shared with the political Right in Israel not only support for a free market economy and opposition to the Soviet Union and communism but also a commitment to Israel's military power and political expansion. The alliance soon solidified.

The strong connection between Israel and evangelicals left many American Jews increasingly worried about what they saw as the anti-Semitism of evangelical teachings. The status of Jews within evangelical theology was, at the very least, ambiguous. In the prophecy literature, Jews held a multifaceted and complex position: on the one hand, most evangelicals were quick to point out that Jews had failed to recognize Christ, and that the collective failure of the chosen people to do so was a cause of particular displeasure to God. On the other hand, dispensationalists believed that at the end times, God would once again be dealing directly with his "earthly people," the Jews, as opposed to his "spiritual people," the Church.[59] Thus the destiny of the Jews as God's chosen people and their central role in God's plan for humanity was a matter of doctrine. (For this reason, perhaps, converted Jews—Derek Price, Charles Lee Feinberg—played a particularly visible role in the prophecy-interpretation genre.) But in a religious tradition in which "earthliness" or "worldliness" was often despised, the positioning of Jews as merely God's people on earth, as opposed to in heaven, certainly seemed like a demotion of Jewish "chosenness." Evangelicals also generally presumed the mass conversion of large numbers of Jews during the tribulation, and the terrible deaths of many others. As one sociologist has pointed out, whatever else these prophecy interpretations suggest, at the very least they indicate the "instrumentality" of Jews for premillennialists.[60] But beyond this particular theological interest in Jewish conversion at the end times—and here one must note that evangelicals viewed all those who had not been converted to Christianity as both recalcitrant and doomed—there was little direct anti-Semitism in the prophecy literature and a good many statements of God's love for the Jewish people.

Anti-Semitism was present in fundamentalist thinking, however, as became clear in a now infamous comment made in 1980 by Bailey Smith, then president of the Southern Baptist Convention. Speaking before a gathering of ministers in Dallas, Smith remarked disparagingly on the ecumenical trends of the major political parties: "It is interesting at great political rallies how you have a Protestant to pray, a Catholic to pray, and then you have a Jew to pray. With all due respect to those dear people, my friends, God Almighty does not hear the prayer of a Jew." The comment reached the national media and set off a storm of criticism. Although Smith's comment sounded like profound anti-Semitism, it might also be interpreted as simple fundamentalist exclusiveness. As William Martin has pointed out, had Smith been asked, he likely would have also argued that God was equally deaf to Hindus, Muslims, and Buddhists.[61] At the very least, however, Smith's statement indicated a stunning insensitivity to Jewish concerns and a more general lack of appreciation for pluralism in American life.

As Smith was being criticized roundly in the U.S. media, Israeli officials and American Jews worked together to craft a response. Smith was immediately invited to come to Israel as a guest of the Israeli government. After his trip, Smith announced, "The bottom line is that you're going to read my name many times in the future in activities supporting the Jewish people and Israel."[62] Of course, there was a conflation of Jewishness with Israel here, one aided by the apparently savvy decision to sponsor Smith's Holy Land trip. In order to deal with Jews and Jewishness, Smith had to go first through Jerusalem. American Jews, and their varied concerns about church and state, civil liberties, domestic policy issues, and so on, were marginalized in this equation. Sidestepping the theological issue of conversion and the political issue of pluralism, evangelical Christian relations with Jewishness were forged through, and exemplified by, their relations to the Israeli state.

Modern Israel's attention to American evangelicals, and evangelicals' attention to Israel, proved useful for both sides. Still, the primary reason for evangelical interest remained biblical. All agreed, drawing on Genesis 12:1–3, that God would bless those who blessed Israel and curse those who cursed it. In their enthusiastic study of Israeli military capacity and their detailed examination of maps, invasion routes, and attack strategies, evangelicals were first and foremost searching for clues to the end times.

This fascination with doomsday sometimes seemed to involve a strange excitement at the prospect of imminent destruction. Lindsey, for example, had apparently thrilled at the prospect of the "billions of dead" and "rivers of blood" that would ensue at the battle of Armageddon: "For all those who trust in Jesus Christ, it is a time of electrifying excitement" (58).[63] Lindsey's swelling phrases brought him criticism and sometimes ridicule by commentators, including liberal Christians who were offended by his weirdly enthusiastic tone, but his attitude was far from unique. In 1971, then-governor of California Ronald Reagan unsettled a group of dinner companions with his apparently hopeful attitude toward the end of history. At a fundraising dinner in Sacramento, Reagan asked one colleague at the table if he had ever read Ezekiel chapters 38 and 39. When the colleague assured Reagan that he had, the governor, who had read and "repeatedly discussed" LGPE in the previous year with other associates, launched into a passionate lecture, insisting that, with the founding of Israel and the development of nuclear weapons, the stage for the final battle was being set. "It can't be too long now," Reagan said heatedly. "For the first time ever, everything is in place for the battle of Armageddon and the Second Coming of Christ."[64] Strange as they might seem to outsiders, such views were understandable, given the premises of evangelical doctrine: if this indeed was the generation that would see the fulfillment of the last of biblical prophecies, it would be witness to the most important events in human history.

This combination of excitement and dread also linked prophecy literature to the New Age, occult, and UFO fascinations that arose at the same time.[65] Each of these genres had a different overt worldview, yet they all shared an iconography of supernatural intervention that challenged secular political logic and undermined liberal humanist assumptions about stable, self-knowing human agency. As the decade progressed, even a mainstream evangelical like Billy Graham became simultaneously more literalist and more focused on the intervention of the spiritual world: his book Angels sold one million copies in just thirty days in 1975.[66] In a period of profound political instability and economic dislocation—the failures of Vietnam, the oil crisis, the economic downturn that began in 1974, fears about the environment and natural resources, and the rise of black radicalism and feminism—the turn to alternative narratives of cause, effect, and meaning was quite common. Fredric Jameson has argued, in his analysis of the rise of the conspiracy film in the 1970s, that the gaps in linear, rational logic apparent in certain kinds of cultural texts highlighted (if only implicitly) the failure of rationality in the face of a dramatically transformed world system—an economic, political, and social universe that no longer seemed comprehensible by the old methods. Or, as one observer put it, quite simply, "In the 1970s, you didn't have to be born-again to reach for notions of the Apocalypse."[67]

After 1967, evangelicals looked around and saw a world spinning out of control; immersed in the post-Vietnam discourse of failure, they harbored doubts not only about the social fabric of American society but also about the nature of U.S. power in the world. In that moment, white evangelicals entered the world of politics for the first time in decades. And they developed a specific (and perhaps otherwise unexpected) interest in military and foreign policy issues, related to their almost obsessive fascination with the question of how and when the last great war—the war to end all wars— would come about. The Apocalypse at Armageddon would be horrific and frightening, but it would also be the one truly just war, with Jesus himself fighting on the side of righteousness.

TERRORISM IN THE NEWS

The evangelical interest in Israel as the site of earth's final battle did not occur in a vacuum. It paralleled, and intersected, a more secular focus on Israel's visible contemporary battles in what soon came to be known as the "war against terrorism." That conflict began in earnest after the 1967 war; as a result of Israel's occupation of Arab territories, Palestinians began to take a more militant stance in the struggle over land. It was during the Olympic Games in Munich, West Germany, however, that the Palestinian-Israeli conflict was brought home to the world. There, on the morning of September 5, 1972, eight Palestinian guerrillas sneaked into the Olympic compound, broke into the rooms of the Israeli team, and took nine Israeli team members and their coaches hostage. In the process, they killed one athlete and one coach; about eighteen others had escaped through a back window. The guerrillas were members of Black September, a strike force for the Palestine Liberation Organization (PLO), though officially disavowed. In return for releasing their hostages, they demanded the release of two hundred Palestinians held in Israeli jails.[68]

Once the attack began, sports reporters from all over the world suddenly became political correspondents. As tense negotiations between the Palestinians and West German authorities continued throughout the day, ABC, the U.S. network covering the games, began continuous live coverage. Sportscaster Jim McKay anchored the broadcast for sixteen straight hours, with the assistance of announcer Howard Cosell. Peter Jennings, a young Middle East correspondent for ABC who was in Munich to do feature stories, managed to sneak into the Italian athletes' quarters and report by phone.[69] Officially, the compound was sealed off, but the high-mounted television cameras captured extraordinary footage: one gunman, his head covered by a dark hood, as he came out to the balcony of the dormitory to examine the situation outside; then German sharpshooters dressed in athletic gear, positioning themselves around the building.

Figure 15. Masked Palestinian gunman on the balcony of the Israeli dormitory at the Munich Olympics in 1972. This image came to symbolize the massacre of eleven members of the Israeli Olympic team by Black September. Photo courtesy of Wide World Photos.

Away from the cameras, the situation grew more and more desperate. From the first, the Israeli government had refused to release any prisoners or to negotiate with Black September. German officials took a gamble: they promised the Palestinians safe passage out of the country, then looked for an opportunity for sharpshooters to pick off the guerrillas. The plan went wrong, and at the airport a gun battle broke out between the Palestinians and German police. Several of the Palestinians were killed, and three surrendered. Before the battle was over, the Palestinians killed all of their hostages, who were tied up and blindfolded in waiting helicopters. One group died when a guerrilla shot into a helicopter and then tossed in a grenade; the second group was machine-gunned down. At first, the information from the airport was confusing. One German official told reporters that all the Israelis had been freed alive; that news was greeted with joy in both the United States and Israel. When the truth came out a few hours later, the response was shock and anger.[70]

The massacre at Munich had an extraordinary impact in the United States. Accounts of the attack and the Israeli deaths dominated U.S. news for more than a week. Reports dissected the Israeli refusal to negotiate, why and how the West Germans had bungled their attack, as well as the controversial decision to continue the Olympic Games in the wake of the murders. American media also detailed the heroism of some of the Israelis during the initial moments of the attack (the two men killed in the dormitory had both died trying to protect their teammates), as well as the names and life stories of the dead.[71] Many accounts pointed out the terrible irony that these deaths had happened at Munich, where the West Germans had been self-consciously trying to counter the memories of the Nazi games of 1936.[72]

Earlier in the spring, Palestinians and their allies had killed dozens of people in terrorist attacks, including both Israelis and international travelers, but none of those events carried the emotional force that Munich had for Americans.[73] Perhaps, as some commentators suggested, it was because the spirit of the Olympics had been destroyed. Or perhaps it was the fact that, this time, U.S. television was on the scene, reporting events as they happened. ABC won twenty-nine Emmys for its work in news and sports at Munich, as well as accolades from the Senate floor to the *New York Times*.[74] Live terrorist TV was born at the Munich Olympics.

Observers in the United States once again made comparisons to Vietnam. By this time, however, the hope of a military victory in Vietnam had all but disappeared. Despite President Nixon's promise of "peace with honor," the war already had spread into Cambodia and Laos, and increasingly people talked about the impossibility of winning against an "unconventional" enemy, one that they believed broke the rules of war by bringing women and children into the battle. For liberals, Vietnam was often mentioned as an example of the limits of military power for solving conflict.

The day after the Olympic massacre, ABC news anchor Howard K. Smith made just such a link, suggesting that the lessons of Vietnam could be used in the Middle East. Despite the Olympic killings, he said, both Israel and the Arab states still had an interest in negotiating a settlement rather than continuing their conflict. Peace was inevitable, Smith said. "The retreat from violence may be slow, but, in the end, sheer weariness with a crisis that has long outlasted any national interest is going to prevail in the Middle East—as it will in Vietnam."[75] Senator George McGovern, the Democratic nominee for president, also drew the comparison, speaking at a campaign rally in Los Angeles. His message was apparently simple: "Stop the killing!" he said. "Stop the killing everywhere around the world!" But in fact, the politics of the Vietnam connection were quite politically charged. Some people remained skeptical of the implicit moral equivalence suggested in that formulation, and the next day, at another meeting with a group of rabbis, one rabbi asked McGovern if he really meant to imply that U.S. pilots in Vietnam could be compared to Arab terrorists. No, McGovern replied, they were on different moral levels. Still, he insisted, killing was killing, and he expressed his "own horror and indignation at the killing that is taking place . . . in Vietnam."[76]

These comments built upon an interpretation of the lessons of the war that had, by the early 1970s, become the dominant one among liberals and some moderates. The quagmire in Vietnam, they argued, was an indication of the changing nature of world power. The United States still relied too heavily on force in situations where political, economic, or diplomatic solutions were more likely to be effective.[77] This "global managerialist" model was certainly committed to maintaining the power and influence of the United States, and to pursuing what its adherents considered to be U.S. economic and political interests. Its proponents insisted, however, that the United States must come to terms with the political realities of a multipolar world, one in which diplomacy and negotiation, rather than military power, should be the key to maintaining U.S. interests.

But just as the debate over Vietnam was far from settled, the response to Munich was also quite divided. Conservatives had a different take than liberals, and mainstream reactions were ambivalent and inconsistent. Even as some observers suggested that the solution to excessive violence was negotiation, others anticipated and supported an Israeli counterattack. When, in response to the Olympic killings, Israeli war planes bombed ten villages in Lebanon and Syria that Israel claimed were guerrilla strongholds, leaving scores of people dead, *CBS Evening News* rather smugly reported the words of one senior Israeli official: "I hope they got the message." Editorialists generally announced themselves able to "understand" and "sympathize" with the Israeli actions, even as they worried that instability and violence in the Middle East would increase.[78]

The instability and violence that did in fact follow were widely reported: the 1973 Arab-Israeli war; the outbreak of civil war in Lebanon; and several major terrorist attacks, in Israel and elsewhere, in 1974 and 1975, including an attack on Israeli schoolchildren at Maalot and the taking hostage of several OPEC oil ministers in Vienna.

Then, in June 1976, four hijackers claiming to be affiliated with the Popular Front for the Liberation of Palestine (PFLP) began what would arguably become the most famous incident of terrorism in a decade obsessed with terrorism. The hijackers, who included two West German radicals and at least one South American, plus several Palestinians, took over an Air France flight from Tel Aviv and forced it to fly to Entebbe, Uganda. There, with the apparent collusion of Ugandan president Idi Amin, the hijackers moved 259 hostages (including the crew) to an old unused terminal at the Entebbe airport, from where they began negotiations, demanding that Israel and several other states release Palestinian or pro-Palestinian prisoners held in their jails.

By 1976, hijacking had already become a dominant international concern. Since 1968, a total of twenty-nine hijackings had been staged by Palestinian or pro-Palestinian groups, while other groups, including several in Latin America as well as the Symbionese Liberation Army (SLA) and the Weathermen in the United States, had carried out kidnappings or assassinations. For many observers, however, there was a particularly close association between Palestinians and terrorism not only because of Munich but also as a result of a widely reported series of hijackings and airport killings in the early 1970s. Perhaps the most infamous of these was Skyjack Sunday in 1970. In one day, the PFLP commandeered three different international flights and forced them to land in Jordan (a fourth attempt failed). Three days later, yet another flight was hijacked. Nearly 450 passengers were held hostage for six days; eventually, all were released.[79]

Realizing that the Palestinian case was damaged by the furious public response to these events, the main faction of the PLO, Arafat's Al Fatah, had pledged after Munich to end all guerrilla or terrorist activity outside of Israel and the occupied territories. The initial goal of the violence had been to bring attention to the Palestinian cause as an independent issue in the Arab-Israeli conflict. After the defeat of the Arab armies in 1967, Palestinians had begun to take leadership in their own movement, and the PLO developed from a front organization controlled by Arab states into a genuinely autonomous Palestinian umbrella. In the wake of the 1967 war and the Israeli occupation of the West Bank and Gaza, and in the context of the appropriation of their land and the ongoing military and political oppression in the occupied territories, many Palestinians believed that violence against Israeli and other civilians was justified. However, the goal of gaining world attention had also included the hope of gaining world sympathy; that hope had been severely undermined by the strong moral condemnation of terrorism in the United States and Europe. Still, the disavowal of international terrorism by major Palestinian organizations did not protect them from blame when smaller factions, such as the PFLP, took matters into their own hands; for those who paid little attention to the political differences among Palestinians (and this included almost everyone in the United States), the distinctions were unintelligible.[80]

Shortly after the PFLP-allied hijackers brought their hostages to Entebbe in late June 1976, the Israelis began planning a secret rescue operation. They were faced with a delicate diplomatic situation, however, since in any such rescue attempt, French or American citizens could possibly be killed. Then, over the course of the week in Uganda, the hijackers inadvertently opened the way for unilateral Israeli action by releasing all the hostages except for the 104 Israeli citizens. Just after midnight on July 4, 1976, Israeli commandos flew the long flight to Uganda and surprised the guerrillas and the Ugandan military. They attacked, killing all the hijackers and loading the hostages into planes bound for Israel. During the raid, which lasted about ninety minutes, three hostages and one Israeli soldier were killed. The Israeli soldier who died, the ground commander of the strike forces, was a young lieutenant colonel named Jonathan Netanyahu. He immediately became a national hero. His brother, then living in the United States with his parents, moved back to Israel shortly thereafter. There, the future prime minister Benjamin Netanyahu's first major public role in Israeli life was that of brother to a national martyr.[81]

Immediately, Israelis poured nearly $3 million in unsolicited contributions into a voluntary fund for the Ministry of Defense, which had recently faced budget cuts. The U.S. news media reported with a sense of awe the unrestrained enthusiasm of Israelis for their military. "Aircraft flew over Jerusalem," *Newsweek* enthused, "skywriting, 'All our respect to Zahal'— the Hebrew acronym for Israeli Defense Forces."[82]

The significance of this support could not have failed to register in a nation that had just watched the disastrous final pullout of American troops in Vietnam the year before. As the North Vietnamese had marched into Saigon, U.S. officials fled, while desperate Vietnamese allies tried to fight their way onto the helicopters. By 1976, the public image of the U.S. military was quite low, and the assessment of Vietnam as a misguided intervention and an unwinnable war was commonplace. In contrast, American observers were riveted by the Israeli raid, and almost as enthusiastic as the Israelis themselves. Newspapers and journalists from across the political spectrum—from the *Nation* to the *National Review*—expressed their support.[83] The U.S. ambassador to the United Nations, William Scranton, defended Israel's action against criticisms that Israel had violated Uganda's territorial integrity: "Under such circumstances," he said, "the government of Israel invoked [*sic*] one of the most remarkable rescue missions in history, a combination of guts and brains that has seldom if ever been surpassed. It electrified millions everywhere and I confess I was one of them."[84] Secretary of State Kissinger was, simply, "immensely pleased."[85]

In fact, given the coincidence of the date (the Fourth of July, on the American Bicentennial), neither public officials nor journalists were above

Figure 16.   Joyful Israelis celebrate in July 1976 as the hostages return from Entebbe, Uganda, where they were freed by a secret Israeli commando unit. Photo courtesy of Wide World Photos.

making grandiose statements implying that the Israelis and the hijackers had orchestrated their crisis with the United States in mind. As one State Department official effused, "The Israelis gave us a very special birthday present this July 4th."[86] Another observer, flush with a vicarious victory, indulged in biblical rhetoric, saying that the Israelis had given a gift to all the world for the U.S. Bicentennial. That gift, he said, was "the Eleventh Commandment: thou shalt not bow down to terrorism."[87]

The Israeli action almost immediately entered the realm of popular culture. Long stories explaining "how they did it" appeared in several major papers and magazines and at least one television news special.[88] The first quickie book on the raid was in the stores within three weeks. Less than a year later, more than six books had been published, including one aimed at a junior high school audience.[89] At least three films were made, one an NBC television movie (*Raid on Entebbe*) and another (*Operation Thunderbolt*) produced by an Israeli film company, Golan-Globus, which in the 1980s would become a major producer of B action movies in the United States.[90]

Figure 17.   The Israeli Superman rescues his people. This editorial cartoon appeared in newspapers and magazines around the country. AUTH © 1976 *The Philadelphia Inquirer*. Reprinted by permission of Universal Press Syndicate. All rights reserved.

In the United States, as in Israel, the Entebbe hijacking was understood as a criminal action inflicted on the innocent. The Palestinian hijackers and their allies likely had a different view, seeing themselves as guerrilla warriors fighting a war on international territory, with civilians less as targets than as weapons. But American responses to Palestinian actions had hardened considerably since Munich. When the eleven athletes were murdered at the Olympics, it led to a surprising number of calls for Israel and the Palestinians to negotiate an end to their ongoing conflict. Four years later, when scores of people were taken hostage, but no one killed (until the rescue raid), links to the larger political conflict were all but invisible.

American interest in the rescue was framed partly as human drama, but also as a discussion of the issue of will. "Once again, and most strikingly," editorialized the *National Review*, "the Entebbe operation showed that in political and military matters, *will* is the decisive factor."[91] As with the framers of National Security Council document 68 in 1950, who had insisted that the cultivation of will was necessary if the United States was going to challenge the "perversions" of the Soviet Union and establish postwar American hegemony, the question of American will was once again paramount. Israel's relative strength of will was taken as the point of contrast, as American observers quickly constructed the lessons of Entebbe for the United States, with U.S. failures in Vietnam as the implicit backdrop. Right after the raid, the military-oriented *Aviation Week and Space Technology* suggested that, while it would not always be possible to duplicate the circumstances of Entebbe, the basic formula—"an uncompromising attack on the international outlaws, wherever they find sanctuary, delivered with the best technical means available"—should become policy.[92] And not only conservatives made the point. Walter Mondale, accepting his nomination for vice president at the Democratic National Convention in August, got one of "the biggest roars of applause" of the five-day event when he said, defiantly, "We reject ... the idea that this nation must sit by passively while terrorists maim and murder innocent men, women, and children."[93]

Despite all the talk about will, however, Entebbe was important to Americans less because the Israelis had exhibited will than because they had won. At Maalot in 1974, the Israelis had shown great force of will by sending in commandos to rescue a group of schoolchildren held hostage, but most of the children were killed in the rescue attempt, and Maalot, despite its iconographic status in Israeli national mythology, was not widely discussed in the United States.[94] Similarly, the U.S. rescue of hostages on the *Mayaguez* in 1975 (in which forty-one Marines died trying to rescue thirty-nine crewmen of a ship seized by the Cambodians) did not evoke nearly as much enthusiasm, precisely because, despite an extraordinary display of the will to fight, the Marines had not managed a clear-cut victory.[95] *U.S. News & World Report* made this clear when it enriched its coverage of Entebbe with a sidebar on the failed U.S. rescue mission into a North Vietnam prison camp in 1970.[96]

In fact, the implicit and explicit comparisons of Entebbe with Vietnam enabled the reinterpretation of the Vietnam War being mounted by conservative intellectuals, who in the mid-1970s had begun to promote the idea of a "Vietnam Syndrome." The concept reiterated an older interpretation of the war, which insisted that the United States could have won in Vietnam with sufficient application of military power. But it was also a claim about the war's legacy: in the wake of its failure to use force properly, the nation was afflicted with a profound failure of nerve. Against those who argued that realism required the United States to recognize a multipolar world, conservatives insisted that realism required a different calculation. The conservative academic theorist Jeane Kirkpatrick (who would go on to become the U.S. ambassador to the United Nations in the first Reagan administration) summarized this view in a 1977 interview: "We are daily surrounded by assertions that force plays no role in the world. Unfortunately it does, in most aspects of society, especially in international relations. Therefore a culture of appeasement which finds reason not only against the use of force but denies its place in the world is a profoundly mistaken culture—mistaken in the nature of reality."[97] In the later 1970s, this interpretation of reality increasingly began to take on the mantle of "common sense." After Entebbe, it did not have to build an argument from scratch; conservatives could—and often did—simply gesture toward the example of Israel. For those who diagnosed the Vietnam Syndrome, Entebbe was a clear example of the positive and successful use of force. Enthusiasts took Israel as a model for American action; they focused on the importance of Israel as both a moral exemplar and an admired military power. Indeed, it was the harnessing of moral discourse *to* military power—in a period in which both were undergoing radical critiques—that made the combination so potent. After Entebbe, and after Saigon, Israel became a prosthetic for Americans; the "long arm" of Israeli vengeance extended the body of an American nation no longer sure of its own reach.

VIETNAM AFTER ISRAEL

In 1977, the movie *Black Sunday* opened to enthusiastic reviews. Directed by John Frankenheimer and adapted from Thomas Harris's best-selling novel of the same name, *Black Sunday* built on the memories of Munich to suggest a nightmare scenario: pro-Palestinian terrorists plotting to attack another iconic sports event, the Super Bowl, where they aimed to kill more than eighty thousand Americans. Working from audience concern and knowledge of recent terrorism and well-known Israeli responses, *Black Sunday* was also perhaps the first film to take the Vietnam Syndrome as its theme. It did so in ways that explicitly linked Israel, Vietnam, television, and reconstructions of a battered American masculinity.

From the beginning, *Black Sunday* takes "realism" as its hallmark, referencing Munich to establish the credibility of a Super Bowl attack and describing the terrorists as Black September members, rather than using a fake organizational name. Although, as several reviewers noted at the time, the plot has some significant credibility gaps, the "aura" of the film depends on its "snatched from the headlines" sensibility and on the audience's belief that the events it depicts are—in the words of the ad campaign—"possibly as near as tomorrow."[98] The major characters in *Black Sunday* are three. The first is the Israeli hero, commander David Kabakov (Robert Shaw). Kabakov discovers the initial indications of the Super Bowl plot while on a raid in Beirut. He goes on to assist, but also to outdistance and outthink, the FBI and other U.S. police agencies. The main Palestinian terrorist is Dahlia Iyad (Marthe Keller), a beautiful, ruthless Black September member who works by sexual manipulation. Dahlia sexually and emotionally controls the third character, Michael Lander (Bruce Dern). Lander is an ex-POW who was taken captive as a navy pilot in Vietnam. After the war, he found work as the pilot of the Goodyear blimp, and the plot revolves around a plan for Lander and Dahlia to use the blimp to fire thousands of steel darts into the crowd at the Super Bowl.

It is Lander who provides the pivotal link between Palestinian terrorism, American soil, and the legacy of Vietnam. The audience is first introduced to him near the beginning of the movie, as Dahlia and her comrades, a group of Palestinians and one Japanese, are watching a black-and-white film. In the film-within-the-film, Lander is a POW in Vietnam who apologizes for his "war crimes" and admits that, as a pilot, he bombed hospitals and children. *Black Sunday* allows its audience to view the black-and-white sequence as if seeing it from within the room; the image is distant and distanced, and Lander is presented both to the guerrillas in the room and to the audience of the film as a strange but important specimen. His statement ends with "I call upon the American people to stop the war."

The fact that the guerrillas have access to the film makes it clear that they have political links to communist Vietnam. More important, the filmed confession establishes Lander's primary identity: he was a POW who did not have the strength to withstand Vietnamese torture and so testified against his country, returning home in disgrace to face court-martial. This initial profile also suggests that he has a continuing problem with his masculinity; Dahlia announces that she can control him and that "he is completely dependent" upon her. Later we learn that he was impotent upon his return home from Vietnam.

Black Sunday's main action unfolds in a dual track: on the one hand, the psychosexual intrigue between Dahlia and Lander, as they plan and prepare the attack; on the other, the attempts to uncover the plot by Kabakov, working in conjunction with American officials. Kabakov has several frustrating encounters with U.S. police and intelligence agencies, since both institutions tend to be too cautious and too bureaucratic to be effective. The Israelis want to act quickly and decisively; the Americans want to make sure of everything before they move forward. Kabakov and his partner resort to their own methods, uncovering the details of the plan bit by bit.

But there is a problem. Kabakov faces another, equally serious, threat—the possibility that at a crucial moment his masculinity will fail him.

BLACK SUNDAY
It could be tomorrow!

Paramount Pictures Presents a Robert Evans production a John Frankenheimer film starring Robert Shaw, Bruce Dern, Marthe Keller "Black Sunday" co-starring Fritz Weaver and Bekim Fehmiu, Music Scored by John Williams, Director of Photography John A. Alonzo, A.S.C., Executive Producer Robert L. Rosen, Based on the Novel by Thomas Harris, Screenplay by Ernest Lehman, Kenneth Ross and Ivan Moffat, Produced by Robert Evans, Directed by John Frankenheimer, Services by Connaught Productions, In Color

[R] RESTRICTED 〔Read the Bantam paperback〕 Panavision,® A Paramount Picture

Figure 18.   Promotional poster for *Black Sunday* (1977).

Kabakov has had a reputation for ruthlessness, but now he is becoming disillusioned with violence. He has, as his partner warns, "come to see both sides—and that is never good." In fact, the film itself seems to present something of "both sides" of the conflict, in that it gives at least minimal background information to suggest Dahlia's motivations (she and her family were made refugees with the founding of Israel in 1948 and suffered under

Israeli occupation in the Palestinian camps). But the issues behind the Israeli-Palestinian conflict are clearly secondary to the film's primary concerns. The threat of Kabakov's becoming less ruthless—and it *is* a threat, within the film—structures the investigation track of the plot and makes gender stability a political issue.

Kabakov's hesitation affects his work just once, very early in the film. During a raid in Beirut, Kabakov and his men attack the Black September stronghold where Dahlia and the others are meeting. The raid, clearly designed to recall the *real* Israeli raid into Beirut that killed three Black September leaders in 1973, is shot in dark half-light. The Israeli soldiers arrive at the headquarters, where they conduct a disciplined room-by-room search-and-destroy mission. (The look of this scene, from lighting to set, would be repeated in several action movies in the 1980s, including *Delta Force* and *Navy Seals*, only with the Israeli soldiers replaced by Americans for raids into Beirut.) At one point in the search, Kabakov bursts in on the "girl" Dahlia, who is in the shower. Seeing her there, beautiful, naked, and afraid, he decides not to kill her.

This decision—Kabakov does not shoot the naked young woman in the shower—is the enabling condition for all the action that follows. Because Dahlia survives the raid, she is able to continue planning the attack; many innocent people die in the hunt for her, and she eventually kills Kabakov's partner. At several points, Kabakov notes that his failure to kill Dahlia was a terrible mistake. But within the logic of the film, it was impossible for him to have killed her: the close-ups of her frightened face, with the camera closer to her than to him, indicate that his decision to let her live is the decision required by the film, not just because she is crucial to the plot but because, from the point of view of the camera, the scene produces her as one-who-will-live. For Kabakov to have shot someone, particularly a woman, who had just been filmed in close-up would have looked like cruel slaughter. At the very end of the film, when Dahlia *is* killed by Kabakov, she is filmed only in medium shot. This refusal to kill Dahlia when she is vulnerable establishes not so much Kabakov's weakness but his fundamental morality and his appropriate heterosexuality. This heterosexual identity offers an anchor, the promise of a dependable masculine entity in a sea of political doubt. When Kabakov's partner is killed, he once again turns ruthless, leading the hunt for Black September and becoming, with the blessing of the plot and the camera, unapologetically and brutally violent. It is only with this renewed commitment to violence that the tide is turned for the Israeli and American efforts to uncover the details of the attack. The film thus anticipates a certain recuperation of violent masculinity several years before the emergence of the militarized post-Vietnam bodies that would dominate Hollywood in the 1980s—beginning, most obviously, with the first of the Rambo films, *First Blood*, in 1982.

Black Sunday switches frequently between the two centers of the plot, thus allowing for a sustained contrast between Kabakov and Lander. Lander is also quite ruthless, showing no feeling for other human beings. But he is also consistently identified through the interconnected tropes of failure of will, sexual failure, and the military failure of the United States in Vietnam, all of which will be linked to his motivations for committing terrorism. The film frequently reminds the audience of Lander's loss in Vietnam: every time he goes through a crisis, a combination of sexual inadequacy and military humiliation is restaged. In one crucial scene, Lander visits his case officer at the Veterans Administration. Decked out and pitiful in his blimp pilot's uniform, he tells the case officer about his relationship with his ex-wife, Margaret. While a prisoner, he was obsessed with her potential infidelity. And before he returned home, Margaret had been visited by a navy officer, who warned her of the high incidences of homosexuality and impotence in POWs. Margaret soon divorced Lander, and it is clear that his impotence played a role. But now, Lander announces proudly (referring to Dahlia), "I don't have that problem anymore." The case officer asks delicately about Margaret's behavior while he was in prison, and Bruce Dern as Lander creates a genuinely sinister moment when he sneers at the officer: "Yeah, she was getting a little *dick* on the side, if that's what you mean." Later, as if to write the Freudian subtext in bold, Lander explains his motivations for killing thousands of Americans at the Super Bowl: "They took it away from me; all those *guys* too, with their two little weenies and a roll, sucking on a Coke; they cheer the big game and they cheer court martials—all the big events."

Fairly late in the film, when Lander believes the plan to attack the Super Bowl has been foiled, he puts on his dress uniform and pulls out all his old medals to show Dahlia. Describing how he has been fired from the Super Bowl job, Lander aims to convince Dahlia that he is, in fact, man enough to have carried out the attack. Dern's acting in this long scene is a tour de force of Method-style intensity, as he careens from humiliation to humiliation, spouting threats against America before finally collapsing into a weeping, self-pitying heap. In this scene, as throughout the film, Lander's failures of masculinity are always knitted right back into the political fabric of the film: his submission to the Vietnamese, the court-martial, and the plot to attack the Super Bowl. Masculinity is never a free-floating trope; it is always tied to national identity and political will.

Lander will try to destroy America; Kabakov will try to save it. At the climactic Super Bowl scene, Kabakov single-handedly stops the blimp and kills Dahlia and Lander.[99] The final third of Black Sunday, centered on the Super Bowl game, carefully orchestrates a sense of "realism" that highlights the film's political salience. Frankenheimer includes crowd and game footage shot at two Orange Bowl games, where Bicentennial flags hang in the background. Famous football players are filmed leaving their bus and entering the stadium. Well-known CBS announcers Pat Somerall and Tom Brooksheir play themselves. They narrate the game in their familiar voices as if the film audience were watching the game "in real life"—that is, on television. The television coverage of the game plays a role in the plot, since the blimp takes pictures for TV, but it also reminds audiences of the famed television coverage of the Olympics, drawing on those media memories as signifiers of "realness." The film uses this reality effect to position football as America's national game, attempting to give it the iconographic status of the Israeli Olympic athletes at Munich. The two teams, the Pittsburgh Steelers and the Dallas Cowboys, were, along with the Green Bay Packers, perhaps the greatest teams in the game in the late 1970s, when football itself was clearly the dominant sport in the country.[100] "You can't cancel the Super Bowl," says NFL commissioner Pete Rozelle, playing himself. "It's like canceling Christmas." As the events unfold and the terrorists seem about to succeed in their attack, the film often intersperses surprisingly long sequences of the game being played, with the announcers in the background. There are shots of actual fans waving signs, of the famous Dallas Cowboys cheerleaders, and of plays on the field. To make the point that the terrorists are striking at the heart of "America," the film (re)produces football as national icon, as symbol of masculinity, and as (implicitly) a kind of "safe war" alternative to the real violence that threatens.

During the Super Bowl, it becomes clear that the properly masculine Israeli, having overcome his doubts and reservations, is in the final instance the only one who has the skill, the experience, and the toughness to stop the terrorists. He is no longer, in Jeane Kirkpatrick's words, "mistaken in the nature of reality." In such a context, it is clear what Kabakov stands for: the Israeli saves America and teaches the nation what is necessary to save itself.

AMERICA'S ISRAEL

In May 1979, Kevin Phillips, a leading conservative intellectual who had worked for Richard Nixon, published a widely cited article on the emerging phenomenon of neoconservatism. In his assessment of the state of conservative politics in the late 1970s, Phillips argued that, despite the media attention they had received, neoconservatives would never manage to achieve real political power. The neoconservative movement, as he defined it, was made up of well-known intellectuals and activists, including Irving Kristol, Daniel Patrick Moynihan, and Norman Podhoretz. He described this group as "distressed ex-liberal Democrats" who had been disenchanted with McGovern in 1972 and who needed a banner to rally around. Several elements, Phillips said, made this specific strain of conservatism "a nonstarter in North Carolina or South Boston," including the "New York city parochialism" and the "intellectualism" of its leaders. In addition, Phillips argued—with more than a suggestion of anti-Semitism—that neoconservatism had "disproportionately Jewish antecedents" and thus focused too strongly on Israel. While he disagreed with those who had suggested that neoconservatism's origins were *primarily* with Jews who had become hawks on issues of Israeli security, Phillips argued that "neoconservatism's strong preoccupation with Israel does suggest a genesis and a partial *raison d'être* not deeply shared by the country as a whole."[101]

This provocative and impressively misguided assessment appeared about eighteen months before the 1980 elections that swept Ronald Reagan to power on a landslide, ushering in a conservative resurgence that fundamentally reshaped the American political landscape. After 1980, neoconservatives *were* influential—active in the Reagan administration, cited in the press, interviewed on television, and consulted for their policy views. Despite what Phillips had said, "real political power" was theirs indeed. Phillips had believed that a concern with Israel was "not deeply shared" outside neoconservative circles, and thus would marginalize the conservative movement. He imagined a focus on Israel as a rather esoteric foreign policy investment, derived from special interest group politics and based on ties essentially ethnic or religious—something akin, perhaps, to Irish American support for the Irish Republican Army. Ten or twelve years earlier, he might have been right. But by 1979, something fundamental had changed in non-Jewish Americans' perceptions of Israel.

The same month that Phillips published his article, Jerry Falwell, working with several other activists of the New Right (including Paul Weyrich, who had founded the Heritage Foundation), announced that he and his colleagues had begun a new organization, the Moral Majority. They were not simply a religious (Christian) organization, Falwell said, but instead were willing to work with anyone "who shared our views on the family and abortion, strong national defense, and Israel." Shortly thereafter, Falwell issued the Moral Majority's platform statement, which listed ten tenets of the new organization. Number 6 read: "We support the state of Israel and the Jewish people everywhere...."[102] As evangelicals and fundamentalists organized themselves, they surprised a great many people in the conservative camp who, like Phillips, had paid little attention to evangelical theology and thus never would have believed that Israel would have mattered in "North Carolina" or in Falwell's Virginia. Like so many others, Phillips did not see how the issue of U.S. support for Israel, far from being an obstacle, helped to secure the conservative coalition that came together to elect Reagan in 1980.

In fact, by 1979, ties between the new Christian Right and Israel had moved from being primarily theological and emotional to quite literal and explicitly political. When the Moral Majority was founded, Falwell had already traveled twice to Israel (in 1978 and 1979) as a guest of the Likud government. In the fall of 1978, he had visited the West Bank settlement of Alon Moreh, where he spoke out in favor of Israeli settlement policy. Falwell told reporters, and later repeated in his preaching, that he believed that Christians must involve themselves politically in such a way as to guarantee that the United States would support Israel:

> In recent years, there have been incidents at the very highest levels that would indicate that America is wavering at this time in her position on the side of Israel. I believe that if we fail to protect Israel, we will cease to be important to God. For the Christian, political involvement on this issue is not only a right, but a responsibility. We can and must be involved in guiding America towards a biblical position regarding her stand on Israel.[103]

Late in 1979, during a fund-raising dinner in New York, Prime Minister Menachem Begin presented Falwell with a medal named in honor of the militant Zionist activist Zev Jabotinsky, making him the first non-Jew ever to receive the honor.[104] A couple of years later, Falwell said again what he had long been preaching: "To stand against Israel is to stand against God."[105]

Despite (or perhaps because of) such success stories, American Jews continued to be concerned about whether the new political power of evangelicals would also mean an increase in anti-Semitism. But as the New Right coalition emerged, several Jewish intellectuals argued for the viability of an alliance between conservative Christians and conservative Jews. Writing in *Commentary*, Irving Kristol, a former Marxist who had gone on to become a major leader of the neoconservative movement, took to task those Jews who, while becoming more conservative on economic and race issues, had remained wary of the Moral Majority. (This move rightward involved only a minority of American Jews, most of whom continued to identify as liberal.) American Jews, Kristol argued, needed to recognize the depth and importance of the Christian Right's pro-Israel politics. Referring implicitly to the incident in which Bailey Smith had said that God does not hear the prayers of Jews, Kristol wrote: "After all, why should Jews care about the theology of a fundamentalist preacher when they do not for a moment believe that he speaks with any authority on the question of God's attentiveness to human prayer? And what do such theological abstractions matter as against the mundane fact that this same preacher is vigorously pro-Israel?" The existence of such support could, Kristol argued, be decisive for Israel's political position in the United States, and thus it mattered more than evangelicals' position on other issues. "This is the way the Israeli government has struck its own balance vis-à-vis the Moral Majority, and it is hard to see why American Jews should come up with a different bottom line."[106]

By 1980, the activism of the Moral Majority and other evangelical groups did include significant support for Israel. Evangelicals had become involved in the electoral process beginning in 1976, with the rallying of evangelical votes for Carter, and continuing into 1977, with support for the antihomosexual referendum organized by Anita Bryant and aided by Falwell in Dade County, Florida. The work continued into 1978, when conservative Christians organized to support pro-life/antiabortion candidates in the midterm congressional elections.[107]

In 1980, pro-Israel evangelicals used their clout quite self-consciously, getting involved early in the Republican primary process. In the spring of 1980, before the Republican nomination was decided, candidate John Connolly had been a strong contender for the conservative vote. But Connolly upset Falwell and others by his attitudes toward Israel, especially when he seemed to assert that the main reason the United States should support Israel was to protect access to Middle East oil, "as if fulfillment of biblical prophecy was not even a consideration."[108] Shortly thereafter, in August 1980, Reagan made a wildly successful appearance before a briefing sponsored by the Religious Roundtable in Dallas. Three months later, as the Republican candidate, he won a decisive victory over President Carter, capturing the traditionally Democratic South by carrying every southern state except Carter's Georgia.

While the question of whether it was the evangelical vote that won the election for Reagan has been hotly debated by scholars and political activists alike, there is little question that Israel was a key issue for the conservative Christians who were involved in the organizing. Thus it was perhaps a case of preaching to the choir when, in early 1981, some prominent leaders of the Christian Right sent a telegram to President Reagan after he took office: "We are concerned about morality and reaffirmation of principles of faith," they wrote, "not only on the domestic American scene but also in terms of our international affairs. From our religious, moral, and strategic perspective, Israel supremely represents our values and hopes for security and peace in the Middle East."[109]

The importance of Israel as an issue in the 1980 elections has often been overlooked. Many evangelical Christians had been educated in detail about the Middle East over the previous decade, and by the year of Reagan's election they shared with many American Jews, and not just conservative Jews, a commitment to supporting Israel both politically and militarily. Of course Israel was not by far the only issue tying conservative factions together; among other things, they also shared a dislike of Carter and of communism. But Israel certainly was one issue, and one that far too often has been ignored or dismissed.

Israel also played another role in the rise of a widespread conservative political culture the late 1970s. For many people, Israel was less the recipient of profound personal allegiance than it was an icon of positive militarism. For the conservative intellectuals who diagnosed the Vietnam Syndrome, Israel was one example of the positive use of force. In addition, Israel emerged as a strategic asset for the United States, especially after its victory in the 1973 war. A new generation of defense planners in the Pentagon argued that Israel could serve American interests in the Middle East precisely because it had the strongest military in the region and could serve effectively to back U.S. political and military goals. After 1973, every branch of the military was involved in strengthening strategic ties, by exchanging military and intelligence information. Journalist Wolf Blitzer has argued that these strategic ties also played a role in the dramatic rise of U.S. military and economic aid to Israel in this period: "If Israel were to be demonstrated to provide a useful military and strategic service to the United States, ... the aid becomes justified on the basis of self-interest as well as national morality."[110] As a strategic asset, Israel could support an active, even aggressive, U.S. posture in the Middle East.

Beyond (and connecting to) these developing policy interests, there lay the more general public enthusiasm for Israel that crystallized after Entebbe. This enthusiasm involved a kind of appropriation: Israel was a model of tough, effective military power used in a just war against terrorism. (Christian evangelicals told the story of Israel as the protagonist in another just war, that of Armageddon.) The fact that Israel was seen as fighting the good fight—and doing it well—made it an icon of all that the Vietnam War was not for Americans. As media and popular culture in the United States focused more on Israel in the 1970s, the image that emerged became implicated in the rethinking of Vietnam that was also a significant component of the conservative resurgence.

Black Sunday provided an extraordinary example of how the connection between the Vietnam Syndrome and Israel was refracted and perhaps even anticipated in popular culture. The connections the film made were indicative of what, in the 1970s, it was possible for audiences to believe. One does not have to think that either the author of the novel or the director of the film had a strong ideological intent to see that their presumptions of what was intelligible to the audience—the nation-saving role that Kabakov could play, for example—were deeply implicated in the cultural and political debates of the moment.

Black Sunday was but one participant in the much larger transformation of U.S. public discourse about Israel in the 1970s. This transformation was the result of an unplanned, uncoordinated, yet quite powerful conjuncture of diverse interests and images. What is perhaps most striking about this history is the remarkable differences in the institutions and practices that constituted it. American Jews, evangelical Christians, military policymakers, and traditional conservative intellectuals all developed their interests in Israel and its military for different reasons, and they did so from diverse sociopolitical locations, with different access to cultural capital, and with varying levels of self-consciousness. The increased identification with Israel that many American Jews felt after 1967 did not immediately seem to map with the evangelical belief that Israel was at the heart of Armageddon prophecy. And prophecy interest overlapped with—but was far from identical to—the mainstream media investments in Israel as the answer to Vietnam. What emerged at these intersections was an increased U.S. investment in an image of a militarized Israel, one that represented revitalized masculinity and restored national pride. In the context of the decade's debate about global managerialist versus conservative militarist models of U.S. world "leadership," Israel's image served to strengthen right-wing views, though the conservative argument would not achieve full hegemony until after the Iran hostage crisis in 1979–1980. To tell the history of this transformation, then, is to find the unexpected points of convergence—the overlap and reinforcement that transformed ideologically charged narratives into the "common sense" of an era.

5 Iran, Islam, and the Terrorist Threat, 1979–1989

The second feature [of terrorism], and vastly the more dangerous, is the principle that no one is innocent of politics. Terrorism denies the distinction between state and society, public and private, government and individual, the distinction that lies at the heart of liberal belief. For the terrorist, as for the totalitarian state, there are no innocent bystanders, no private citizens. Terrorism denies that there is any private sphere, that individuals have any rights or any autonomy separate from or beyond politics.

—Senator Daniel Patrick Moynihan,
"Terrorists, Totalitarians, and the Rule of Law"

"What do you want for Christmas?" [reporter to young girl]
"I want to get Daddy out of Iran."

—*ABC News*, December 25, 1979

In the United States, the 1980s began with the nightly spectacle of Americans held hostage by Iranian militants in Tehran. During the 444 days of their captivity, which began on November 4, 1979, and ended on January 21, 1981, the day Ronald Reagan was inaugurated as president, the hostages in Iran became a national symbol. Many Americans marked their solidarity with the captives with yellow ribbons or white armbands. People in coffee shops and on radio talk shows debated what should be done to free them. And for more than a year, Walter Cronkite, who in 1979 was rated in polls as the most trusted person in the United States, closed his nightly news broadcast with a reminder of the hostages and their fate: "And that is how it was on January __, the __ day of the hostages' captivity."[1] Similarly, ABC's late-night newscast *Nightline* began with a marker of the hostage crisis: Day 148 and Day 233 became signifiers in a tally whose referent needed no explanation. The United States existed on two calendars, with the number of days in captivity superimposed over the Gregorian dates. In fact, the Iran crisis became one of the most widely covered stories in television history, gaining as much sustained attention as civil rights, Vietnam, or Watergate. One Kennedy School of Government study summarized the overall coverage this way: "Instead of receding with time, eclipsed by fresh-breaking news, the story of the 'hostage crisis' mushroomed, becoming a virtual fixation for the nation and its news organizations throughout much of the fourteen-month embassy siege."[2]

On the day of the hostages' release in January 1981, President Reagan used his inaugural address to announce that "terrorism" would replace "human rights" as the nation's primary foreign policy concern. Over the next decade, the "war against terrorism" played a significant role as the theoretical structure that supported the Reagan-Bush military buildup and the determined reassertion of U.S. political and military hegemony in the Middle East, a reassertion that included, among other things, U.S. military intervention in Lebanon (1981–1983), military and logistical support for Iraq in the Iran-Iraq war (1980–1983), the sale of arms to Iran in the Iran-Iraq war (the Iran-Contra deal, 1983–1985), the U.S. bombing of Libya (1986), and the expansion of arms sales to Saudi Arabia (1985–1988).[3]

As we have seen, terrorism was already a visible concern in foreign policy and an available plot device for films and novels in the 1970s. In the 1980s, however, the discourse of terrorist threat developed in new and important ways as public reactions to the Iran hostage crisis were staged in the speeches of policymakers, in television news reports, and in the activities of communities around the country. These accounts brought Americans, rather than Israelis, into the primary position as victims of—and eventually fighters against—terrorism. For the fourteen months that it dominated the U.S. nightly news, and for nearly a decade after in various cultural texts, the Iran story became the paradigmatic signifier of America as a nation imperiled by terrorism. Debates over U.S. national interest continued in the 1980s, but debates about the relevance of antiterrorism and the Israeli model did not: Iran ended that discussion and structured a national narrative of victimization and longed-for revenge.

The discourse of terrorist threat formed in the context of the Iran hostage crisis depended on the underlying structure of a captivity narrative—those stories of whites taken by Indians that had dominated the literature of early America.[4] The hostages in Iran, like those early captives, came to represent an entire nation in its conflict with another culture; the public concern over their captivity was part of a larger story about national identity, foreign policy, and racial constructs. Gender was central to the Iranian captivity story, as it was significant at earlier points in American history, and family, domesticity, and marriage figured visibly in public understandings of the crisis. The United States was distinguished from Iran (and captives distinguished from captors) in large part by the ways that the hostages were positioned within their families, as part of the private sphere. The private sphere, identified with the activity of women and the affective life of the family, and imagined as separate from public life and politics, became politicized precisely through the staging of an imminent threat to its autonomy.[5] With the family under siege as a highly visible trope, the preservation of a privileged site for the nonpolitical life of individuals became the signifier of American national identity.

As the discourse of terrorist threat developed, during the Iran crisis and after, it helped to construct a subtle but crucial change in the imagined geography of the Middle East, a change that was marked by a reclassification: "Islam" became highlighted as the dominant signifier of the region, rather than oil wealth, Arabs, or Christian Holy Lands. None of these other constructs disappeared, of course, but they were augmented and transformed by a reframing of the entire region in terms of proximity to or distance from "Islam," which itself became conflated with "terrorism." On one level, these constructs referred to genuine changes in political identities in the Middle East in the 1970s and 1980s. Revivalist Islam *did* become a more prominent political force in places like Egypt and Lebanon, and eventually Iran, in the wake of the failure of secular nationalism to produce the promised political and moral victories against the vestiges of Western imperialism (including military victories against Israel, which was seen as an outpost of European power). The representation of this reality in U.S. public culture, however, often transformed an emergent political-religious phenomenon into the essential character of an entire region. Ironically, perhaps, this cognitive mapping of the Middle East in terms of Islam made non-Arab Iran the new synecdoche for the whole area: what had been understood, albeit incorrectly, as "the Arab world" in the 1960s and 1970s became, again, incorrectly, "the Islamic world" in the 1980s. (Islam was the majority religion in forty states and territories in 1983, including many non–Middle East states such as Indonesia, parts of Africa, and Turkey, as well as parts of Yugoslavia [Bosnia] and significant areas of what was then the Soviet Union.)[6]

The story of terrorism, captivity, Iran, and Islam was also a story about television. It highlighted the centrality of the mass media, particularly television, in the public consumption of the hostage crisis. It was television that brought the Iran hostage crisis into the homes of millions of Americans night after night, thus providing Iranians with a stage on which to air their grievances against the United States. Television came to be perceived as an actor, as implicated in some of the activities it proposed to report. The issue of the complicity of news coverage became central to policy debates about terrorism and also to television news programs' own self-representation.

After Iran, the problem of terrorism and the problem of television became intimately intertwined.

This chapter traces the cultural and political work that the representation of terrorism did in mapping certain moral geographies, and the role of that mapping in supporting U.S. expansionist nationalism. In focusing on terrorism as a construct in this way, I have no intention of minimizing the significance or the moral gravity of hostage taking, bombings, or killing. Of course, holding hostages in the embassy was both politically and morally wrong, and, as much as one might understand the anger directed against the United States by Iranians, that anger does not justify systematically enacting revenge on noncombatants. At the same time, it is not my purpose to theorize terrorism per se or to analyze what distinctions can or should be made among types of political violence. Nor is it to suggest what kinds of military activity might be more acceptable, more politically or morally justifiable, and in what circumstances. That project has been undertaken, in great detail and with varying degrees of success, by others.[7]

If my analysis does have an underlying theorization of terrorism, it is this: that of the many kinds of activity that might fit various definitions of terrorism, the discourse of terrorist threat in the 1980s focused on only one set—those highly visible and dramatic actions, such as hijackings and bombings, that came to dominate news coverage in the United States. I suggest that this narrowed definition of terrorism did important political work. As a cultural symbol, terrorism came to carry an "excess of meaning" that had powerful nationalist implications in the United States.[8] Antiterrorism then came to be central to the construction of U.S. national interests in the 1980s, finding its way into a wide range of cultural and political sites. In the discussion that follows, I first examine the television news coverage of the Iran crisis, then link the extraordinary visibility of the hostage story to the production of the icon of "media terrorism" in academic and policymaking circles in the mid-1980s. The chapter ends by tracing the trope of hostage rescue in the proliferation of popular narratives in the 1980s, focusing particularly on rescue dramas in film. In each of these very different institutional locations, I argue, terrorism, hostage taking, and captivity worked to construct the United States as a nation of innocents, a family under siege by outside threats and in need of a militarized rescue that operated under the sign of the domestic. Terrorism in the 1980s was a gendered trope that figured centrally in the imagined geography of a nationalist and expansionist narrative that staged "Americans" and the "Middle East" in a drama of conflict, threat, and rescue.

CAPTIVITY AND ISLAM

Seven years after the Munich Olympics, ABC television was once again catapulted to prominence by a terrorist event. On November 4, 1979, the U.S. embassy in Tehran was taken over by Iranian militants. Sixty-five Americans were taken hostage on the first day of what was to become the 444-day Iranian hostage crisis. Acting quickly, ABC managed to get a reporter and camera crew on the scene in Tehran. Shortly after the ABC correspondents' arrival, Iran began refusing entrance to other news teams. For more than four days, ABC was the only network able to produce its television coverage from Tehran, and it fully exploited the advantage. On November 8, ABC ran a special broadcast at 11:30 P.M., after the local news, called *The Crisis in Iran: America Held Hostage*. The show opened with exclusive footage of American hostage Barry Rosen being paraded before the cameras by his captors. "Look at this," the anchor began, "one American, blindfolded, handcuffed, today in the courtyard of the American embassy in Tehran." The hour-long news special went on to showcase the images and themes that would soon become nightly rituals: Iranians marching in the streets, U.S. flags burning, tearful interviews with families of the hostages, a concerned president considering various diplomatic and/or military options, and interviews with angry U.S. citizens. "When I see what they do to that flag," said one longshoreman, "it just gets me in the heart."[9]

Initially, both the U.S. and the Iranian governments expected the hostage crisis to be resolved relatively quickly. The takeover of the U.S. embassy by a group of students loyal to the Ayatollah Khomeini had taken most Iranian officials by surprise, and Prime Minister Mehdi Bazargan promised that his government would assure the hostages' safety and quick release. But the actual politics on the ground in Iran were more complicated. Bazargan was one of the more moderate leaders in a country still in the midst of consolidating a revolution, and he soon lost the internal power struggle to hard-liners close to Khomeini. Khomeini threw his support behind the students at the embassy, and the hostages quickly became national symbols in Iran, caught up in the new government's determination to prove Iran was capable of defying the United States.

The United States had long played a highly visible role in Iran, as the primary ally of the recently deposed Shah. The Shah had ruled Iran since 1941; in the early 1950s, he had maintained his throne in the face of an emerging democracy movement only with the help of the CIA. A Westernizing, secular leader, the Shah had established a certain base of support among the urban middle classes but had maintained his rule through the

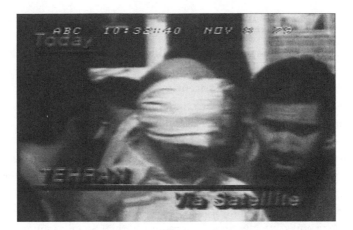

Figure 19.   Hostage Barry Rosen is brought into the courtyard and shown to the television cameras in the early days of the hostage crisis.

ruthless suppression of dissent. The internal security police in Iran, SAVAK, were known for torture and murder; they were also known to be trained and funded by the CIA. By the late 1970s, the Shah had inspired opposition that included both liberal, secular elements opposed to his antidemocratic rule and religious leaders opposed to the rapid secularization and Westernization he had introduced into the country.

Despite this opposition, the Shah was widely considered to have a stable hold on power, in large part because of the very strong alliance between Iran and the United States. That alliance had provided him with a wide range of military and political resources, the most important of which was access to advanced weapons technology. In the 1960s and 1970s, successive U.S. governments cultivated the relationship because, perhaps more than any other ruler in the Middle East, the Shah could and did shore up the stated goals of U.S. foreign policy in the region: the supply of oil, support of Israel, and containment of the Soviet Union. A major oil-producing nation, Iran consistently supported the continuing flow of oil to the United States and its allies; it was one of the few Middle Eastern nations that had not participated in the 1973 oil embargo.[10] The Shah also had positive relations with Israel, which included security and intelligence sharing. Most important, Iran under the Shah was strongly anti-Soviet and served as a valued cold war partner for the United States. The Nixon Doctrine of 1969 had declared that, in the wake of Vietnam, the United States would shore up its international military and political position by supporting regional allies. In the Middle

East in the 1970s, Israel, Saudi Arabia, and Iran became the primary pillars of that policy, each of which then provided the United States with some combination of military support, intelligence data, and political backing. (After the Camp David Accords in 1978, Egypt also became a major U.S. ally.) President Nixon had apparently explained U.S. expectations to the Shah with remarkable candor at a 1972 meeting. At the end of talks aimed at expanding U.S.-Iranian relations, Nixon looked across the table and said to the Shah, simply: "Protect me."[11]

The Shah played the role of regional client to the hilt, and as the oil wealth flowed in, the United States allowed Iran to buy virtually any and all weapons (except for nuclear weapons) in the U.S. arsenal. One analyst has described the Shah's buying frenzy as "a stampede": in the period between 1972 and 1976, the Shah ordered more than $9 billion worth of U.S. weaponry, including more advanced planes, tanks, and artillery than the Iranian army could easily absorb.[12]

With this kind of backing, neither U.S. officials nor the Shah himself expected his government to be overthrown, and certainly not with the extraordinary rapidity that it was. But opposition to the Shah's rule had mounted significantly in the later 1970s, as "modernization" proceeded with little regard for most people's religious sensibilities, and oil wealth remained in the hands of a few, while calls for democracy were ruthlessly suppressed. Despite his well-deserved reputation for ruthlessness, however, the Shah, secretly ill with cancer, was increasingly unwilling or unable to repress the mounting demonstrations that developed at the end of the decade. The protests, which were staged by a coalition of religious organizations (with different views about the role of Islam in the state), secular moderates, and leftists, soon became a call for the Shah's removal. In January 1979, the Shah left the country, effectively abdicating his throne. Shortly thereafter, the Ayatollah Khomeini returned to Iran from exile to lead what political scientist Richard Cottam has described as "quite possibly the most popular revolution in human history."[13]

The Iranian government under Khomeini's leadership was, like most postrevolutionary governments, composed of a complex set of disparate elements that had little in common but their desire to get rid of the Shah and a broadly shared hatred of the United States as the Shah's backer. With the Shah gone, the struggle over power and policy ensued in earnest. The Shah and his rule were still the source of enormous anger and frustration; the wealth he had apparently taken out of the country when he fled was a potent reminder of the misrule and corruption of the monarchy. When, just eight months after the revolution, the Carter administration decided to allow the ailing Shah to come to the United States for medical treatment, angry students stormed the U.S. embassy in protest. The hostages who were taken on November 4, 1979, became both symbol and stake in the internal struggle to define the nature of postrevolutionary Iran. Over the next fourteen months, as the Carter administration negotiated with various members of the Iranian leadership, U.S. officials often found themselves talking to Iranian officials who were soon replaced, as the Iranian government became more and more dominated by radical Islamic clergy.[14] As long as the hostages remained in Iran, they were a living symbol of the new government's refusal to be dominated by the United States; the students later called the takeover "the second revolution."[15] The hostages, Khomeini sometimes said, would not be released until the United States learned a lesson about the new realities of power in Iran.[16]

The captivity of the hostages riveted U.S. audiences, who watched the evening news in unprecedented numbers in the first weeks after the embassy takeover. The role of television at such moments was already firmly established. In 1972, ABC had televised the events surrounding the hostage taking and murder of Israeli athletes at the Munich Olympics. Four years later, the rescue of Israeli hostages at Entebbe had dominated U.S. news for weeks. This time, six days after the takeover of the embassy, ABC began running a news special on Iran every night. The head of ABC News, Roone Arledge (who had been promoted from the sports division after overseeing the Munich coverage), made the decision, he said, because everyone he saw was obsessed with the crisis. From his elevator man to his taxi driver to the pilot on his plane—"all these people care about now are the hostages in Iran."[17] Most people at ABC expected the news special to be a two- to three-week commitment; instead, "America Held Hostage" went on the air every night for four months, until March 1980, when ABC replaced it with the more generic late-night news program *Nightline,* anchored by Ted Koppel. In the early months of the broadcast, ABC estimated that the hostage specials reached an average of twelve million viewers each night.[18] The show regularly beat *The Tonight Show* in audience share, prompting one columnist to comment that "ABC has finally found someone who can beat Johnny Carson. Khomeini."[19]

The task of putting together thirty minutes of daily coverage on the same story was made considerably easier by the Carter administration's decision to keep the crisis in the public eye. According to Hodding Carter, then assistant secretary of state for foreign affairs, "the decision was made for there to be a very visibly concerned president who said in effect that the hostages' fate is a primary concern of the president of the United States."[20]

Figure 20.   Iranian protesters burn an American flag outside the U.S. embassy in Tehran in late 1979. The scene would become a familiar one to Americans over the 444 days of the hostages' captivity. Photo courtesy of Wide World Photos.

On reflection, one ABC staff member made clear the interdependence of news makers and policymakers: "We needed a daily news peg. If they had said, 'No, we're not going to talk about the hostage crisis anymore,' that show would have ultimately perished."[21] Regular evening news broadcasts were also dominated by the hostages: one analyst has estimated that, over the entire year of 1980, coverage of the hostages in Iran took up more than 20 percent of all television news; on ABC, coverage averaged 4.1 minutes out of every 22-minute broadcast.[22]

ABC's initial presentation of the crisis stressed the innocence of the hostages, their captivity, and their national identity. The first shots had focused on the humiliating vision of "one American" held captive. As *America Held Hostage* continued, the initial shot of hostage Barry Rosen in a blindfold became a staple image, a constantly invoked symbol, used at least once in most broadcasts as the illustrative on-screen icon. Updates on the hostages or reports on Iranian demonstrations and flag burnings were often introduced with this photo, which became perhaps the single most visible symbol of the crisis overall. This image soon came to represent the nation itself: if the hostages were important in Iran because of their symbolic meaning, they were important to Americans for the same reason. Both sides saw the people held inside the embassy as representing the United States, and the question of how the "United States" should be treated became the underlying political stakes of the drama being played out in Tehran.

Within the television news accounts, the hostages represented the United States not because they worked for the U.S. embassy but because of their status as private individuals, as "typical Americans." The fact that most of the hostages were American diplomatic personnel ("official Americans," in State Department lingo) was all but ignored. Instead, the hostages were consistently identified by their positions within their families, by their relationship to "home." Throughout the months of the crisis, the human drama of parents, wives, and children waiting for the hostages' return structured the news stories of Iranian demands, diplomatic negotiations, and foreign policy complexities. Gary Sick, an official in the Carter administration, described the coverage as "the longest running human interest drama in the history of television": "Never had a news story so thoroughly captured the imagination of the U.S. public. Never had the nation sat so totally transfixed before its television sets awaiting the latest predictable chants of 'Death to America' alternating with the day's interview with a brave relative of one of the hostages."[23] Although the reporters narrating the interviews and family stories usually indicated whether the hostage was in the military or part of the diplomatic staff, and listed briefly his or her title, those were not significant distinctions; very little was ever said of the specifics of a particular hostage's job within the embassy, or of his or her political convictions. Instead, television audiences learned the names of the hostages and saw frequent interviews with their families. The hostages were individualized—they had weeping mothers and stoic fathers—but not distinguished from each other.

The suffering of the families of the hostages was painfully clear, as, in interview after interview, they struggled to maintain hope for the safe return of their family members. At Christmas the first year, and again the second year, television crews went to homes and church services, inter-

Figure 21.   Barry Rosen's blindfolded visage became the icon
for ABC's coverage of the hostage story.

viewed children and neighbors, filmed presents being opened around Christmas trees in families with missing fathers or sons or daughters. As the
months wore on, the "hostage families" became a new kind of figure in
American public life: they gave interviews, held their own press conferences,
and attended commemorative events in local communities. They also had a
powerful status as moral agents in the realm of politics. Families traveled to
meetings with government officials in Europe, and on one occasion, Ted
Koppel arranged for the wife of one of the hostages to confront an Iranian
diplomat on *Nightline*.[24] These families represented their husbands or children in the Tehran embassy, but they also became more broadly representative; they were not the nation-state as public institution but the national
community constituted through its families, and now under siege. The
hostages were identified with the private sphere, allied with family, emotions, and domesticity, rather than diplomacy, officialdom, or politics.

The yellow ribbons that soon became the predominant public symbol of
concern for the hostages were another important instance of this framework: the ribbons appeared on streetlights, pinned to blouses, and on
bumper stickers. In January 1980, a gigantic yellow ribbon was wrapped
around the outside of the Super Bowl stadium. The yellow ribbons had a
complicated history as a symbol of female fidelity to husbands or boyfriends
in times of war; they symbolized the promise of love and reentry into private life for soldiers, and now for hostages. The practice of placing yellow
ribbons was a material part of the construction of meanings about Iran; it

also provided private citizens with a simple way to identify as part of the "family" that would welcome the hostages home.[25] The location of the hostages in the world of "private life" became a way of marking them as nonpolitical, and their "freedom from politics" became one of the primary aspects of the political narrative that developed around them.

In a similar way, ABC's icon of Barry Rosen invited the audience to see the crisis as a simple story of human suffering. The moral distinction between Iranian "fanaticism" and the haunting image of a single, blindfolded man's face was the not-very-subtle subtext of many of the ABC reports. This depoliticization of the individual, his or her insertion into a position of virtuous selfhood, is the classic move of the captivity narrative; it identifies the hostage with the feminized space of family and sexuality. Identification with the private sphere is the guarantee of "innocence"; it is what constitutes the captive as the virtuous victim resisting illegitimate domination. In the case of Iran, these private individuals were counterposed to the mass of Iranians chanting outside the embassy, fists raised, their fury turned either on the people inside or on the effigies of Carter they burned outside the gates. The contrast invited those in the American audience to feel their own furious bewilderment. And despite the fact that some news accounts explained something of the history of U.S.-Iranian relations under the Shah, a determined incomprehension remained the dominant stance.[26] The news media made something of a virtue of this incomprehension. In February, after more than three months of near-saturation reporting, CBS anchor Walter Cronkite could still open his report on diplomatic developments in the hostage situation with the comment that the breakthrough might help solve "the gigantic puzzle that for the last 103 days has been Iran."[27]

The Iranian students at the embassy and their supporters, on the other hand, did everything in their power to emphasize the "guilt" of the hostages and their status as U.S. government representatives. Statements by Khomeini or other Iranian officials often referred to the embassy as a "den of spies," a designation that emphasized the official, and potentially hostile, status of the embassy employees. In fact, as is the case with almost all embassies, some of the U.S. personnel stationed in Tehran did have espionage responsibilities. (David Martin and John Walcott have argued that the eventual rescue attempt in April 1980 was made considerably more difficult by the fact that most of the CIA agents in Tehran were now hostages at the embassy.)[20] The Iranian threat to put some of the hostages on trial for spying was taken quite seriously by the Carter administration. Carter also made it clear to his staff that any such trials would have elicited immediate U.S. military action against Iran.[29] Later, many of the official papers and documents seized in the embassy takeover were published in Iran. Though they showed relatively little evidence of spying, they did indicate what the Iranians wanted to emphasize: the public and official nature of the work done at the embassy. For the captors, this was the significance of the flags and the Carter effigies, which were accompanied by repeated statements from the Iranian militants that they had no quarrel with the American people, only with the U.S. government.

The Iranian attempt to stage an ideological rather than personal confrontation was perhaps most evident in the decision, two weeks after the initial takeover, to release some of the hostages. Right after the embassy attack, boxer Muhammad Ali had volunteered to replace the hostages, saying that the militants' actions were against the spirit of Islam.[30] His offer was ignored, but soon thereafter, with the PLO serving as negotiator, the students agreed to release any women and black men who were not being held as suspected spies, on the argument that neither of these groups was as central as white men to the dominant power structure in the United States. The goal was also apparently to split U.S. public opinion; on the day the release was announced, a demonstrator in Tehran was filmed carrying a sign obviously meant for the U.S. television cameras on the scene: "American Blacks! Rais[sic] Up against Carter!"[31]

Although this rather crude attempt at revolutionary incitement got little hearing, the Iranian students had more success in getting their views across to one of the first group of released hostages. One young marine, Sergeant William Quarles, told reporters in Tehran that he had made some friends among his captors. Quarles's statement also indicated that he had been receptive to some of the political frameworks the Iranians had presented. "In a way, I kinda hate to leave them. Some of them are pretty nice people," Quarles told reporters. "I've learned a lot from what I've read and what I've seen, and I'm very saddened by some of the things that went on under the Shah's regime." The history of the U.S. relationship with the Shah, he seemed to suggest, might deserve some inquiry. Before televising this apparently shocking statement, the ABC reporter explained to viewers that Quarles's apparent sympathy for his captors was a syndrome well known to psychologists. American officials later admitted that they were "concerned about some of the statements the freed hostages have made since their release."[32]

But the explanatory power of such explicitly political approaches was overridden by the personalist and ahistorical approaches of the hostage captivity narrative. When that narrative did attempt to explain Iranian actions (rather than simply assume a posture of appalled bafflement), it did so through Islam, rather than the specific history of U.S.-Iranian relations.

Figure 22.   Sergeant William Quarles speaks to reporters after
being released by his captors at the U.S. embassy in Iran,
November 1979.

"Militant Islam" quickly became the primary narrative device for the U.S.
news media; long essays and editorials in many major publications explained "Islam" as a single, unchanging cultural proclivity to mix faith with
politics, and to express both through violence. The vast variety of Muslim
beliefs and practices, spread across four continents, were summarized in
simplistic, often overtly hostile summaries of the "essence" of Islam, which
was now allegedly on display in Tehran.[33] This explanation of events as both
produced by, and exemplary of, Islam also enabled a certain categorization
of persons: Muslims were those who made politics out of simple human
suffering.

Islam was contrasted explicitly with Christianity, and perhaps in no other
political situation in the 1970s did the mainstream media and politicians so insistently present the United States as a "Christian" nation. In 1979, after almost two decades of slow secularization of U.S. political life (and just before the
political victories of the emerging Christian Right), it was relatively uncom-
mon for the mainstream media to evoke Christianity as a public symbol of nationalism. In the discourses surrounding the Tut exhibit, for example, tropes
like modernity, rationality, and humanism were more commonly linked to
American identity. But as "Islam" emerged as the category for understanding
Iran, Christianity became remarkably prominent in the media accounts.

This mobilization of religion-as-nation was particularly evident in one
dramatic segment of ABC's *America Held Hostage* on December 21, 1979,

six weeks after the takeover of the embassy. The anchor introduced a report on a demonstration in support of the hostages by commenting that Americans and Iranians were "worlds apart in their view of the world, their values, their principles, and surely in their demonstrations." This American demonstration, the anchor opined, "was totally unlike *anything* we have seen in Iran." In fact, the "demonstration" was a gathering of foreign service officers and marines, the colleagues of the hostages, who marched silently in Washington, D.C., then gathered for a short service, where they sang "God Bless America" and several other songs. With only a minimum of voice-over (which explained that the songs were being sung at the request of one of the hostages), the camera panned the crowd, first in straight-on close-ups, then in medium close-ups shot from below, so that the camera and the television audience looked up into the faces of those singing. The camera then pulled back to a wide-angle shot of the crowd with one large American flag waving in the middle. That shot seemed to end the broadcast; anchor Frank Reynolds signed off with the American flag and the crowd in a still image beside him. But before the credits rolled, the film of the demonstration recommenced, serving as a kind of coda: a young marine, in full-dress uniform, went to the front of the stage to sing "Go Down Moses." The (white) marine's performance of the old African American spiritual was formal, almost operatic, but its resonance with the exodus story and its African American revisions were clear—this time, "the people" were not African American slaves or their descendants, nor new nations struggling against colonialism, nor even just the hostages in Iran, but the entire American nation those hostages were seen to represent. This reinvocation and reinterpretation of the black Christian use of the exodus narrative mobilized its nationalist connotations. As the singer intoned the repeated phrase "let my people go," the camera lingered on his face; when the young man stepped away from the podium, the camera pulled back to medium shot. The final frozen image was of a serious but proud marine, smiling slightly at the applause that greeted his evocative rendition of the ancient story of captivity and redemption.[34]

The reporting on the hostage crisis took on a different tone when, in April 1980, five months after the initial embassy takeover, the U.S. government attempted a military rescue of the hostages, code-named Operation Eagle's Claw. The rescue plan called for helicopters to be flown to the Iranian desert, from where they would carry members of the Delta Force special operations team (formed in 1977 in part in response to the successes of the Israelis at Entebbe) into the heart of Tehran. The team would then drive pre-positioned vehicles to the embassy, extract the hostages, and bring them back to the desert for pickup.[35] On April 24, a visibly shaken President Carter announced that the mission had been aborted at stage one, after three of the helicopters had been taken out of service for malfunction or navigational problems. Then, as the rescue team had prepared to leave the Desert One staging area outside of Tehran, one of the helicopters accidentally collided with one of the transport planes, killing eight military personnel and seriously wounding five others.

Television news coverage of the rescue failure was extraordinary in both its intensity and its tone. Several long news specials described the mission, naming the members of the rescue team who had died, interviewing their families, and detailing the furious reactions of people from across the political spectrum. The Carter administration defended its decision to launch the rescue, and the decision to abort it, amid a storm of protest from those European allies and congressional representatives who said that military measures should not have been used, as well as the outcry from those who strongly supported the idea of a rescue but who angrily discussed the mission's failures of planning and execution. Meanwhile, both television and print media produced in-depth accounts of the attempted rescue, to the extent that information was available, showing detailed maps and step-by-step illustrated explanations of the rescue plan, with arrows and charts explaining what had gone wrong, and where, and why.[36] No one who had seen the gleeful enthusiasm that greeted similar illustrations three and a half years earlier, after Entebbe, could have missed the contrast.

Then, too, there was the issue of the bodies. Left in the burned wreckage of the plane, the bodies of the eight servicemen quickly became tangible signifiers of national failure. After the Israeli rescue, U.S. television cameras had recorded the arrival home of the victorious rescue team and the flag-draped coffins that had accompanied them. Now the U.S. operation would be symbolized by the humiliation of those bodies left behind. The day after the mission, ABC anchor Frank Reynolds opened his broadcast with a melodramatic summary: "We tried, we failed, and we have paid a price: the bodies of eight young Americans still lie in the Iranian desert, victims of a daring and tragic end to the rescue mission in Iran." Unremarkable in its casual claim to "we"—by this time, television news had become all but the official mouthpiece for an outraged nationalist response to the crisis—the report also signaled what would be television's near-universal narration of the event: it was good to have tried a rescue but inexcusable to have failed. The tenor of helpless anger only increased when the bodies were taken to Tehran, where some religious authorities joined the Iranian students in unwrapping charred corpses before a gathering of demonstrators—

and, of course, the television cameras. No network showed the exposed bodies, but ABC allowed close-ups of the cloth-covered bodies and footage of the beginning of the unwrapping process, thus getting close enough to the display to be shocking.[37]

In the months following the April rescue attempt, the hostage story stayed in the news, with hopes for a negotiated end rising and waning. Conventional wisdom had it that another rescue had been made impossible, though in fact the Carter administration began planning a second try two days after the failure of the first.[38] But during the next months, little else happened to promise hope, despite ongoing negotiations.

In August 1980, news accounts focused attention on an issue that had arisen periodically since the embassy attack: the rights and opinions of Iranians living in the United States. At the end of July, almost two hundred Iranian students were arrested when a pro-Khomeini demonstration in Washington, D.C., escalated into a violent conflict with a few American counterdemonstrators. Although criminal charges against the Iranians were quickly dropped, the students were held in a New York detention center until their immigration status could be checked. The August events were certainly not the first time that public attention had been focused on Iranian students in the United States; the vocal anti-Shah or pro-Khomeini opinions of some of the students had been the source of considerable media outrage from the first weeks of the crisis. But by August, tensions were at a high point. After the demonstration, there were many calls in the press and Congress for all of those arrested to be deported, but, as one CBS reporter wearily announced, quoting a Justice Department official, "The Constitution protects even visitors to this country, and some Iranians have learned to take advantage of that."[39] Almost all the demonstrators were soon found to be in compliance with their visas and were released, going immediately from New York back to Washington for another demonstration, which was met by a group of Americans (white and African American) who staged another counterdemonstration. The Americans, carrying U.S. flags and effigies of Khomeini, chanted for the Iranians to "go home." Although the two groups were separated by a long corridor of District of Columbia police, some fights broke out, and some Iranians were hit by bottles and eggs. The Iranian demonstrators were protected by police from serious violence, but at this point, American demonstrations did not look so different from Iranian demonstrations after all.[40]

Anti-Iranian sentiment in the United States drew heavily on the stereotyped representations of the Arab Middle East that had become so prevalent in the 1970s, particularly the image of "Arab terrorism." The Israeli battle against terrorism had, as we have seen, very high visibility in the U.S. press, and the reporting of those events often had not explained Arab nationalism or Palestinian grievances with any more nuance than the current media explained Islam or Iran. The post-1973 iconography of the oil crisis was also redeployed, as the angry fascination with Arab oil wealth and "oil sheiks" reappeared, this time organized around Khomeini and Iran. For example, "Nuke Iran" or "Don't Waste Gas, Waste Khomeini" bumper stickers had been available from the early days of the crisis. More than twenty anti-Iran novelty songs were produced within the first month or so of the embassy takeover; two of them became national hits. Dart boards and toilet paper with Khomeini's image popped up for sale, in an odd kind of commodification that in some ways paralleled the irreverent purchase of King Tut T-shirts and coffee mugs. To purchase was to contain.[41]

Perhaps the weirdest example of how anti-Arab sentiment morphed into anti-Iran sentiment (and back again) is that of an Iranian wrestler who, in the early 1980s, called himself the "Iron Sheik." Here again, the "Arab Sheik" image was used to carry over oil crisis anger and resentment onto representations of Iran. As media scholar Hamid Naficy has discussed, this Iranian wrestler was often paired with a bad Soviet wrestler, and the two of them were pitted against blond "American" wrestlers, particularly Hulk Hogan. The Iranian would wave the Iranian flag and shout anti-American slogans, which then became a cue for the audience to shout and wave placards reading "Iran Sucks." (Later, with the onset of the 1991 Gulf War, this wrestler rather cleverly remade himself into an Iraqi general.)[42]

The last six months of the hostages' captivity were dominated by reports of the possibility of their release. From late July to September, a negotiated solution looked very likely. But on September 22, 1980, Iraq invaded Iranian territory, crossing four strategic junctures, including the disputed Shatt al-Arab waterway, and launching what would become the eight-year Iran-Iraq war. Many Iranians were convinced that the Iraqi attack was instituted, or at least backed, by the United States, so the onset of hostilities with Iraq made negotiations with the United States much more difficult.[43] With the hostages still in Tehran, Jimmy Carter proved to be unelectable and on November 4, 1980 (the first anniversary of the embassy attack), Ronald Reagan won the presidential election decisively. Another Christmas passed, commemorated in television specials and, once again, long interviews with the hostage families. The Iranian government was by then engaged in furious negotiations with the Carter administration. The conservative clerics in power had now become convinced that the continued holding of hostages was doing their government more harm than good. Finally, in the last weeks of the Carter administration, terms for the release of the hostages were settled upon and enacted. These terms included the release of more than $8 billion in Iranian assets held in the United States. On January 21, 1981—the day of Reagan's inauguration, and thus the last day that Iran could be sure that the arrangements it had made with Carter would be honored—the hostages were released. As a result of their 444-day captivity, the United States had, indeed, been taught a lesson about the limits of its power. But over the course of the 1980s, the impact of that lesson was surely not what any of the revolutionary elements in Iran would have hoped.

"TERRORIST THEATER"

In October 1984, *Harper's* magazine published a forum on terrorism and the media that brought together some of the nation's most prominent journalists to consider the responsibility of the news media in reporting terrorist events. The problem, as *Harper's* presented it, was the development in recent years of the "terrorist theater": a staged performance of violence in which the terrorist had become "the master of ceremonies at a media spectacle."[44] By the mid-1980s, the issues of media, representation, and visibility had become intimately tied up with the public discourse on terrorism. Inevitably, descriptions of the problem of "media terrorism," as it was increasingly known, took the television coverage of the Iranian crisis as their backdrop. By 1984, the developing mainstream consensus looked back at the embassy takeover as an exemplary moment in this new kind of terrorism. It had become something of a truism to argue that the hostage crisis had been prolonged by the daily presence of television cameras in Tehran. Television, in the words of one of the commentators, had "managed to turn the American embassy into a television stage. The Iranians had merely to appear on it in order to impose any message they wanted on the world."[45] Both liberals and conservatives tended to agree that the ongoing problem of terrorism was inexorably linked to the public visibility that the news media gave to terrorist events. In the years after the hostage crisis, a new public figure, the terrorism expert, joined with policymakers and politicians in articulating the phenomenon of media terrorism. The knowledge about terrorism produced in this circuit included its own very distinct definitions of what terrorism was, and a new articulation of why it was so dangerous.

The development of an expert consensus on terrorism had begun to take shape before the embassy crisis in Iran. In July 1979, the First International Conference on Terrorism met in Jerusalem, where it had succeeded in bringing together an impressive roster of primarily conservative international political leaders, including Israeli prime minister Menachem Begin, presidential candidate and former CIA director George Bush, columnist George Will, *Commentary* editor Norman Podhoretz, Senator Henry Jackson, and author Claire Sterling, who would soon go on to write a popular book on terrorism.[46] The conference was organized by the Jonathan Institute, which had been founded in 1976 by Benjamin Netanyahu in memory of his brother Jonathan, the Israeli army officer who was killed while leading the rescue at Entebbe. Before his brother's death, Benjamin Netanyahu had served for several years in the special forces of the Israeli army. After founding the Jonathan Institute, he became a frequently quoted expert on terrorism. He would later serve as a diplomat in Washington and as Israel's representative to the United Nations before returning to Israel in 1988. There he quickly became the leader of Israel's right-wing Likud party and, in 1996, prime minister.

At the end of the 1979 meeting in Jerusalem, the conferees adopted a joint definition of terrorism that looked back at the hijackings and airport massacres of the 1970s: "Terrorism is the deliberate and systematic murder, maiming, and menacing of the innocent to inspire fear for political ends." But the conference also looked forward: by bringing together Americans and Europeans with Israelis, the makeup implicitly suggested that terrorism was an international problem; by focusing on conservative political leaders, the roster also reflected the alliances that were developing between the United States and the Israeli right.

Although the first conference achieved a good deal of positive press coverage, it was eclipsed by the high public visibility of the Second International Conference on Terrorism, which was held in Washington in 1984 and served as the primary source for the *Harper's* special forum. Between 1979 and 1984, a great many changes had taken place on the international political scene, including not only the Iran hostage crisis and the arrival of the Reagan administration in Washington but also a complex series of events in the Middle East: the Israeli invasion of Lebanon in 1982, the subsequent U.S. military intervention in Lebanon that was effectively ended by the bombing of the U.S. Marine barracks in Beirut in 1983 by Shiite militants (in which 243 marines were killed), and the ongoing Iran-Iraq war. The 1984 conference brought together many of the same public figures as the 1979 event, but it carried a very different kind of political weight in the United States. The symbolism of moving the conference from Jerusalem to Washington was not lost on anyone; now the United States, rather than Israel, would be acknowledged as the leader in the struggle against terrorism. The conference was covered extensively in the media and was treated as an im-

portant policymaking event. When Secretary of State George Shultz addressed the gathering, his speech was reported as the top story of the day
in the *Washington Post*, despite the fact that Shultz had already given
dozens of similar speeches on the topic of terrorism.[47]

Perhaps nothing so indicates the surprising success of the 1984 meeting
as the publication history of the conference proceedings, which were first
excerpted in *Harper's* in 1984 and then published in 1986 under the title
Terrorism: How the West Can Win, with Benjamin Netanyahu as editor.
How the West Can Win was widely reviewed, including glowing assessments on the front pages of both the *Los Angeles Times Book Review* and
the *Washington Post Book World*. In both cases the reviewers were other
leading political figures: Dennis DeConcini, the Democratic senator from
Arizona who had authored antiterrorism legislation, and Robert McFarlane,
Ronald Reagan's national security adviser, who called it "the best assessment we have of ... international terrorism."[48] Other reviewers were far
less enthusiastic, and several liberals criticized the book as simplistic and
militaristic. Writing in the *Nation*, Edward Said argued that the book included several essays by academic specialists on Islam that "would be considered the rankest racism or incompetence in any other field."[49] In general, however, *How the West Can Win* presented itself, and was received by
the press, as *not* simply another analytic text but rather as a strategic manual for the war on terrorism, offering "a clear and comprehensive plan,"
formulated by experts, "with which world democracies can act to free themselves from the threat that holds every person hostage."[50] Less than a year
after its original publication, *How the West Can Win* was reissued in a
mass-market paperback format complete with lurid cover art featuring two
crossed assault rifles over a globe (and an endorsement by the well-known
liberal governor of New York, Mario Cuomo, among others).

The need for coordinated international action against the "threat that
holds *every person* hostage" was one of the central messages of both the
conference and the book. "Terrorism is the cancer of the modern world,"
declared one essay. "No state is immune to it. It is a dynamic organism
which attacks the healthy flesh of the surrounding society."[51] This trope of
an international terrorist cancer attacking the body of the West managed
to expand the definition of potential victims, while retaining the Middle
East as site and source of the infection. Cancer infects one organ but soon
threatens the whole body; Israel may have been on the front line, but now
it was the entire West, and in particular the United States, that was under
attack. This was very much Secretary of State George Shultz's argument:
"Wherever it takes place, [terrorism] is directed in an important sense

against *us*, the democracies, against our most basic values and often our fundamental strategic interests."[52] Just three months before the opening of the conference, in April 1984, Shultz had articulated the Shultz Doctrine, which called for the increased use of force in combating terrorism.

Several participants at the conference highlighted the supposedly special relationship between "Islam" and terrorism. No other cultural or religious group was singled out in this way, despite the fact that many of the participants discussed terrorist activities in Europe, Latin America, and Asia. With some caveats and a small amount of complexity, three basic reasons were given for considering Islamic terrorism to be a particular concern. First, as Bernard Lewis, perhaps the country's best-known expert on Islam, explained, Islam is a "political religion," since Muhammad founded and led a state as well as a faith. Or, as one of the other experts put it, "Politics itself has been viewed as a variant of religion, if not religion incarnate."[53] This particular fusion of state and religion was presented as in the "nature" of Islam, but not of course of Judaism or Christianity.

Second, the "world of Islam" invented terrorism. Two of the three experts devoted a significant part of their presentation to the rise of the tenth-century sect, the Assassins, as an early and emblematic example of the Islamic use of terror—and of the ultimate failure of the tactic. In addition to the dubious intellectual worth of explaining modern politics through medieval examples, it is important to note the ways in which those examples worked by inference. Khomeini's government had often been described as "harsh medieval rule," as if the Iranian revolution were simply an anachronism rather than a specific response to modernity. By explaining modern Islam in terms of tenth-century antecedents, these experts extended that association, making the implicit argument that Islam itself (not just in Iran) had a medieval character—that Muslims, unlike Western people, lived outside of time.

Finally, the expert panel posited an essential opposition between "Islam" and the "West." P. J. Vatikiotis, author of several well-known books on Middle Eastern politics, argued that "Islam" was essentially hostile not only to ideas of democracy or pluralism but also to the Western concept of the nation-state itself. In the Middle East, he insisted, the nation was considered in religious terms, so that the "community of believers" was necessarily in a constant clash with the idea of a nation-state. Muslims were thus particularly inclined to *international* types of terrorism, since they were disinclined to comprehend state boundaries. (Vatikiotis mentioned the PLO as one major source of terrorism, but he failed to mention both its secular orientation and the fact that, far from being hostile to the concept, it was fighting to *establish* a state.) Islam was hostile to democracy, and thus, "as European influence receded ... [t]he return of the traditional politics of violence was inevitable."[54] The overall effect of these presentations was to make clear that, whatever caveats they might offer, these experts were convinced of the existence of a particular Islamic tendency toward terror. This "tendency" seemed to be rooted in the idea that Islam was at once ahistorical, still operating from its medieval structures, yet also *hyper*political in its refusal to recognize a boundary between church and state.

The hyperpoliticization of Islam linked it to terror; it also connected Islam to totalitarianism. Conference participants labeled all three as antidemocratic and anti-Western, but also as instruments for the expansion of "politics" to the whole society. As Jeane Kirkpatrick, U.S. ambassador to the United Nations, argued, "The affinities between terrorism and totalitarianism are multiple. Both politicize society."[55] This was also the underlying force of Senator Moynihan's argument that the threat of terrorism lay in its challenge to the liberal belief in the separation of public and private spheres. Just as the coverage of the hostage crisis had resolutely inserted the hostages into the private space by focusing on the hostage families at home, expert discourse insisted that terrorism in general was defined by its refusal to acknowledge the "innocence" of the "private" citizen. By focusing on this alleged refusal of terrorists, Muslims, and totalitarians to acknowledge the privileged status of the private sphere, the conference participants forged one enemy from diverse political and ideological trends.

Within this formulation, "media terrorism" became the code for a certain, particularly heinous, kind of violence that seemed to be primarily interested in the television coverage the action would generate. The heart of the "global battle" against the "cancer" of terrorism lay with Western public opinion and the media that (presumably) influenced it. One centerpiece of the conference was the journalists' symposium mediated by ABC's *Nightline* anchor, Ted Koppel.[56] The symposium included several of the most prominent journalists and columnists of the 1980s, including Norman Podhoretz, editor of *Commentary*; Charles Krauthammer of the *New Republic*; syndicated columnist George Will; Bob Woodward of the *Washington Post*; Daniel Schorr, then of Cable News Network; and two European columnists, Alain Besancon and John O'Sullivan.[57] Koppel began the discussion with a provocative introduction, suggesting that the media and terrorists had developed "a symbiotic relationship." "Without television," he said, "terrorism becomes rather like the philosopher's hypothetical tree falling in the forest: no one hears it fall and therefore it has no reason for being. And television without terrorism, while not deprived of all the interesting things in the world, is nonetheless deprived of one of the most interesting."[58] In the lively exchange that followed, the discussants disagreed strongly and sometimes vociferously on questions of censorship, media culpability, and the issue of self-restraint in reporting. At one point, Daniel Schorr rather pointedly commented that it was entirely appropriate that Koppel mediate the discussion, since (referring to Koppel's rapid rise to journalistic prominence as a result of his role as anchor of *Nightline* during the Iran hostage crisis) "you are one of few Americans, along with Ronald Reagan, whose career has benefitted from terrorist activities."[59] But despite the disagreements among the participants, whose political opinions ranged from strongly conservative (Will and Podhoretz) to liberal (Woodward and Schorr), there was one remarkable convergence: media reporting of terrorist activities, it was agreed, helped to give those activities legitimacy.[60]

The journalists of the forum agreed that Western, and particularly American, media were trapped in a dilemma. The national ideals of openness and freedom of speech (and, of course, the competition among the businesses that are the media) meant that any highly spectacular event would be covered, and covered even to excess. But the representation of terrorist events, it was argued, served the terrorists in their cause. Media coverage of hijackings and bombings offered a "magnifying effect," functioning, in the words of Charles Krauthammer, as a "form of political advertising.... Like the sponsors of early television who produced shows as vehicles for their commercials, media terrorists now provide drama—murder and kidnaping, live—in return for advertising time."[61] More or less successfully, terrorists used the media as a stage; and more or less consistently, the media gave the hijackers and bombers the kind of political status they were seeking.

Within this logic, the news media was represented as terrorism's coconspirator through its insistence on reporting the activities that allowed terrorists an audience for their grievances. Television's presentation of the story was also said to inhibit the military or law enforcement activity that would actually stop and punish terrorists—that is, having the cameras there limited the kind of violent responses national governments might choose. At the same time, the media, and in particular television, was said to be *like* terrorism: its pursuit of a story violated the sanctity of the private individual; it recognized no national boundaries; it refused to "avert its eyes" in the face of what should not be shown.[62]

Although it was never said quite so explicitly, a significant underlying problem with "media" terrorism, as opposed to other types, had to do with its targets. While terrorists who focused on a "local" population were rarely a threat to Americans and Europeans, when those same terrorists wanted to get international media attention, they chose nonlocal targets to get their actions beamed into the living rooms of those Americans and Europeans. Krauthammer, for example, defined "media terrorism" by way of an oddly nostalgic comparison between the "classical terrorism" of the FLN in Algeria, in which violence was aimed directly at the French colonizers, versus a more insidious violence that was not directed at the oppressors per se. In this new terrorism, the hostages or the airline passengers were only the means, not the real object. The goal of the violence was not revenge, it was air time.[63] In this logic, "old terrorism," though admittedly violent, at least had the virtue of being uncommodified by a dependence on mass media. In this new age, relatively rare actions could nonetheless terrorize a "nonlocal" (and thus presumably "innocent") population; international news media gave the violence of third world actors salience in first world homes.

Krauthammer's delineation of the historical progression of types of terrorism—from direct and local to international and mass-mediated—was remarkably partial, even partisan. It ignored, for example, the continuing reality of terrorist activities that were *not* dependent on the media. As Bob Woodward attempted to point out, a great deal of the military activity aimed at instilling terror in a civilian population did not need television to get its point across. Woodward used the assassination of the president-elect of Lebanon in 1982 as his example, but he was largely ignored by other participants, who seemed uninterested in this merely "local" violence.[64] In essence, the distinction between "classic" and "media" terrorism was a distinction between victims; when attacked within their own borders, civilians and noncombatants simply did not hold the interest of most of the conference participants. (In fact, when the panel became part of the book, none of the liberal panelists were asked to contribute.) The panel's focus on "media terrorism" was entirely congruous within the conception formulated by the conference as a whole, which defined terrorism as a cancer and television as the agent of an infection that moved violence from the third world to the first world by attacking the innocent across state lines.

In a deft series of moves, then, the Second International Conference on Terrorism translated a rather broad understanding of terrorist activity as the deliberate and systematic targeting of civilians (to paraphrase the definition adopted at the 1979 conference), which theoretically could include a range of activities from an IRA bombing to the murder of nuns in El Salvador to the Israeli bombing of Palestinian camps in Lebanon, into a very specific focus on *international* events, particularly hostage taking, that made extensive use of the media as part of their strategy. The link between media and terrorism was constructed as both instrumental (what the media did to further actual terrorist events) and metaphoric, in the shared tendency of both the media and terrorism to refuse to respect the "right to privacy" of American and European citizens. The flexibility of this definition—and something of its essentially nationalist nature—becomes clear when one considers the near-universal habit among conference participants of referring to the bombing of the U.S. Marine barracks in Lebanon in 1983 as a terrorist event. The horrors of that attack notwithstanding, it was obviously an attack on a military installation—the U.S. Marine base. In that case, the language indicated a convenient insensitivity to the distinction between civilian and military targets on the part of those who declared themselves most committed to it.

How the West Can Win was a respectfully reviewed best-seller, but it was hardly alone in the kinds of arguments it made about the terrorist threat. While the high positions held by many of its contributors surely contributed to the book's unusual visibility, it was part of an avalanche of academic and semipopular books about terrorism published in the 1980s. These books, and the associated reviews, plus major articles in popular journals, meant that the discussion of the proper American and/or Western response to terrorism had become a noticeable popular and policy preoccupation. Walter Laquer, himself the author of one of the best-known of these studies, pointed out in 1986 that "the literature on terrorism has grown by leaps and bounds."[65] Another observer complained, "Every think tank, police force, subway system, and fast food restaurant has its own mandatory 'terrorism expert.' "[66] These productions of knowledge, simply by their extraordinary volume, helped to construct what Edward Said has called "the sheer knitted-together strength" of a dominant discourse.[67] Although the specific policy suggestions varied, as did the particular political affiliations of those producing this discourse, the presumptions about what defined "terrorism" were remarkably similar. The real crime of terrorists was not their killing of civilians (which, after all, happened in wars all the time) but their targeting of private life. The Iran crisis was the paradigmatic and originating event for a discourse that combined concerns about the victimization of "innocents," the active role of the media, and a direct attack on the "West."

RETURN OF THE HOSTAGE STORY

In the mid-1980s, as antiterrorism was dominating the concerns of policymakers, the rescue of hostages taken by Middle Eastern terrorists became a near obsession in U.S. cultural texts, inspiring films, novels, and true-story narratives. These stories inevitably took the Iranian hostage crisis as their reference point, either directly or indirectly, but they enacted a crucial transformation: in these accounts, the hostages in question were rescued, not negotiated for. They returned home as symbols of victory, not as reminders of decline.

In 1983, for example, the renowned spy novelist Ken Follett published *On the Wings of Eagles,* which recounted how billionaire businessman H. Ross Perot had organized a rescue operation to free two executives of his company, who had been wrongfully imprisoned in Iran. Publicity for the book went directly to the point: "There were two major American rescue efforts in Iran. One failed—and made grim headlines. The other succeeded...." Follett's account received ecstatic reviews and quickly became a best-seller; it was soon made into a television movie, starring Burt Lancaster.[68] Also in 1983, John le Carré published *The Little Drummer Girl,* one of the best-selling novels of the decade, which focused on the efforts of a covert Israeli team to capture a Palestinian terrorist with the aid of a naive young woman. The climax of the novel was the dramatic, last-minute rescue of the heroine by her Israeli lover. When the movie became a film a year later, the British heroine became an American, played by Diane Keaton. Although le Carré's tale was a complicated meditation on the moral complexities of violence, it was also something much simpler: a detailed exegesis of the elements of a successful rescue attempt.

In addition, hostage rescue quickly became a staple of American action movies. The film landscape had already been transformed by the success of action/sci-fi films like *Star Wars* (1977), *Alien* (1979), and *Raiders of the Lost Ark* (1981), which broke both budget and box office records. By the middle 1980s, action films dominated the box office, spawning new stars like Harrison Ford, Sylvester Stallone, and Arnold Schwarzenegger.[69] The low-budget imitators that came in the wake of these successful films made hostages and rescue a recurrent plot device, often organized around a wishful revision of the Iran crisis in militarized terms. In *Iron Eagle* (1986), for example, a teenager dreams of being an air force pilot. He finally gets his chance when he must launch his own operation to rescue his father, who is being held hostage by Khomeini-like Middle Eastern despots. Although not a big-budget film, it was successful enough to spawn two sequels.[70] In fact, Hollywood produced so many, mostly minor, films about terrorism and rescue in this period that when the Bruce Willis blockbuster *Die Hard* was released in 1988, the audience's presumed familiarity with the genre was part of the point. Just as the terrorists (who were really only robbers pretending to be terrorists) counted on FBI antiterrorism protocol to carry out their heist, the film counted on the audience to know, and to enjoy the film's commentary on, the various routines of a hostage event: the issuing of statements and demands, the arrival of the media, the bumbling of high-level officials, and the vulnerability of frightened captives. By the time Sylvester Stallone was preparing to star in *Rambo III*, *New York Times* film critic Vincent Canby felt obliged to warn the filmmakers that they had better get their film out soon, since "if they wait much longer, there won't be any hostages left."[71]

The proliferation of militaristic action films in the 1980s often has been misunderstood as primarily a right-wing reaction to Vietnam. But the political currency of the action genre is far more complicated. On their surface, action films often exhibit rather different ideological positions: the range extends from the firmly militarist *Delta Force* series to the anticapitalist populism of several Steven Seagal movies (*Under Siege*, *On Deadly Ground*), from the right-wing populism of the *Rambo* films to the mildly liberal *Die Hard* movies, which construct snobbish Europeans, right-wing Central American dictators, and the Army Special Forces as the enemies. The terrorists in the action genre are sometimes third world radicals and sometimes ex-CIA operatives; sometimes they are just evil individuals. The films' attitudes toward the official state enforcement apparatus, be it the military or the police, is similarly varied, ranging from selectively contemptuous (in the *Rambo* and *Die Hard* films) to adoring (in *Navy Seals* and *Delta Force*). It does seem clear that any understanding of the politics of action films as a genre cannot simply be read off their plots, which seem to gleefully insert left- and right-wing (or apolitical) bad guys, as well as racially diverse male and female protagonists, with barely a ripple on the surface. Ultimately, the significance of the genre derives not from the films' choice of enemies, nor from the race and gender of their heroes, but from their construction of the American family as that which must be saved.[72]

The 1986 action thriller *Delta Force* is a particularly interesting example of the post-Iran antiterrorist film, not because it has a more sophisticated plot or more developed characterizations than other films of the genre but precisely because it does not. *Delta Force* is outstanding only in the degree to which it is animated by a virulently racist and patently militarist fantasy of rescue and revenge, which manages to place only the thinnest gloss of plot and characterization over its love affair with military hardware, body counts, and men on motorcycles. (When it was released, the film was the object of a nationwide protest by the American-Arab Anti-Discrimination Committee.)[73] But as part of the routine B-level output of the studios, *Delta Force* is telling because of the ways in which it makes ob-

vious its own adherence to a sense of the emerging formulas and requirements of a genre-in-the-making.

The film opens with a shot of a single helicopter in a desert at night. A
caption reads, "Iran, Desert One, April 25, 1980," the date of the U.S. military's failed hostage rescue attempt. As the camera lingers on the helicopter,
it explodes. In the ensuing scene, the Americans begin a rapid evacuation,
but one marine, Captain McCoy (Chuck Norris), goes back into the burning
helicopter to pull a trapped comrade from the wreckage. As flames leap behind him, Norris carries the wounded man in his arms across the desert toward the last departing military plane. On board, he complains to his colonel
about the poor planning of the hostage rescue attempt. "They [the top lead-
ership] thought their plan was better," the colonel tells him. Norris responds:
"I spent five years in Vietnam watching them do the planning, and us the
dying. As soon as we get home, I'm resigning." Norris's character makes
what is essentially a generational link between the iconic status of Vietnam
for baby boomers and the reality that, by the mid-1980s, the film's target
audience of teenage males would not have been born when the war in Vietnam ended. For this younger generation, at least, *Iran* was the touchstone for
American failure.

The plot that unfolds over the course of *Delta Force* is not about the Iranian hostage situation, however, but about another hostage taking and another rescue attempt. It is a fictionalization of the 1985 TWA hijacking, in
which an Athens–New York flight was forced to fly to Beirut. *Delta Force*
recounts the story of the actual hijacking in great detail, including the fact
that the plane was flown several times back and forth between Beirut and
Algiers before the approximately twenty hostages were dispersed into various holding cells in Beirut. In the end, all the hostages were eventually released after negotiations between the U.S. government and the Shiite faction, Hizballah.[74] Despite its obvious interest in reproducing a sense of
"authenticity," however, it is this real-life ending that *Delta Force cannot* reproduce. In the movie, negotiations with the terrorists quickly prove futile,
and the army's Delta Force, with help from the Israeli military, rescues the
hostages in an impressively pyrotechnic operation. (Norris's Captain
McCoy returns from retirement for the express purpose of joining this rescue.) If the opening credits of the film were not clear enough in situating
Iran as the back story to the retelling of this new hostage crisis, the characters repeatedly refer to the failed rescue attempt. On at least four occasions,
Norris or one of his comrades makes reference to the Iran "fiasco," asking
themselves or their commanding officers whether "this time" they will be
allowed to go in and "get those people out of there."[75]

The story of the hijacking begins in the Athens airport, with vignettes that introduce several of the passengers and establish their embeddedness in families. Two happily married older Jewish couples strike up a conversation; one of them has just returned from celebrating their twenty-fifth wedding anniversary in Israel. The two women go off to shop, sharing stories of their grandchildren, and one woman shows the other her wedding band, which is inscribed in Hebrew. Also on the ground, several suspicious-looking dark-skinned men signal each other, then board. Once the plane is off the ground, it is taken over by the fanatic-looking terrorists, who are clearly Arab (they speak Arabic) and apparently Shiite Muslims (they ultimately make a connection with Ayatollah Khomeini).

As events unfold onboard, long, often melodramatic sequences outline the relationships among passengers and establish types: the brash-but-lovable Jewish women and their caring husbands; a noble Gentile priest and the two nuns who act as his family; a brave stewardess; three loyal young American navy divers; and a young family with a small daughter. Several connections unfold around the little girl and her doll, and when her father is separated from the other passengers, she gives him her doll for comfort. These sentimentalized characters caused more than one reviewer to complain that *Delta Force* was really trying to be one of the *Airport*-style disaster films that had been popular in the 1970s, "complete with a not-quite-all-star supporting cast."[76]

What the reviewers missed, however, were the ways in which these airplane scenes owed an even greater debt to the iconography of the films made about the Israeli rescue at Entebbe. In *Delta Force*, Entebbe functions as the successful (Israeli) model that could revise the U.S. failure in Iran. This link can be traced literally: *Delta Force* was made by the Golan-Globus production company and directed by Menachem Golan, the same Israeli team that made the Entebbe movie *Operation Thunderbolt*, which Israel submitted as its official entry to the Academy Awards in 1977. But it can also be seen on screen: *Delta Force* employs several of the actors from *Operation Thunderbolt* as passengers/hostages and draws on a similar set of characterizations of the passengers. The Arab terrorists, the Holocaust-scarred Jews, and the noble Gentiles are all near-direct replications. The final scenes of *Delta Force* and *Operation Thunderbolt* are also virtually identical: on the flight home after the rescue, the joyful hostages celebrate in part of the plane while the soldiers attend to one of their members who is dying. The fact that only one commando dies in *Delta Force* is also a direct reference to the loss of Jonathan Netanyahu at Entebbe. Thus *Delta Force* constructs a layered palimpsest in which the failures of the U.S. military in Iran are revised through the production of narrative and iconographic links with the successes of the Israeli military.[77]

Delta Force also adds several new elements, however, which serve to both update and Americanize the film. The most obvious is the significance of television. Television is a character in *Delta Force*, albeit one that plays a rather contradictory role. At the level of plot, the film is very critical of television. Lee Marvin's Colonel Alexander comments knowingly that the terrorists "have gotten the attention of the world, so now they manipulate the media. Perfect." But at the level of the image, the film depends on television as its authenticator. *Delta Force* is meticulous in re-creating some of the images made famous by television and print media during the actual TWA hijacking. In one scene, for example, the American pilot of the hijacked plane, with a terrorist holding a gun to his head, leans out the cockpit window on the ground in Beirut to answer questions from reporters—an exact replica of a famous news photograph. The reporters in the movie roll their cameras and snap photos, making the images that the film's viewers are invited to "remember" from the coverage of the hijacking story only a year earlier. *Delta Force* thus references news reporting of the original event, using television images to establish a relationship of authenticity between the film and the historical events it recounts and revises. Like *Black Sunday* almost ten years earlier, the film depends on the audience's memory of television to signify its own "realism."

Despite this commitment to realist signifiers, *Delta Force* is also clearly a film that inserts itself in "history" in order to revise that history's unwelcome outcome. After the plane lands for the final time in Beirut, and hostages are dispersed to areas around the city, the Delta Force team is dispatched to rescue them. From that moment on, the film begins energetically telling a story that definitively did *not* happen, but that the film invites its audience to imagine as the superior alternative to the mere negotiations that in reality ended the crisis. After the team arrives in Beirut, there is plenty of action, as the rescuers blast their way through the city, basically leaving Beirut in shambles. They whoop joyously as they race through the streets in a car chase, dispatch dozens of terrorists, blow up buildings, and—along the way—get the hostages to safety.

Even once the hostages have been saved, the hero McCoy stays behind to confront the head of the terrorists, Abdul (Robert Forster). In this penultimate scene, the film's vengeful fantasies are highlighted, as McCoy refuses to use his superior weapons to dispatch Abdul, instead lingering over a hand-to-hand battle. Of course, this extended scene gives Norris an opportunity to display his martial arts skills, but since Abdul is not a martial arts master, this is not one of the impressive showdowns that sometimes climax such films. Instead, it functions as something like a torture session, where vengeance is enacted slowly on the body of the Arab. He is badly beaten, slowly enough for the audience to enjoy each close-up of his increasingly bloody face, before he is finally dispatched with a small rocket launcher. The scene ends with McCoy back on his motorcycle once again; vengeance enacted, he smiles slightly and takes off to rejoin his team.

The final moments of *Delta Force* are focused on reunion and return. Once aboard the plane that will take them home (first via Israel), the hostages shower the military with thanks. The shots of the plane landing in Israel, where the waiting families stand anxiously on the tarmac, are designed to recall the mass-mediated memory of both the homecoming of the Iranian hostages and the Israeli return from Entebbe. Families introduced at the beginning of the film are reunited; couples kiss; the little girl gets her doll back from her daddy. The sober military men disembark silently, separate at first from the happy homecoming. But as the rescuers get on their military jet, with the U.S. flag emblazoned on the side, the hostages cheer them, throwing flowers at the departing plane. In this moment, the civilians recognize the movie's fundamental truth: the protection of their domestic tranquillity requires active military intervention. Public institutions must act to keep the private safe, and in that sense, private life is a public concern.

A year after *Delta Force*, another captivity and rescue drama appeared on the U.S. cultural landscape, this one in the form of the autobiographical account *Not without My Daughter*. Betty Mahmoody, the author of the book, was a middle-class housewife in Michigan, married to an American-ized Iranian doctor. In 1984, she and her daughter went with her husband, Moody, on what they thought was a family visit to Tehran; instead, they were forced to stay in Iran for more than seventeen months, during which time her husband and his family apparently colluded in keeping them from leaving the country. Mahmoody's captivity eventually ended with a desperate and dangerous, but successful, run across the border into Turkey. When *Not without My Daughter* first appeared, in 1987, it was reviewed positively and prominently in the major book publications; reviewers called it "compelling drama" and a "riveting inside look at everyday life in the Ayatollah Khomeini's revolutionary paradise."[78] Mahmoody's story of being held hostage in Iran was considered to have great commercial potential, and the movie rights were sold before the book was even begun.[79]

Mahmoody's tale was yet another hostage story but with a crucial difference; the site of her captivity was the home, not an embassy or a cell, and the domestic nature of her drama was significant. Mahmoody's rescue came not with the arrival of the Delta Force but through her manipulation of her husband's expectations and the strength of her determination to protect her daughter. Unlike action movies and spy novels, her maternal melodrama seemed to solicit a female audience. When the movie *Not without My Daughter* was released in 1991, it starred Sally Field, whose acting roles had long identified her with emotional, female-centered characters.

In fact, gender is the central structuring problem of *Not without My Daughter*, as it was, in a different way, in *Delta Force*. Mahmoody's deep investments in what she sees as appropriate gender roles frame not only her understandings of Iran and Islam but also her sense of what has happened to her family. At first, Mahmoody focuses on her belief that she has been taken hostage by her husband because *he* has been taken hostage by a fanatical religion that teaches him that women should be submissive. As time goes on, however, Mahmoody seems convinced that the real horror of Iran and the bankruptcy of Islam are signified less by Iranian women's restricted lives than by their domestic failures.[80]

When Mahmoody first arrives in Tehran, she resists the imposition of Islamic dress and codes of behavior, claiming her rights as an American woman to live and dress freely. Over the course of the coming months, however, she (and eventually her daughter) are forced to wear increasingly restrictive clothing: the chador on the street and conservative, heavy clothing at home. Mahmoody painstakingly details these impositions and links them to the narrow, shallow lives the other wives lead. She describes the women as fearful and dependent, the husbands as selfish and brutal men who often beat their wives: "Iranian women were slaves to their husbands, . . . their religion as well as their government coerced them at every turn" (34). In her account, the political nature of Islam creates a particular gender ideology, which insists that women are limited to the private sphere, the servants of men.

There is no reason to doubt either the reality of Mahmoody's suffering or her general account of an increasingly restrictive environment for women in Iran. Although Mahmoody does get a good many facts about Iran and Shiite Islam wrong, she clearly is giving her best understanding of events and beliefs that obviously confound her. Unquestionably, an American woman living in Iran in this period would have found herself subject both to her own sense of cultural disjuncture and to condemnation by patriotic Iranians. In the mid-1980s, Iran was still a revolutionary society, one in which increasingly strict interpretations of Islamic law were imposed, including rigid rules about the appearance and behavior of women. The combination of these constraints, enforced by harsh punishments meted out by the courts, and the impact of the terrible war with Iraq, made life in Iran, particularly Tehran, difficult—even oppressive—for many of its inhabitants. By the time Mahmoody arrived in Tehran, many exiled Iranians, even those opposed to the Shah, were speaking out against the new government.[81]

The remarkable, and deeply problematic, aspect of Mahmoody's account is not that she raises questions about the treatment of women in Iran, albeit in a crude way. Rather, it is that even as she raises those questions, they are secondary. Instead, much of the book is devoted to enumerating the failure of Iranian women to live up to a particularly American domestic ideal. From the minute Mahmoody arrives at her in-laws' home in Tehran, the one thing that bothers her more than the restrictions on her as a woman is the failure of other women to keep house properly. She is appalled by the lack of cleanliness in the homes of various family members, particularly the bathrooms. She insists that neither men nor women shower enough, that their clothes are filthy, that everyone around her stinks (26). And she is deeply offended by the food, by the fact that Moody's mother is such a bad cook. She fumes over the improper washing of rice and the inability of her in-laws to use utensils properly.

In contrast, Mahmoody takes real pride in the kind of housekeeping she does for her family, despite her furious hatred of her husband. As described on page after page, she carefully picks through the bug-infested rice; she thoughtfully shops for fruits and vegetables that are not moldy; she sweeps and mops the various houses she and her family live in, keeping them scrupulously clean, despite the fact that she can't get Saran Wrap (35) and even though her rude in-laws drop their sugar on the floor when they make tea (292). The months are punctuated by the "real American" meals she occasionally manages to cook; at the same time, she prides herself on her ability to cook Iranian food that is better than Moody's mother makes. If cleanliness is next to godliness, then American life and the American home are symbolized by Good Housekeeping.

Whether or not the upper-class Iranian women in Mahmoody's circle were in fact terrible cooks or their homes were in fact covered in cockroaches is less the point than how these images are used to bolster the larger logic of the book. The fanatical adherence to Islam has made something go very wrong for the domestic lives of these women and their men. Mahmoody's reaction connects her story to the long history of imperialist writing, and specifically to nineteenth-century European depictions of the colonized world. As Anne McClintock and others have shown, the "cult of domesticity" in the Victorian era meant that middle-class homes came to be characterized by their cleanliness and "refinement." Scrubbed floors, washed curtains, and polished boots not only distinguished the private home from the public world of work but also differentiated the middle-class European from others less clean. "Housework," McClintock argues, "is a semiotics of boundary maintenance."[82] These "dirty" others included both the industrial working class and the racialized inhabitants of Europe's colonies. By the late nineteenth century, the use of soap (made available through raw materials from the colonies) became a central symbol of the progress of the imperial nations over the "primitives" in the empire.[83] Mahmoody's disgust also resonates with the long history of anti-Semitic stereotypes: the dirty Jew, which in other circumstances becomes the dirty Arab, now the dirty Muslim.[84] Mahmoody's story mobilizes that history, focusing particularly on women and their homes as a site of uncleanliness.

The kind of confinement and limitation Mahmoody faced in Iran was, in her view, based not on nature or social convention but on politics. The threat to the family created by Islam came from the ideology that overly confined women in the home, making them "slaves" to men. Yet Mahmoody also insisted that "free" women would carry out their household duties properly. She suggested that seclusion in the home made Iranian women not *more* feminine but less so; covered in Islamic dress and thoroughly domesticated, the women of Iran had nonetheless failed as housewives.

Mahmoody presented her existence before Tehran as a life of gender freedom that was simultaneously universal and particularly American. Mahmoody's freedom did not consist in *not* being responsible for cooking and cleaning but in being able to dispatch those responsibilities with relative autonomy. The status of women as independent-minded caretakers of the domestic order looked a lot like the "freely chosen subordination" of women that had signified the privileged nationalist spaces in the biblical epics. But the idea that the liberalization of American women's roles might have come about through political and even ideological struggle was precisely *not* the argument of Mahmoody's book. Instead, the white suburban domestic arrangements she defined as "American" were understood as natural, and the specific position of women in the United States was presented as the gender order that emerged when there was no ideology present. The implication, therefore, was that only people and cultures who were hyperpoliticized by religious ideology would see gender any other way.

Mahmoody's account was symptomatic of the ways in which the developing sense of American militancy in the 1980s was framed by the logic of the captivity story: a private person, wrested from his or her home by savages, wants nothing more than to return to the family he or she left behind. But the time spent in captivity also teaches the hostage that the private life that makes one "innocent" of politics is also the thing that makes her most representative of her nation. Indeed, well before the Iran crisis, the foun-

dation of Western liberalism had been its promise of a "private citizen"—
the private sphere as protected by national citizenship.

PRIVATE LIVES IN PUBLIC

In the years after the Iran hostage crisis, an impressive array of cultural and
political texts described American bodies as vulnerable to a terrorist threat
mapped as Islamic and Middle Eastern. The problem of the decline of American world power in the years after Vietnam and the militant answer symbolized by Israel were brought home by the failures of the Iran hostage crisis. The discourse of *America Held Hostage* was energized by the implied
contrast between U.S. humiliation and Israel's successes in rescuing its
citizens.

U.S. nationalism in the 1980s insisted that its self-justification lay in
America's respect for the public-private distinction, in the protected interi-
ority of its citizens. This vision of Americans as private individuals living in
families characterized by proper domesticity was certainly not new, or
unique to this period, or to writings about Islam or terrorism. But the image
of that private domesticity as imperiled, as under imminent and severe
threat from the outside, and particularly from the Middle East, underlay a
significant strain of nationalist discourse in the years after the Iranian
hostage crisis.

In this logic, the nation-state itself was identified with the private sphere
that it was said to protect. Thus the nation's necessarily public character was
concealed by the logic that constructed its legitimacy. The United States'
interventionism abroad was justified because this world of personal feeling
and domestic ties was threatened from the outside. State-sponsored activities like counterterrorism or military force could be undertaken for the sake
of something identified as private—love, the family, revenge.

Several years after the publication of Mahmoody's book, in early 1991,
the film version of *Not without My Daughter* opened at what turned out
to be a fortuitous time, just after the launch of the Gulf War against Iraq.
Although the war pitted the United States against Iraq, not Iran, and although Iran had in fact just ended its own long and devastating war against
Iraq, the spillover effect was remarkable. With the movie's release, a mass-
market paperback issue of *Not without My Daughter* was catapulted onto
the best-seller list, where it stayed for almost four months.[03] It was perhaps
not surprising that as the United States turned to a major military action
against Iraq, the Iranian captivity story was revitalized. Terrorism's presence on the world stage enabled a narrative that constructed the United

States as an imperiled private sphere and the Islamic Middle East as the pre-eminent politicized space from which terrorism effected its invasions. For more than a decade, that narrative had worked to produce a certain type of American identity, defined by the production of individuals who were "free of politics." Within this world of vulnerable families and lovers, terrorism threatened precisely what *had* to be threatened in order to establish the dis-interested morality of the state's militarized response in the international arena. In the early 1990s, that sense of threat would be mobilized again, when, with the start of Operation Desert Storm, the United States launched its first all-out war against a Middle Eastern nation.

6 Military Multiculturalism in the Gulf War and After, 1990–1999

The point is, that history and destiny have made America the leader of the world that would be free. And the world that would be free is looking to us for inspiration.... We must play that role in whatever form it presents itself.... We cannot step back away from this position of leadership. If we can make a difference, we must make that difference.

—General Colin Powell, speaking
to the National Press Club, 1992

[The immigrants] appear as the result of colonization and decolonization and thus succeed in concentrating upon themselves both the continuation of imperial scorn and the resentment that is felt by the citizens of a fallen power, if not indeed a vague, phantasmatic longing for revenge.

—Etienne Balibar, "Racism and Nationalism"

In the early fall of 1990, the United States–led coalition against Iraq began what would become one of the largest military operations of the post–World War II period.[1] The multinational coalition of troops was initially mobilized in response to Iraq's invasion of Kuwait; the official goal was to defend the border of Saudi Arabia and also to protect U.S. and Western "interests" in the Gulf. Operation Desert Storm involved almost seven hundred thousand troops, including more than five hundred thousand Americans, in the task of avenging what President George Bush described as the "rape" of Kuwait.[2] Ensuring the continued "flow of oil" was the most common argument for massive military response; protecting the "friendly" and "stable" monarchy in Saudi Arabia was another. Yet when the president announced the deployment of U.S. troops to the Gulf region, he did so in a short speech that linked the strategic argument to an explicitly moral plea: he asked Americans to support "the decision I've made to stand up for what's right and condemn what's wrong all in the cause of peace." He backed his justification for doing "what's right," however, with a strong statement of the national interest of the United States in the Middle East:

> My administration, as has been the case with every president from President Roosevelt to President Reagan, is committed to the security and stability of the Persian Gulf.... Our country now imports nearly half the oil it consumes and could face a major threat to its economic independence. Much of the world is even more dependent upon imported oil and is even more vulnerable to Iraqi threats.... Let us be clear, the sovereign independence of Saudi Arabia is of vital interest to the United States.[3]

By 1990, then, the president was able to call upon what seemed to be a widespread understanding of U.S. interests in the region, and to have those interests serve as a common currency in the justification of a massive commitment of U.S. military power.

As a political operation, the United States–led action was extraordinary: the American government managed to pull together a coalition that included eleven Middle Eastern states and twenty-five others. With the end of the cold war, the Soviet Union was no longer a major opposing force, so there was no fear of igniting a war against a more powerful opponent. Although some people in the United States clearly did have concerns about the *biblical* consequences of American involvement—a reissue of John Walvoord's *Armageddon, Oil, and the Middle East Crisis* sold more than six hundred thousand copies in ten weeks—in the secular world, the war seemed blessed.[4] Under some pressure from the United States, even the United Nations backed the decision to intervene, issuing multiple Security Council resolutions demanding Iraqi withdrawal. Thus by the time the air war began, the forces of more than a dozen countries were staged in Saudi Arabia and elsewhere in the Middle East, all of them effectively operating under U.S. command.

As a military operation, the action was equally successful. At every stage, from the initial deployment of defensive troops in August 1990, to the bombing attack on Iraqi positions in both Kuwait and Iraq that began on January 16, 1991, to the start of the ground war in February 1991, the United States and its allies brought together an unprecedented display of military force. The military actions succeeded in driving the Iraqis out of Kuwait and in inflicting severe damage on the Iraqi military and economic infrastructure, though they did not manage to kill or overthrow Iraq's leader, Saddam Hussein. Estimates on the number of Iraqi casualties have varied widely, ranging from one hundred thousand (including civilians who died as a result of war-inflicted damage) to fifteen hundred.[5] What is quite clear, however, is that the United States achieved its major goals with an extraordinarily low allied casualty rate—fewer than three hundred Americans died in the conflict.[6] In the years that followed, the United States led the world politically in part because it operated a high-tech, high-powered military machine that seemed, at least on this battlefield, invincible.

The American armed forces that were untouchable on Middle Eastern battlefields were equally inviolable in public discussions of Desert Storm at home. In the self-consciously post-Vietnam discourse about the Gulf, those who supported the war donned yellow ribbons and bought "Support Our Troops" bumper stickers. For the most part, not even the most vocal opponents of the war found it appropriate to criticize the troops or their conduct. Antiwar protestors displayed banners and placards that called for the U.S. government to "Support the Troops: Bring Them Home." Both sides seemed to agree that "the troops" were indeed "ours"—to send or bring home, that the military meant America, and that Americans (in their diverse ways) were supporting the military.[7]

Many commentators, at the time of the Gulf War and since, have analyzed the celebratory and nationalist slant of the coverage of Desert Storm in the U.S. news media. Their criticisms have been important in establishing the limits of what the public knew, or could know, through the saturation news coverage that made the war into a television event. The televisuality of the war also has seemed, to some, to mark its "postmodern" nature: its apparent immediacy in terms of news coverage and yet its strange unreality, despite its nightly presence in American homes. In this, the coverage of Desert Storm was less a transformation than a consolidation of earlier trends. Engaging that nexus of television, representations of the military, U.S. nationalism, and the Middle East that had been forged in the coverage of Israeli actions and then in the Iran hostage crisis and its aftermath, it was the perhaps inevitable end result of more than two decades in which the Middle East functioned as a signifier for the post-Vietnam decline of the American empire. Yet the story being told about the Gulf War, by both policymakers and journalists, was that it was the beginning of something quite new. "Our troops" would represent the United States in what President Bush called the "New World Order," even as their strength and invincibility made that order possible.

In two very different ways, the success of military action in the Gulf War vanquished the ghost of Vietnam from American discourse. For the Right, the Gulf War provided the final proof that the U.S. military defeat in Vietnam, and later in Iran, had been caused by the failure of the national lead-

ership to authorize the use of adequate force and allow the military freedom
of action. The Vietnam Syndrome could be overcome with the proper
demonstration of an alternative to the Vietnam experience. Given enough
will and resources, the Israeli model of quick, decisive action would work;
new military doctrine, advocated by General Colin Powell, among others,
called for the early use of "decisive force" in any engagement. The failures
of the 1960s and 1970s could be blamed on the lack of political will to use
the military force available. As President Bush stated in a nationally televised speech at the start of the ground war: "I've told the American people
before that this will not be another Vietnam and I repeat that here tonight.
Our troops ... will not be asked to fight with one hand tied behind their
backs."[8] After Desert Storm, the specter of Vietnam would no longer haunt
the halls of the Pentagon.

To the degree that Vietnam symbolized the possibility of effective antiwar protest and large-scale social mobilization *against* the exercise of U.S.
power, the Gulf War also revised the legacy of Vietnam for the Left. Antiwar sentiment was widespread and rather well organized in the early days
of the Gulf War; large national demonstrations were held in both Washington, D.C., and San Francisco on January 26, 1991.[9] But this opposition
failed to have the slightest effect on the outcome of the conflict, nor did it
have a significant impact on public discussion of the war. The peace movement of the 1980s and 1990s was organized to oppose "another Vietnam."
The assumption was that war *meant* Vietnam and that what the Vietnam
War had shown was that, over time and with enough information, the U.S.
public would likely turn against intervention. But the Left had simply failed
to understand the changes in geopolitical circumstances that had transformed the meanings of intervention. As the cold war sputtered to an end,
third world nations could no longer count on alliances with the Soviet
Union to counter potential U.S. military action. For that reason, the situation for Iraq, isolated and without powerful allies, was very different than
that in Vietnam. Nor had the Left paid sufficient attention to the Pentagon
debates about U.S. military strategy: the advocates of "decisive force" argued that the United States should not pursue any more "low-intensity"
conflicts that might prevent the full use of airpower and military hardware.
By the time of Desert Storm, the changes in global political alliances and
U.S. military theory had made a protracted engagement unlikely.

In addition, the Left had not fully accounted for the changes in what the
military signified in American culture. For those leftists and liberals who
had lived through the Vietnam era, had feared the draft, and had seen the
returning body bags, the military was a dangerous part of a state apparatus

that disproportionately took the lives of people of color and the poor. But over the course of the 1980s, the all-volunteer army had come to mean something very different to most people: it signified not only patriotism but also opportunity; it was not an example of the racism in American life but a potential counter to it. The racially diverse families who sent their sons and daughters to the Gulf were often ambivalent about the risks and the dangers, but they were almost uniformly certain that the "new army" represented them, and that they, in all their diversity, represented America.

In this context, televised news coverage meant something new as well. After Vietnam, most people, including the Left, had assumed that the fundamental impact of television was to bring war to the living room and thus increase the public's opposition to violence.[10] For people across the political spectrum, this understanding of the antiwar impact of television was fundamentally challenged by the relationship forged between the hyper-representation of Desert Storm and its joyful public embrace.

THE WAR AS IMAGE

The Gulf War was simultaneously a major military action and a staged media event, and from the beginning the undeniable marriage of these two aspects has required observers to account for its new kind of media politics. From the time Iraq crossed the border into Kuwait in August 1990, the United States and its allies responded with military actions that were also consciously staged with the media in mind. In August, the United States began sending troops and supplies to Saudi Arabia in a long, slow buildup of force. Officials argued that the combined forces of the allied coalition would at least prevent Iraq from going farther and invading Saudi Arabia; eventually, the mission was expanded to include driving Iraq out of Kuwait. As hundreds of thousands of troops and untold millions of dollars worth of equipment made their way to the Middle East, the world's press corps was invited to explain their movements as a display of U.S. resolve. Also over the course of the fall, the U.S. military began a massive call-up of reserve forces still at home. As the reservists began to report to their bases, American newspaper and television correspondents were there to chronicle the human drama of those who left their families, work, and communities to fulfill their duty. Working through the United Nations, the allied coalition even managed to set a date for the start of the war: for more than eight weeks, television and newspapers reported that Saddam Hussein faced a January 15, 1991, deadline for withdrawal from Kuwait. If he did not withdraw—and few expected he would—the coalition would launch its air war.

As the media descended on Saudi Arabia to await the countdown, many observers argued that the fundamental rules of reporting had shifted in this war. The misrepresentations and absences that would typically be expected in mainstream media coverage of U.S. foreign policy had become something more insidious, an intensification of "coverage" of the events and the military apparatus that actually seemed to destroy the very possibility of critical distance or an informed citizenry.[11] The specific military actions of the coalition were of course followed in minute detail. CNN, the all-news cable network that had begun operating in 1980, set a standard of saturation coverage that was followed by the traditional networks.[12] In January, as the UN deadline for the Iraqi pullout from Kuwait approached, newscasts excitedly counted the days or hours left before the expected beginning of the action. As one observer commented, "All through the winter of 1990, the production had its own built-in 'coming attractions'—the many variations on 'showdown in the Gulf' that teased the viewer with a possible January opening on all screens in domestic multiplexes throughout the nation."[13] People in the United States watched the buildup and then the war on their televisions; they soon spoke of Patriot missiles, AWACS aircraft, and "pinpoint" bombings with a kind of insider's knowledge.[14]

Despite the amount of time devoted to reporting, the quality of the information being relayed was quite poor. The allied coalition placed tight limits on the movement of reporters in the field and prevented most "unauthorized" access to military personnel or military information.[15] Despite television's self-representation as offering "dramatic live coverage" of the conflict, there was often very little to be seen. Some of the best footage was provided by the military itself: film from the radar screens inside the airplane cockpits as they targeted and bombed selected Iraqi targets. Such images were utterly internal to the view of the U.S. military; thus they led to the frequent claim that, on TV, the war looked like a video game.[16] Even the CNN reporters in Baghdad, the only television crew to cross behind Iraqi lines, were strictly limited in where they could travel. Many times they were reduced to describing what they could see from their hotel rooms.[17] Often, in the absence of other material, the primary story became the emotions, suffering, and bravery of the reporters themselves, combined with similar stories of the emotions, suffering, and bravery of the U.S. soldiers' families back home.

For many critics of the war, however, the problem of the representation of Desert Storm went well beyond questions of censorship or adequate reporting. The dynamic of saturation live coverage led to a discussion, especially in academic circles, of the Gulf War as the first postmodern war. This was the first time, it was sometimes said, in which representation of the event *was* the event. Media scholar Tom Engelhardt has described the war as heralding the beginning of "total television"—a package of TV/movie/newspaper/bumper sticker/theme park info-tainment that was being offered to viewers by new multimedia giants like Time-Warner or Rupert Murdoch, which owned stakes in each of those cultural industries.[18] Like the Tut exhibit and the Iran crisis, the Gulf War was marketed through a broad range of commodities: American flags, of course, and yellow ribbons, which returned in force with the Gulf War.[19] There were T-shirts, too, one with an image of Saddam Hussein that said "Nuke Their Ass and Take the Gas"; another showed a camel in target sights, saying "I'd Fly 10,000 Miles to Smoke a Camel"; a third showed the mushroom cloud of a nuclear explosion with the caption "The New Iraq: Parking Lot of the Middle East." One could also buy Desert Storm bubble-gum cards or Ralph Lauren red, white, and blue coffee mugs, or perhaps settle for watching patriotic advertisements by companies like Coca-Cola. Participation in watching and shopping did not *reflect* experience, it *was* the experience.[20]

Benedict Anderson has argued that in the early development of nationalism in seventeenth- and eighteenth-century Europe, cultural consumption, particularly of novels and newspapers, helped define the parameters of the "imagined community" that made local populations into nations, fusing differences of region, language, class, or religion into a "common culture" that reorganized both time and space.[21] In the late twentieth century, the central role of television during the Gulf War suggested a hyperextension of that logic, with time organized by the disruption of routine television programming for twenty-four-hour news. The generalized social practice of watching the war on TV was, as Engelhardt points out, "perhaps the purest imagined community ever achieved—the most complete erasure of complicating social difference through the convergence of private selfhood and social identity."[22] Television had been, from its beginnings, a technology that inserted public discourse into private space. Now the crisis produced a sense that what we did in our homes was nonetheless a shared experience of great intensity.

Just before the fighting broke out in January 1991, the postmodernist philosopher Jean Baudrillard published an article in the British newspaper the *Guardian* that described the impending war as a mass-media simulacrum, that is, an event that did not need to happen, precisely because the media bombardment of the Western public with video game imagery had already created the "experience" of war in advance.[23] Even Christopher Norris, a British theorist who had spent years criticizing the tenets of Baudrillardian postmodernist theory, described the Gulf conflict as "in some sense, a 'postmodern' war":

> How else could one explain the extraordinary inverse relationship between extent of coverage and level of informed public grasp; the profusion of meaningless statistical data served up to create an il- lusory sense of objective, factual reporting; the absurd claims about "precision bombing" and "pinpoint accuracy," designed to convince us that civilian casualties were almost non-existent ... amounting, one could argue, to a wholesale collapse of the "public sphere" of informed critical debate.[24]

This profound discomfort with the media-ization of the war expressed more than uneasiness with the patriotic outpouring that accompanied it. The problem was often expressed in relationship to the earlier conflict in Vietnam, and to the received assumptions that it was television coverage— bringing a war to the dinner table via the nightly television news—that had been at the heart of the breakdown in public support for Vietnam. In fact, most observers assumed that television news had, as a medium, "a pacifist bias," in that showing the horror of war on television was likely to lead the public to tire of violence in almost any situation.[25] In the Gulf, however, the United States was winning a war that was being represented as essentially bloodless. Antiwar activists struggled with the problem of how to explain the new realities of a "living room war": the more the media covered the op- erations, the more the U.S. public supported the war.[26]

Vietnam was only part of the history being elicited and vanquished in the Gulf. The history of the Iran hostage crisis, or rather, the history of the news coverage of that crisis, was signified everywhere. ABC, for example, began each night's coverage with an icon that consciously echoed the earlier mo- ment: "War in the Gulf: Day X."[27] It was the discourse of Iran that brought out the yellow ribbons the minute the troops were dispatched and then al- lowed President Bush to define the nature of the "threat" in the Gulf as Sad- dam Hussein's "terrorist regime." When Saddam Hussein obliged expecta- tions by taking nearly one thousand Americans as hostages for several months before the bombing began, the news accounts were a frenzy of re- play and recapitulation: stories of the hostage families, this time against a backdrop of the near certainty of retaliation.[28] In fact, the layered history of television coverage of earlier crises was part of what television news aimed to evoke. With the self-promoting Iran-derived icons and the self-important narrative of hostages, captivity, and reporter bravery, the news of the war was a markedly narcissistic affair that depended for its legibility on the television-watching history of its audience.

Ironically, the legacy of Iran was also a crucial aspect of the U.S. diplomatic and political failures that proceeded and enabled the war with Iraq. During the eight-year-long war between Iran and Iraq (1980–1988) that had followed the consolidation of the Ayatollah Khomeini's rule in Iran, U.S. policy had generally tilted toward Iraq. The general assumption among policymakers was that U.S. interests lay in keeping either side from building up too much strength or becoming a preeminent military power in the region, but the emotional pull of anti-Iranian sentiment was a strong force. No one in Washington was under any illusions about Saddam Hussein, whose secular nationalism and moderate economic egalitarianism provided only the smallest fig leaf for his dictatorial and repressive rule. But the United States nonetheless provided Iraq with satellite photos and information, as well as weapons and equipment, in the hopes of ensuring that if Iraq did not win the war with Iran, it at least would not lose. It was this history, perhaps, that encouraged U.S. planners to underestimate the extent of the Iraqi threat to Kuwait and led the U.S. ambassador to Iraq to signal in the summer of 1990 that the United States would not intervene in "Arab-Arab" conflicts over borders. Fearing Islamic fundamentalism in Iran, American policymakers allowed themselves an uneasy alliance with Saddam Hussein that lasted almost a decade.[29]

Some scholars have suggested that much of the anxiety evoked by the Gulf War among media and cultural critics had to do with the fact that television news played such a key role in the public discourse. In a certain sense, the critics of the media war were expressing not only their concern about the war but also their anxiety about television as a medium. The Gulf War was a spectacle, they argued, and as such it represented "the ascendancy of the visual and ... its frantic, continuous, and ultimately hollow deployment."[30] For these observers, the problem with television news—or often television in general—was that it evacuated "history," discouraging analysis and contextualization. Visuality itself appeared the culprit: things moved too fast, critics said; language was emptied; images replaced thought. In fact, the evacuation of critical discourse in the Gulf War likely had less to do with any kind of inevitable distortion by television's images and more to do with what was *not* on-screen: few American soldiers in body bags; almost nothing of the grittiness of ground battle and its associated injuries; remarkably little of the devastating effects in Iraq. The form could become content only if the content was uninformed.[31]

But critics of the "spectacle" of the Gulf War assumed that spectacle was in itself a problem, that elaborate visual displays were by definition opposed to knowledge, history, and truth. This denigration of the visual as a source of information connected back to the earlier Orientalist fascination with spectacle. Nineteenth-century Europeans and Americans were ambivalent about the image: they trusted *only* that which could be "rendered up to be viewed" and yet simultaneously distrusted precisely those mechanisms (the photograph, the panorama, even vision itself) that promised unmediated access to the real. The instability of viewing became a metonym for the uncertainty of all knowledge: If seeing was *not* necessarily believing, then how could anyone secure access to truth?[32]

Public debates about television have long participated in this equivocal evaluation of the powers of the visual. Utopian suggestions that TV (then cable TV, then the Internet) could be a great democratic leveler in providing information to the public have generally existed side by side with dire warnings of the consequences of television: the supposed dumbing-down that detractors claimed comes with "passive" viewing rather than "active" reading; the claims about the loss of community or family conversation once everyone sits in front of the TV; the low moral values TV was said to impart. These criticisms have generally been present when television was being discussed as an entertainment medium; when its role was as the primary source for news and information, the anxieties were compounded.

With the Gulf War, an earlier concern with the partiality of the visual and the problems of epistemology reasserted itself full force. Without denying the fact of hyperrepresentation or the specific problems of the ownership and control of the media, it is important to move beyond this dichotomy of spectacle versus knowledge, the visual versus history, television versus truth. The seemingly sophisticated analyses of the Gulf War that focused on the formal effects of the television medium, along with the political discussions of the postmodern loss of history, often shared a common limitation: they assumed a prelapsarian world in which "the visual" did not interfere with the production of a more honest historical narrative, in which history itself was somehow available as a content for contemplation, separate from the narratives that framed it and made it readable. Such analyses ignored both the contents and the contexts of what was shown in favor of a general, categorical dismissal.[33] But instead of seeing visual media as an evacuation of history, we need to see them *as* history—not just because culture is part of larger politics, and vice versa, but also because, from the Holy Land panoramas to the biblical epic films to 1980s action movies, visual representations have both framed and claimed history. They have done so in ways that linked them to, rather than separated them from, other forms of cultural production and other forms of history writing. It *is* true that form does matter, since formal conventions are the language in which cultural products speak. But the meanings of cultural forms lie not in the forms themselves but in their deployment in a larger discursive field. As Bourdieu and others have suggested, meanings are made in the interaction of different cultural practices. In the case of the Gulf War, we must, of course, ask what role the hyperextension of visual images played, but in order to understand that, we need to know the intertexts and contexts of Gulf War television—how it engaged with other narratives about history and identity to envision the world it was helping to create.

THE MULTICULTURALISM SCARE

In April 1991, just after the Gulf War ended, the conservative columnist George Will suggested in *Newsweek* that the chair of the National Endowment for the Humanities (NEH), Lynne Cheney, had a tougher task than her husband, Secretary of Defense Dick Cheney, since she was facing an escalating battle over multiculturalism at home. "In this low-visibility, high-intensity war," Will wrote, "Lynne Cheney is secretary of domestic defense. The foreign adversaries her husband, Dick, must keep at bay are less dangerous, in the long run, than the domestic forces with which she must deal." At the NEH, Lynne Cheney was faced with "domestic forces" that were politicizing literature, challenging the traditional literary canon, and supporting the "theater of victimization" that was increasingly apparent in academic life. Will argued that these forces, comprising literature scholars and student radicals, among others, were imposing issues of "group politics"—racial, ethnic, and sexual—onto literature, and thus were "fighting against the conservation of the common culture that is the nation's social cement." The battle for the future of the NEH was crucial, Will argued, because as much as any Supreme Court justice or political player, Cheney was in charge of "constitutional things": she was engaged in a battle for the maintenance of those habits, mores, and ideas that make up the "national mind" that "truly constitutes America."[34]

Will's battle cry, his insistence that the campus literature curriculum was emerging as the site of a major cultural and political struggle, was part of a groundswell. As the conflict with Iraq heated up, the U.S. news media launched a fiery debate not about the pros and cons of the war but about the meanings of multiculturalism and its much-derided twin, "political correctness." Over the course of six months, the supposed rise of "p.c." on university campuses rated the cover of *Time*, *Newsweek*, and the *New Republic*, as well as long stories in the *New York Times* and the *Los Angeles Times*, to name just a few.[35] As the 1990s began, the mainstream media took up conservatives' clarion call against the putative takeover of university campuses and intellectual life by radicals who championed "group rights" in the name of people of color, women, gay men and lesbians, and others.[36]

The tone of the initial articles in the major newspapers and magazines was almost uniformly incredulous, even hysterical. The basic traditions of education and democracy were said to be under attack by what the headlines called "The Victims' Revolution" or "The Thought Police."[37] Colleges were often the focus, not only because they were the sites of student activism but also because colleges were assumed to be part of the ideological cement of American identity and nationalism. "For most of American history," *Time* explained, "the educational system has reflected and reinforced the bedrock beliefs of the larger society."[38] Presumably, one purpose of education was to teach students to experience their national identity as primary over other ties, be they racial or political or cultural. Now, critics argued, professors and students seemed determined to privilege "minor literature" and "victims' history" over the unifying narratives that were the basis of national cohesion.

The attack on political correctness was multifaceted and often diffuse, but it had its roots in a complex network of conservative organizations and think tanks that, beginning in the 1980s, had made support for conservatism on campuses a primary organizational priority. Conservative political leaders and foundations supported a network of student newspapers that they hoped would bring conservative ideas to key universities; they also began to help student organizations bring nationally known leaders of the Right to speak on campus. In 1985, the organization Accuracy in Academia was founded to expose the presence of radical faculty members on campus and to monitor professors who failed to include conservative views in their lectures or who demonstrated Marxist leanings. Overall, these and other efforts were designed to counter what many conservatives believed was the liberal bias in higher education. Right-wing activists also argued that intellectual standards were being lowered by affirmative action and even by the expansion of financial aid.[39]

Certainly it was the case that campuses had changed in the 1970s and 1980s. By the time of the Gulf War, universities had become far more racially and ethnically diverse, registering in microcosm the changing character of the U.S. population. In 1965, new immigration laws had altered the previous system of immigration quotas, which had been heavily tilted in favor of Europeans, to allow an increased number of immigrants from Asia, Africa, and the Middle East. By 1990, the share of U.S. immigrants designated as white had decreased to approximately 50 percent, down from 90 percent in 1970. And the absolute number of newcomers was rising rapidly: in 1990, one out of four foreign-born residents had been in the United States less than five years.[40]

At the same time, the identity movements of the 1960s and 1970s, from Black Power to Chicano and American Indian movements to feminism, questioned the older model of assimilation. They suggested that certain cultural differences would not, and should not, simply fade into a national mosaic. This new generation would no longer necessarily "Americanize" their names or put aside their languages. Those coming out of the identity movements also tended to celebrate the new immigration as part of a larger challenge to the post–World War II homogenization of American life. After the 1960s, college students frequently organized themselves along lines of race, gender, sexuality, religion, or politics, often with little attention to nationalist frameworks.

Critics of the new multiculturalism feared that these identity movements would undermine the common culture, that they were a threat to the nation precisely because they might lead—in a frequently repeated phrase—to the "balkanization" of America. At the heart of the issue lay the question of how the nation as a whole, now newly self-conscious about the diversity of its population, would come to engage issues of race, nation, gender, and sexuality. It was perhaps not surprising, then, that the racial and political tensions that were erupting across the United States (the police beating of Rodney King would be caught on videotape in April 1991) were also playing out in complicated ways on college campuses.[41]

For conservatives, "political correctness" in the academy was the final holdout of feminism and radical racial politics, both of which had been defeated or otherwise driven underground by the New Right resurgence of the 1980s. As outlined in countless media reports, political correctness was a composite of at least three related issues, which were often presented as one. First, college students were supposedly no longer learning the traditional humanities canon focused on "great literature" and "Western civilization." That is, professors were teaching a left-wing version of the humanities that emphasized the literature and experiences of people of color and women, thus Amy Tan and Frances Harper were displacing the truly great writers like Melville and Hemingway. Anti-p.c. critics decried these changes as "politicizing" the teaching of literature, as if before p.c. arrived on campus there were no political choices involved in deciding how to teach writings from the Civil War or the work of socially aware writers like William Faulkner or Richard Wright. Sometimes this criticism was paired, implicitly or explicitly, with echoes of the affirmative action debate as commentators suggested that, these days, certain groups of students at the university were only interested in seeing "themselves" represented.[42]

Second, critics attacked the rise of poststructuralist epistemologies among academics. Intellectuals were no longer teaching students to search for truth and to believe in the possibility of objective knowledge, critics argued; instead, they were undermining the very foundations of democratic culture by challenging the idea of timeless values and universal truths. Moving away from an approach that emphasized aesthetic appreciation, academic critics "strip[ped] literature of its authority" and put relativism and relevance in its stead.[43]

In fact, there *had* been important changes in how many scholars viewed issues of cultural value and historical truths; these faculty might not dominate academic departments, but they did change how history, literature, and culture were taught, at least in some courses. Some college teachers did begin, for example, to teach Shakespeare less as a great author of universal literature and more as a writer deeply steeped in the political and cultural developments of his time, including issues of colonialism, gender, and race.[44] Some of these teachers and scholars insisted that all ideas about aesthetics and beauty were matters of historical construction, neither self-evident nor universal. Others made a narrower claim: that the aesthetic greatness of certain works of art could not be separated from their worldliness. According to the critics of political correctness, academics of this new school were forcing political values onto students; those who taught literature or history in the traditional way, on the other hand, were not forcing *their* values on students but instead were helping to produce a "common culture."

Finally, the critics of p.c. concluded that this new orthodoxy in the classroom was leading both students and administrators to censor unpopular speech on campus. The most frequently discussed manifestation of this supposed censorship was the development of university speech codes that prohibited "hate speech" such as racist or homophobic epithets. In one oft-cited example, a Brown University student was suspended after he wandered through campus in the middle of the night, drunk, shouting racist epithets. In another case, a University of Connecticut sophomore was required to move off campus after she posted a sign on her dorm room that listed "people who would be shot on sight": the list included "preppies," "bimbos," and "homos."[45]

On this last point, constitutional protections of speech were in fact sometimes at issue. Some of the administrative decisions about the rules of student conduct appeared to be little more than rule by fiat; they seemed to rest on an assumption that students were a particular class, whose youth and close proximity to each other (and to campus administrators) denied them their constitutional privileges. But despite their claims to be defending free speech, the anti-p.c. forces avoided the discussion of how to support democracy in the university. They failed to engage in any reasoned debate about the parameters of free speech in the specific situation of college campuses or even to acknowledge that the learning environment for some students could be poisoned by the actions of others. The speech codes, critics claimed, were nothing more than an effort by the politically correct to force their (multicultural) values on others. As Michael Kinsley pointed out in the *Washington Post*, however, most of the "p.c. scare" was based on a very few widely publicized incidents and a cobbled-together conglomeration of unrelated examples of campus racial or sexual tensions in which parties disagreed about appropriate remedies. The anti-p.c. diatribes simply produced "lists of things the writer [found] objectionable and would like—in the spirit of toleration and free inquiry—to expunge from the college curricula."[46] Or, as another observer described it, the red menace of the 1950s became the rainbow menace of the 1990s.[47]

The furor—and it was an extraordinary furor—over issues of multiculturalism on campus had an explicitly political agenda. A young woman who graduated from Harvard in 1991 described the partisan nature of the debate in *Harper's*. Majoring in U.S. and British history and literature, she wrote that she had not seen much evidence of the supposed multiculturalism of the curriculum: none of her courses at Harvard had, for example, ever required her to read a work by a black woman writer. Nor had she ever felt that the discussion of ideas was limited in her classes or, in general, on the campus. She did have one experience of feeling censored, however. When she went to an open rally called to "support our troops" during the Gulf War, she tried to speak in favor of the troops but against the war. The organizers turned off the microphone, and the audience shouted her down. The next day, supporters of the war were allowed to speak freely at an antiwar rally. Such intolerance of antiwar dissent was not unusual in the nation at large, of course, so it was not surprising to see it mirrored on campuses. By 1991, the tone of national discussion about the Middle East and the Gulf War had its own orthodoxy; as the student described it, she was silenced not by the politically correct but by the "*patriotically* correct."[48] An officer from the Los Angeles Police Department suggested a similar link between war abroad and conflict at home: "Saddam Hussein scared the shit out of us with chemical weapons and even though ... he didn't use the gas, we still made him pay the price. Same with Rodney King."[49] With such commentaries in mind, some observers on the Left suggested that a commitment to simplistic nationalism and racism underlay the near-simultaneous launch of the Gulf War and the attack on political correctness. But these critics missed a far more important connection. The concerns of multiculturalism were not, in fact, ignored or undone by the discourse on the Gulf War. They were incorporated by it.

ALL THAT WE CAN BE

The public representations of the Gulf War did not focus solely on images of technical mastery and precision bombing; many news reports also emphasized the changing character of the U.S. armed forces that were winning the war, highlighting the racial diversity of the new military. As newspapers and television reported the call-up that would mobilize regular duty and reserve forces from communities across the nation, their predominant theme was that the U.S. soldiers were a microcosm of the U.S. population—a heterogeneous mixture of races and ethnicities, drawn from small towns and local communities all around the nation, and including not only black and white men but also Latinos, Asian-Americans, Native American Indians, and even women (presumably of all races).

The image of the soldier has a long and important history in the construction and reinforcement of national identity. As historian Oscar Campomanes has argued, the soldier, as both historical referent and contemporary embodiment, often becomes "the common sign in which a whole nation must recognize itself."[50] In a situation in which most commentators agreed that the representations of the war were a crucial part of its meaning, it made sense that the images of the military took on a particular emotional investment. At stake was the self-representation of the nation, and thus the political status of the United States at the height of its reconstituted global power. After the Gulf War, politicians and the press alike expected that the United States would now be able to intervene whenever and wherever its leaders felt necessary. The representations of the military provided the mandate for that power: the diversity of its armed forces made the United States a world citizen, with all the races and nations of the globe represented in its population. As the military would represent the diversity of the United States, the United States, as represented in its military, would contain the world.

It was true that the soldiers who went to the Gulf were in some ways significantly different from those who had fought in Vietnam. The all-volunteer army was more racially diverse, older (the average age of those who went to the Gulf was twenty-seven), more likely to be married, and better trained than the army of the 1970s. In addition, a relatively high percentage of the soldiers who went to Saudi Arabia and Kuwait were reservists. The increased reliance on reserve forces came about as a result of policy changes in the 1970s that aimed to develop a smaller standing army more dependent on reserve forces for large-scale conflict. Acting in the wake of Vietnam, policymakers believed that the draft was no longer politically feasible; reserve forces were also cheaper than a full standing army. One result of this decision was that any major conflict would require a call-up of the reserves, presumably making it harder for the government to carry out a war without the general support of the population (which would be sending off its civilian family members and employees to the war).[51]

Commentators enthusiastically highlighted the composition of the all-volunteer "new army"—an army that now visibly included women. More than forty thousand American women served in the Gulf; they represented only 11 percent of the total force, but that was up from 1.5 percent in Vietnam. Both *Newsweek* and *People* featured "women warriors" on their covers within a month of the call-up.[52] The policy forbidding women to operate in combat missions on the front lines was still in place during the Gulf War, and columnists in several major newspapers discussed the impact of women's increased participation, debating whether the war would signal a change in the military's stance. Women were already allowed to operate in support positions (refueling, communications, medical rescue) that took them to the front lines; sixteen women died during the deployment, eleven of them in combat.[53]

The public discourse acknowledged women as potential combatants in complicated ways. When women soldiers themselves were interviewed, they insisted that "combat has no gender," and that "you can be tough and still be a female." Many of the reports simply lionized the women, though some stories focused on the virtually unprecedented phenomenon of dual-career military families: What happened to children, for example, when their fathers *and* mothers went to fight? The issues of morale and sexuality were never far from the surface, however, as when conservative commentators suggested that women in combat would be subject to so much sexism and sexual harassment that their presence would be disruptive to discipline.[54]

Other discussions, particularly prominent in the African American press, centered around whether black soldiers and families were bearing "too much of the burden." Black soldiers made up 30 percent of active troops in Desert Storm, but polls showed support for the war to be consistently lower among African Americans than among whites: in February 1991, only 48 percent of blacks supported the war while 85 percent of whites did.[55] The disproportionate representation of black (male and female) soldiers on the battlefield led many African American leaders to speak out against the risks and to oppose the war.[56] Several commentators, even those who supported the war, wondered whether "this time" black servicemen would be afforded a better deal on their return home.[57]

Latinos, Asian-Americans, and American Indians also served in the Gulf. Military officials often touted this diversity while simultaneously portraying it as essentially irrelevant. "Well, see, we just have soldiers," one officer told a reporter who asked about race relations. The soldiers themselves told a more complicated story—of racial tension that coexisted with camaraderie, of racially segregated socializing, and of "jokes" that not infrequently got out of hand. One private, born in Jamaica of East Indian and Chinese parents, said he felt it was impossible to complain about the constant racial humor: "It's a tricky subject, and word gets around sometimes. You gotta be careful."[58] Despite these signs of conflict and dissent, however, the general tenor of the reporting about the war was that the nation had pulled together in the face of crisis, and that Americans were forging on the battlefield the respectful "rainbow" that seemed so elusive at home.

That enthusiasm was nowhere more evident than in the televised coverage of Super Bowl XXV, played just ten days after the bombing attack began in January 1991. The fortuitously timed athletic contest, already a major media event, provided an opportunity for a multilayered patriotic display. Fans brought thousands of small American flags and posters to the game, with made-for-TV signs reading "America's Best Citizens Support Our GIs" and "Go USA." As the game began, the African American singer Whitney Houston performed the national anthem; as she sang, the camera dissolved to images of an African American marine in close-up and long shots of rows of enlisted men and women lined up on the field. At halftime, ABC presented a highly produced news summary of recent events in the Gulf, including live shots of soldiers in Saudi Arabia watching the Super Bowl in their barracks. On the field, the halftime show included a solo by a young boy who dedicated his song "to the real heroes in the Middle East protecting freedom for all of us kids." At another point, a large group of children whose parents were serving in the war paraded across the field wearing yellow ribbons and carrying flags, while the cameras zoomed in to highlight their ethnic and racial diversity. The final performance came from the crowd itself, which on cue turned over red, white, and blue cards that made the Super Bowl shield, visible only to the television cameras over-

Figure 23.   The multiracial brotherhood of war: an African American and a Native American soldier take a break together. The diversity of the U.S. forces was the subject of countless articles before and during the Gulf War. Photo by Margaret Thomas. Courtesy of *The Washington Post*.

head in the Goodyear blimp. As Jim Castonguay has argued, ABC and the NFL presented the Super Bowl as a morale booster for both the troops and the folks at home, "performing an indispensable USO-like function for the troops who were enjoying the game along with the home TV viewer."[59] In this Super Bowl, unlike the fictional one in *Black Sunday*, the United States represents itself, to itself, as having the will to fight.

It was within this narrative that General Colin Powell came to embody the preeminent soldier-statesman, the sign of the nation in its expansionist mode. Powell, the first African-American chairman of the Joint Chiefs of Staff, was perhaps the most respected public leader to emerge from the war.[60] During the conflict, Powell served as a dignified and highly visible leader whose no-nonsense approach to winning the war made him an apt symbol of both multiculturalism at home and the New World Order abroad. Powell seemed above the fray of day-to-day politics, the consummate soldier whose sense of duty to his country transcended partisan allegiances. He publicly supported the overall aims of the war and was a passionate defender of both the honor and the prowess of the U.S. military.[61] He thus played a key role in revitalizing the image of the armed forces, still tainted by events in Vietnam and the failed hostage rescue mission in Iran.

At the daily press briefings during the war, Powell's straightforward style and plain speech won him a great deal of admiration. His famous explanation of the U.S. strategy against Iraq was a case in point. "Our strategy in going after this army is very simple," he said in a televised news conference. "First we are going to cut it off, and then we are going to kill it."[62] Powell was also a primary spokesperson for the notion of an expanding international role for the United States. Although he believed that the use of military power should be circumspect (he supported U.S. intervention in Haiti but opposed it in Bosnia), he had played a key role in developing military strategies that focused on deep strikes into enemy territory and the quick achievement of all-out victories. (He was also a significant player in the bureaucratic reorganization that had, in the 1980s, dramatically increased the influence of military officers in determining the goals and conduct of war.)[63] In his autobiography, released after the end of the war, Powell stated proudly that no other nation could "hope to match or challenge the military and economic power of the free world led by the United States."[64]

Like a lot of African Americans facing limited job opportunities, Powell had joined the military as a young man and had stayed on. He never tired of saying that the military was an excellent career for black Americans: "I wish that there were other activities in our society and in our nation that were as open as the military is to upward mobility, to achievement, to allowing [blacks] in."[65] Since the post-Vietnam move to an all-volunteer military, black participation in the armed forces had jumped noticeably: in the early 1990s, 23 percent of all military personnel were black, compared with 11 percent in the general population.[66] Although many commentators correctly described this disproportionate representation as the "poverty draft," it was nonetheless undeniable that the military had become something of a haven for black men. African Americans reenlisted at almost twice the rate of whites, and their opportunities for advancement and promotion were better in the armed forces than in virtually any civilian corporation. In 1991, blacks made up 32 percent of the army's enlisted personnel and 11 percent of its officers; this was not, of course, an equitable ratio, but it compared favorably with the Fortune 500, where only 1 percent of upper management was African American.[67] The numbers suggested something similar for black women. While the discussions of "women in the military" often erased racial differences among women, or ignored nonwhite women altogether, the rates of participation for black women were strikingly high: 48 percent of all women in the Gulf were African American.[68] The record of

African American leadership and achievement in the military, and General Powell's role as one of the highest-ranking and most influential black men in recent history, meant that the military was also held up by many commentators, both black and white, as a model of successful efforts to end racism and discrimination in employment.[69]

Powell became, in this context, the nation's premier citizen-soldier, the living embodiment of the institution in which the whole nation must recognize itself. At the time he retired from service in 1993 (after clashing with President Clinton over several issues ranging from gays in the military to women in combat), Powell was introduced at one farewell dinner as "the only man who could today win either the Democratic or the Republican presidential nomination without ever setting foot in New Hampshire."[70] Journalists from liberal to conservative embraced him. The right-wing *National Review* described him as "America's Black Eisenhower,"[71] while the *New York Times* suggested that, should Powell elect to run for president, he could be a "transformative historical figure" who would add "dignity" to American political life.[72] He was, like the military he embodied, "untouchable."[73] He stood for the nation not because the United States was figured as black but because it was figured as open-minded, as multicultural, as pluralist, and thus as having *already* successfully achieved the aims that "p.c." college professors and their students were agitating for.

Despite Powell's extraordinary status, the figuration of the United States through the sign of the multicultural military was fraught with tensions, as the military traditions of masculinity and (hetero)sexualized discipline ran up against the multicultural narrative of inclusion. One *Washington Post* report on the relationships among soldiers in a multiracial platoon offered a noteworthy glimpse into the gender and sexual exclusions of the new army and showed how heterosexual masculinity provided the narrative by which racial inclusion was effected. As one soldier explained to a reporter, there were some racial tensions among the members of his platoon, but there was also reciprocity and camaraderie. Everybody shared music and reading material, he said. "People had black literature or white literature, like *Jet* magazine, *Ebony* magazine.... It went around, everybody read it.... You got your pornography, black, white, or whatever. That went around."[74] The unmistakable presumption here was that the soldiers passing around multiracial pornography were men, and were heterosexual. Older narratives of the military as the cookstove of the melting pot were thus updated in a masculine dream of the multiracial brotherhood of sex and war.

Women were still expected to be external to the fighting, represented but not present. As one soldier's discussion with a reporter made clear, the most popular pinup in the Gulf—a jeans-clad white woman who was, in her daily life, a policewoman—was a display that embodied both women's status as sexual objects and their putative liberation: "We are in a country [Saudi Arabia] where women are treated different than in the States, and are not as beautiful. [Her] picture is a constant reminder why we are here."[75] The sexual politics of this masculine narrative were already under siege, however. Despite real resistance on the part of the official services, it was clear that women soldiers *were* being incorporated, that the presumptions about the nature of the military and the required conditions for platoon bonding would not last forever. In fact, within a few years of the end of the war, two major Hollywood films, *Courage under Fire* (1996) and *G.I. Jane* (1997), took women in combat as their subject; both suggested that the biggest barrier to full female participation was retrograde sexism that could, in time, be overcome.

If the position of women as soldiers seemed to threaten the logic of women as pinups, the traditional function of war as a staging ground for masculinity did not entirely disappear. The extraordinary display of U.S. military technology on the television news may have helped to rescue the more traditional narrative of male power now potentially under threat from feminism, women soldiers, and American decline. As Robyn Wiegman has argued, the high-tech images of high-tech military equipment—the detailed attention to the Patriot attacks, the Scud missiles, and the "surgical" bombings that were displayed through cameras mounted on the U.S. planes—allowed the technology itself to stand for a kind of public and phallic masculinity that might once have been symbolized by the male bodies of warriors, but which was no longer (quite) available in the new military. The display produced a warrior discourse that solicited and signified male power but separated it from any specific embodiment.

But the reporting of the war also affirmed a certain type of femininity. The narratives about the Gulf echoed the family stories that had dominated coverage of the Iran hostage crisis, drawing on specifically feminized modes of discourse, in particular melodrama, which privileged personal stories of fear, suffering, and tragedy. The stories of the soldiers, their children, and their worried parents and siblings became the human drama of the conflict; these tales of hope and loss seemed to solicit a female audience. The almost equal visibility of both kinds of narration—high-tech *and* high drama—involved the dissolution of the stark gendered divisions of public man/ private woman. These family-war stories allowed narratives coded as "feminine" to represent the nation in its public mode, even as they also served to rearticulate masculinity as more mobile, more interior, and more "domestic" than ever before.[76]

Gender presumptions were being altered as they were being reinscribed, but the heterosexual imperative remained. Gay and lesbian soldiers were conspicuously absent from the Desert Storm discourse of diversity. The policy banning lesbians or gay men from serving in the military came under attack by gay organizations as soon as the mobilization began, as a result of several stories of witch-hunts for homosexuals.[77] Gay magazines and political organizations quickly took up the cause of the "right to serve." It made sense: if the military was to be the sign of the nation, and the sign of the nation was to be multiracial and to include both men and women in uniform as its signifiers, then the exclusion of gays from the military was an exclusion from citizenship, from national representation.

This demand for military equality exposed the contradiction that lay at the heart of any vision of the nation as signified and embodied in its armed services. On the one hand, the military's self-representation as a microcosm of a pluralist American society opened the way, or even made inevitable, the claims made by gay men and by women of whatever sexual orientation that the role of the solider as sign of the nation *required* their full participation. On the other hand, the military's traditional dependence on racial bonding forged through the ideology and rituals of heterosexual masculinity *required* a policy that excluded gay men and lesbians and severely limited the role of women. (In this context, General Powell's opposition to openly gay soldiers in the military was well known; he also opposed women serving in all-ground-combat units.)[78] The inherent tensions meant that even success would not be unproblematic for excluded groups, since the military, as an institution run on discipline and uniformity, has traditionally required something far more stringent than "assimilation" from its members. The politics of representativeness would invoke the diversity of the military, but the military would tend to demand the erasure of difference in the service of discipline.

Arab Americans were reminded of this assimilationist imperative as the war began. News accounts often seemed fascinated by the very fact of an Arab American community. The media tracked the fact that the community itself was divided about the war, and Arab Americans in the military were the subject of quite a few human interest stories.[79] Ever since the Iran hostage crisis, Middle Eastern immigrant communities had received sporadic attention in the U.S. press. In the late 1960s, new groups of Arab and some Iranian immigrants had begun to arrive in the United States, following the 1965 change in immigration laws and especially after the 1967 Arab-Israeli war, when increasing numbers of Palestinians, Iraqis, Yemenis, and others began to join the Lebanese and Syrians of earlier generations. Many of the Palestinians had been displaced by the Arab-Israeli war; others were fleeing political instability elsewhere in the region. In contrast to earlier immigrants, these new arrivals were more likely to be Muslims, more nationalist, and, after the Black Power and identity movements of the late 1960s and 1970s, more conscious of race and culture, as well as more critical and political, than previous generations. They soon began to organize. The first self-consciously political Arab American organization was founded right after the 1967 war; it was followed by many others in the 1970s. In 1980, James Abourezk, a former U.S. senator from South Dakota, founded what would soon become the largest and most effective political voice for Middle Eastern immigrants, the American Arab Anti-Discrimination Committee (ADC), which took a determinedly mainstream and pluralist approach to challenging anti-Arab bias in American culture. In the 1980s, ADC organized a series of demonstrations, letter-writing campaigns, and call-ins to protest the virulent anti-Arab racism that was common in films and television shows. The group also protested the anti-Iranian and anti-Islamic slant of *Not without My Daughter*, since they understood quite well (and long before the Gulf War) that such sentiments were eminently transferable: the fact that Iranians are not Arabs would not alter the impact of the movie on U.S. perceptions of Arabs and Arab Americans.[80]

Many Arabs in the United States felt threatened by the overall rhetoric of the Gulf War. In the conflict with Iraq, the presumption of both the U.S. government and much of the public seemed to be that after almost two decades of doubt and decline, the multicultural United States could pull together in the face of a Middle East that was clearly an outside threat. The images of Saddam Hussein in the U.S. press drew on both analogies with Hitler and the history of anti-Arab images from the 1970s and 1980s to create a composite figure of terrorism, fascism, and greed. The position was one Hussein filled particularly well, given his record of repression at home and his embrace of virtually every opportunity for confrontation. But the fact that there were Arab nations in the allied coalition, including not only Saudi Arabia and Kuwait but also Syria and Egypt, barely rippled the surface of the rhetoric; as with Vietnam, these allies were praised in press briefings and then marginalized in the debate about what the United States was actually at war to protect. In this context, Arabs and Iranians in the United States had reason to worry about their new visibility on the international stage, as well as reason to doubt their incorporation into multicultural America. Despite the occasional discussion of Arab Americans in side-bars on "opinion at home," the images of the diversity and strength of U.S. armed forces simply did not include Arab Americans.

At some level, the process of constructing a "multicultural" national iden-tity for Americans was not so much different from the earlier task of making a "white" one. The idea of a "white" nation forged from a conglomeration of Germans, Italians, Irish, Swedes, and others depended on masking differences of language, religion, and values in order to forge a new unity. This unity did not require that all its members be treated equally; in fact, it could serve pre-cisely to deflect attention from "internal" injustices, be they class distinctions or ethnic hierarchies, as long as everyone within the group was "compen-sated" by the externalization of another, racialized group. Nationalism is not the same as racism, but in this instance it used a similar logic: the production of "multiculturalism" as a militarized national construct imagined a multi-cultural family that offered an appropriately hierarchical and yet affective tie among peoples and groups. The militarized nation needed an "outside" to mark its boundaries; that outside was the Middle East.[81]

As part of the trajectory of nationalist discourse, the representations of the Gulf War were indeed "postmodern" not only because of their focus on spectacle and display but also in their extension and revision of the racial logics of modern nationalism. The United States was constructed as supe-rior and expansive—as having a right both to sovereignty over its own cit-izens and to hegemony in other parts of the world—precisely because the war helped to define (multicultural) America as different from, and superior to, the putatively less liberal identities of other nations, particularly those in the Middle East. But if the vision of military multiculturalism had solved the dual dilemma of decline abroad and "political correctness" at home, it had produced an aporia of its own: What would happen when America was forced to acknowledge the Arabs within?

THE SIEGE

Edward Zwick's film *The Siege* opened in November 1998, just a few weeks before President Clinton, on the day before an impeachment vote was scheduled in the House of Representatives, ordered renewed bombing of Iraq as punishment for its failure to comply with the protocols of the UN inspections established after the Gulf War. Despite the film's timely subject matter (Muslim Arab terrorists attacking New York City) and its star power (Denzel Washington and Bruce Willis), the film did not do very well, earn-ing only $41 million in its initial theater run (compared with the $80 million for *The Rugrats Movie* in approximately the same period). When it was released on video, however, *The Siege* topped the rental charts for several weeks.[82] Initially subject to a boycott by the American Arab Anti-Discrimination Committee, *The Siege* actually presented a view of Arabs and Arab Americans that was almost unprecedented in American movies—not because of its plot, which seemed to be a straightforward tale of terrorism-at-home, but because of the way in which it was such a definitively and self-consciously post–Gulf War film. Through its interest in visuality and surveillance, the film redeployed and commented on the type of images that were highlighted by Gulf War television coverage. Even more important, its interest in Arab Americans as an immigrant population challenged, though it did not entirely explode, the logic of military multiculturalism.

The Siege mobilizes the major elements of the action/terrorism genre to construct a distinctly liberal narrative of race and foreign policy. The basic plot elements are simple: an African American FBI counterterrorism specialist, Tony Hubbard (Denzel Washington), is faced with an escalating series of terrorist bombings in New York City. His task is to find the terrorists, who are soon revealed as Islamic fundamentalists. When, despite great bravery, he fails to end the attacks, Congress puts the city under martial law. The military commander (Bruce Willis) invades the city and rounds up Arab American males, herding them into a makeshift concentration camp at Yankee Stadium. The final part of the film is then organized around Hubbard's two key tasks: stopping the terrorists through legal and proper means, and stopping the abuse of authority represented by Willis's general and exemplified in the concentration camp.

As an action film, *The Siege* is interested in many of the same things as other (more conservative) films in the genre: the workings of technology and surveillance; the role of the media, especially television; the play of gender and sexuality; and of course the thrill of threat and the satisfaction of rescue. Also like many 1980s and 1990s action movies, *The Siege* presents, and thus posits, the multiracial makeup of military and/or police forces. Overall, though, the particular way in which this film situates itself and its audience distinguishes it from apparently similar films. For that reason, its mixed success at the box office is quite interesting, in part because of what it suggests about the promise and the limits of a more liberal version of multiculturalism at the turn of the twenty-first century.

The Siege tells its story of race, terrorism, and desire through complex layers of representation; images from television news and the surveillance operations of various security forces structure both the form and the content of the film narrative. At key moments, the act of viewing forms a crucial subtext to the surface events of the film's plot. While the movie is about terrorism in New York, and secondarily about the problem of race and national identity, it is also a movie about television—particularly television news. These levels of narrative reinforce each other, drawing on the complex ways that terrorism, race, television, and the Middle East had long been linked in U.S. discourse.

The movie opens with an image of a bomb exploding and a building crumbling; the shot looks grainy, in a square frame. We hear a voice-over; Saudi Arabia is mentioned, as is a U.S. military installation. As an audience, we know from the look of the image that we are watching television news; it is likely that many viewers would also remember the bombing of the U.S. military housing complex in Dhahran, Saudi Arabia, in 1996. Next, another fictional news broadcast talks about a suspect in the bombing, "Sheik Ahmed Bin Talal." The character of the "Sheik" suggests the bombing of New York's World Trade Center five years earlier, for which the Egyptian sheik Omar Abdel-Rahman and other several other Islamic fundamentalists living in the United States were arrested and ultimately convicted.[83] That connection is only underlined when, a few scenes later, a muezzin is shown offering the Muslim call to prayer from a mosque. Playing on the audience's assumption that the setting is still the Middle East, the camera slowly zooms out to reveal the streets of Brooklyn, with the Manhattan skyline in the background. The movie will return several times to this reality: Middle Eastern Muslims are no longer only in the Middle East.

What the audience sees in the film is often presented via the technologies of satellite imagery, surveillance equipment, and television. Vision mediated by technology is almost a character in this movie; television and surveillance equipment appear at key moments in the plot, enabling action and commenting on events. Unlike earlier films such as *Delta Force*, in which television news is an enemy, here television represents history and signifies truth. The film opens by soliciting its viewers with news sequences, encouraging them to think intertextually, to remember recent terrorist events through their experience of watching those events on TV. Frequent television and radio news reports punctuate the rest of the story; narrated by well-known television and radio anchors (several from National Public Radio), they invite the audience to see the film as true to life. Of course, use of news accounts within films is hardly unusual, but the sophistication of the "news" sequences and their repeated use throughout the narration gives *The Siege* a distinct self-consciousness about information. Knowledge about the techniques of viewing becomes knowledge about the security state—the threats it poses, and the threats it contains.

The security state is represented by two types of institutions. The first is the military, which, along with the CIA, is defined by its intrusiveness, its massive resources, and its ruthlessness. The other type of institution is represented by the FBI, which, as personified by Denzel Washington's Agent Hubbard, is defined by its commitment to antiterrorism, its integrity, and its relative lack of resources. In the world of the film, the FBI is both competent and human—negotiators get stuck in traffic; agents lose perpetrators; and the authority of the agency is undermined by the military takeover. The portrayal of the FBI is aided by Washington's star persona; in the Hollywood of the 1990s, he was known as a gentle, generous person, who usually played sympathetic, if sometimes flawed, characters in serious films. (Washington had also starred as a conscientious military man in the Gulf War film *Courage under Fire,* also directed by Zwick.) The humanity of the FBI is also signified by its exemplary racial diversity and its (relative) feminist consciousness. Hubbard oversees a team that includes another African American man, an Asian American woman, two white men, and an Arab American man, Frank Haddad (Tony Shalhoub).[84] The FBI is also aided by a tough, white female CIA agent (Annette Benning), whose ownership of her own sexuality is paralleled by her tough competence. She manages her Palestinian informer in part through sexual manipulation, just as she manages the FBI team in part by lying about her true identity. Benning's character is a long way from the "freely chosen submission" of the women of the biblical epics, but the film is ambivalent about her power; the film, like the FBI, needs her to do its work, but neither is quite sure what to do with her.

The fundamental division between security state agencies is paralleled by another division, that between Arab citizens and Arab terrorists. Although one of the interesting things about *The Siege* is its relatively sympathetic portrayal of the motivations of the bombers—Sami Bouajila gives a marvelously nuanced performance as the Muslim fundamentalist Samir—the structuring logic of the film requires a sharp distinction between those within and those outside the law. Just as the violence and authoritarianism of Willis's conniving general are paralleled and balanced by the integrity and reasonableness of Washington's Agent Hubbard, so the fanaticism and violence of Samir and the terrorists are balanced by the gentleness and humor of the law-abiding figure, that of the Arab American Agent Haddad. Frank, the number two person on the counterterrorism team, is a practicing Muslim, a U.S. citizen born in Lebanon, and a proud family man. He is located within a much larger *immigrant* community, people who have made the United States their home, and the film explores this community fondly and in some detail: the Arab markets and coffee shops in Brooklyn, the streets with signs in Arabic, the mosques and community centers. But somewhere in that world, the terrorists are hiding, waiting to carry out another in the series of bombings. The terrorists are not immigrants but wayfarers, whose primary identity is with the political struggles involving the United States and Arabs in the Middle East. No one is more anxious than Haddad to catch them.

For Frank, and for the film itself, the roundup and internment of Arab Americans brings a moment of truth. Throughout *The Siege*, the immigrants in Brooklyn are represented as generally law-abiding citizens, part of the national mosaic, and their roundup is depicted as a horror. The scenes of mass arrests are punctuated with the voice-overs of a call-in radio talk show, in which some people offer racist commentary but others angrily point out the comparisons to Japanese internment in World War II and suggest that in the 1990s this could not happen to any other ethnic group in America. At the height of the crisis, Frank's thirteen-year-old son is brought to the stadium where Arab men are being held, and Frank desperately searches for him. Hubbard then goes after Frank and finds him wandering through the barbed wire, absolutely astounded that after twenty years in the United States, and ten years with the FBI, this could happen to his family. He angrily resigns from the FBI on the spot, insisting to Hubbard that he simply won't be "their sand nigger" anymore. Shortly thereafter, however, Hubbard convinces Frank to rejoin the team; the threat posed by the terrorists is simply too great, the requirements of the nation too compelling. At the end of the film, Haddad and Hubbard have found and killed the last of the terrorists and have reasserted civilian control over the city. The system works.

By the time *The Siege* was released in 1998, its critique of anti-Arab racism had been enabled by nearly three decades of Arab American activism. That activism had not prevented the outrageous, cartoonish representations of Arabs in a film like *True Lies* just four years earlier, but it did allow *The Siege* to credibly posit anti-Arab sentiment as a political distortion rather than as a reflection of the nature of Arabs. The film suggested that the threat of terrorism at home could be managed by distinguishing the "immigrant" from the wayfarer, thus allowing for the reality of Arab immigration in a narrative of liberal embrace. Its focus on the presence of Arab immigrants drew on the logic of Gulf War multiculturalism but challenged its enabling assumption: that the Middle East could be fully externalized and that "Arabs" or Islam could reliably serve as one half of a moral binary, with "America" on the other side.

The Siege was a post–Gulf War film in another sense, however, in that it served less as a challenge to the discourse of U.S. global reach than as an

Figures 24 and 25.   In *The Siege* (1998), Arab immigrants behind the barbed
wire of a concentration camp (top); and an Arab American FBI agent, played
by Tony Shalhoub, is convinced to return to the job by his boss, played by Denzel
Washington.

extension and refinement of it. As much as the film refused some of the
racial and nationalist assumptions of the dominant news coverage of the
Gulf War, it depended on its audience to understand that issues of terrorism and media were connected to debates about U.S. power in the post-Vietnam world. And in suggesting that the Middle East and its politics profoundly infected and infiltrated the United States, the film knew what its
audience knew: that, as a result of the oil crisis, terrorism, Iran, and the Gulf
War, the Middle East had become a site of extensive U.S. investment, in
every sense of that term.

The Siege also shared with the Gulf War coverage some fundamental
fascinations: TV and surveillance; the questioning of the United States' international role after Vietnam; the love and fear of covert power; and the
transformations in the role of women in the gendering of the nation-state.
Most important, both the film and the news accounts were part of an increasingly self-conscious diversity in images of the nation, and both manifest the assumption (derived in part from their civil rights precursors) that

only a genuinely multicultural nation deserves world power. Indeed, as a culmination of almost fifty years of post–World War II nationalist discourse, the public narrative of the Gulf War was remarkable precisely for the way it set the terms of a debate that fused a contained racial liberalism with a confident reassertion of U.S. global power. Capturing what once had been a resistant strain of cultural politics, the Gulf War changed the face of American expansionist nationalism, not simply in the way it managed, in short order, to make a demon out of a former U.S. ally and to construct an urgent national interest in protecting the sovereignty of a faraway Middle Eastern nation, but through the extraordinary work it did in incorporating the challenge of multiculturalism into the logic of the New World Order.

Conclusion
9/11 and After: Snapshots on the Road to Empire

INTRODUCTION

All profound changes in consciousness, by their very nature,
bring with them characteristic amnesias. Out of such oblivions,
in specific historical circumstances, spring narratives.
                        —Benedict Anderson, *Imagined Communities*

In January 2003, the *New York Times Magazine* published a cover story by Michael Ignatieff, one of the nation's leading advocates for human rights, titled "The Burden." In it, the liberal Ignatieff argued that Americans needed to recognize and accept that they were now at the helm of an empire. Considering the confluence of U.S. military, economic, and cultural preeminence, he said, "What word but 'empire' describes the awesome thing that America is becoming?"[1]

It was one sign of the remarkable transformation in American politics after September 11 that a leading human rights activist and liberal political commentator would now make the case for empire in the *New York Times.* Americans might think of their nation as the "friend of freedom everywhere," Ignatieff said, but the realities of U.S. power since the end of the cold war had ignited a great deal of resentment, as the nightmare of the terrorist attacks of September 11 surely made clear. Looking ahead at the war that was about to be launched in Iraq, he argued that nonetheless there were cases where the promotion of human rights actually required war; it was, sometimes, the only "real remedy for regimes that live by terror." But if Americans were to invade Iraq under the banner of freedom, they would have to assume the responsibility that comes with imperial power, including the responsibility to remain involved in Iraq for at least a decade, as well as the imperative to "enforce a peace" on the Palestinians and Israelis.

Ignatieff's argument was both an heir to and a departure from the "benevolent supremacy" discourse that had dominated the early cold war era. Benevolent supremacists had supported direct military intervention in the name of fighting the "tyranny" of communism, but they generally did not support U.S. colonialism, which was itself presented as a kind of

266

tyranny. Ignatieff wore the mantle of benevolent supremacy when he argued that U.S. actions were necessary to support freedom and defend human rights, and that, in fact, self-determination for Iraq would be best supported by the imposition of U.S. power. But while the discourse of benevolent supremacy had included a rejection of formal colonialism, Ignatieff now made a case for formal U.S. rule in Iraq, conceding that the U.S. military was "producing a form of imperial rule for a post-imperial age." Ideally, of course, this new kind of empire would not be necessary, but Americans no longer had the luxury of refusing to rule the world: "Those who want America to remain a republic rather than become an empire imagine rightly, but they have not factored in what tyranny or chaos can do to vital American interests. The case for empire is that it has become, in a place like Iraq, the last hope for stability and democracy alike."[2] Igantieff's essay did not appear in isolation; it was part of a rash of books, articles, and reviews about the issue of "American empire" that were no longer restricted to liberals or the left. Its appearance was part of the emergence of a new "common sense" about American power. This vision of America helped to refigure not only the U.S. role in the world, particularly the Middle East, but also the language and images that Americans used to understand themselves.

As a result of September 11 and the wars that followed it (the "war on terrorism," the war in Afghanistan, and the Iraq war), previous constructions of national and transnational identities have been both reaffirmed and revised. Both the Middle East as a moral geography and a variety of religious beliefs have continued to play significant roles. My contention, however, is that what happened after September 11 was neither the inevitable result of developments in post–cold war foreign policy nor a natural response to a terrorist attack. Although the attacks gave rise to a broad outrage, this was not the only thing Americans felt. Nor did Americans uniformly support any one policy response. Initial public reactions to the attacks were varied and unstable: Internet postings and emails offered responses that ranged from anger to grief to numbness, from pro-war to pacifist. Foreign policy in the wake of the 9/11 attacks was also contested and changeable. The "war on terrorism" was part of a larger post–cold war vision that was fractured between two competing models. One model focused on an inevitable "clash of civilizations" between the West and Islam; the other argued for what might be described as a "domino democracy theory," which assumed that people in the Middle East and the Muslim world had aspirations to be as much like the West as possible. International responses to developments post–September 11 were often quite different from American ones, and in the pages that follow I highlight some of the reactions from Europe and the Middle East. This remains, however, a story focused primarily on the ways that diverse groups of people in the United States perceived the Middle East at a time of unprecedented crisis and violence. The shape of U.S. responses to 9/11 emerged not only from rational debates about policy but also through the cultural work done by media accounts, popular culture, and television images.

This chapter is organized as an analysis of the contested meanings and compressed history made visible in five well-known images from the period beginning September 2001 and ending summer 2004, i.e., from 9/11 to Abu Ghraib. Each photograph or television image represents a moment, a problem, and a set of political and intellectual debates. As Susan Sontag has argued, "the Western memory museum is now mostly a visual one."[3] What we know is inextricably intertwined with what we have seen recorded on film or in digital memory. By asking the right questions of a photograph, we may discover what rendered it powerful at a particular place and time.

Of course, from an epistemological perspective, there is also a danger in using photographs as the basis for writing history. Photographs invite us to see them as transparent representations, as a kind of historical record. Yet, photographs are inevitably fragments. Sontag argues that the moral and political meanings of an image are established by the context in which it appears. And that context is changeable and changing: a single image, particularly a political image, may be inserted in different historical circumstances, matched with other and different photographs, and used as evidence for divergent points of view. Over time, the reproduction of certain photographs (starving children in Africa, Palestinians throwing stones at Israeli tanks) may actually work to abstract the events they depict, to make them seem less real as events precisely because they are so familiar as images.[4] Such familiar images carry a message about how to read them and what to feel: guilt, outrage, piety, hope, etc. But precisely because they do this, they stop conveying meaningful information about the world. "The knowledge gained through still photographs," Sontag writes, "will always be some kind of sentimentalism, whether cynical or humanist." To avoid these limits, photographers and their publishers often try to fix the meaning of the image with captions. But the caption cannot forestall sentimentalism, Sontag argues, nor can it prevent the "argument or moral plea" of a photograph from being revised or undermined by its inherently ambiguous meanings and multiple potential contexts.[5]

In some sense, this chapter is a sustained engagement with the question of whether it is possible to caption a photograph. To write a caption—and each section of this chapter might be considered an impossibly extended caption—might make it possible if not to fix the image, at least to insist on its historicity. My aim here is to remember the moments in which the images were made and the ways in which they circulated, to take note of their fluidity, and, finally, to articulate the cultural work done by these photographs as interventions in their historical moment. I do not wish to imply that the photographs analyzed here are the only route to the ideological and cultural problems they open up, but to argue that the images participated in the process of meaning-making that, from the ashes of 9/11, forged the imperial reach of the Iraq war. Each commentary-caption does suggest a preferred reading of the photograph, offering a particular set of contexts and conversations as the most relevant and politically salient. If the conversations that surround the image sometimes also seem to operate at some distance from it, that is not surprising. Instead, it highlights the sly way that culture works. Culture packs associations and arguments into dense ecosystems of meaning; it requires us to know a thousand things about politics, social life, and correct feeling in order to "get it"; and then, in a remarkable sleight of hand, it makes the reactions it evokes seem spontaneous and obvious.[6] The project of this chapter is to insist on reading the emotions evoked by these highly charged photographs as historically constituted feeling. It is to refuse these images their future as sentimentalism by giving them feet of clay.

SNAPSHOT: FIREMEN RAISING THE FLAG

The photograph shows three firemen at the site of the World Trade Center on September 11, 2001. They are attaching an American flag to a wildly leaning pole. They are dusty and dirty, but the afternoon light shining on them makes the blues and yellows of their uniforms shimmer. All three are white; the one most fully facing the camera is stocky and powerful. They are looking up. Behind them, barely in focus, rises a pile of debris that goes well above their heads.

The photograph was taken by Thomas Franklin, a photographer with a New Jersey paper, and has become one of the most widely reproduced images associated with September 11. Franklin later said that he immediately recognized the parallel to the famous image of U.S. marines raising the flag at Iwo Jima in 1945. And just as the Iwo Jima image became the informal icon of American courage and sacrifice in World War II, the image of the firemen became a potent symbol of American resilience and bravery after the 9/11 attacks. The photograph circulated widely on the Internet, was

Figure 26.   Photo by Thomas E. Franklin. Courtesy of *The Record* (Bergen County, N.J.), 2001.

reproduced in newspapers and magazines, and was sold on T-shirts and posters. Both the Associated Press and *Editor & Publisher* named it the best picture of the year. A woman in Kansas made a mosaic of it using ten thousand colored beads. Later, U.S. troops in Afghanistan left copies of the photo as "calling cards" on the battlefield. The following year, it was issued as a "Heroes of 2001" postage stamp.[7]

The photograph was only one of dozens of searing images produced on September 11. Its elevation to iconic status is the story of one particular process of constructing an understanding of the attacks on New York and Washington, D.C. and of the history that produced them. In fact, for most people it was television news, not newspapers, that most immediately provided the visual record of the day's events. As news of the attacks spread, most TV channels switched to full-time live coverage. At first there was no clear narrative and the television networks had not yet branded the event. (Before long each news team labored under its own title: "Attack on America" at both CBS and NBC, "America Attacked" on ABC.) The cameras were there immediately, however, and the events and emotions of that morning were soon encapsulated in extraordinary images: the first stricken tower throwing up plumes of smoke over lower Manhattan; a plane slicing through the second tower; then the crumbling collapse of both buildings into mountains of debris. In Washington, D.C., where a plane was flown into the Pentagon, the smoke could be seen from downtown, several miles away. Both the White House and the Capitol building were hastily evacuated.

On the streets of New York, people watched, frozen in shock and disbelief. As the buildings collapsed, many fled the area, just ahead of a billowing tidal wave of dust. Others emerged from it, covered in ash and often struggling to breathe. As the hours passed, television cameras also conveyed haunting images of firefighters and police officers, breathing through masks, as they picked doggedly through the rubble looking for survivors. Around the perimeter of the destruction, the friends and families of the victims gathered, holding pictures of their loved ones, which they hoped would bring them information or inspire rescuers. Approximately three thousand people died on September 11, several hundred of them firefighters, police officers, and rescue workers.[8]

Satellite television and the Internet quickly propelled live news and images around the world, prompting expressions of global sympathy and solidarity. In Germany and in Britain, flags flew at half-mast; in Prague, people placed lighted candles at the base of the statue of Saint Wenceslas. The French newspaper *Le Monde* famously ran an editorial with the headline "We Are All Americans." Palestinian spokesperson Hanan Ashrawi told CNN, "We feel your pain, we feel your sorrow, we will do everything we can to help."[9]

The rush of supportive global responses was complicated by fears of how the United States would react to the attacks. A young man who lit a candle in Prague said he felt a great deal of sympathy, "But I hope the U.S. will be careful how it responds and will find the right culprit and that no other innocent victims will die."[10] Chilean author Ariel Dorfman argued in an editorial that Americans would now have to acknowledge the end of their sense of exceptionalism; they could no longer imagine themselves "beyond the sorrows and calamities that have plagued less fortunate people around the world." Noting the worldwide outpouring of support, he remarked, "It remains to be seen if this compassion shown to the mightiest power on this planet will be reciprocated."[11] In the Middle East as well, responses at the grassroots level were decidedly mixed. While ordinary Jordanians gathered outside the U.S. embassy for a candlelight vigil, other Arabs praised the attack on the United States.[12] By September 2001, the year-old second intifada of Palestinians against the Israeli occupation had devolved into an escalating cycle of violence. More than seven hundred Palestinians had been killed in the previous year, along with almost two hundred Israelis, and among Palestinians ongoing anger about U.S. support for Israel was at an all-time high. CNN and NBC both aired footage of Palestinians celebrating the news of the attacks by dancing and shooting rifles in the air.[13]

In the United States, a prominent initial response was what the *New York Times* called the "hero hunt." The bravery and determination of New York firefighters had already captured the public imagination. After escaping from the World Trade Center, many people told of seeing firefighters going up into the buildings they themselves were trying desperately to flee. Those stories were repeated over and over again in newspaper and television accounts. "We needed to balance out the grief," the *Times* said simply, in one of its dozen editorials and features lionizing the firefighters.[14]

Throughout September and October, firehouses in New York were inundated with cookies, candles, and sympathy cards for those who had died. Several weeks after 9/11, former Reagan speechwriter Peggy Noonan wrote of finding herself standing on the sidewalk with other New Yorkers, mostly white-collar professionals, as a convoy of firefighters and construction workers involved in the recovery drove by. The bystanders shouted and cheered for the workers, waving flags and signs and throwing kisses. Noonan commented on the irony of class reversal: professionals, writers, and lawyers who had been "kings and queens of the city," were now cheering men who probably "hadn't been applauded since the day they danced . . . with their bride at their wedding."[15]

The image of the firemen raising the flag crystallized this self-conscious search for heroes. Under the banner of heroism, both the media and folk culture complemented a recognition of enormous loss with a vision of national pride. "American-ness" became defined through ideals of courage and self-sacrifice. Within that framework, however, two rather different visions emerged. One might be called "ordinary heroism," the other, "heroic masculinity." The two were thoroughly intertwined, even as they offered contrasting narratives of the meanings of September 11. Both were embodied in the idealized image of the firemen.

When commentators began to insist, as they immediately did, that "everything had changed" after 9/11, they meant in part that the country had a new zeitgeist, for which "hero" became a shorthand. This vision of ordinary heroism exuded hopefulness and democratic idealism. Media and popular culture imbued the "heroes" with the qualities they now extolled as exemplary of Americans in general—bravery, generosity, stalwartness, and self-sacrifice. The multinational backgrounds of the victims at the World Trade Center were heralded as emblematic of the U.S. embrace of multiculturalism. Many Americans described themselves as transformed by a longing to be of service, to help those in need, to act with greater civic spirit.[16] There was an outpouring of altruism: the lines to give blood were hours long, and the size of monetary donations to the victims' funds was truly staggering. A nationwide survey showed that Americans overall felt stronger connections across racial and class divides, and generally exhibited "a more capacious sense of 'we' than we have had in the adult experience of most Americans now alive."[17]

In chapter 5, I documented the cultural work done during the Iran hostage crisis by the production of iconographic American ordinariness—people whose ability to represent the United States lay in the very fact that they were not leaders or public figures, but rather ordinary people in extraordinary circumstances who refused to be only victims. After 9/11, the rescuers, survivors, and victims were all described as heroes. However much these affirmations of solidarity and self-sacrifice were also constructions—in the end there was no permanent transformation of Americans into heroes—the trope of ordinary heroism affirmed the kind of compassion that Ariel Dorfman had hoped Americans would be able to bring to the world at large.

Very quickly, however, the idealism of ordinary heroism was overshadowed by a vision of Americanness as heroic masculinity. The firefighters hailed in the public sphere were working-class people, mostly men and mostly white, who for many weeks were as close to military heroes as the new "war on terrorism" would have. Those searching for a more militarized heroism offered a rush of enthusiastic commentary claiming the firefighters as ideals of masculinity. The *New York Times* trumpeted "The Return of Manly Men"; "Welcome back, Duke [John Wayne]," enthused the *Wall Street Journal*.[18] For some observers, these men were constructed as "ideal Americans" more easily than most of the 9/11 victims, who tended to be clustered at either end of the social spectrum—many of those who died were bankers or investment brokers; others were the undocumented immigrant workers who served them. The firefighters were icons of the lower-middle-class "working-man," whose idealized "let's do it" pragmatism has often been recuperated in times of crisis as the folk embodiment of national strength.

The photograph of the firemen was also a photograph of flag-raising, and soon, the American flag itself was flying everywhere—on the side of buildings, in front of homes, on bumper stickers, in advertising, and as part of the window displays in stores. The flag in these contexts bespoke a level of defiance that, for example, the yellow ribbons of the hostage crisis had not. Nonetheless its meanings were contested and fluid.[19] When family members placed a small flag in an impromptu memorial for a loved one who had died, or when a group of surfers in Australia formed a human American flag on a beach, they apparently did so simply to offer remembrance and to acknowledge victims, including noncitizens who had made the United States their home.[20]

Within a few weeks, however, the connotations of the flag subtly changed. The heroism of community sacrifice merged into a masculinized heroism that was equated with nationalism and ultimately with jingoism. For some the flag meant righteous anger; it symbolized commitment to revenge. Later, the flag was often connected to support for the war in Afghanistan—those "calling cards" left by soldiers in Afghanistan turned the photo of the firemen and the flag into a symbol of war as revenge. A few months after 9/11, country singer Toby Keith released a hit song, "Courtesy of the Red, White, and Blue (The Angry American)," that succinctly summarized the new mood:

> Justice will be served
> And the battle will rage . . .
> And you'll be sorry that you messed with
> The U.S. of A.
> 'Cause we'll put a boot in your ass
> It's the American way.

The song offered a cowboy toughness, a promise to fight, and, elsewhere in the lyrics, an insistence that "the eagle will fly" to enact the revenge that some commentators clearly longed for. (Later, just before the Iraq war, a pro-war hit single by Darryl Worley, "Have You Forgotten?," mobilized the memory of the attacks in a similar fashion: "Some say that America is just looking for a fight/ Well, after 9/11, man, I'd have to say they're right.")[21]

As the flag became a militarized icon, it also served, for others, as a self-defense mechanism. People who "looked" Muslim, Arab, or merely brown-skinned often visibly displayed the flag in their places of business, hoping to blunt the potential for hate crimes. In times of war, patriotic fervor has consistently included racial, ethnic, and/or political repression, from the Palmer raids of World War I to the internment of Japanese Americans in World War II to police violence against antiwar protestors during Vietnam.[22] This war was no different. Hundreds of Arab and Muslim men were arrested in broad rounds of detentions, and thousands more were hauled in for "voluntary" interviews, while many of those who simply appeared to be Arab or Muslim were profiled at airports and other public places. In November 2001, Congress passed the USA PATRIOT Act, which limited certain civil and legal rights for both citizens and noncitizens. The law included a significant expansion of the ability of government agencies to use electronic surveillance without a warrant. It also severely limited the legal rights of anyone U.S. officials declared an "enemy combatant"; those so designated were caught in a limbo, treated neither as domestic criminals nor foreign prisoners of war, and denied the legal protections offered to either.[23]

Despite President Bush's calls for tolerance and his public meetings with Arab and Muslim leaders, there were more than one thousand incidents of violence against Arab and Muslim Americans (or those perceived to be Arab or Muslim) in the fall of 2001, and at least five people were killed. "I see flags everywhere," one American of Palestinian descent told a reporter, "yet my first instinct is apprehension."[24]

Anti-Muslim and anti-Arab sentiment was common, but it was not the only response. A number of Arab and Muslim Americans also reported that they had been embraced and supported by their neighbors and friends. When a store owned by a Palestinian was vandalized outside of Washington, D.C., people in the community sent dozens of cards, bouquets of flowers, and written notes of apology for the behavior of others. The Council on American-Islamic Relations reported being inundated with calls and letters from members relating acts of kindness and support around the country.[25]

Still, the sense of threat was palpable, and Muslims and Arabs were not the only Americans who felt targeted. Right after 9/11, the government began to issue a series of alerts, color-coded yellow, orange, or red, about possible additional terrorist attacks. Someone sent anthrax-poisoned letters to congressional leaders; there were warnings about possible attacks on the New York subway. In the general climate of fear, dissent—and even certain kinds of discussion about the motivations or backgrounds of those who committed terrorist acts—was rendered by some as unpatriotic and dangerous. A few days after September 11, White House press secretary Ari

Fleischer warned reporters that "people have to watch what they say and what they do." Those who criticized the administration for civil rights violations against Arabs or Muslims were told by Attorney General John Ashcroft that "Your tactics only aid terrorists, for they erode our national unity and diminish our resolve."[26]

In the post-9/11 moment, the photograph of firemen raising the flag had done a complicated kind of cultural work. It had been mobilized, for one moment and for some people, as a symbol of ordinary heroism—of generosity, diversity, and strength—for those in and outside of the United States struggling to forge their own understandings of what had happened and what it meant. But, as with all photographs, its meanings were fluid and contested. As a symbol of heroic masculinity, it also became linked to nationalism and to an aggressive patriotism that equated Americanness with revenge, militarism, and the silencing of dissent. In that version of the photograph, the right to nationalist revenge was carried with the flag. The target of that revenge was generally named as Osama bin Laden, and his image also circulated as a tightly compacted site of meaning-making.

SNAPSHOT: OSAMA BIN LADEN

The video was released October 7, 2001, showing bin Laden dressed in fatigues and a traditional headdress, with a rifle by his side. He was somewhere in Afghanistan, standing in front of a cave. The video sometimes showed him gesturing and pointing; other times, he was smiling. The rifle signified his militancy; the headdress showed his conservatism and piety; and the very fact of the video recording marked his self-aware modernity. The video was enabled by a world in which images and ideologies flowed promiscuously across old borders. It had been recorded by al-Qaeda and then sent to the Arab satellite news network al-Jazeera, which, as U.S. interest in Afghanistan and Iraq intensified, would soon become a global media force, much as CNN had during the 1991 Gulf War.

Bin Laden was not only the war on terrorism's major target, he was also its most potent symbol. The still of the video was soon broadcast all over the world and plastered on magazine and newspaper covers in the United States. It was on Internet sites ranging from stopviolence.com to lifeisajoke.com. There were bin Laden video games on the Web and bin Laden piñatas for sale—a quick and unerring consumer culture response to bin Laden's iconization that paralleled the proliferation of anti-Khomeini products during the Iran hostage crisis era.

Figure 27.   Courtesy of AP/Wide World Photos.

In the United States, bin Laden's performance on the tape, from his ready way with a rifle to the deliberate fashion in which he combined symbols of piety and militarism, meant that he ideally represented the cruelty of what al-Qaeda did, of what terrorists do. Bin Laden himself was (and remains as of this writing) a genuine danger. Many commentators at the time suggested a range of possibilities for addressing the threat he posed. Some argued for hunting down bin Laden and putting him on trial for crimes against humanity; others, including liberals and parts of the left, supported military action against Afghanistan along the lines of what the United States ultimately pursued. But bin Laden as icon was something else: a densely packed set of associations and justifications that served as the visible backdrop for Bush's self-proclaimed transformation of the U.S. posture in the world.

The ability of non-state actors to exact a price from powerful states was not new, but the end of the cold war coincided with the intensification of globalization in a way that raised serious questions about whether traditional state power might soon be rendered obsolete. The increased role of international organizations like the WTO and IMF; the movement of transnational capital and the continual relocation of production to chase lower labor costs; the extraordinarily rapid global flow of information, culture, and ideas enabled by new technologies like the Internet; and the development of diasporic communities as loci of emotional affiliation were all symptoms and engines of the phenomenon broadly and loosely defined as "globalization." Whatever the limits of the term, it marked a transformation that clearly was under way. The division of the world into two great superpower orbits and the larger set of nonaligned or marginally aligned nations that served as the superpowers' battleground and their prize—what Michael Denning has called the "era of three worlds"—was coming to an end.[27]

Both scholars and politicians have often described terrorism as one example of how global networks can make mockeries of traditional models of state power and outmoded military structures. Thus, when in October 2001 President Bush announced the "war on terrorism," he insisted that the United States was about to begin a "new and different war" that would need to be fought "on all fronts." Bush argued that unlike World War II, which brought clear-cut victory, or Vietnam, which ended in a quagmire, or even the high-tech Gulf War, the new war would be "a different kind of war that requires a different type of approach and a different type of mentality."[28] Speaking to a reporter a few days later, Vice President Dick Cheney put it more bluntly, "It is different than the Gulf War was, in the sense that it may never end. At least, not in our lifetime."[29]

War is nothing if not politics, or as Karl von Clausewitz famously said, "diplomacy by other means."[30] But despite having "declared war" on terrorism, U.S. leaders insisted on defining terrorism in terms that marginalized it as a political issue, by focusing on terrorism as a moral failing. The terrorists hate us because they hate freedom, President Bush told audiences repeatedly; the war on terrorism was, he insisted, "a monumental struggle of good versus evil."[31] The attacks of 9/11 were of course immoral acts, but that statement can only be the beginning, not the end, of analysis. Not only are definitions of good and evil historically constituted, but the participation by relatively large numbers of people in murder or other kinds of violence (that is, in numbers that cannot be explained by any individual pathology) always requires a historical explanation. There are no questions about the causes of social violence—from the Nazi perpetration of the Holocaust, to the Khmer Rouge genocide in Cambodia, the European colonization of Africa, or the endemic violence in U.S. urban areas—to which "because they were evil" is a satisfactory explanation. Evil is a historical problem, and historical problems require politically informed analysis (just as political problems require historically informed analysis).

Ervand Abrahamian has argued that in covering the war on terrorism, the U.S. media abetted the administration's framing of the conflict in de-politicized terms by systematically avoiding any discussion of links between the September 11 attacks and U.S. policy in the Middle East, particularly the Israeli-Palestinian conflict. In one tape released after September 11, bin Laden stated that his attacks were aimed not only to destroy the Western "crusaders" but also to "revenge our people killed in Palestine"—a position he had taken many times before. But, having already been advised by the White House not to air such "inflammatory" messages, U.S. television networks simply refused to show the video.[32]

Of course, the fact that bin Laden claimed to be fighting for the liberation of Palestine does not make that claim true, and it would not in any case justify the mass murder of civilians. The issue is simply what Americans (at least those who got their news from U.S. television) were allowed to know, what information they had available to compare with the Bush administration's framework or their own previous understanding of the issues. Even if bin Laden's claims about al-Qaeda's motivations were false or perhaps irrelevant, the political arguments he made nonetheless did matter to the millions of people in the Middle East who, though they might oppose terrorism, nonetheless felt some sympathy for bin Laden's hatred of the United States. In Europe, and certainly in the Middle East, the fact that many Arabs and Muslims were angry about the ongoing Israeli occupation and the brutalization of Palestinians was taken as a given; even British Prime Minister Tony Blair regularly made the connection. To say that these issues were relevant was not to say that U.S. policies made terrorism justifiable, or that the United States somehow deserved the violence aimed against it. But the fact that, in the United States, those larger questions about the relationship between U.S. Middle East policy and terrorist acts were effectively marginalized promoted a de-politicized language that made the 9/11 attacks almost personal in their abstractness. Framed as an act of "evildoers" who hated something as broad and vague as "freedom"—rather than, say, something as concrete and specific as U.S. foreign policy—the violence of September 11 seemed incomprehensible as a political act.

In the 1970s and 1980s, policymakers and pundits had framed terrorism as a problem of hyper-politicization: terrorists destroyed the sacred private space of individualism by insisting that no space was free of politics. After 9/11, the problem was understood differently; terrorists might be speaking in political terms, but those terms were literally invisible, and so their acts became evidence of private pathology. In both cases, however, the hallmark of terrorism in these debates was that it blurred boundaries between

Figure 28. Courtesy of Reuters.

public and private: it failed to separate the home from the world and, by claiming Islam as a mantle, brought faith into politics. By crossing the line between state and non-state, private and public, legitimate and illegitimate violence, terrorism constituted a problem of categorization. And categories mattered: the power to define the terms of the new war, and the moral geographies of global politics, was at stake.

SNAPSHOT: AFGHAN WOMEN IN BURQAS

She is covered head-to-toe in heavy blue fabric, with a small vent for her face. She may be in a group, or alone, but the image appears designed to exhibit her invisibility. She is presumed to be the silent testament to her own oppression. As a Muslim woman under the draconian rule of the Taliban, she cannot be seen uncovered in public, cannot work or go to school, can barely get health care, so that Afghan women have one of the highest mortality rates in the world. Sometimes the photos of the women in burqas also show a young girl in the group, uncovered and lovely. She is there, it seems, to make clear what has been lost to these women—perhaps to suggest the energy and sexuality that the burqa is presumed to have destroyed.

Within a week of 9/11, Americans were inundated with information about Afghanistan, about Islam, and about the oppression of Muslim women in Afghanistan. The images and stories were everywhere, on the covers of *Time* and *Newsweek,* on the nightly news, in women's magazines, on the *Oprah* show. There was no question that the Afghan government severely limited the education and freedom of both men and women. The religiously ultra-conservative Taliban had come to power at the end of a civil war that left much of the population at the mercy of lawless factions. Once in power, the Taliban instituted a particularly oppressive and ideologically driven form of Islamist rule. Under their regime, the most quotidian functions of government, from road repair to economic policy, were all but ignored, while violations against "Islamic law" were aggressively punished.

Like other revolutionary movements in other contexts, the Taliban's leaders used women's bodies as a symbol of their struggle.[33] They came to power in part by claiming that Islam would protect women from the dangers of secularism and immorality and from the ravages of the previous civil war, in which rape and assault had been common.[34] Once in power, they demanded that all women don the burqa as a signifier of the virtue of Islam, and kept women and girls from going to school and from many forms of professional work. In August 2001, a Physicians for Human Rights survey found that a majority of Afghan women and men said the Taliban had worsened their lives. Over 80 percent of respondents also said that the Taliban's persecution for dress code violations was an unimportant matter; they were far more concerned about health care, poverty, and war.[35]

Afghan women's bodies—their covering or uncovering—were also mobilized by U.S. feminists as a symbol of their opposition to the Taliban. Eventually, the figure of the Afghan woman covered in a burqa helped to justify the U.S. war against Afghanistan in the winter of 2001–2002. For many years, U.S.-based feminist activists, particularly the Fund for a Feminist Majority, had organized a campaign to "End Gender Apartheid in Afghanistan," which had successfully worked with Afghan women's groups to educate Americans about the Taliban's draconian rule. But the campaign was often controversial. Other feminists argued that the Feminist Majority's approach, particularly its intensive focus on the burqa as a "symbol of the total oppression of women," was sensationalist and culturally insensitive.[36] For example, in the spring of 2001, at an all-star performance of Eve Ensler's "Vagina Monologues" in Madison Square Garden, Oprah Winfrey did a reading of a segment Ensler had recently added to the show, called "Under the Burqa." "Imagine a huge cloth/hung over your entire body/like you were a shameful statue," Winfrey read. The performance ended with the appearance of a burqa-clad woman whom Winfrey dramatically unveiled. Eighteen thousand audience members were then invited to wear bits of burqas on their lapels as a remembrance of Afghan women's suffering.[37]

In reviews and discussions of the show, several critics suggested Winfrey should not have lifted the burqa from the woman, who was herself a woman's rights activist in Afghanistan. The woman should have lifted her own burqa, they argued; the show should not have implied that she needed an American woman to symbolically free her. Feminists both inside and outside the United States argued that such fantasies of rescue, connected to a long history of imperialist cultural rhetoric, had positioned European or American women as having the responsibility to "save" the women of the Muslim world from their own culture.[38]

At the same time, feminist critics of the crusade against the burqa were also opposed to the Taliban's treatment of women, and argued for international feminist activism that engaged productively with women activists in Afghanistan. The problem with mainstream U.S. feminism came when it selectively highlighted issues that resonated with American or Western women, who often were most energized by limitations on personal and sexual liberty, rather than the economic, political, and educational issues prioritized by women in Afghanistan. Those approaches functioned not as a way of representing Afghan women's lives but as a way of refusing to see them, of failing to engage the complex political and economic situation that for many women in Afghanistan made the burqa either a low priority or a non-issue.[39]

When members of the Bush administration spoke to the American people about the war, they also, from the beginning, used women's rights language, arguing that the war was necessary not only to retaliate for 9/11 but also because the Taliban deserved to be deposed from power due to their history of misrule, and particularly their record on women's issues. In November, First Lady Laura Bush gave the president's weekly radio address and echoed the official administration position: "The brutal oppression of women is a central goal of the terrorists . . . [and] the fight against terrorism is also a fight for the rights and dignity of women."[40] U.S. foreign policy justifications had been intertwined with women's rights rhetoric before, as with the language that had linked "benevolent supremacy" to a vision of the "freely chosen subordination" of women in democratic heterosexual marriage. But in 2001 the convergence of a new war on terrorism and a rhetoric of women's liberation was uncomfortable for many U.S.-based feminists, and it launched a heated debate about whether feminists should in this case—or in any case—support a war that claimed the liberation of women as one of its justifications.

The U.S. invaded Afghanistan in November 2001, and the Taliban were deposed from power within a matter of weeks. Osama bin Laden and several of his key advisors apparently escaped, however, so there could be no pretense that the "war on terrorism" had been won. During and after that war, the rule of the Taliban was presented as the exemplar of the kind of world the terrorists wanted to create. The image of the oppressed Muslim woman in the burqa, and by extension the status of women in Islam, became central to a debate that soon began to rage about the roots of terrorism and the role of religion or culture in fueling it. Analysts and policymakers regularly insisted that neither the Taliban nor bin Laden were "true" Islam, but despite those caveats and qualifiers, and despite even the good intentions of those who showed solidarity with their Muslim neighbors in the United States, the Taliban's militancy and Afghan women's invisibility had come to be dual signifiers that together evoked the idea of an inherent difference between "Islam" and the "West." That difference had been famously termed by Samuel Huntington "the clash of civilizations."

The phrase, and the concept it succinctly encapsulated, came from the title of Huntington's influential book, *The Clash of Civilizations and the Remaking of World Order*, published in 1998. Huntington was one of the nation's most respected and influential scholars of international relations; the book was an expansion of a controversial article he had published in *Foreign Affairs* three years earlier.[41] When Huntington's analysis first appeared, it was hotly debated among international relations scholars, many of whom criticized it for the broad strokes of its argument, simplistic statements, and harshly negative views of Islam, but the discussion remained largely within the academic and policy communities.[42] Then, in the aftermath of September 11, *Clash of Civilizations* was reissued and became a national bestseller, and Huntington became a media star. He was interviewed in the *New York Times*, wrote a commissioned essay for *Newsweek*, and was profiled in *The Atlantic*. More importantly, "clash of civilizations" suddenly became media shorthand, a presumption, a coded way of "explaining" the origins of terrorism and the nature of Islam.[43]

The full content of *The Clash of Civilizations* presented a fairly complicated argument about the future of global politics. Huntington argued that with the end of the cold war, culture, particularly religion, would take over from economics and ideology as the glue holding groups of people together. The "civilization" (a term he resurrected from the early twentieth century, when it had distinctly racialist connotations) would replace the nation-state and the cold war bloc as the primary organizing site for identity—and thus as the nexus of conflict. Civilizations, he argued, are coherent, generally large-scale cultures that tend to have distinct values and world views. They are long-lived and relatively unified, based on fundamental ties of "blood, language, religion, and way of life" (42). Members of any given civilization tend to define their identity through the articulation of an "other," an "outside." Thus, Huntington argued, the prospects for peaceful intercivilizational integration were not good: "Relations between groups from different civilizations . . . will be almost never close, usually cool, and often hostile" (207).

Within this overall view of world history as essentially a contest between warring factions, Huntington believed that the West would face its greatest challenges from Asia, which was gaining in economic strength and power, and Islam, which was the most dangerous threat. Muslims, he said, were growing in numbers and strength and were in general more inclined toward violent conflict than people from other civilizations (254–265). Against those who argued that the conflicts between Western nations and Muslim ones emerged from clashing political interests, such as the history of U.S. intervention in the Middle East, the situation in Israel/Palestine, or the corruption of Arab governments supported by the United States, Huntington posited something far more elemental:

> The underlying problem for the West is not Islamic fundamentalism. It is Islam, a different civilization whose people are convinced of the superiority of their culture and are obsessed with the inferiority of their power. The problem for Islam is not the CIA or the U.S. Department of Defense. It is the West, a different civilization whose people are convinced of the universality of their culture and believe that their superior, if declining, power imposes on them the obligation to extend that culture throughout the world. (217–218)

As one proof that this cultural tension had reached a state of "quasi war," Huntington cited the fact that between 1980 and 1999 the United States had engaged in seventeen military operations in the Middle East, all against Muslims. There was, he said, no comparable pattern of U.S. military operations against any other people (217).

Huntington used a relativist argument to posit a deeply conservative position. Western culture, he suggested, should stop trying to assert its values and beliefs as if they were universal. Western values such as rationality, individualism, human rights, and separation of church and state had little relevance for other cultures. Western leaders may claim to act in the interests of the "world community," but such statements are presumptuous and wrong. The West does not speak for the rest of the world, it confronts it, Huntington argued. In this confrontation, Western civilization would have to accommodate other civilizations, renouncing its universalist pretensions, but it should above all aim to protect its own interests, maintain its global position, and prevent its "subordination to other economically and demographically more dynamic civilizations" (303). An honest particularism in defense of Western values, Huntington posited, would be far better than disingenuous talk of a universal world community.

Huntington's general arguments about culture were mobilized in the media to support a broad discourse about the dangers of "the clash of civilizations," one that did not always maintain his realist policymaking assumptions. That discourse, as it was constructed in journals of elite opinion and in small-town newspapers, on television and on radio talk shows, frequently claimed that the United States was the last defender of the noble values of individualism and human rights, which Islamic civilization did not respect. An editorial writer for the *San Diego Union-Tribune*, for example, described his fact-finding trip to the Middle East by contrasting a mosque and a church standing side-by-side in Istanbul:

> The two nearby monuments symbolize the age-old rivalry
> between two cultures—the largely democratic and secularized
> West, built on the Enlightenment ideals of reason and individual
> liberty spawned in 18th century Europe and America; and the
> largely authoritarian and theocratic societies of the Muslim world,
> shaped over the past 14 centuries by the unchanging orthodoxy of
> the Holy Koran.[44]

Huntington had been similarly, if implicitly, scornful of non-Western civilizations, but he had insisted that they should be treated as competitors, not potential converts. *Newsweek*, on the other hand, published a long, sweeping cover story by the conservative political scientist Fareed Zakaria, which argued that while the culture of the Middle East "fuels the fanaticism" at the heart of terrorism, the only way out of political and economic stagnation for Middle Eastern Muslims was to come to terms with Western hegemony. "If the West can help Islam enter modernity in dignity and peace, it will have done more than achieved security," Zakaria wrote. "It will have changed the world."[45] In the U.S. media, then, the concept of a "clash" was mobile: it hovered between a despairing vision of the inevitability of conflict and a determined manifesto for America's mission to the world.

Nowhere was the threat of a cultural clash discussed with more intensity than among American evangelical Christians. In the aftermath of 9/11, several evangelical leaders made incendiary comments. Franklin Graham, son of Billy Graham and leader of a mission organization that had programs in Afghanistan and later in Iraq, called Islam "a very evil and wicked religion." Jerry Falwell made an infamous declaration on *60 Minutes* that "Mohammed was a terrorist." The National Association of Evangelicals and the Southern Baptist Convention held a meeting shortly thereafter to try to undo some of the damage that those kinds of statements were inflicting on the U.S. image abroad, and *Christianity Today* published several articles that addressed in a more complex way the teachings of Islam.[46] Yet statements like Falwell's spoke to a larger Manichean vision in which the forces of "false religion" were at war with the followers of Jesus. Lay people evidenced a similar outlook as they enthusiastically purchased the dozens of critical evaluations of Islam published by evangelical publishers, with titles like *Secrets of the Koran, Inside Islam,* and *Married to Mohammed.* Polls in fall 2002 showed that evangelicals in general had an unfavorable view of Islam, and that 79 percent did not believe that Muslims and Christians worship the same God.[47]

Huntington subscribed to a far more subtle sense of the cultural differences at hand, and certainly would not have agreed with the idea of a moral crusade against Islam. He could not control the ways in which the notion of a "clash of civilizations" became meaningful shorthand for different groups of people, any more than New York City firefighters controlled the meanings that people made of their heroism or their image. There was a particular irony, however, in the way that Huntington's argument was eventually taken up by the Bush administration in its push for war against Iraq. While Huntington supported aggressive action in the war on terrorism and had backed the war in Afghanistan, the logic of his argument suggested a more cautious view about the advisability of turning to Iraq as the next target, as the Bush team began to do in full force as soon as the major fighting in Afghanistan was over. In *Clash,* Huntington had continually insisted that, while conflict was inevitable, Western leaders had to realize they could not forcefully transform other nations: "Western belief in the universality of Western culture suffers from three problems: it is false; it is immoral; and it is dangerous. . . . Imperialism is the necessary logical consequence of universalism" (310). Huntington clearly saw other civilizations as inferior to the "West," but argued that Western nations should defend their interests, not promote their ideologies. For Huntington, unlike Ignatieff, imperialism was always to be avoided.[48]

The Bush administration, however, would find in Huntington's turn of phrase the silent justification for its invasion and subsequent occupation of Iraq, even as its policymakers claimed to be opposed to the concept of a clash. In a televised address on March 17, 2003, President Bush succinctly summarized his administration's three reasons for going to war with Iraq. The president argued, first, that Iraq's nuclear, chemical, and biological weapons capabilities posed a clear and present threat to the United States; second, that Hussein's government aided and abetted terrorism generally and al-Qaeda specifically; and third, that the regime was a tyrannical one, guilty of gross violations of human rights. Toppling it was promoted as a pivotal step in facilitating democratization throughout the region.

The first two of these arguments might have resonated easily with a defensive foreign policy posture and a realist worldview, especially if the threat of an Iraqi attack could be shown to be potentially imminent and if the purported link between Hussein and bin Laden could be shown to be solid and operationally significant. Neither of these contentions proved to be sustainable, however. In the case of Iraq's supposed weapons of mass destruction, policymakers had self-consciously exaggerated the slim evidence obtained by U.S. intelligence services in order to make the case for war.[49] Regarding the terrorism connection, members of the administration knew that the evidence for Iraq's ties to al-Qaeda was very weak, but they continued to argue publicly that, as the president put it, Iraq had "aided, trained, and harbored terrorists, including operatives of al-Qaeda."[50] According to Secretary of State Colin Powell's testimony to the official commission investigating the U.S. response to 9/11, members of the Bush foreign policy team had come into the White House with the agenda of toppling Hussein. Deputy Secretary of Defense Paul Wolfowitz had argued for using the events of 9/11 "as a way to deal with the Iraq problem." The final report of the 9/11 commission argued that there was no evidence that Iraq and al-Qaeda ever had "a collaborative operational relationship" or that Iraq had been involved in any attacks on the United States. Nonetheless, polls taken in the run-up to the war showed that 68 percent of Americans believed that Saddam Hussein had a direct hand in the attacks on the United States.[51]

Although both these arguments, concerning Iraq's weapons and its terrorist ties, were critical in bringing the nation to war, once the war was under way the Bush administration had to increasingly rely on the third justification—that the war was to be fought for liberty. Announcing the imminent start of the war, Bush had articulated his vision in a statement directed to the Iraqi people:

... We will tear down the apparatus of terror and we will help
you to build a new Iraq that is prosperous and free. In a free Iraq,
there will be ... no more executions of dissidents, no more torture
chambers and rape rooms. The tyrant will soon be gone. The day of
your liberation is near.[52]

President Bush's promise to use U.S. military power as a force for freedom was a dramatic departure from a realist framework of pursuing only
limited U.S. national interests (even when those interests were justified by
claims of U.S. benevolence or stewardship). This stance represented the as-
cendance within the administration of a strongly ideological group of neoconservative defense intellectuals and policymakers. As I argued in chapter
4, the term "neoconservative" originally emerged in the 1970s in reference
to a specific group of people who had defined themselves as newly conservative after turning against the social liberalism of the 1960s. By the 1990s,
however, "neoconservatism" referred to a fairly broad set of foreign policy
ideas subscribed to in various degrees by a range of people who would come
to have great influence in the Bush administration. Neoconservatives generally supported a more proactive or offensive U.S. military posture, a
strong pro-Israel Middle East policy, and the aggressive promotion of free
markets. They also argued strongly for developing U.S. goals that were
based as much on ideological or moral precepts as on realist ones, though
the actual practice of that moralism proved to be selective and self-inter-
ested, as I will argue.

The neoconservative, offense-oriented military approach has now been
codified as the "Bush Doctrine" of preemption; that is, the assertion of a
U.S. right to strike against foes who pose a potential but not necessarily imminent threat to U.S. interests. Bush began to lay out the basic components
of that doctrine in his State of the Union address in January 2002, when he
declared that the United States now confronted an "Axis of Evil" that included Iraq, North Korea, and Iran. All three states, he argued, were trying
to get access to weapons of mass destruction. The United States, however,
would not "permit the world's most dangerous regimes to threaten us with
the world's most destructive weapons."[53] Bush finalized his doctrine in
June 2002 during a speech at West Point, when he declared that "If we wait
for threats to fully materialize, we will have waited too long. ... We must
take the battle to the enemy, disrupt his plans and confront the worst
threats before they emerge."[54] Both scholars and observers in the press
noted that the Bush Doctrine of preemption overturned not only certain
basic premises of international law but also the fundamental principles of

U.S. foreign policy over the previous five decades.[55] As Bush stated it, the doctrine had no limits; wherever U.S. policymakers saw a *potential* threat, they would reserve the right to respond with military action, including the overthrow of governments.

Administration officials generally accompanied articulations of the Bush Doctrine with broad statements about the U.S. commitment to promoting liberty, fighting tyranny, and supporting democracy. Indeed, the heart of neoconservatism—that which most clearly distinguished it from other contemporary and historical forms of conservatism—was the claim that U.S. foreign policy should be formulated on the basis of (conservative) morality as well as strategic interests. Many of the most prominent neoconservative intellectuals and activists, including Francis Fukuyama, Paul Wolfowitz, William Kristol (son of Irving Kristol), William Bennett, and Allan Bloom had been influenced, either directly or indirectly, by the political philosopher Leo Strauss. In the three decades following World War II, Strauss had taught that modern politics was being destroyed by the moral relativism that was increasingly central to intellectual and public life in the United States and Europe. That lazy relativism had led to an unwillingness to argue for the value of any particular moral insight or way of life. (It also led to a lack of interest in the great classics of Western literature, Strauss's other passion.) What was needed, Strauss argued, were strong leaders willing to stand up for what was right and to do battle against "tyranny."[56] The Bush team's characterization of terrorists as those who "hate freedom," and certain nation-states as part of an "Axis of Evil," was fundamentally aligned with this kind of morals-based vision of international politics.

The neoconservative position seemed directly opposed to the pragmatic culturalism of Huntington's "clash" model, which had eschewed both universalism and moralism. Speaking at West Point, President Bush made the contrast explicit: "When it comes to the common rights and needs of men and women, there is no clash of civilizations. The requirements of freedom apply fully to Africa and Latin America and the entire Islamic world."[57] Neoconservatives liked to argue that the fall of Saddam Hussein would work something like the fall of the Berlin Wall; it would set off a tidal wave of democratic change, in the Middle East and elsewhere. Leaders of the exiled Iraqi opposition and their supporters offered their enthusiastic concurrence, insisting that Iraqis would greet U.S. troops with sweets and flowers.[58] Thus the ideological backing for remaking the Middle East was the language of idealism. To oppose U.S. policy was to suggest that Arab or Muslim peoples did not have the right to democracy; support for the push toward war was brandished as an antiracist credential.[59]

For neoconservative policymakers, however, "democracy" meant quite specific things: basic formal democratic institutions, such as voting, certainly, and specific protections for civil rights (including for women and minorities); but also, just as centrally, individualism, capitalism based on a free market, and protection of private property. Democracy also was defined as having good relations with the United States.[60] The Bush Administration's National Security Strategy of September 2002 explicitly committed the United States to lead other nations toward "the single sustainable model for national success."[61] The nations of the Middle East, considered specifically resistant to democracy, uniquely dangerous to the United States, and particularly oppressive to women, were marked as ripe for transformation.

In reality, then, neoconservatives never separated the embrace of liberal democracy from the assumption that the United States exemplified that ideal and should dominate any "universal" order that would emerge—much as "the common heritage of mankind" argument about oil in the 1970s had assumed that the United States and its allies would manage the world's valuable resources. In fact, those valuable resources were never far from the surface of the debate about Iraq. For many years, U.S. policy toward Iraq had rested on the reality that it had enormous oil reserves, was located strategically in the Middle East, and had the capacity as well as the ambition to be a major regional power. With a hostile government in power in Iraq, as it had been for more than twenty years under Saddam Hussein, U.S. military and economic power in the Middle East was lessened. The presence of a pro-American government, on the other hand, would potentially allow the United States to influence oil flow and oil prices, and would likely facilitate the installation of another U.S. military base in the Middle East, at a time when other U.S. bases, including those in Saudi Arabia, were the source of considerable resentment. In the early 1990s, during the administration of George H. W. Bush, a series of defense planning documents had established a set of aggressive and entirely non-moralistic long-term policy visions for the Pentagon. Those documents were written under the watch of key players in the George H. W. Bush administration, all of whom would be leaders in the future George W. Bush team: Dick Cheney was Secretary of Defense, Colin Powell was Chairman of the Joint Chiefs of Staff, and Paul Wolfowitz was Undersecretary of Defense for Policy. Focused on the importance of maintaining absolute U.S. military hegemony in the Middle East and elsewhere and on the necessity of ensuring U.S. access to oil, they did not mention the importance of fighting tyranny or spreading democracy.[62] By the time of the Iraq war, however, the U.S. "national interest" in oil supply had been established with such success that it was rarely highlighted in discussions of the war, except by the U.S. left and in the Middle East, where newspapers and cartoons commonly asserted—indeed, almost assumed—that the United States was acting in Iraq to secure its own access to Iraq's oil.

Neoconservatives were not only more oriented toward pursuing narrowly defined national interests than they claimed to be, but also they were far from immune to the "clash" model proposed by Huntington. During the lead-up to the war in Iraq, a forty-year-old book by Rafael Patai, *The Arab Mind*, was popular reading among members of the Bush administration; one observer called the book "the bible of the neocons on Arab behavior."[63] Patai's patently racist text argued, among other things, that Arabs did not really understand time (because of the structure of the Arabic language) and that they were at once sex-obsessed and sexually repressed, both due to perverse childrearing practices. (The implication could be drawn, then, that Arabs were particularly vulnerable to sexual humiliation.) The underlying message of the crudely argued book was that the Arab world was fundamentally different from the "West" and, in key ways, contemptible. Despite their critiques of realism, then, neoconservatives were in no way starry-eyed democratic idealists. They were fully capable of racist theorizing about Arabs and Islam, and also completely committed to promoting U.S. strategic and economic hegemony in the Middle East and elsewhere.

Perhaps no one in the Bush administration better represented the neoconservative combination of democratic idealism, hard-nosed realism, and pure nationalist arrogance than National Security Advisor (and now Secretary of State) Condeleezza Rice. Rice was trained as an expert on the Soviet Union, had been an official in the George H. W. Bush administration, became the provost of Stanford University, and was now one of the administration's leading hawks. She had once defined herself as a realist, but by the time she joined the George W. Bush administration, she had become an ideal neoconservative: a proponent of the just cause of U.S. muscle-flexing who also insisted that moral visions were central to American political identity. "Power matters," Rice told the *National Review.* "But there can be no absence of moral content in American foreign policy, and, furthermore, the American people wouldn't accept such an absence. Europeans giggle at this and say we're naive and so on, but we're not Europeans, we're Americans—and we have different principles."[64]

Rice was also the first African American woman to hold a cabinet-level position in foreign affairs, and as such, was a highly visible symbol. In her very person, standing by the side of the president or speaking on the evening news, she represented a vision of the United States as a place where a woman of any race might achieve extraordinary success and power. In the 1991 Gulf War, Colin Powell had become the embodiment of military multiculturalism and confident U.S. global leadership in the post–cold war order. But as Secretary of State, Powell had expressed doubts about the invasion of Iraq and had been marginalized in the Bush administration. Rice, on the other hand, was at the center of policymaking and had the ear of the president.

As a symbol, Rice was presumably the exact opposite of the Afghan woman covered in a burqa. Growing up in the segregated South, she had faced racial discrimination, but now she was highly educated, supremely accomplished, and—quite simply—the most powerful woman in the world. If women in Muslim lands supposedly faced the threat of erasure, Rice, with her impressive public presence, her obvious intelligence and self-confidence, and her truly stunning record of accomplishment, was a visible symbol of the possibilities for women born in a land of opportunity. That fact, and her deeply held right-wing beliefs, made Rice an ideal spokesperson for the neoconservative vision of the United States in the world: a multicultural meritocracy, confident of its own moral superiority, certain of its power, and willing to use that power to reshape the globe in its own, democratic, image.

SNAPSHOT: SADDAM HUSSEIN'S STATUE COMES DOWN IN BAGHDAD

It was the most compelling image of the fall of Baghdad, signaling to the world that the United States had liberated Iraq from a brutal dictator. On April 9, 2003, less than one month after the onset of the war, the giant statue of Saddam Hussein at a prominent square in downtown Baghdad, draped in an Iraqi flag, was pulled to the ground and smashed with the help of American marines, as cheering Iraqis joined in. The photographs and TV images showed a gathering of those who were being liberated, jeering at the image of the dictator who had, without a doubt, oppressed them for decades. President Bush was elated as he watched the events unfold live on television. Reports from around the United States were ecstatic: this was "just the evidence the Coalition needed," *Newsweek* enthused, "to show the world that Iraqis saw the Americans as liberators."[65]

At the time, the reports told of only one problem with the scene, which was soon remedied. At first, one marine, Cpl. Edward Chin of New York, had climbed the statue of Hussein and draped it with an American flag.[66] Later, after protests by the Iraqis, the U.S. flag was replaced with an Iraqi one. Then, with help from the U.S. marines, the statue was delivered to the

Figure 29. Courtesy of Reuters.

crowd. The next day, a commentator on al-Jazeera said the U.S. flag had been an apt symbol: "Everything that happens in Iraq now will have an American flavor and smell."[67]

Before long, reports started to emerge that perhaps the crowd had not been as big as reported, and had not arrived at the square so spontaneously. In July 2004, the rumors that the statue's fall had been an exercise in image fixing were confirmed when the *Los Angeles Times* reported that an internal U.S. Army report had strongly criticized the actions of the soldiers on site. It turned out that it was a U.S. marine colonel who had decided to topple the statue, not Iraqi civilians. Once the events were under way, a group of Army psychological operations officers on the scene realized that there was a problem—and an opportunity. They quickly used their loudspeakers to gather Iraqis to join the action. A few did—not the large crowd that most news accounts implied, but a hundred or so. When the army tank finally pulled down the statue, the psychological operations people managed to gather Iraqi children to sit on the tank.[68]

The irony was both obvious and painful: the iconic symbol of the "liberation of Baghdad" was a staged event designed by the propaganda wing of the U.S. Army, with cheering Iraqis who were imported onto the scene and then named its protagonists.[69] Just as remarkable is the fact that the television reporters on site, who covered the events live, failed to question the Army's assurance that the Iraqis had organized the event, and also, seemingly deliberately, did not show the small size of the crowd. Working within an ideological frame that predisposed them to see smiling Iraqis, they showed only those aspects of the scene that fit the frame.

Many Iraqis did in fact welcome the overthrow of Saddam Hussein, and some met the U.S. troops waving American flags and offering cigarettes. There was, for a time, the sense that many segments of the Iraqi population were willing to consent to the imposition of U.S. power if it meant the chance to be free from Hussein's rule. The majority Shiites in the south had long been marginalized and often brutally suppressed, as had the Kurds in the north, whose autonomous areas had been protected militarily by the United States since the end of the first Iraq war in 1991. Almost everyone in Iraq—Sunni or Shiite, Arab or Kurd—had a family member or a close friend who had been imprisoned, murdered, or in some fashion silenced by the regime. Despite the flurry of world protest over the unilateralism of the invasion, the United States began its takeover with a deep well of anti-Hussein and pro-American sentiment in place in Iraq itself.

Nonetheless, the sentiment was less universal and more short-lived than media reports led many Americans to believe. There was strong Iraqi opposition from the beginning, and many signs indicated that the invasion was not uniformly welcomed or consistently successful. American media coverage of the invasion was, from the beginning, remarkably credulous— so much so that in 2004, both the *New York Times* and the *Washington Post* issued public apologies for their handling of the war. The reporting of the story of Hussein's statue was emblematic of several larger problems that marred the information people in the United States received about the war: first, the direct manipulation of the media by the military and political leadership; second, the compromised role of embedded reporters; and third, the general frenzy of media patriotism.

Perhaps the least noted of these has been the kind of direct manipulation of the media that happened around the Hussein statue in Baghdad. As military analyst Carl Conetta has argued, even before the war in Afghanistan, members of the defense establishment had begun to argue that they needed to reconceptualize the media as a "battlefield" and public affairs as a "weapon."[70] Of course militaries in general are likely to try to spin events according to their liking, and the U.S. military has long included an informations arm, but in this war, the Pentagon's commitment to the role of "public affairs" and "information operations" was unprecedented. Research by retired Air Force colonel Sam Gardiner only confirmed the success of that commitment. He found more than fifty major events in the Iraq conflict whose reporting showed signs of a media manipulation campaign by the Pentagon.[71] The mainstream media's tendency to rely on official sources for quick and easy news made them more vulnerable to "directed" stories. One analyst reported that in the period from September 2002 to February 2003, just before the ground war in Iraq began, NBC, ABC, and CBS ran 414 stories on Iraq. All but 34 of them issued from the White House, the Pentagon, or the State Department.[72]

Military planners also decided to try to influence news coverage by increasing the media's access to the military perspective on the war. In the 1991 Gulf War, the Pentagon had allowed reporters very limited access to the battlefield, and then only as a part of a reporters' pool. That highly restrictive policy had outraged the media, as I discussed in chapter 6, and eventually led to an about-face. In operation "Iraqi Freedom," approximately six hundred reporters were "embedded" within U.S. military units during the initial fighting.[73] Just under half of those participated in a weeklong "Embed Boot Camp" before leaving for Iraq, in which they rose at 5 a.m., ate rations, and were taught some basic military skills by Marines. Andrew Jacobs of the *New York Times* described the experience as "alternatively enlightening, entertaining, horrifying, and physically exhausting," and said he felt a bond with the marines even before leaving for Iraq.[74] David Zucchino, an embedded reporter for the *Los Angeles Times*, assessed his experience as extremely valuable in giving an unscripted view of the day-to-day realities of soldiers. But he also saw it as dramatic, dangerous, and deeply compromised. At one point, Zucchino reported, he was in a tank with a group of soldiers who came under fire. Short-handed, an officer told him to staff a vision block and search for targets. "Placed in a soldier's seat," he wrote, "I had been asked by an officer to perform a soldier's job."[75] He did, and wrote that he was only glad that he had not seen anyone to target. Reporters knew from the beginning that they would tend to become part of the "organizational culture" of the military and that their stories were likely to be skewed by their identifications with their units, on whom they depended for food, access, and safety in the battle zone. In addition, all media outlets had signed a contract promising that they would not describe U.S. combat losses—a stipulation that led some commanders to refuse to allow reporters to film American dead. Editors and reporters argued that they were fully cognizant of these limits, and that they balanced coverage from embedded reporters with other news stories.[76] Indeed, U.S. news outlets did have other non-embedded reporters in Iraq, but the stories from the "embeds" were often highlighted as the most dramatic and exciting. Three-quarters of the embedded reporters were Americans; most other countries received the majority of their news from independent reporters on the ground. As a result, audiences in the rest of the world saw more Iraqi perspectives and more casualties, both Iraqi and Allied, than did people in the United States.[77]

In addition to the direct media manipulation and the impact of embedded reporters, there was also the unabashed patriotism and even jingoism of much of the coverage of the Iraq war, which went much further than the already enthusiastic tone set during the first Gulf War. The right-wing Fox network had established early on its determination not only to report but also to promote the war. (As the war began, Fox anchors paraded a "Wall of Heroes," showing family snapshots of soldiers who were fighting in Iraq.) Even the more traditional news networks, which insisted on their own objectivity, pulled back from the kind of adversarial reporting that they had once prided themselves on. In February 2003, Dan Rather was strongly criticized by the White House and even by other networks for interviewing Saddam Hussein, on the argument that even allowing Hussein to present his views was tantamount to undermining the war effort. (In fact, during the interview Hussein looked like the demagogue he was.)[78] This kind of criticism would have been unimaginable during the Iran hostage crisis, when U.S. reporters regularly trooped to Tehran to interview the Ayatollah Khomeini and other clerics. It was no wonder, then, that Sam Donaldson of ABC made clear that he understood the new ground rules for media quiescence. Criticized for failing to ask hard questions of President Bush during a prewar press conference, Donaldson commented that it was difficult for the media "to press very hard when they know that a large segment of the population doesn't want to see a president whom they have anointed having to squirm."[79] Setting aside this rather stunning dismissal of the primary justification for the fourth estate—that through independent reporting the media might provide some kind of check on political power—Donaldson was onto something. A July 2003 survey by the Pew Research Center for the People and the Press found that 70 percent of respondents thought news outlets should be strongly pro-American. (At the same time, 64 percent said news coverage of the war on terrorism should be neutral.) With public opinion demanding patriotism, most major television outlets complied. As Project for Excellence in Journalism director Tom Rosenstiel put it: "Some of that rallying around the flag was really a rallying for eyeballs."[80]

The fall of the statue of Saddam Hussein was not, certainly, the only example of media misrepresentation. In fact, perhaps nothing so crystallized the combination of official manipulation, a credulous press, and the rush to patriotism as the enthusiastic reporting of the story of Pfc. Jessica Lynch, the army supply clerk who was taken prisoner by the Iraqi military at the beginning of the invasion, then lionized as a heroine by the U.S. media for her valor in fighting the Iraqis who had attacked her unit. Her "rescue" by U.S. military special forces was an event staged and filmed by the Pentagon, which then released dramatic footage of the nighttime raid. Lynch's story ran in the United States as the classic American fantasy of the captivity narrative. As I discussed in chapter 5, the hostage or the captive has frequently stood as a symbol of victimized yet heroic national identity in a time of crisis. Six weeks after the rescue, however, a BBC documentary revealed that the tales of Lynch's heroism were rumor at best and manufactured at worst: she had apparently been knocked unconscious when her vehicle went off the road: the only injuries she suffered were broken bones from the accident. While Iraqi eyewitnesses reported that the U.S. Special Operations forces had received no resistance either outside or inside the hospital, because the Iraqi forces had left the area the previous day, the Army had edited the video to make it appear that the team faced armed resistance and that the raid inside the hospital was dangerous and heroic. The BBC called the videotaped rescue "one of the most stunning pieces of news management ever conceived."[81]

Both Lynch's rescue and the destruction of Hussein's statue, which happened within a week of each other, were presented by most U.S. media sources as heralds of a rapid U.S. victory in Iraq and the moral legitimacy of the war. The revelation that each was built in part on misleading information or outright fabrication was only the beginning of a more profound disillusionment. Within eighteen months, the Bush administration's reasons for going to war would lie in shreds, and the American image in the world would be shattered. The moment of triumph was short-lived and illusory.

SNAPSHOT: A PRISONER AT ABU GHRAIB

The photograph went around the world: a man in a black hood and some sort of black robe—probably a blanket with a neck hole cut into the center—standing on a cardboard box, his arms stretched out, with electrodes attached to his hands and apparently to his genitals. The photograph was one of dozens that showed members of an Army reserve unit at Abu Ghraib prison brutalizing Iraqi prisoners. A small number of photographs were first shown by CBS in late April 2004. By the next morning, they were on the front page of newspapers and the lead story on television all

Figure 30.   First printed in *The New Yorker*.

over the world. Over the next few weeks, additional photographs were discovered and published. In one, two soldiers were smiling brightly at the camera, standing behind a group of naked men who had been hooded and piled into a pyramid.[82] Another showed a man naked on the floor of a cell block, a female soldier holding a leash attached around his neck. Other images showed beatings, men chained and hooded, and men forced to simulate oral sex. In some, male and female soldiers alike gloated over what appeared to be dead bodies.

The image of the hooded man was not the most horrific or dramatic of the photographs, but it was a particularly haunting one. In part, this was due to unintentional resonance with the politics of race in the United States. The hood and robe on the Iraqi man looked oddly like a Ku Klux Klan outfit, though the robes were black rather than white, and the face hidden was not that of the perpetrator, but of the victim. In addition, while the man on the box was almost certainly a Muslim, the way in which he had been forced to stand, with arms outstretched to the sides, positioned him in a classic reference to Jesus on the cross. Whatever this man was in real life, his pose, his dress and hood, and the obvious violence being threatened him, stood as stark reminders of the links that connected this moment of violence in Iraq to the history of racial violence in the United States and to the Christian beliefs that had been used both to justify that violence and to organize opposition to it.

Several commentators have pointed out that the soldiers in the photos appeared to have no guilt or concern about what they were doing. Indeed, the very fact that they were taking pictures and then sending them by email to each other and to friends was part of what made the photos so shocking. At the same time, the reality that even these horrific acts were photographed had its own logic in a culture inundated by images and consumed with self-representation. For Americans accustomed to taking tourist photos, family portraits, and college group shots, the taking of pictures was very much part of most experiences. As Sontag argued about the photographic impulse at Abu Ghraib: "The events are in part designed to be photographed. The grin is a grin for the camera. There would be something missing if, after stacking the naked men, you couldn't take a picture of them."[83]

The damage done by the Abu Ghraib photographs to the reputation of the United States in the Arab world was incalculable. Just after the first images were aired, an announcer on al-Jazeera commented that "the pictures released by the U.S. CBS News network showing repulsive and immoral practices by U.S. soldiers . . . have caused great shock and dismay." The pan-Arab paper *Al-Quds al-Arabi* was more harshly critical: "What the U.S. forces did and are doing in Iraq confirms to us what we have always warned of, namely, that the aim of this invasion and occupation was primarily to humiliate the Arabs and Muslims and was never for changing the Iraqi dictatorship or establishing a model democracy, justice, and human rights."[84]

When the photos were first published, the Bush administration responded with outrage and statements of regret, but insisted that the "abuse" (Defense Secretary Rumsfeld argued that there was a "technical" difference between abuse and torture) had been perpetrated by a small number of troops acting illegally and without sanction. The president went on Arabic-language television to say that he was appalled: "What took place in that prison does not represent the America that I know." However, he assured his audience, what they saw in the pictures were "the actions of a few people." A small group of unsupervised reservists, working in a tense, overcrowded prison, had acted in an unprecedented fashion; the conditions would be remedied and those responsible punished. Six officers in Iraq were reprimanded, while seven of the soldiers in the photographs faced criminal charges. Within a month, one of the reservists was convicted in a court-martial and sentenced to one year in jail and dishonorable discharge.[85]

The quick and sure punishment of these lower-level soldiers was necessary if the U.S. project in Iraq was to be rescued from the harsh reality of Abu Ghraib. Before the photos were released, the triumphant image of U.S. power projected to the American people and to the world was already in danger of collapse due to the many failures of the occupation authorities to provide security and basic services for the population. Now, the revelations of torture at Abu Ghraib presented an even more profound threat: that the U.S. occupation would come to be widely seen not only as flawed, or as suffering from failures of logistics and management, but also as a project of racialized domination. In the face of that perception, presidential apologies did little to stem the tide of anger in the Middle East. In Iraq, an opposition newspaper published a simple, powerful editorial cartoon: a woman, shown from behind, is labeled "Iraq." Her back is riddled with bullet holes; one of them is covered by a useless band-aid that says "apology."[86]

Despite the administration's claim that the torture at Abu Ghraib was an aberration, evidence showed otherwise. By the summer of 2004, a series of investigative reports and analyses undertaken independently by human rights organizations, journalists, and scholars made clear that U.S. military officers knew of the abuse months before it was reported in the press. Those reports left many questions unanswered about exactly what was approved, and when, and by whom; the full story was not likely to be uncovered for months or years, if at all. But the information that emerged in the wake of the Abu Ghraib scandal pointed toward high-level administration support, both implicit and explicit, for what Anthony Lewis has described as the process of "making torture legal."[87]

Beginning in the immediate aftermath of September 11, the Justice Department, the White House counsel, and ultimately an ad hoc team of lawyers working for Defense Secretary Rumsfeld all issued arguments that the United States could carry out interrogations of some prisoners—those designated "enemy combatants," most of whom were held at the U.S. military base in Guantanamo, Cuba—that broke the ban on torture, despite the fact that the United States was a signatory to the Geneva Conventions.[88] With those guidelines in place, a set of specific policies was developed in Iraq, and especially at Abu Ghraib, that authorized practices of physical and psychological coercion.[89] Military commanders in Iraq were briefed on interrogation methods at Guantanamo, which could in some cases include sleep deprivation, exposure to extreme heat and cold, and holding prisoners in "stress positions" for long periods of time. All of the reservists accused of abusing Iraqi prisoners at Abu Ghraib told investigators that military intelligence officers encouraged such techniques, as well as others, like confining inmates naked in rooms without beds, forcing them to wear female underpants, and handcuffing them to cell doors.[90] (In addition, at least two of those reservists had worked as prison guards in the United States, where physical and emotional abuses by guards are routine.)[91] The actions at Abu Ghraib were also not very different from behaviors exhibited by U.S. troops elsewhere. Iraqis taken prisoner in other parts of the country reported being forced to stand in stressful positions and to engage in personally and sexually humiliating acts. The pattern suggests what journalist Mark Danner calls a "purposefully devised and methodically distributed" script for abuse.[92]

Overall, then, several streams of evidence pointed to a policy or series of policies supported by high officials that enabled and authorized a great deal of what went on in Abu Ghraib. The U.S. reservists at the prison were not just a few young men and women gone bad. They were part of a system—a historically constituted process—for which, once again, "they were evil" was not an adequate explanation.

Still, there were the photos. Whatever policies or practices were in place, whatever instructions were given or abuses encouraged, they cannot explain the smiles we see in the photos of torture. No memo requested those images, and no order from a superior officer could elicit those smiles. There have been other examples of soldiers taking photographs of dead bodies or battlefields, but there are few other cases where they place themselves in the frame, anxious to show their own participation in the suffering. The clearest historical parallels to the Abu Ghraib photographs are the images of lynching that circulated in the early decades of the twentieth century. From 1890 to 1940, hundreds of people, the vast majority of them African Americans, were murdered by mobs in the South. The threat of death and torture aimed to keep African Americans in fear and to prevent them from challenging the Jim Crow system of the post–Civil War South. But in many instances, lynchings were also public activities staged for the benefit of whites. Announced in advance, they were orchestrated outings, where families came to watch and cheer.

Photographs taken during lynchings often depicted images very similar to those from Abu Ghraib: young men smiling as they stand in front of a charred body; people gathered in groups to stare at a mutilated corpse and to pose for the camera. There was often a sexual overtone, since lynching was frequently justified by accusing African Americans of sexual crimes against white women and children. And the lynching pictures, too, were circulated among friends, sent as postcards through the U.S. mail.[93] There was no sense of shame in the lynching photos; the subjects believed themselves to be free from any censure. The racial violence depicted was entirely justified, in their eyes, by their own racial hate. The photographs from Abu Ghraib were images of a new kind of racial politics, one that brought the symbolics of domestic racism—itself a product of the history of colonialism and imperialism—into the service of new, overtly imperial American power. In his essay "Is There a Neo-Racism?" Etienne Balibar argues that nationalism is always supported by an ideology that constructs those outside the nation as racial "others." This is true even in contexts in which the inhabitants of a nation are not of the same race: nationalism binds them, and works to collapse their differences into a single national identity. Culture, Balibar argues, can "function like nature," or like the ideas of nature that have for centuries divided human beings into racial categories. The production of any culture, including national culture, can "function as a way of locking individuals and groups a priori into a genealogy, into a determination that is immutable and intangible in origin."[94] After 9/11, despite the fact that policymakers and pundits were careful to insist that they were not vilifying all Muslims, "Islam" functioned as a synecdoche for a particular series of pathologies—an excessive devotion to religion, a tendency toward violence and jihad, the oppression of women, failure of democracy, and irrational hatred of the United States.

Those American soldiers featured in the photographs at Abu Ghraib were white, but the officers and policymakers in charge of setting U.S. policy, at Abu Ghraib and elsewhere, were white, black, Latino, and Asian American. The culture that tied these Americans together was, quite simply, an imperial one; it offered a moral geography that positioned the multicultural United States as an island of liberty in a sea of danger. The danger, it was understood, came from Muslims, and in the post-9/11 climate, "radical Islam" developed racialized overtones. Through categories of culture that worked like race, a confused but powerful mapping fused Islam, the Middle East, and terrorism; it marked entire groups of people as immutably and intangibly inferior. Earlier constructions of race had imagined that categories of difference were borne on the body; the racialization of religion inscribed them in the soul.

CONCLUSION

In the preceding chapters, I have highlighted the often invisible significance of the Middle East to Americans. That significance has been anything but invisible since September 11, but in this new visibility, the long history of U.S.–Middle East cultural encounters has frequently been occluded. In the epigraph to this chapter, Benedict Anderson describes the way in which terrible traumas often bring about "characteristic amnesias," which then allow for the construction of narratives. In the case of 9/11, one highly visible narrative that emerged from the trauma asked, "Why do they hate us?" Because, it answered, "They hate liberty and freedom." The history forgotten in that narrative was both political and cultural—the history of U.S. foreign policy toward the Middle East and the complex cultural work that had represented the Middle East to Americans, and thus Americans to themselves.

The Middle East has been central to American nationalist constructions in part because it has been a rich site for developing U.S. political and economic power. During the cold war, the U.S.–Middle East relationship offered the potential for incorporating third-world nationalisms into a U.S. sphere of influence, containing the Soviet Union, and, of course, controlling or managing oil. In the 1990s, as the United States emerged as the world's one great superpower, the Middle East remained of great strategic and economic interest. The Middle East has been arguably the single greatest source of fear and concern for U.S. policymakers, largely because a range of groups in the region, from Islamist movements to Palestinian nationalists to Israeli settlers, have used violent tactics in their political struggles. I have suggested that, however real the threats or material the gains, none of these "national interests" was staged in isolation. The Middle East was mapped for Americans through the intersecting deployment of cultural interests and political investments.[95]

In making this argument, I have posited a succession of moral geographies that mapped the Middle East in a meaningful relationship to the United States. My task has been to produce a study of representation that takes into account the discursive power of conjuncture, and to show how the intersection of different meaning-making activities can create a cultural logic strong enough to reach well beyond the operations of any given text. The chapters thus traced a discourse of expansionist nationalism as it was produced in certain historical moments, while remaining attentive to difference, contradiction, and moments of disruption. In writing a cultural history that takes international relations as its topic, I have aimed to intervene in several ways in current scholarship in cultural studies, international affairs, American studies, and postcolonialism.

First, I have argued that Orientalism cannot, in itself, explain U.S. representations of the Middle East in the post–World War II period. The nineteenth- and early-twentieth-century constructions of the Middle East *can* be fairly described as Orientalist—they followed the operations described by Said, and neatly divided the world into East and West, "us" and elsewhere. Even then, however, the representations of "the Orient" were marked by ambivalence, constructing it as both exotic and dangerous, alluring and disgusting. The moral geography that contrasted East and West did not disappear entirely in the postwar period, although as "the Orient" became the "Middle East," it was less often seen as even marginally exotic or attractive and more often represented as merely dangerous or backward. Versions of Orientalism were apparent in policymakers' disdain for Nasser in the 1950s, in the public outrage over "oil sheiks" in the 1970s, and in the recent images of bin Laden. In *Clash of Civilizations*, Huntington posited a neo-Orientalist framework, one that insisted that the primary division in the world was between the "West and the Rest," with "the Rest" led by an Islamic civilization that was fundamentally different from the Western one.

In other ways, however, the construction of post-9/11 Americanness, like earlier nationalist formulations, has been distinctly post-Orientalist. In the period after 1945, I have argued, there was a slow move away from the modern construction of a unified (white, masculine) national and racial identity toward the positing of national subjects as disjointed and diverse, gendered both masculine and feminine, and ultimately multiracial. The unified European or Western subject was replaced with one far more protean and changeable, and the "West" itself was often split, as the United States began sometimes to define itself as operating against Europe. Thus the meanings of the Middle East in the United States have been far more mobile, flexible, and rich than the Orientalism binary would allow. Appropriation, affiliation, distinction, and mobilization were all, at times, central to an evolving set of uneven relationships.

Looking beyond Orientalism allows us to see the emotionally charged and politically contested meanings that the Middle East has had for a range of people living in the United States. As the founding site for Judaism, Christianity, and Islam, the spaces of the Middle East have been mobilized as part of several alternative moral geographies. These geographies undergirded the claims—made by Muslims, Jews, and Christians, both black and white—to ancient Middle Eastern history as sacred history. Sometimes, those claims have been explicitly nationalist: the biblical narratives of the epics and the anti-Islamic "Americanness" that emerged in the Iran crisis are two examples. But the identities that mobilized the Middle East were not always or only national: the alliance with Israel helped to establish a certain type of transnational alliance for evangelical Christians, much as American women's appropriation of the problem of Afghan women's oppression helped to define one type of transnational feminism.

Similarly, ancient Egypt and contemporary Islam framed the transnational and often anti-imperial arguments of African Americans. If, as I have argued, the Middle East has been particularly important in the negotiation of black identities, it is partly because religion, culture, and myth have mattered enormously to a population that often saw itself as under siege within the United States. Non-Christian religions and non-Western histories promised an alternative narrative to that of dispossession and discrimination. The Middle East did domestic work for African Americans. And the sense of affiliation that was created made space in which to challenge the dominant narratives of U.S. global power.

The second intervention of this study has been to highlight the protean, complicated, and influential relationships between gender, race, and nationalism. The "domestic" politics of race and gender have been central to U.S. representations of the Middle East, and representations of the Middle East have been fully implicated in the formations of racial and gender identities. The *content* of these formations, however, has often been unexpected. Gender has played a central role in imagining Americanness, but discourses of national identity and citizenship have *not* been only male. Undoubtedly, the construction of a proper masculinity has remained a part of the narratives of race and nationalism traced in this study, from the image of the tough Israeli operative who saves a feminized post-Vietnam America to the construction of a heroic masculinity for the 9/11 firemen.

In conjunction with ideologies of national manhood, idealized images of women and/or highly restrictive ideologies of family life have also been frequently mobilized in the discourse of nationalism. In these formulations, women, constructed as signifiers of private life, have represented what the nation *protects*, but not what the nation *is*. I drew on those images to argue for the importance of the idea of the "freely chosen subordination" of women to constructions of postwar benevolent supremacy. In that construct, women were folded into a narrative of nation that centered maleness, but which required the signs of domestic tranquility as its support.

At other times, however, women, and even feminized domesticity, have been at the heart of the nationalist imaginary, as the nation was constructed through a refusal of its own publicness. In the Iran hostage crisis, for example, it was family status that proffered public authority and constructed a feminized national citizenship that could be held by either men or women. Both the mothers and fathers of the hostages represented the nation *because* they were aligned with family, domesticity, and the private sphere.

Finally, there are times when Americanness is signified by women's freedom. The "freely chosen subordination" of women in the biblical epics was idealized by contrasting it with slavery, or with the older imperial model of pure subjugation. When Betty Mahmoody was trapped in Iran, she held fast to her Americanness by contrasting her proper femininity with that of Iranian women, who were at once too subservient, in their acceptance of veils and dependence on men, and yet not quite subservient enough, in their refusal to clean or cook properly. American women, by contrast, had just enough freedom. As women became more prominent in U.S. public life, and feminist ideas (if not a feminist movement) became mainstreamed, it made sense that a woman like Condeleezza Rice would come to stand as a representative for American identity and American power. She represented the "just right" amount of freedom enjoyed by American women, a freedom that now included serving at the highest levels of U.S. public life. In contrast to "Muslim women," her image was all but severed from any requirement of representing proper domesticity (though her sober manner and conservative dress were an asset). Still, gender was far from absent: it was in part through her specifically female freedom that Rice represented the moral superiority of the United States.

It also mattered a great deal, of course, that she is African American. This study has argued that just as postwar American national identities were *not* imagined simply as male, they were also not always or uniformly white, even when racial divisions were being insistently re-inscribed. Instead, the task of nationalist discourse after World War II—facing the civil rights movement, then black liberation and feminism, as well as increases in non-white immigration, and the rise of ethnic identity movements—was to claim the terrain inhabited by a population able to insist on its own diversity. When U.S. nationalism succeeded, it did so because racial diversity and gendered logics were incorporated into the stories told about the moral geographies that underlie U.S. power. Increasingly, the expansionist nationalism of the United States has depended on "multiculturalism" as its authorization. Even when the horrific behavior of U.S. soldiers at Abu Ghraib drew upon the long history and current practices of racial oppression, the fact that U.S. policymakers and military leaders are racially diverse was mobilized as the silent signifier of American democracy.

The third intervention of the book has been its argument, both implicit and explicit, for the centrality of culture to the study of foreign policy, and the importance of centering the U.S. global role in any history of American culture. The analyses in each chapter have positioned transnational, national, and subnational identities as complexly intertwined. The goal has been to denaturalize national identity as a category, to insist that it is a complex cultural construct that must be accounted for, rather than presumed as the foundation of analysis. That project of denaturalization extends as well to the presumed baseline material reality of "national interest." The Middle East has long been posited as central to that interest, but what Americans need, or want, or are willing to fight for, has in practice been a matter of cultural construction, negotiation, and contest. That contest has never been more important than now, as, at the beginning of the twenty-first century, the United States takes on the role of acknowledged imperial power.

The most fundamental goal of the book, however, has been to provide a detailed case study of the intersection between cultural texts, foreign policy, and constructs of identity. My animating assumption has been that culture matters; my aim has been to show *how* culture has mattered to specific groups of people in particular moments. To highlight the centrality of representation is not to suggest that cultural products "stand in for" or "express" other realities. Each of the institutional sites examined in the book has its own logics and its own language; they should not be reduced to reflections of each other or of some larger, less visible structure. But in their uncoordinated conjunctures, they have the knitted-together power of a discourse. Thus, if culture is central to the worlds we regard as political and social, it is not only because culture is part of history, but also because the field of culture is history-in-the-making.

Acknowledgments

In the years that I have been working on this project, I have been extraordinarily fortunate in the debts I have incurred. My teachers, friends, and colleagues have taught me by their example and their support that scholarship is anything but solitary. For the exchange of ideas, the institutional backing, and the encouraging words, I owe to many people more gratitude than these pages can ever convey.

I first learned about the Middle East, and a great deal more besides, from my undergraduate teacher at the University of North Carolina-Chapel Hill, Herbert Bodman, and from his wife Ellen Fairbanks Bodman. They have been treasured mentors and friends. I am thankful also to two other extraordinary teachers, Peter I. Kaufman and Weldon Thornton.

I also owe a profound debt to those who advised and shepherded the Brown University dissertation on which this book is based. Robert Lee first convinced me that my life as a political activist and my interest in U.S. foreign policy could both be relevant to cultural studies. He remains a wonderful critic, colleague, and friend. Philip Rosen opened up new intellectual avenues for cultural studies and film analysis; I am grateful for his perceptive, demanding readings. Mari Jo Buhle read every chapter with an equal amount of rigor and enthusiasm; her generosity and her political and intellectual engagements have been an inspiration. I remain grateful as well to Neil Lazarus for his astute criticism and intellectual example. Thanks also to Richard Meckel, Susan Smulyan, and Sasha Torres for advice and interventions.

Monica McCormick at the University of California Press was a wonderful editor for the first edition, and Mari Coates has been a great pleasure to work with on the updated version. My sincere thanks also to the editors of the American Crossroads series, particularly Peggy Pascoe and George Lipsitz, who read the manuscript at an early stage and gave it their careful attention.

I would like to thank Robert Wuthnow and the Center for the Study of Religion at Princeton University for the fellowship that made it possible to finish the manuscript and for the intellectual home CSR provided. The W. E. B. DuBois Institute at Harvard University was also an excellent resource during the year I was a nonresident fellow. The early research and writing for this project was generously supported by a Mellon dissertation fellowship, administered by the Woodrow Wilson National Fellowship Foundation. George Washington University supported first the completion of the book and then the revised edition with grants for research and financial support for illustrations. I am also indebted to John Lynch and the Vanderbilt University Television Archives; Tom Porter of Son Boy records; the Egyptological staff at the Boston Museum of Fine Arts, especially Peter Manuelian, Joyce Haynes, and Timothy Kendall; the curatorial staff at the Metropolitan Museum of Art; and the Schomberg Library of African American Culture. Earlier versions of chapters of this book were published in *American Quarterly* and *Representations* and are used here with permission. Joanne Meyerowitz solicited an article for the *Journal of American History*'s special issue on *September 11 and History,* which provided my first opportunity to think through the ideas that became the basis of the new final chapter. I would like to thank the editorial boards and outside readers at all three journals for their comments.

At key stages of the project, I was fortunate to have help from several outstanding research assistants. Laura Schiavo provided creative, diligent research assistance at early stages. Later, Tim Walsh and Michele Gates-Moresi went well beyond the call of duty, patiently looking up obscure facts and tracking down citations while also offering generous and energetic moral support. For the new edition, I benefited greatly from the enthusiasm, creativity, and compulsive diligence of Sandra Heard and Julie Passanante. I am deeply grateful to all of them for their hard work; the book would have been very much impoverished without their help.

This study developed out of an intellectual community, and I owe my most profound debt to those friends and colleagues who have seen it through from the earliest stages, when it was little more than a series of hunches and hopes. At Brown University, "the Group" met regularly for more than five years to read each other's work, comment on the results, and push ourselves forward through the dissertation-writing process. I can't offer enough in terms of thanks and praise for this living monument to sisterhood-is-powerful, whose members included, at various times: Lucy Barber, Gail Bederman, Krista Comer, Dorothy Cox, Jane Gerhard, Ruth Feldstein, Elizabeth Francis, Louise Newman, Donna Penn, Uta Poiger, Miriam Reumann, Laura Santigian, and Jessica Shubow. In addition, I am very grateful to my other friends and colleagues from Brown, who read chapters, offered research advice, and shared long evenings of food and talk and ideas. I particularly want to express my appreciation and affection to Nathan Angell, Mark Cooper, Kirsten Lentz, Ezra Tawil, Jennifer Ting, and Mari Yoshihara.

My colleagues in the American Studies department at George Washington University have been welcoming and generous since my arrival. Howard Gillette, Chad Heap, James O. Horton, Bernard Mergen, James A. Miller, and John Vlach have made our department a pleasurable and exciting place to work. I owe particular thanks to Phyllis Palmer and Teresa Murphy, who as department chairs worked hard to ease my transition into teaching and to make sure I had time to write. In addition, the graduate students in my classes at GW have consistently challenged and improved my thinking on the links between cultural products and the public. While it would be inappropriate to single out specific individuals, I have benefited in more ways than I can name from the generosity and intellectual comraderie that these students/scholars/friends have provided.

My thanks and appreciation also to those folks at GW and elsewhere who read parts of the manuscript and/or provided intellectual and emotional sustenance in the process of writing: Amal Amireh, Johanna Bochmann, Jennifer Brody, Jeffrey Cohen, Denis Doyon, R. Marie Griffith, David Gutterman, Bill Hart, Kerric Harvey, Matthew Frye Jacobson, Michael Kazin, Christina Klein, David Lamberth, Kate Masur, James A. Miller, Teresa Murphy, Patrick Rael, Roy Rosensweig, Kirsten Swinth, Rosemarie Thompson, Brad Verter, Robert Vitalis, Gayle Wald, Stacy Wolf, Andrew Zimmerman, and Samuel Zipp. Several people read all or most of the manuscript at key stages. Amy Kaplan, George Lipsitz, Peggy Pascoe, Michael Rogin, Priscilla Wald, and one anonymous outside reader offered astute criticism and demanding, encouraging advice. For the updated edition, Stephanie Batiste and Ted German read the new chapter carefully and generously, and offered insightful comments, political wisdom, and much-needed support at the end game.

I am especially grateful to several people for their years of intimate engagement with this study. Ruth Feldstein's ability to take a chapter apart and put it back together again transformed the project. In the years since we graduated from Brown, she has been a consistent intellectual partner, both in research and teaching, and a source of sane counsel and valued friendship. I cannot imagine writing this book, or much of anything else, without her. Jane Gerhard is a trusted friend and colleague who reads with great insight, an unerring sense for what matters, and an insistence on keeping the big picture in place. Uta Poiger lent her creativity and keen intelligence to my work as well as her own; she discussed everything, read every chapter in multiple drafts, and offered moral support and intellectual sustenance beyond all reckoning. These friends are also comrades and role models, and I see their words and their ideas on every page of this manuscript.

Any intellectual project of such length and complexity is also sustained, if one is lucky, by friends and family who insist, against all evidence, that there is life beyond the book. Many thanks to Wan Chi Lau, Laura Cherry, Jeffrey Covington, Wendy Eudy, Ted German, Doug Hazen, Marlena Rupp, and Marc Salit for talk, meals, and laughter. My dear friend Gayle Wald is the source of both book talk and book avoidance, and I couldn't do without either. I would also like to thank a few people who, simply by doing their own jobs so well, made it possible for me to finish mine: Rosemary Dalton, Jehan el-Bayoumi, Yaron Gal, Samuel Potolicchio, and Donald Schomer.

My gratitude and love always to my family: my parents Gene McAlister and Katie Slater McAlister and to my sister, Julie McAlister. They have remained patient, good-humored, and unfailingly supportive, even when it sometimes appeared as if this whole seemingly masochistic process would never end. Through many phone calls and visits, each of them has taught me, in different ways, that while scholarship is a wonderful way to expand one's universe, family love is the path to home.

For many years, I have also made my life with three other important families. My goddaughter and special niece Ella Wechsler-Matthaei, and her parents Nancy Wechsler and Julie Matthaei, have given me their trust and their love, which I return with deep gratitude. Carla Lillvik has been my beloved friend for more than twenty years. She, her husband Gary Simoneau, and their daughter Camille have been an anchor and an inspiration. Ann Munson, my treasured confidante, has shared not only her extraordinary friendship but also the warmth of her family circle. She, her husband Tony Palomba, and their children Nathaniel and Joanna are lights in my universe. Since I left Boston, I have lived at a distance from each of these families, and I miss them every day.

Finally, my deepest thanks to my life partner, Carl Conetta, who has been a brilliant reader and my most demanding critic. I have learned more than I can say from his deep knowledge of U.S. foreign and military policy, his political passion, and his ability to remember in detail the plot of every movie he has ever seen. He has read every part of this book, talked about nascent ideas over dinner, encouraged me through long days of writing, and then remembered for both of us to laugh and go to the movies. Carl's ideas are here, absolutely. But even more than that, his extraordinary faith—in this book, in me, and in us—has made all the difference.

Notes

PREFACE

1. Ali Behdad describes this moment from his own life in the preface to *Belated Travelers*, vii.

2. Karl Marx, "The Eighteenth Brumaire of Louis Bonaparte," 595.

INTRODUCTION

1. Amy Kaplan, "Left Alone with America," 11.

2. Michael Shapiro, "Moral Geographies and the Ethics of Post-Sovereignty," 482. Edward Said, in *Orientalism*, uses the phrase "imaginative geography" to a similar effect.

3. Benedict Anderson, *Imagined Communities*, 3.

4. Both Edward Soja, in *Postmodern Geographies*, and David Harvey, in *The Condition of Postmodernity*, have argued persuasively that critical social theory has prioritized a theorization of time to the near exclusion of space.

5. David Campbell, *Writing Security*, 12. See also Richard Ashley, "Foreign Policy as Political Performance."

6. Pierre Bourdieu, *Field of Cultural Production*, 32.

7. These two examples are not ones Bourdieu specifically uses; for his examples, see ibid., 180–181.

8. Ibid., 57.

9. More general discussions of the images of Arabs in the news media include Edward Said, *Covering Islam*; Michael Suleiman, *The Arabs in the Mind of America*; Edmund Ghareeb, *Split Vision*; and Janice Belkaoui, "Images of Arabs and Israelis in the Prestige Press." Studies of stereotypes of Arabs in popular culture include Jack Shaheen, *The TV Arab* and "The Hollywood Arab"; and Kathleen Christison, "The Arab in Recent Popular Fiction." See also three pamphlets published by the American-Arab Anti-Discrimination Committee:

Laurence Michalak, *Cruel and Unusual;* Suha Sabbagh, *Sex, Lies, and Stereotypes;* and Dan Georgakas and Miriam Rosen, eds., *The Arab Image in American Film and Television.*

10. Some of the book-length studies that draw on Said include Ali Behdad, *Belated Travelers;* Rana Kabbani, *Europe's Myths of Orient;* Lisa Lowe, *Critical Terrains;* Anne McClintock, *Imperial Leather;* Christopher Miller, *Blank Darkness: Africanist Discourse in French;* and Mary Louise Pratt, *Imperial Eyes: Travel Writing and Transculturalism.* Writers who do not explicitly draw on Said's model but who nonetheless have written studies that clearly are a product of the extraordinary interest in the cultural politics of imperialism that has followed upon Said's work include Malek Alloula, *Colonial Harem;* Sarah Graham-Brown, *Images of Women: Portrayal of Women and Photography in the Middle East, 1860–1950;* and Zeynep Celik, *Displaying the Orient.*

11. Edward Said, *Orientalism,* 12.

12. Eric Hobsbawm, *Age of Empire,* 57. See also Michael Doyle, *Empires,* 141–146, 251–253.

13. Etienne Balibar, "Racism and Nationalism," 62.

14. On Islam, see, for example, Said, *Orientalism,* 65–72.

15. Lisa Lowe, *Critical Terrains,* 12. See also Ali Behdad, *Belated Travelers,* 10–17. One study that productively attends to the complexities of sexuality in Orientalist discourse is Robert Lee, *Orientals.*

16. Edward Said, *Orientalism,* 230. This argument about Said's humanism is made, in a slightly different way, by James Clifford, "On *Orientalism,*" in *Predicament of Culture.*

17. In the last third of his book, Said also discusses the United States as the twentieth-century heir to nineteenth-century European Orientalism. His argument assumes that Orientalism operated in much the same way in the United States as it had in Europe.

18. See Homi Bhabha, "DissemiNation: Time, Narrative, and the Margins of the Modern Nation," 301.

19. On the gendering of the political subject, see Nancy Fraser, *Unruly Practices;* Jean Elshtain, *Public Man, Private Woman.* This argument is complicated by Mary Ryan, *Women in Public;* Mari Jo Buhle, *Women and American Socialism;* and Lori Ginzberg, *Women and the Work of Benevolence.*

20. Lauren Berland discusses this dynamic in *The Queen of America Goes to Washington, D.C.* This is not, of course, unique to the United States. Two very useful books on the social history of the family and the state in France are Roddy Reid, *Families in Jeopardy;* and Jacques Donzelot, *Policing of Families.*

21. From John Berger, *Ways of Seeing.*

22. Bruce Kuklick, *Puritans in Babylon,* 4–5.

23. Lester Vogel, *To See a Promised Land,* 59.

24. Bruce Kuklick, *Puritans in Babylon,* 21–24.

25. John Davis, *Landscape of Belief,* 16–17.

26. Lester Vogel, *To See a Promised Land,* 59.

27. Anne McClintock, *Imperial Leather*, 40. For a fascinating and evocative discussion of the modern uses of the Holy Land, see W. J. T. Mitchell, "Holy Landscape."

28. Lester Vogel, *To See a Promised Land*, 105; John Davis, *Landscape of Belief*, 45–48

29. Mark Twain, *Innocents Abroad*, 342. Also quoted by John Davis, *Landscape of Belief*, 46. As Davis explains, Twain refers to Prime as "Grimes" throughout.

30. Moody's teaching was based on the teachings of the Irish minister John Darby, who had begun preaching in the 1830s. After the Civil War, it was taken up enthusiastically by large numbers of American evangelicals. On Darby, see Paul Merkley, *Politics of Christian Zionism*, 62–63; and Paul Boyer, *When Time Shall Be No More*, 183–186.

31. On Moody and early evangelical views of the Holy Land, see James Hunter, *American Evangelicalism* and "Evangelical Worldview since 1890"; William Martin, *With God on Our Side*, 7–8; Paul Boyer, *When Time Shall Be No More*, 86–100; Steve Brouwer, Paul Gifford, and Susan Rose, *Exporting the American Gospel*, 33–40; and George Marsden, *Fundamentalism and American Culture*.

32. Pratt discusses the "monarch" genre in *Imperial Eyes*, 201–208.

33. Angela Miller, "The Panorama, the Cinema, and the Emergence of the Spectacular"; John Davis, *Landscape of Belief*, 55, 65–72.

34. Timothy Mitchell, *Colonising Egypt*, 4, 13. The Cairo Street viewed at the European exhibition described by Mitchell was mobile. It came to the Chicago world's fair in 1893 and the St. Louis world's fair in 1904. See Zeynep Celik, *Displaying the Orient*.

35. The phrase "the certainty of representation" is Mitchell, *Colonising Egypt*, 7, quoting Heidegger, "The Age of the World Picture," in *The Question Concerning Technology and Other Essays*, 127.

36. Jonathan Crary, *Techniques of the Observer*, 97–136. Angela Miller's discussion of Crary in "The Panorama, the Cinema, and the Emergence of the Spectator," is particularly useful.

37. Jonathan Crary, "Modernizing Vision," 34.

38. Although both Crary and Mitchell use Foucault to talk about a modern preoccupation with spectacle and visuality, they have somewhat different interests. They both point out the ways in which the nineteenth century made knowledge into that which could be *seen*, but Mitchell is far better at delineating the direct political consequences of the move, while Crary is better at pointing out the contradictions and complexities within it.

39. John Davis, *Landscape of Belief*, 73–74.

40. Ibid., 89–94.

41. Lester Vogel, *To See a Promised Land*, 71.

42. "Regression and decrepitude" is from Charles Elliott, *Remarkable Characters and Places of the Holy Land*, 1867; "Ottoman rule" and "Mussulman character" are from Jacob Freese, *The Old World*, 1869; both quoted in Lester Vogel, *To See a Promised Land*, 75.

43. Lee Scott Theisen, "General Lew Wallace and *Ben-Hur*," 36. The stage production of *Ben-Hur* ran in New York in 1899; Bruce Babington and Peter William Evans, *Biblical Epics*, 5.

44. Lew Wallace, *Ben-Hur*.

45. Matthew Jacobson, *Barbarian Virtues*, and Emily Rosenberg, *Spreading the American Dream*. Both discuss the political resonance of this concern with markets. On the general climate of the time, see James Livingston, *Pragmatism and the Political Economy of Cultural Revolution;* and Martin Sklar, *Corporate Reconstruction of American Capitalism;* and Alan Dawley, *Struggles for Justice.*

46. Joseph Conrad, *Heart of Darkness*, 33.

47. Patrick Brantlinger, *Rule of Darkness*, 227–254.

48. Sumiko Higashi, *Cecil B. DeMille and American Culture*, 89–90. On department stores and Orientalism, see also Mari Yoshihara, "Women's Asia"; and Susan Porter Benson, *Counter Cultures*.

49. William Leach, *Land of Desire*, 111.

50. Ibid., 105.

51. John Kasson, *Amusing the Million*, 50–53.

52. See Patricia Hanson and Alan Gevinson, eds., *The American Film Institute Catalog of Motion Pictures*, listings under "Arabia" and "Arabs."

53. Gaylyn Studlar, "Out-Salomeing Salome," 116–117. On the anagram of "Arab Death," see Antonia Lant, "Curse of the Pharaoh," 91.

54. Joel C. Hodson, *Lawrence of Arabia and American Culture*, 11–82.

55. Gaylyn Studlar, *This Mad Masquerade:* "woman-made man," 151; "full torrent," 101. "When an Arab sees a woman he wants, he takes her": Miriam Hansen, *Babel and Babylon*, 256. See Hansen's discussion of women fans as sexual agents, 259–262.

56. Miriam Hansen, *Babel and Babylon*, 261.

57. Ibid., 257, 260.

58. Richard Carrott, *Egyptian Revival*. James Stevens Curl focuses more on architecture and design in Europe in *Egyptomania*.

59. Bruce Kuklick, *Puritans in Babylon*, 19; Brian Fagan, *Rape of the Nile;* John Wilson, *Signs and Wonders upon Pharaoh*.

60. Antonia Lant, "Curse of the Pharaoh," 85.

61. Ronny Cohen, "Tut and the '20s," 87.

62. Sumiko Higashi, *Cecil B. DeMille and American Culture*, 182–183. See also Bruce Babington and Peter William Evans, *Biblical Epics*, 44–46.

63. William Appleman Williams, *Tragedy of American Diplomacy*.

64. Stuart Creighton Miller, *"Benevolent Assimilation,"* 88. See also Kristen Hoganson, *Fighting for American Manhood*.

65. Emily Rosenberg, *Spreading the American Dream*, 29. On missionaries, see Jane Hunter, *Gospel of Gentility*. Oscar Campomanes's work on the cultural production of U.S. imperialism in representations of the Philippines has significantly influenced my own. See "American Orientalism at the Turn of the Century and Filipino Postcoloniality" (Ph.D. diss., Brown University, forthcoming). See also Vicente Rafael, "White Love."

66. Stuart Creighton Miller highlights the rhetoric of "benevolence" in the imperialism debates in *"Benevolent Assimilation."*

67. See Walter Benn Michaels, "Anti-imperial Americanism"; and Matthew Jacobson, *Barbarian Virtues,* 220–259. On the earlier debate about absorbing Mexicans, see Richard White, *New History of the American West;* and Reginald Horsman, *Race and Manifest Destiny.*

68. Lisa Lowe's *Immigrant Acts* charts this tension as it developed in the twentieth century.

69. Emily Rosenberg, *Spreading the American Dream,* 23–58.

70. Ibid., 100.

71. Richard Maltby, *Hollywood Cinema,* 69; Robert Sklar, *Movie-Made America,* 216.

72. Robert Sklar, *Movie-Made America,* 224–225; and John Izod, *Hollywood and the Box Office,* 114–118.

73. On the complicated history of Zionism, for example, see Bernard Avishai, *Tragedy of Zionism;* and Mark A. Raider, *Emergence of American Zionism.* On anti-Zionism among Jews, see Thomas A. Kolsky, *Jews against Zionism.*

74. William Quandt, *Decade of Decisions,* identifies these (minus religious attachment) as the three primary pillars of U.S. policy in the region. This analysis is supported, variously by Alan R. Taylor, *The Superpowers and the Middle East;* and Walter LaFeber, *America, Russia, and the Cold War.*

75. Emily Rosenberg, *Spreading the American Dream,* 123–128.

76. Joe Stork, *Middle East Oil and the Energy Crisis,* 27; Daniel Yergin, *Shattered Peace,* 179–180.

77. Quoted by Emily Rosenberg, *Spreading the American Dream,* 197. As President Truman explained in a letter to King Ibn Saud in 1950, "The United States is interested in the preservation of the independence and territorial integrity of Saudi Arabia. No threat to your Kingdom could occur which would not be a matter of immediate concern to the United States." Daniel Yergin, *The Prize,* 427–428. See also David Painter, *Oil and the American Century.*

78. For discussions of the coup in Iran, see Richard Cottam, *Iran and the United States,* 95–109; and Walter LaFeber, *America, Russia, and the Cold War,* 157–158.

79. George Lenczowski, *American Presidents and the Middle East,* 57–66.

80. Joe Stork, *Middle East Oil and the Energy Crisis,* 82.

81. Thomas McCormick, *America's Half-Century,* 186–190, calls this policy "subimperialism" and argues that between 1967 and 1985, the policy was carried out by both the United States and the Soviet Union, which turned to Iraq and Syria. See also Alan Taylor, *The Superpowers and the Middle East,* esp. 112–120.

82. Timothy Mitchell, "Middle East Studies."

83. Vincente Rafael, "Cultures of Area Studies in the United States"; Timothy Mitchell, "Middle East Studies."

84. Edward Said, *Orientalism,* 6.

85. Timothy Mitchell, "Middle East Studies."

86. Gregory Orfalea, *Before the Flames*, 60–78.

87. Ibid., 78.

88. The Naturalization Act of 1790 allowed naturalization only for "free white persons." It was amended and reauthorized several times in the nineteenth century. In 1870, the law was revised to include "persons of African nativity and descent," in order to accommodate the naturalization of former slaves, though this also had the effect of allowing naturalization of immigrants from Africa, while disallowing naturalization of any other "nonwhite" persons. Chinese were specifically disallowed from naturalization by the 1882 Exclusion Act. Later, various Supreme Court rulings declared that Japanese and Indians were ineligible for citizenship. See *Ozawa v. United States* (1922); *United States v. Bhagat Singh Thind* (1923); and the summaries in Ronald Takaki, *Strangers from a Different Shore*, 111–114, 207, 299; and Matthew Jacobson, *Whiteness of a Different Color*, 15–38; 223–275. The McCarran-Walter Act of 1952 nullified the racial restrictions on naturalization.

89. On the history of racial science, see William Stanton, *Leopard's Spots;* Stephen Jay Gould, *Mismeasure of Man;* Richard Lewontin, Steven Rose, and Leon J. Kamin, *Not in Our Genes;* and Daniel Kevles, *In the Name of Eugenics.*

90. Matthew Jacobson, *Whiteness of a Different Color*, 230–233; quotations on 233.

91. *Dow v. United States et al.*, Circuit Court of Appeals, Fourth Circuit, September 14, 1915. See also Matthew Jacobson, *Whiteness of a Different Color*, 239.

92. Joseph Massad, "Palestinians and the Limits of Racialized Discourse"; and Therese Saliba, "Another 'Other': Ambivalent Constructions of Arab Americans" (paper presented at the meeting of the American Studies Association, Boston, November 1993).

93. Gregory Orfalea, *Before the Flames*, 60.

94. Sameer Y. Abraham, "Detroit's Arab-American Community," 90–91.

95. Hamid Naficy, *Making of Exile Cultures.*

96. See Matthew Jacobson, *Whiteness of a Different Color*, 171–200. On the history of U.S. anti-Semitism, see Leonard Dinnerstein, *Antisemitism in America*, especially 58–77 on ideas about race.

1. "BENEVOLENT SUPREMACY"

1. "The Ten Commandments," *Time*, November 12, 1956, 122. See also "In the Grand Tradition," *Newsweek*, November 5, 1956, 112.

2. Bosley Crowther, "The Ten Commandments," *New York Times*, November 9, 1956, 35.

3. William Herberg, *Protestant, Catholic, Jew*, 102. By 1960, 63 percent of Americans claimed some affiliation with a religious denomination, compared with 48 percent in 1940. James Patterson, *America in the Twentieth Century*, 344.

Lorem ipsum dolor sit amet

4. Reported in the religion column "Mt. Sinai to Main Street," *Time*, November 19, 1956, 82, 85.

5. 1950: *Samson and Delilah*, no. 1, $11 million; 1951: *David and Bathsheba*, no. 1, $7 million; 1952: *Quo Vadis*, no. 2, $10.5 million; 1953: *The Robe*, no. 1, $20–30 million; 1956: *The Ten Commandments* brought in $34 million. Cobbett Steinberg, *Film Facts*, 21–22. *Ben-Hur* (1959) was the biggest box office draw of the decade 1951–1960. It won eleven Oscars, including Best Picture. Bruce Babington and Peter William Evans, *Biblical Epics*, 5–6; Lee Scott Theisen, "General Lew Wallace and *Ben-Hur*," 38.

6. On individualism as a national signifier, see Steven Whitfield, *The Culture of the Cold War*.

7. Charles Higham, *Cecil B. DeMille*, 278; Thomas H. Pauly, "Way to Salvation," 469.

8. On the rhetoric of totalitarianism, see George Lipsitz, *Rainbow at Midnight*, 182–203; and Ruth Feldstein, *Motherhood in Black and White*, 40–61.

9. Bosley Crowther, "The Ten Commandments," *New York Times*, November 16, 1956, 35.

10. Donald Neff, *Warriors at Suez*, 391.

11. Jonathan Boyarin discusses the complex history of exodus as a metaphor in "Reading Exodus into History."

12. "Benevolent Supremacy" is the title of chapter 8 in Charles Hilliard, *The Cross, the Sword, and the Dollar*, 64–74. On the other end of the political spectrum, a left-liberal rhetoric of American power and responsibility organizes Reinhold Niebuhr's work in the 1940s and 1950s; see *The World Crisis and American Responsibility* and *The Irony of American History*.

13. *Life*, February 17, 1941, 61–65; published in Henry R. Luce, *The American Century*, 3–40.

14. Nikhil Pal Singh discusses Luce in his intellectual context in "Culture Wars," 479–482.

15. William Jackson, *Withdrawal from Empire*, 21–25. The Atlantic Charter is reprinted in Walter LaFeber, ed., *Origins of the Cold War*, 32–33.

16. For discussions of the assumptions of U.S. policymakers about the postwar period, see Thomas McCormick, *America's Half-Century*, 44–98; and Walter LaFeber, *The American Age*, 434–508.

17. Daniel Yergin, *Shattered Peace*, 152.

18. Ibid., 180, quoting James Forrestal to Secretary of State Byrnes.

19. Typical of the plans and providing the basic template for several of them is *Joint Basic Outline War Plan; Short Title: Pincher*, Joints Chiefs of Staff, December 1945 (declassified January 1976).

20. Daniel Yergin, *Shattered Peace*, 179–192.

21. Richard Cottam, *Iran and the United States*, 55–109.

22. On the Truman Doctrine and its impact, Walter LaFeber, *America, Russia, and the Cold War*, 49–73; and Melvyn Leffler, *A Preponderance of Power*. Truman's speech is reprinted in LaFeber, *Origins of the Cold War*, 151–156.

23. Daniel Yergin, *Shattered Peace*, 176. See also Nikhil Singh, "Culture Wars," 480–482.

24. Dean Acheson, *Present at the Creation*, 374.

25. Gaddis Smith, *Dean Acheson*, quoted in Ernest May, "NSC 68: The Politics of Strategy," 15.

26. Jerry Sanders, *Peddlers of Crisis*, 30. "NSC-68," document text in Ernest May, *American Cold War Strategy*, 38.

27. Dean Acheson, *Present at the Creation*, 375.

28. See Ernest May, *American Cold War Strategy*, 130–151. May's collection brings together highly edited versions of some of the major interpretations of NSC-68 and the conduct of the cold war. Also see John Gaddis, "Strategy of Containment."

29. "NSC-68," document text in Ernest May, *American Cold War Strategy*, 27. Further references are given in parentheses in the text.

30. On the often blurred distinction between gender inversion and homosexual orientation, see Robert Corber, *Homosexuality in Cold War America*, 1–23, 79–104; and George Chauncey, *Gay New York*, 47–130.

31. Jerry Sanders, *Peddlers of Crisis*, 45, quoting Chester Barnard, chair of Rockefeller Foundation and CPD member.

32. In 1952, *Newsweek* ran two stories on Queen Elizabeth II and one on Princess Margaret. In 1953, articles appeared on April 6, June 1, June 8, October 12, and December 21.

33. "Wife, Mother, and Queen to Be," *Newsweek*, January 9, 1950, 24.

34. "Elizabeth and Philip: At the Edge of Empire," *Newsweek*, December 21, 1953, 44–46. See also William Roger Louis, *British Empire in the Middle East*.

35. Charles Hilliard, *The Cross, the Sword, and the Dollar*, 71.

36. The military actions were in Iran (1953), Suez (1956), Jordan (1957), Lebanon (1958), and Syria (1957).

37. On spectatorship and extrafilmic discourses, see Miriam Hansen, *Babel and Babylon*, and Linda Williams, *Hardcore*.

38. Bruce Babington and Peter William Evans's *Biblical Epics* is a very useful analysis. Their summary of recent scholarship on the films discusses several shorter treatments, including Michael Wood's chapter on epics in *America in the Movies*, Stephen Neale's discussion in *Genre*, and Giles Deleuze's analysis in *Cinema 1: The Movement-Image*.

39. In *Widescreen Cinema*, John Belton barely mentions the genre that dominated the early widescreen, describing them simply as "historical costume pictures" designed to appeal to an older audience (83). One analysis that does attend to religion is Thomas H. Pauly, "Way to Salvation."

40. Alan Nadel, "God's Law and the Wide Screen," 421.

41. Vivian Sobchack, "'Surge and Splendor,'" 26. See also Philip Rosen, "Securing the Historical."

42. "In the Great Tradition?" *Newsweek*, November 28, 1949, 70.

43. Gladwin Hill, "Most Colossal of All," *New York Times*, August 12, 1956, reprinted in *Encyclopedia of Film*, vol. 6, ed. James Monaco; "The Ten Commandments," *Time*, November 12, 1956, 122–123.

44. Henry Noerdelinger, *Moses and Egypt*, 1.

45. Widescreen films in one or another format dominated the box office in the 1950s. Of the top-grossing films from 1953 to 1959, eleven of the top twelve were released in a widescreen format. Examples of nonbiblical epics include *Around the World in Eighty Days* (1957); *20,000 Leagues under the Sea* (1955); *El Cid* (1961); and *The Last Days of Pompeii* (1960). David Pratt, "Widescreen Box Office Performance to 1959," 65–66. On the introduction of widescreen, see Douglas Gomery, *Shared Pleasures,* 238–246; John Belton, *Widescreen Cinema;* Richard Hincha, "Selling CinemaScope."

46. "6,500 See Debut of CinemaScope, New Film Process, in 'The Robe,'" *New York Times,* September 16, 1953, reprinted in *Encyclopedia of Film,* vol. 6, ed. James Monaco.

47. Quoted in "Birthday of the Revolution," *Time,* October 12, 1953. Thomas Pauly discusses the popularity of the early biblical epics in "The Way to Salvation," 469–471.

48. Some additional examples: Robert Coughlan, "The General's Mighty Chariots," *Life,* November 16, 1959, 118ff. (on *Ben-Hur*); "The Robe," *Look,* September 8, 1953, 70–73; and "DeMille's Greatest," *Life,* November 12, 1956.

49. "Mr. DeMille and Moses," *Look,* November 27, 1956, 77; "In the Grand Tradition," *Newsweek,* November 5, 1956; Gladwin Hill, "Most Colossal of All," *New York Times,* August 12, 1956, reprinted in *Encyclopedia of Film,* vol. 6, ed. James Monaco.

50. "DeMille Directs His Biggest Spectacle," *Life,* October 24, 1955, 143.

51. "The Ten Commandments," *Time,* November 12, 1956, 122.

52. Metz describes the spectator's "preliminary identification with the (invisible) seeing agency of the film itself as discourse," in "Story/Discourse (A Note on Two Kinds of Voyeurism)," in *The Imaginary Signifier,* 98.

53. Homi Bhabha, ed., *Nation and Narration;* Philip Rosen, "Making a Nation."

54. This same basic plot element is characteristic of most of the religious epics of the period, including *Samson and Delilah* (1949), *David and Bathsheba* (1951), *The Robe* (1953), *The Egyptian* (1954), *Demetrius and the Gladiators* (1954), and *Land of the Pharaohs* (1956).

55. Bruce Babington and Peter William Evans also point out the individuation of the Hebrews in their *Biblical Epics,* 63.

56. See, for example, William Hutchison, *Errand to the World.*

57. Alan Nadel, "God's Law and the Wide Screen," 427. Bruce Babington and Peter William Evans discuss the appropriation of Jewish history briefly in *Biblical Epics,* 34.

58. The films included *Gentleman's Agreement* (1947), *Mr. Skeffington* (1944), and *Crossfire* (1947). On these films, see Michael Rogin, *Blackface, White Noise,* 209–250; Robert Corber, *Homosexuality in Cold War America,* 79–104; and Bruce Babington and Peter William Evans, *Biblical Epics,* 37–39. Matthew Jacobson discusses the novel *Gentleman's Agreement*

(1947) and Jewish assimilation in *Whiteness of a Different Color,* 171–199, esp. 187–192.

59. The evil Nero in *Quo Vadis* is played by British-born Peter Ustinov, and Petronis is played by Briton Leo Glenn. Yul Brynner (Ramses in *The Ten Commandments*), was born in 1915 on Sakhalin Island (which passed back and forth between Japanese and Russian sovereignty from 1853 to 1945, when it became part of the Soviet Union) and had later become a Swiss citizen. In *Ben-Hur,* American Charlton Heston faces the Irish-born Stephen Boyd, although William Wyler originally wanted Heston to play the Roman Messala. In 1988, radio show host Terry Gross interviewed Kirk Douglas (producer and star of *Spartacus*), who explained his decision to cast British actors as Romans because he believed they had a more aristocratic bearing; *Fresh Air,* April 7, 1995, rebroadcast of interview from August 8, 1988.

60. Truman had a complicated and sometimes vexed attitude toward Zionism and the partition of Palestine; as late as 1945, he went on record as opposed to the establishment of a Jewish state in Palestine. He came to support the establishment of Israel via a combination of electoral pressure, pro-Zionist lobbying by both Jewish and pro-Zionist Christian groups, and the rising sense of the moral claims of Israel in the wake of the Holocaust. This history is traced by Michael J. Cohen, *Truman and Israel;* and Zvi Ganin, *Truman, American Jewry, and Israel.*

61. This argument is made by Bruce Babington and Peter William Evans, *Biblical Epics,* 54.

62. On the black church, see Gayraud S. Wilmore, *Black Religion and Black Radicalism;* James Cone, *Black Theology and Black Power;* Albert Raboteau, *Slave Religion;* and Lawrence Levine, *Black Culture and Black Consciousness,* 3–80.

63. Published in James Weldon Johnson, *God's Trombones.*

64. Jonathan Kaufman, *Broken Alliance,* 35.

65. Jonathan Boyarin, "Reading Exodus into History"; see also Michael Walzer, *Exodus and Revolution;* and Wilson J. Moses, *Black Messiahs and Uncle Toms.*

66. Roosevelt complied by issuing Executive Order 8802. On the Negro March on Washington, see Lucy Barber, "On to Washington."

67. Juan Williams, *Eyes on the Prize,* 1–36; and Derrick Bell, *Race, Racism, and American Law,* 542–551.

68. Ruth Feldstein, "'I Wanted the Whole World to See.'"

69. Quoted in Howard Raines, *My Soul Is Rested,* 69

70. Michael Walzer, *Exodus and Revolution,* 1. Walzer's overall project is to articulate a liberatory interpretation of the Exodus narrative, in contrast to the one he sees being developed by the Israeli Right. Edward Said takes issue with what he sees as Walzer's selective reading of the biblical story in "Michael Walzer's *Exodus and Revolution.*" Jonathan Boyarin usefully analyzes the underlying assumptions of the debate between Walzer and Said in "Reading Exodus into History."

71. *Stride toward Freedom*, King's account of the Montgomery struggle, received highly favorable reviews in both black and white papers, and James M. Washington describes it as very influential within the black community—"the handbook of the movement," in Martin Luther King Jr., *A Testament of Hope*, 417. Also see David Garrow, *Bearing the Cross*, 110–115. On Gandhi, see Martin Luther King Jr., "My Trip to the Land of Gandhi" (originally published in *Ebony*, 1959), reprinted in *Testament of Hope*, 23–30.

72. Martin Luther King Jr., "The Current Crisis in Race Relations" (originally published in *New South*, March 1958), reprinted in *Testament of Hope*, 86.

73. Martin Luther King Jr., "I See the Promised Land" (speech given on April 3, 1968, at the Mason Temple in Memphis), reprinted in *Testament of Hope*, 280–281, 286.

74. Martin Luther King Jr., "The Rising Tide of Racial Consciousness" (speech given to the National Urban League in 1960), reprinted in *Testament of Hope*, 146.

75. Penny Von Eschen, "Challenging Cold War Habits," 630.

76. On Sampson and White, see Helen Laville and Scott Lucas, "The American Way"; and Gerald Horne's commentary, "Who Lost the Cold War?"

77. Mary Dudziak, in "Desegregation as a Cold War Imperative," discusses several incidents. See also Penny Von Eschen, *Race against Empire*, 96–100; and Ben Keppel, *Work of Democracy*, 61–96.

78. Anna Lord Strauss of the League of Women Voters, quoted in Helen Laville and Scott Lucas, "The American Way," 570.

79. Mary Dudziak, "Desegregation as a Cold War Imperative," 61.

80. *Washington Post* editorial, May 19, 1954, quoted in Juan Williams, *Eyes on the Prize*, 35.

81. James Baldwin, *The Fire Next Time*, 87.

82. The phrase is Laura Mulvey's, from "Visual Pleasure and Narrative Cinema."

83. See Elaine Tyler May, *Homeward Bound;* Jane Gerhard, *Desiring Revolutions;* and Mari Jo Buhle, *Feminism and Its Discontents.*

84. Of the voluminous material on the public-private distinction, the following are particularly useful: Morton Horowitz, "History of the Public/Private Distinction"; Nancy Fraser, *Unruly Practices.* On bourgeois narratives, see Nancy Armstrong, *Desire and Domestic Fiction*, 108–134; and Nancy Armstrong and Len Tennenhouse, *Imaginary Puritan*, 1–46.

85. Amy Kaplan, "Romancing the Empire," 677.

86. Ibid.

87. On Suez , see J. C. Hurewitz, "Historical Context [of Suez]"; Robert Bowie, "Eisenhower, Dulles, and the Suez Crisis"; and Diane Kunz, "Economic Diplomacy of the Suez Crisis." See also Donald Neff, *Warriors at Suez;* and Peter Hahn, *The United States, Great Britain, and Egypt.*

88. George Lenczowski, *American Presidents and the Middle East*, 46, quoting Eisenhower, *White House Years.*

89. On Egypt in this period, see Robert Vitalis, *When Capitalists Collide;* and Joel Beinin and Zachary Lockman, *Workers on the Nile,* 395–447.

90. John Spanier, *American Foreign Policy,* 123; George Lenczowski, *American Presidents and the Middle East,* 40–55.

91. John Waterbury, *Egypt of Nasser and Sadat,* 83–100.

92. Diane Kunz, "Economic Diplomacy of the Suez Crisis."

93. Donald Neff, *Warriors at Suez,* 390–391.

94. George Lenczowski, *American Presidents and the Middle East,* 52.

95. William Quandt, *Decade of Decisions,* esp. 121–123, 183–185, 284–290.

96. Edward Said uses the phrase "knitted-together strength" in *Orientalism,* 6.

2. THE MIDDLE EAST IN AFRICAN AMERICAN CULTURAL POLITICS

1. The quotations are from Martin Luther King Jr., "Facing the Challenge of a New Age," 135–136 (address before the First Annual Institute on Non-Violence and Social Change, in Montgomery, Alabama, in December 1956), reprinted in *A Testament of Hope,* ed. James Washington.

2. W. E. B. Du Bois, "Suez," in *The Creative Writings of W. E. B. Du Bois,* ed. Herbert Aptheker, 45–46.

3. Paul Gilroy, *Black Atlantic.*

4. James Baldwin, "The Harlem Ghetto" (1948), reprinted in *Notes of a Native Son,* 55.

5. On the history and wide-ranging definitions of black nationalisms in the United States, see Wilson Moses, *The Wings of Ethiopia;* E. U. Essien-Udom, *Black Nationalism;* and William Van Deburg, *New Day in Babylon.*

6. Martin Delany, 12–13, quoted by Paul Gilroy, *Black Atlantic,* 22–23.

7. Hollis Lynch, *Edward Wilmot Blyden,* 64. Both Paul Gilroy and Kwame Anthony Appiah have argued that Blyden was likely influenced by Jewish thought on conceptions of peoplehood as he developed his ideas about "racial personality." See Gilroy, *Black Atlantic,* 208–212; and Appiah, "The Invention of Africa," in *In My Father's House,* 3–27. See also Wilson Moses, *Black Messiahs and Uncle Toms,* 62–129.

8. Text of the Balfour Declaration in Walter Laquer and Barry Rubin, eds., *Israel-Arab Reader,* 18.

9. Robert Weisbord and Richard Kazarian Jr., *Israel in the Black American Perspective,* 13–14. See also Appiah's discussion of Du Bois and Zionism, "Illusions of Race," in *In My Father's House,* 42–44.

10. Robert Weisbord and Richard Kazarian Jr., *Israel in the Black American Perspective,* 16.

11. On the founding of Israel, see Michael J. Cohen, *Truman and Israel;* and Simha Flapan, *Birth of Israel.*

12. On Bunche, see Ben Keppel, *Work of Democracy,* 31–96.

13. Robert Weisbord and Richard Kazarian Jr., *Israel in the Black American Perspective,* 20–22.

14. Jonathan Boyarin, "Reading Exodus into History," 540, argues persuasively that the influence of the exodus trope also worked in the other direction: the civil rights connotations of exodus played a role in the increasing tendency to use that rhetoric to represent the Israeli state.

15. Penny Von Eschen, *Race against Empire*, 96–121.

16. Martin Luther King Jr., "The Ethical Demands for Integration" (speech delivered in Nashville, Tennessee, on December 27, 1962, and published in *Religion and Labor*, May 1963), reprinted in *A Testament of Hope*, ed. James Washington, 117–125; quotations from 117.

17. See Brenda Gayle Plummer, *Rising Wind*, 257–272.

18. Different articles and editorials in the *Baltimore Afro-American*, quoted in Penny Von Eschen, *Race against Empire*, 168–169.

19. Richard Wright, *The Color Curtain*, 140.

20. Brenda Gayle Plummer, *Rising Wind*, 258.

21. Ibid., 278.

22. On Suez and African American reaction, see ibid., 259–261. In *Israel in the Black American Perspective*, 29–32, Robert Weisbord and Richard Kazarian Jr. discuss African American reactions at the time, including those of Joel A. Rogers and Horace R. Cayton. Quoting an interview with Bayard Rustin, they also make the argument for the retrospective significance of Suez (31).

23. On the day after the fight, Clay announced that he "believed in Allah"; at a second press conference the following day, he clarified his membership in the Nation of Islam. Thomas Hauser, *Muhammad Ali*, 81–84; John McDermott, "Champ 23: A Man-Child Taken in by the Muslims," *Life*, March 6, 1964, 38–39; Huston Horn, "The First Days in the New Life of the Champion of the World," *Sports Illustrated*, March 9, 1964, 26ff.; "Prizefighting: With Mouth and Magic," *Time*, March 6, 1964, 66–69.

24. On Clay, see "Cassius Marcellus Clay," *Time*, March 22, 1963, 78–81; Pete Hamill "Young Cassius Has a Mean and Sonny Look," *New York Post*, March 8, 1963; Howard Tuckner, " 'Man, It's Great to Be Great,' " *New York Times*, December 9, 1962; and "C. Marcellus Clay Esq." *Sports Illustrated*, June 10, 1963, 19–25. On his relationship with Malcolm X, see *The Autobiography of Malcolm X*, 349–356; Bruce Perry, *Malcolm*, 245–250; also Stan Koven, "The Muslim Dinner and Cassius Clay," *New York Post*, January 23, 1964; William Braden, "Muslims Claim the Credit for Clay's Victory," *New York Post*, February 2, 1964; "Cassius X," *Newsweek*, March 16, 1964, 74.

25. Ali quoted by Robert Lipsyte, "Cassius Clay, Cassius X, Muhammad Ali," *New York Times Magazine*, October 25, 1964, 29ff. On Ali and the Nation: Ted Poston, "Clay in Malcolm X's Corner in Black Muslim Fight," *New York Post*, March 3, 1964; "Cassius Clay Says He Is Not 'Scared' of Killing Reprisal," *New York Times*, February 24, 1965; Milton Gross, "The Men around Cassius Clay," *New York Post*, May 28, 1965; "FBI Probes Muhammad and Clay," *New York Post*, February 28, 1966. See also Alex Haley's *Playboy* interview with Ali in October 1964, reprinted in *Alex Haley: The Playboy Interviews*, 46–79.

26. Bill Jaus, "Cassius: I'm Still Unfit," *New York Post*, February 21, 1966; Henry Hampton and Steve Fayer, *Voices of Freedom*, 321–334; Thomas Hauser, *Muhammad Ali*, 142–201.

27. Sanchez is quoted in Henry Hampton and Steve Fayer, *Voices of Freedom*, 328.

28. For a very useful discussion of Baraka's early work, see James A. Miller, "Amiri Baraka," 3–24. On the founding of BARTS, see Komozi Woodard, *Nation within a Nation*, 63–68.

29. Baraka describes writing the play in his *Autobiography*, 210; he discusses his affiliation with Sunni Islam, 267–269. Baraka says that Jaaber "buried Malcolm X," but Peter Goldman mentions only Sheikh Ahmed Hassoun, the Sudanese cleric who had returned with Malcolm X from Mecca, in *The Death and Life of Malcolm X*, 302.

30. The designation of Baraka came from a poll of thirty-eight prominent black writers published in the January 1968 issue of *Negro Digest*. The writers also voted Baraka "the most important living black poet," and "the most important black playwright." Werner Sollors, *Amiri Baraka/LeRoi Jones*, 264 n. 6. On Baraka's transformation to Maoism, see his *Autobiography*, 308–314.

31. Marvin X and Faruk, "Islam and Black Art," 134. Jones used the phrase "post-American" earlier as well, in his essay "What the Arts Need Now" (1967), reprinted in *Raise, Race, Rays, Raze*.

32. Mattias Gardell, *In the Name of Elijah Muhammad*, 65; E. U. Essien-Udom, *Black Nationalism*, 84.

33. See John Voll, *Islam*. Perhaps Elijah Muhammad was also incorporating some reference here to Asia Minor, which comprises most of modern Turkey.

34. James Baldwin, *The Fire Next Time*, 46.

35. Mattias Gardell, *In the Name of Elijah Muhammad*, 57–85.

36. On Muslim slaves and early Muslim communities in the United States, see Richard Turner, *Islam in the African-American Experience*. There is some indication, however, that Muslim Africans were *less* likely than others to be taken and sold as slaves; see Morroe Berger, "Black Muslims," 49–64.

37. According to C. Eric Lincoln, *Black Muslims in America*, 120.

38. Elijah Muhammad, *Message to the Blackman in America*, 31.

39. Ibid., 58.

40. Ibid., 59.

41. Ruth Feldstein, *Motherhood in Black and White*, 139–164.

42. On the theological difference between the Nation of Islam and both Christianity and orthodox Islam, see Mattias Gardell, *In the Name of Elijah Muhammad*, 144–186.

43. Described in *Autobiography of Malcolm X*, 224–225. Also in Bruce Perry, *Malcolm*, 142.

44. Malcolm X, "Message to the Grassroots" (1963), collected in *Malcolm X Speaks*, 5–6.

45. Elijah Muhammad, *Message to the Blackman*, 95–96.

46. Of the many that explore this history, perhaps the best single source is Jack Salzman, ed., *Bridges and Boundaries*. On the prewar period, see Hasia Diner, *In the Almost Promised Land*.

47. *Autobiography of Malcolm X*, 320.

48. Speech at Boston University, February 15, 1960, quoted by C. Eric Lincoln, *Black Muslims*, 169.

49. Malcolm X, "Message to the Grassroots" (1963), collected in *Malcolm X Speaks*, 5–6.

50. Brenda Gayle Plummer, *Rising Wind*, 284–285; Louis Lomax, *When the Word Is Given*, 72–73.

51. For example, a strong editorial in one early NOI publication, *The Moslem World and the U.S.A.*, quoted by E. U. Essien-Udom, *Black Nationalism*, 302.

52. Brenda Gayle Plummer, *Rising Wind*, 261. Also quoted by C. Eric Lincoln, *Black Muslims*, 225. Karl Evanzz discusses Nasser's return cable, dated January 23, 1958, in *The Messenger*, 181.

53. There is some debate about whether Elijah Muhammad actually made the hajj, or pilgrimage to Mecca, or simply visited during a non-hajj period. Bruce Perry says that neither Malcolm X nor Elijah Muhammad was in Saudi Arabia during the period of the hajj in 1959; *Malcolm*, 205–206. Karl Evanzz's *The Messenger*, however, describes Muhammad's trip in late 1959 as a hajj, 212–215. He also discusses the role of the U.S. government in thwarting Muhammad's trip (192–196). Given that the hajj occurs just once a year, and both studies agree that Malcolm just missed the one in June 1959, it seems unlikely that Elijah Muhammad's trip constituted a genuine hajj, even though he (unlike Malcolm in 1959) visited Mecca.

54. The television special "The Hate That Hate Produced," produced by Mike Wallace and Louis Lomax, aired in 1959. See Karl Evanzz, *The Messenger*, 196–199. Already in 1959 and 1960, the "Black Muslim" movement had been covered in articles in *Time* ("Black Supremacists," August 10, 1959); *Newsweek* ("The Way of Cults," May 7, 1956); the *New York Times* ("Rise in Racial Extremism," January 25, 1960); *Christian Century* ("Despair Serves Purposes of Bizarre Cult," August 10, 1960); and *Reader's Digest* (Alex Haley, "Mr. Muhammad Speaks," March 1960). The first book-length study, C. Eric Lincoln's scholarly *The Black Muslims in America* was first published in 1961; a year later, James Baldwin's "Letter from a Region in My Mind" came out in the *New Yorker*, and E. U. Essien-Udom published *Black Nationalism*. Louis Lomax's popular account of the Nation of Islam, *When the Word Is Given*, came out in 1963, and in that same year, Malcolm X was interviewed by *Playboy* (May 1963), while Alfred Black and Alex Haley published a long article in the *Saturday Evening Post* ("Black Merchants of Hate," January 26, 1963). Some of this coverage is discussed in the third edition of C. Eric Lincoln's *Black Muslims*, 174–176.

55. The book was excerpted in the *Saturday Evening Post*, September 12, 1964, before its official publication. It was widely reviewed; see, for example, I. F. Stone, "The Pilgrimage of Malcolm X," *New York Review*, November 11, 1965.

56. *Negro Digest* ran several articles on the "Black Muslims" in the early 1960s, including an essay by Elijah Muhammad called "What the Black Muslims Believe," November 1963, 3–6. *Jet* covered the impact of Muslim identity on the career of Cassius Clay: Bobbie E. Barbee, "Will Link with Malcolm X Harm Clay's Career?" March 26, 1964, 50–57. Coverage in the black press was often ambivalent: when Malcolm X was killed, *Sepia* magazine's headline was "The Violent End of Malcolm X: He Taught Violence, He Died Violently," May 1965.

57. C. Eric Lincoln, *Black Muslims*, 128. On the black public sphere, see *Public Culture* (fall 1994), now available as *The Black Public Sphere*, in particular Manthia Diawara, "Malcolm X and the Black Public Sphere."

58. C. Eric Lincoln, *Black Muslims*, 108.

59. Amiri Baraka, *Autobiography*, 203. For a contemporary discussion of the response, see Larry P. Neal, "Malcolm and the Conscience of Black America," *Liberator* 6, no. 2 (February 1966): 10–11. Mance Williams discusses the impact of Malcolm X's *Autobiography* on the Free Southern Theater company in *Black Theatre*, 62.

60. Amiri Baraka, *Autobiography*, 204.

61. Komozi Woodard, *A Nation within a Nation*, 63–74. For a useful discussion of the publishing scene, see Henry Louis Gates and Nellie McKay, eds., *The Norton Anthology of African American Literature*, 1791–1806.

62. See Ed Bullins, "Short Statement on Street Theatre," *Drama Review*, summer 1968, 93.

63. Amiri Baraka, *Autobiography*, 249.

64. Harold Cruse, "Intellectuals and the Theater of the 1960s," in *Crisis of the Negro Intellectual*, 531. See also the penultimate chapter of the book, "The Harlem Black Arts Theater." The special issue of *The Drama Review* (*TDR*) on black theater was summer 1968.

65. Pierre Bourdieu, *Field of Cultural Production*, 51.

66. See Peter Burger, *Theory of the Avant-Garde*.

67. Interview with Ed Bullins, *New Plays from the Black Theatre*, ed. Ed Bullins, vii.

68. Stokely Carmichael, "We Are Going to Use the Term 'Black Power' and We Are Going to Define It Because Black Power Speaks to Us," in *Black Nationalism in America*, ed. John Bracey, August Meier, and Elliot Rudwick, 472. Carmichael is also quoted by Phillip Brian Harper, *Are We Not Men?* 51.

69. Addison Gayle, "Cultural Strangulation: Black Literature and the White Aesthetic," 46.

70. Amiri Baraka, "The Need for a Cultural Base to Civil Rites and Bpower Mooments," in *Raise, Race, Rays, Raze*, 43, 46. On the broad diffusion of cultural nationalism, see William Van Deburg, *New Day in Babylon*.

71. C. Eric Lincoln, *Black Muslims*, 72.

72. Elijah Muhammad explained the story of Yakub frequently, including in *Message to the Blackman*, 117–119. This myth was dropped from Nation of

Islam theology after Wallace D. Muhammad took over leadership of the community following Elijah Muhammad's death in 1975. See Aminah Beverly McCloud, *African American Islam,* 72–88.

73. The play was then published in the little magazine *The Liberator* the following month and in 1969 collected in Baraka's *Four Black Revolutionary Plays.* Publication history from Jeff Decker, ed., *The Black Arts Movement,* 120–121. The following discussion quotes from the text *Four Black Revolutionary Plays.* Subsequent page numbers are given in parentheses in the text.

74. For example, in Baraka's pamphlet "Seven Principles of US Maulana Karenga & the Need for a Black Value System," later reprinted in *Raise, Race, Rays, Raze.*

75. Larry Neal, "The Black Arts Movement," 73; K. William Kgositsile, "Towards Our Theater: A Definitive Act," *Negro Digest,* April 1967, 15.

76. The transformation of the name of the villain Yakub into a name (and a spelling) that looks more like Jacob may have anti-Semitic overtones, though this is not explicit elsewhere in the play.

77. Werner Sollors, *Amiri Baraka/LeRoi Jones,* 211. Sollors usefully focuses on the science fiction references and structure of the play. He argues that Baraka's use of the "mad scientist" character ultimately undermines the "antiwhite" logic of the play: the beast is as pitiable as was Frankenstein's creature, and ultimately the responsibility for evil lies with the black creator, Jacoub.

78. Larry Neal interprets the play as a critique of the Western aesthetic in "The Black Arts Movement."

79. See LeRoi Jones, *Blues People.*

80. The link between sexuality and classic horror films has been extensively discussed; one interesting recent example is Robin Berenstein, *Attack of the Leading Ladies.*

81. Phillip Brian Harper, *Are We Not Men?* 50.

82. There have been several other important studies of the masculinist bias of much of the Black Arts movement, including Joyce Hope Scott, "From Foreground to Margin." On cultural and gender conservatism in African American political movements, see also E. Frances White, "Africa on My Mind."

83. Andreas Huyssen, "Mass Culture as Modernism's Other," in *After the Great Divide.*

84. For example, Amiri Baraka, "From: The Book of Life," written after the Newark riots in 1967 and collected in *Raise, Race, Rays, Raze.*

85. LeRoi Jones (Amiri Baraka) and Larry Neal, eds. *Black Fire.* Essays with Islamic themes in the anthology include David Llorens, "The Fellah, the Chosen Ones, The Guardian," and Nathan Hare, "Brainwashing of Black Men's Minds." In the Bullins anthology, *New Plays from the Black Theatre,* other examples of NOI-influenced plays are "El Hajj Malik: A Play about Malcolm X," by N. R. Davidson Jr., and "The Black Bird (Al Tair Aswad)," by Marvin X. See also Dudley Randall and Margaret G. Borroughs, eds., *For Malcolm.*

86. Amiri Baraka, *Four Black Revolutionary Plays,* vii–viii.

87. Larry Neal, "The Black Arts Movement," 77.

88. Useful descriptions of the 1967 war can be found in William Quandt, *Decade of Decisions;* and Donald Neff, *Warriors for Jerusalem.*

89. Milton Himmelfarb, "In the Light of Israel's Victory," 57. A similar description is given in Charles Silberman, *A Certain People,* 183.

90. Charles Silberman, *A Certain People,* 185. For an excellent account of the meanings of the 1967 war for American Jews, see Paul Breines, *Tough Jews,* 57–62.

91. Charles Silberman, *A Certain People,* 185. "The People," *Time,* June 16, 1967, 18. Michael Staub argues that American Jews had been talking about the Holocaust well before the 1967 war in "Holocaust Consciousness, Black Masculinity, and the Renegotiation of Jewish American Identity, 1957–1967" (paper presented at the annual meeting of the American Studies Association, Kansas City, November 1996).

92. Arthur Hertzberg, "Israel and American Jewry," 69.

93. Ibid., 72.

94. "The Six-Day War and Jewish Power," *New Republic,* June 8, 1987, 7.

95. Frantz Fanon, *Wretched of the Earth,* 206–248.

96. Cleaver quoted in Irene Gendzier, *Frantz Fanon,* 264; Alvin Pouissant, "Overview of Fanon's Significance."

97. Amiri Baraka, "Last Days of the American Empire (Including Some Instructions for Black People)," reprinted in *Home,* 189–209.

98. Clayborne Carson, *In Struggle,* 192–198, 266. See also Stokely Carmichael and Charles Hamilton, *Black Power.*

99. Robert Weisbord and Richard Kazarian Jr., *Israel in the Black American Perspective,* 33.

100. "Third World Round Up: The Palestine Problem: Test Your Knowledge," *SNCC Newsletter,* June–July 1967. The cartoons and photos are described in Robert Weisbord and Richard Kazarian Jr., *Israel in the Black American Perspective,* 33–36; and Clayborne Carson, *In Struggle,* 267–269.

101. Clayborne Carson, *In Struggle,* 265–269.

102. Clayborne Carson, "Blacks and Jews in the Civil Rights Movement."

103. Murray Friedman, *What Went Wrong,* 227–233. Jonathan Kaufman's wonderful study, *Broken Alliance,* also makes a similar presumption. For an interesting revisionist account, see Gary Rubin, "African Americans and Israel."

104. Whitney Young, A. Philip Randolph, and Baynard Rustin sharply criticized the SNCC leaflet, and Martin Luther King Jr. made several statements of support for Israel after the 1967 war. In 1975, several major leaders, including Bayard Rustin, William Fautnoy, and Andrew Young, formed Black Americans in Support of Israel Committee (BASIC). Pamphlet in Schomberg clipping file, labeled "Israel."

105. Cornel West points out the significance of the principle of Palestinian rights in "On Black-Jewish Relations," 144–153. Alice Walker makes a similar argument in "To the Editors of *Ms.* Magazine," in *In Search of Our Mothers' Gardens,* 347–354. See also Waldo Martin Jr., "Nation Time!"

106. James Baldwin, "Negroes Are Anti-Semitic Because They Are Anti-White" (1967), reprinted in *The Price of the Ticket: Collected Non-Fiction, 1948–1985.*

107. "Black Art," originally published in *The Liberator* (January 1966) and collected in *Black Magic* (1969), reprinted in *Selected Poetry*, 106–107. See Amiri Baraka, "I Was an Anti-Semite," *Village Voice*, December 20, 1980, 1.

108. Clayborne Carson (*In Struggle*, 268) points to one such example in the press conference given by SNCC program director Ralph Featherstone in the wake of the crisis. Since the Nation of Islam was revived by Louis Farrakhan in 1975, these kind of statements have been frequent. Mattias Gardell, *In the Name of Elijah Muhammad*, 246ff. See also Ellen Willis, "The Myth of the Powerful Jew, with Prologue."

109. Amiri Baraka, "From: The Book of Life," in *Raise, Race, Rays, Raze*, 52.

110. See Reginald Martin, *Ishmael Reed and the New Black Aesthetic Critics.*

111. Zora Neale Hurston also constructs Caribbean voodoo as an authentic heritage for African Americans, in *Mules and Men*, though she does not posit it as originally African. My thanks to Krista Comer for pointing out this link.

112. Ishmael Reed, *Mumbo Jumbo*, 161–191. Further references are given in parentheses in the text.

113. Henry Louis Gates, *Signifying Monkey*, 229.

114. Benedict Anderson, *Imagined Communities*, 24–25.

115. Fredric Jameson, "Modernism and Imperialism." See also Edward Said, *Culture and Imperialism*, esp. 62–110.

116. Lisa Lowe, *Immigrant Acts;* George Lipsitz, *Dangerous Crossroads;* José David Saldívar, *Border Matters.*

117. Paul Gilroy, *Black Atlantic*, 208.

118. Addison Gayle, "Introduction," in *Black Aesthetic*, xxiii.

3. KING TUT, COMMODITY NATIONALISM, AND THE POLITICS OF OIL

1. David Harvey, *Condition of Postmodernity*, 121–200.

2. Fredric Jameson, *Postmodernism*, 1–54; Fredrick Buell, "Nationalist Postnationalism."

3. The exhibit was scheduled for six cities: Washington, D.C. (November 1976); Chicago (April 1977); New Orleans (September 1977); Los Angeles (February 1978); Seattle (July 1978); and New York (December 1978). It was later extended to San Francisco and Toronto.

4. See Emily Rosenberg's *Spreading the American Dream.* On the display of cultural imports and empire, see Timothy Mitchell, *Colonising Egypt.* For an excellent discussion of the ways that other countries use and transform cultural imports from the United States, see Uta Poiger, *Jazz, Rock, and Rebels.*

5. Thomas Hoving, *Making the Mummies Dance*, 401.

6. Ibid., 402.

7. Hoving's role at the Met was discussed in detail by Grace Gluck, "The Total Involvement of Thomas Hoving," *New York Times Magazine*, December 8, 1968. Reviews of Hoving's memoir also provided an opportunity for assessments of his tenure at the Met. See Robert Hughes, "Masterpiece Theater," *New York Review of Books*, March 4, 1993, 8–14; Arthur C. Danto, "Rocking with the Minister of Fun," *New York Times Book Review*, January 3, 1993, 1ff.; and Calvin Tomkins, "More or Less True Confessions," *New Yorker*, February 8, 1993, 106–108.

8. Thomas Hoving, *Making the Mummies Dance*, 429.

9. Ibid., 33.

10. Ibid., 404.

11. Ibid., 103.

12. Quoted descriptions from the official catalog and from an interview with the new director of the Met, Philippe de Montebello, aired as part of the PBS Skyline special "The Tut Phenomenon," December 8, 1978.

13. Hilton Kramer, "Tutankhamen Show in New York at Last," *New York Times*, December 20, 1978, C10.

14. Laurie Prothro, "Young King Tut," *National Review*, February 19, 1977, 211. The "official story" of Carter's find is generally drawn from Howard Carter's three-volume account, written with A. C. Mace, *The Tomb of Tut Ank Amen*. On archaeological plots, see Ella Shohat, "Imagining Terra Incognita," 51.

15. Quoted in Howard Carter, *Wonderful Things*, 27, which is the Metropolitan's reprint of excerpts from Carter's three-volume account.

16. Critics of the 1984 exhibit *"Primitivism" in 20th-Century Art* charged that it evacuated the history of colonialism by insisting on seeing African art through modernist categories. See Marianna Torgovnick, *Gone Primitive*, 119–137; Hal Foster, "The 'Primitive' Unconscious of Modern Art"; and James Clifford, "Histories of the Tribal and the Modern," in *Predicament of Culture*, 189–214.

17. Thomas Hoving, *Tutankhamun*, 275.

18. Kwame Anthony Appiah discusses how art from Africa has been incorporated, via a modernist aesthetic, into museum culture in Europe and the United States, in "The Postcolonial and the Postmodern," in *In My Father's House* 137–157. Annie Coombes analyzes the role of museums in forwarding a popular ideology of imperialism in *Reinventing Africa*.

19. On commodification and the increasing market for museum reproductions, see Michael J. Ettema, "History Museums and the Culture of Materialism." David Harvey (*Condition of Postmodernity*, 62–62) briefly describes the rapid increase in the number of museums and the takeoff of the "heritage industry" in the 1970s. See also Eilean Hooper-Greenhill, *Museums and the Shaping of Knowledge*.

20. *New Yorker*, December 25, 1978, 21.

21. Matthew Stevenson, "A King Tut Book of Etiquette," *Harper's*, January 1979, 97.

22. On the 1973 war, see William Quandt, *Decade of Decisions*, 165–206.

23. "A Time of Learning to Live with Less," *Time*, December 3, 1973, 29–32ff. See Daniel Yergin, *The Prize*, 615–618.

24. Thomas McCormick, *America's Half-Century*, 162.

25. "The Arabs' New Oil Squeeze," *Time*, November 19, 1973, 88.

26. Simon Head, "The Monarchs of the Persian Gulf," *New York Review of Books*, March 21, 1974, 29.

27. Thomas McCormick, *America's Half-Century*, 195–203.

28. Joe Stork, *Middle East Oil and the Energy Crisis*. See also J. E. Peterson, ed., *Politics of Middle Eastern Oil*, and Robert Lieber, *Oil Decade*.

29. Jerry Sanders, *Peddlers of Crisis*, 173.

30. Daniel Yergin, *The Prize*, 633–652.

31. A typical critique that portrays the U.S. government and the oil companies capitulating to the "oil threat" is Jack Anderson with J. Boyd, *Fiasco*.

32. Walter Levy, "The Years That the Locust Hath Eaten," 288.

33. On the Nixon Doctrine, see Thomas McCormick, *America's Half-Century*, 191–215; also Robert W. Tucker, "The American Outlook." Specifically vis-à-vis Iran, see Richard Cottam, *Iran and the United States*, 147–154.

34. Walter Levy, "Oil and the Decline of the West," 1014.

35. Edward Said discusses U.S. media coverage of the oil crisis in *Covering Islam*. Examples of the ways in which even respectable media outlets produced versions of such arguments include Leonard Mosley, "The Richest Oil Company in the World," *New York Times Magazine*, March 10, 1974; and Simon Head, "The Monarchs of the Persian Gulf," *New York Review of Books*, March 1974.

36. Thomas Hoving, *Tutankhamun*, 31.

37. Copy of the Tut resolution on microfilm at the Schomberg Library in New York, in the vertical file labeled "Egypt-Antiquities."

38. Herbert Scott-Gibson, *Tutankhamun and the African Heritage*, caption text for figure 11.

39. *Treasures of Tutankhamun*, discussion of catalog no. 19, unnumbered page.

40. On the decline of black political movements, see Michael Omi and Howard Winant, *Racial Formation in the United States*. On developments in black cultural nationalism, see William Van Deburg, *New Day in Babylon*. See also Edmund Gaither, afterword to the Boston Museum of Fine Arts publication, Joyce Haynes, ed., *Nubia: Ancient Kingdoms of Africa*, 58–59, which discusses black interest in Ancient Egypt, 58–59.

41. One example is Stanley Alpern's "The New Myths of African History," in *Bostonia*, summer 1992, 26–32.

42. Legrand H. Clegg II and Lisbeth Grant, "Big Tut *Rip-Off!*" *Sepia*, November 1977, 39–47.

43. "Tutankhamun: A Different Perspective," television broadcast, December 1978; producer Gil Nobels interviewed John Henrik Clarke and Josef Ben-Jochannan. An edited version of the transcript was reprinted as "Early Egypt: A Different Perspective," *Journal of African Civilizations* 1, no. 1 (April 1979), 6–15.

44. Mel Tapley, "Tut: The Black Boy King," *New York Amsterdam News*, December 16, 1978, 69.

45. Sylvester Leaks, "Tutankhamen: Black Art Overlooked by White Eyes," *New York Amsterdam News*, April 7, 1979, 17.

46. A highly technical argument for this point is made in Martin Bernal's *Black Athena*. Robert Young rightly criticizes Bernal for ignoring the central role of Egyptology in U.S. racial discourse in the nineteenth century in *Colonial Desire*, 118–141.

47. Cited in Reginald Horsman, *Race and Manifest Destiny*, 129.

48. See Stephen J. Gould, *Mismeasure of Man*, 61–69; Reginald Horsman, *Race and Manifest Destiny*, 117–138, 142; and William Stanton, *Leopard's Spots*.

49. This is discussed extensively by Reginald Horsman in *Race and Manifest Destiny*. Hegel is quoted to this effect by Martin Bernal in *Black Athena*, 256. Mainstream Egyptologists did continue to address this debate; see Kathryn Bard, "Ancient Egyptians and the Issue of Race," *Bostonia*, summer 1992; James Brunson, "Ancient Egyptians: 'The Dark Red Face Myth,' " and Ivan Van Sertima, "Black Dynasties and Rulers."

50. W. E. B. Du Bois, *The Negro*, 9. Du Bois later published versions of this argument in *Black Folk, Then and Now* (1939) and *The World and Africa: An Inquiry into the Part Which Africa Has Played in World History* (1947). On Du Bois's dilemma on racial classifications, see Anthony Appiah, "Illusions of Race," In *In My Father's House*, 28–46.

51. From Edward A. Johnson, *Adam v. Ape-Man and Ethiopia*, cited in James G. Spady, "Cheikh Anta Diop and Freddie Thomas," 16.

52. Joel Rogers, *World's Great Men of Color*. Also see George G. M. James, *Stolen Legacy*.

53. Shirley Graham Du Bois, "Egypt as Africa," 26. Shirley Graham Du Bois was W. E. B. Du Bois's second wife, and occasionally his collaborator, until his death in 1963.

54. Cheikh Anta Diop, *African Origin of Civilization*, includes sections from *Nations, nègres et culture* (Paris, 1955) and from *Antériorités des civilizations nègres: Myth ou vérité historique* (Paris, 1967). See also UNESCO, *Peopling of Ancient Egypt*.

55. Cheikh Anta Diop, *African Origin of Civilization*, 53.

56. Ibid., 249.

57. This representation of slavery as causing the destruction of proper patriarchy in black families found its most famous articulation in the Moynihan report of 1965. On the history of representing black women as damaging to black men, see Ruth Feldstein, *Motherhood in Black and White*.

58. Legrand H. Clegg II and Lisbeth Grant, "Big Tut *Rip-Off!*" *Sepia*, November 1977, 47.

59. Paul Gilroy, *Black Atlantic*, 187–223.

60. Fred Pfeil makes the argument for postmodernism as the cultural expression of a particular class fraction in "Makin' Flippy-Floppy: Postmodernism and the Baby-Boom PMC," in *Another Tale to Tell*, 97–125.

61. Eric Lott has argued that the use of blackface has been central to the construction of white American masculinity for more than two hundred years. See

"White Like Me," and *Love and Theft*. See also Alexander Saxton, *Rise and Fall of the White Republic*, esp. 165–182.

62. Kobena Mercer, "1968: Periodizing Politics and Identity," 433.

63. Here I am drawing on Fredric Jameson's definition in *Postmodernism*, as well as David Harvey's *Condition of Postmodernity*.

4. THE GOOD FIGHT

1. "The Home-Front War," *Newsweek*, May 8, 1967, 31–36, quote on 36.

2. Paul Boyer et al., *Enduring Vision*, 987. See also Ronald Spector, *After Tet*.

3. Hendrik Hertzberg, "Why the War Was Immoral."

4. "Foreign Relations," *Time*, June 16, 1967, 15.

5. "Middle East: The Scent of War," *Newsweek*, June 5, 1967, 47; "Intermission: 'Too Late and Too Early,'" *Newsweek*, June 12, 1967, 39.

6. "The Quickest War," *Time*, June 16, 1967, 22; "The Three-Day Blitz from Gaza to Suez," *U.S. News and World Report*, June 19, 1967, 33; "Terrible Swift Sword," *Newsweek*, June 19, 1967, 24. See also "U.S. Believes Israel Can Hold Its Own," *Chicago Tribune*, June 6, 1967, sec. 1:8.

7. "The People," *Time*, June 16, 1967, 18; Joseph Zullo, "Call March Urging U.S. to Back Israel," *Chicago Tribune*, June 6, 1967, sec. 1:7.

8. Russell Baker, "Needed: Agency to Allocate Wars," *Chicago Tribune*, June 1, 1967, sec. 1:10; Edward Tivnan, *The Lobby*, 69.

9. "The Three-Day Blitz from Gaza to Suez," *U.S. News and World Report*, June 19, 1967, 33.

10. The film was released in December 1960; it came in fifth on the list of top moneymaking films for 1961. The listings, based on reports in *Variety*, are strictly by calendar year; they would thus account only for revenues in 1961 (ignoring the lucrative first weeks in December). In a more accurate count, it is likely that the film would have ranked even higher. Cobbett Steinberg, *Film Facts*.

11. "*Exodus*," *Time* review, December 19, 1960, 69.

12. Edward Tivnan, *The Lobby*, 51.

13. Leon Uris, *Exodus*.

14. Bosley, Crowther, "Exodus," *New York Times*, December 16, 1960.

15. *Time*, December 19, 1960, 69.

16. Daniel Boorstein, *The Image: A Guide to Pseudo-Events in America* (1961), quoted in Paul Breines, *Tough Jews*, 53.

17. See Thomas Kolsky, *Jews against Zionism*; Mark Raider, *Emergence of American Zionism*, 172–201; John Frankel, *Prophecy and Politics*. See also Bernard Avishai, *Tragedy of Zionism*, especially his meditation on the role of Israel in contemporary American Jewish identity, 349–362.

18. "To the Editors of *Ms.* Magazine," in Alice Walker, *In Search of Our Mothers' Gardens*, 349.

19. Michelle Mart, " 'Tough Guys' and American Cold War Policy."

20. Leonard Dinnerstein, *Antisemitism in America*, esp. 58–149; and on the lynching of Leo Frank, 181–185.

21. Edward Tivnan, *The Lobby*, 61, citing Melvin Urofsky, *We Are One! American Jewry and Israel*.

22. Michael Rogin, *Blackface, White Noise*, 266.

23. Paul Breines, *Tough Jews*, 62–73. On representations of Jewish women, see Stacy Wolf, *How Do You Solve a Problem Like Maria?*

24. Paul Breines, *Tough Jews*, 1–75; quotation on 54.

25. Thanks to David Gutterman for pushing me to clarify this point. On masculinity and U.S. nationalism, see Gail Bederman, *Manliness and Civilization*.

26. Hal Lindsey, *Late Great Planet Earth*. All subsequent page references are in parentheses in the text. Ten million copies reported sold: Edwin McDowell, "Publishers: A Matter of Faith," *New York Times Book Review*, April 6, 1980, 18. Best-seller of the decade: Mark Silk, "Religious Books: Seven That Made a Difference," *New York Times Book Review*, March 30, 1976, 21. William Martin also repeats this claim, without attribution, in *With God on Our Side*. Later sales: Leo Ribuffo, "God and Contemporary Politics"; Paul Boyer, *When Time Shall Be No More*, 6.

27. Paul Boyer, *When Time Shall Be No More*, 126–127.

28. John F. Walvoord, *Israel in Prophecy*, 1962. Another example, *Israel in the Spotlight*, by Charles Feinberg, was published in 1964.

29. Dwight Wilson, "Armageddon Now!" quoted in Paul Boyer, *When Time Shall Be No More*, 2.

30. Ray Walters, "Paperback Talk," *New York Times Book Review*, April 6, 1980. Some of the publishing history from jacket and inside cover of Zondervan edition, thirteenth printing, August 1971. (In 1988, Zondervan was acquired by Harper and Row, later to become HarperCollins, and *LGPE* was reissued in 1990 once again under the Zondervan imprint.)

31. Edwin McDowell, "Publishers: A Matter of Faith," *New York Times Book Review*, April 6, 1980, 8; Ray Walters, "Paperback Talk," *New York Times Book Review*, March 12, 1978, 45–46.

32. Most histories of the fundamentalist and evangelical movements address this long retreat from politics. See, for example, James Reichley, "The Evangelical and Fundamentalist Revolt."

33. Nancy Ammerman, "North American Protestant Fundamentalism," 95–97; Robert Liebman, "Making of the New Christian Right," 230; William Martin, *With God on Our Side*, 100–143.

34. Anne Loveland, *American Evangelicals and the U.S. Military*, 122–166.

35. Paul Merkley, *Politics of Christian Zionism*, 62–63; David Rausch, *Zionism within Early American Fundamentalism*, esp. 79–126. See also George Marsden, *Fundamentalism and American Culture*.

36. James D. Hunter, "Evangelical Worldview since 1890," 21–22; Nancy Ammerman, "North American Protestant Fundamentalism," 59–71.

37. Hertzel Fishman, *American Protestantism and a Jewish State*, 83–122, 140–150.

38. "Could the Rapture Be Today?" *Moody Monthly*, May 1960, quoted in Paul Boyer, *When Time Shall Be No More*, 187.

39. *Christianity Today*, 21 July 1967, quoted in Hertzel Fishman, *American Protestantism and a Jewish State*, 152.

40. Grace Halsell, *Prophecy and Politics*, 72–73; Merrill Simon, *Jerry Falwell and the Jews*, 57–100, esp. 61–65.

41. *His Land*, videocassette; Paul Boyer, *When Time Shall Be No More*, 206.

42. Carl F. Henry, ed., *Prophecy in the Making*, 9.

43. Herman Ridderbos, "Future of Israel," 322; Wilbur Smith, *Israeli-Arab Conflict and the Bible;* Carl F. Henry, ed., *Prophecy in the Making*, 133, 141, 89, 343; Paul Boyer, *When Time Shall Be No More*, 188.

44. Harold John Ockenga, "Fulfilled and Unfulfilled Prophecy," 309; Wilbur Smith, "Signs of the Second Advent of Christ," 207.

45. John Walvoord, "Future of Israel."

46. On evangelicals and TV overall, see Peter Horsfield, *Religious Television*, 9, 13–23. On Falwell specifically, see David Snowball, *Rhetoric of the Moral Majority*, 46–49; Frances Fitzgerald, "Disciplined, Charging Army," 58, 88.

47. Robert Wuthnow, "Political Rebirth of American Evangelicals," 173; Eithne Johnson, "Emergence of Christian Video."

48. James Hunter, *American Evangelicalism*, 46; Frances Fitzgerald, "Disciplined, Charging Army," 59.

49. On Carter, see Robert Wuthnow, "Political Rebirth of American Evangelicals," 177. *Newsweek*, October 21, 1976, quoted by Anne Loveland, *American Evangelicals and the U.S. Military*, 212. See also Richard Neuhaus, "What the Fundamentalists Want," 9; Paul Boyer, *When Time Shall Be No More*, 11–13; William Martin, *With God on Our Side*, 173–190.

50. In addition, Pastor Chuck Smith, who had a national audience on 125 radio stations and 20 TV stations, plus a successful line of paperbacks, films, audiocassettes, and videocassettes, frequently discussed Israel and the end-times scenario. On Jack Van Impe, see Paul Boyer, *When Time Shall Be No More*, 129, 160; on Smith, see Randall Balmer, *Mine Eyes Have Seen the Glory*, 12–30. On newsletters and videos, see William Martin, "Waiting for the End"; Eithne Johnson, "Emergence of Christian Video," 196.

51. Ray Walters, "Paperback Talk," *New York Times Book Review*, March 12, 1978, 45–46. Lindsey's books included *Satan Is Alive and Well on Planet Earth* (1972) and *The Terminal Generation* (1976); see John Nelson, "Apocalyptic Vision in American Culture."

52. Gary Wilburn, "Doomsday Chic." Paul Boyer also describes this trend in *When Time Shall Be No More*, 11.

53. John F. Walvoord and John E. Walvoord, *Armageddon, Oil, and the Middle East*, 52.

54. Paul Boyer, *When Time Shall Be No More*, 6. John F. Walvoord was president of Dallas Theological Seminary from 1952 to 1986, and became chancellor in 1986.

55. Thomas McCall and Zola Levitt, *Coming Russian Invasion of Israel,* 33–35, 13.

56. Tim LaHaye, *Coming Peace in the Middle East,* 13–24.

57. John F. Walvoord, *Armageddon, Oil, and the Middle East Crisis* (1990), 32, 48. Not "biblically important": 51. Like other prophecy writers, Walvoord reiterates this point repeatedly. In the 1976 edition: "The enigma of how the underdeveloped Middle East could ever become the center of world history again has suddenly been solved [by the rise of Arab oil power]": 55–56.

58. Wolf Blitzer, *Between Washington and Jerusalem,* 193–194; Paul Boyer, *When Time Shall Be No More,* 204.

59. See also John F. Walvoord, "Future of Israel," 332; and Hal Lindsey, *Late Great Planet Earth,* 131.

60. Charles Strozier, *Apocalypse,* 204.

61. William Martin, *With God on Our Side,* 215.

62. Grace Halsell, *Prophecy and Politics,* 122; Wolf Blitzer, *From Washington to Jerusalem,* 198.

63. Boyer also discusses Lindsey's tone in *When Time Shall Be No More,* 128. See also Michael Barkun, "The Language of Apocalypse."

64. Reagan discussed *LGPE* with Herb Ellingwood, cited by Grace Halsell, *Prophecy and Politics,* 43. James Mills's article detailing his conversation with Reagan appeared in *San Diego Magazine,* August 1985. The article is also discussed by Paul Boyer, *When Time Shall Be No More,* 142–143. For a rather different assessment of Reagan's religious views in this period, see William Martin, *With God on Our Side,* 208.

65. John Saliba, "Religious Dimensions of the UFO Phenomenon."

66. John Pollock (*Billy Graham,* 280–281) describes *Angels* as having sold, by the end of 1976, "more copies in hardback than any book in American history except the Bible." An ad for the "Billy Graham Bicentennial Festival of Faith" claimed over one million sold in July 1976, in the *Philadelphia Inquirer,* July 5, 1976, B8.

67. Fredric Jameson, *Geopolitical Aesthetic;* quote from Mark Silk, "Religious Books: Seven That Made a Difference," *New York Times Book Review,* March 30, 1986, 21. On the economic transformations in this period, see David Harvey, *Condition of Postmodernity;* Barry Bluestone and Bennett Harrison, *The Great U-Turn.* On the failures of liberal ideology, see also Steve Brouwer, Paul Gifford, and Susan Rose, *Exporting the American Gospel,* 24–25.

68. The description of these events is drawn from several sources: from contemporary newspaper and television accounts, particularly ABC and CBS evening coverage September 6–9, 1972, as well as Serge Groussard, *Blood of Israel.*

69. Marc Gunther, *House That Roone Built,* 19.

70. "Horror and Death at the Olympics," *Time,* September 18, 1972, 28.

71. For example, "A Father Three Weeks, He's Slain," *Atlanta Constitution,* September 6, 1972, A1; "Israel's Dead Were the Country's Hope," *Time,* September 18, 1972, 26; "Israeli Team Had Eighteen Athletes and Coaches," *New York Times,* September 6, 1972, A19.

72. Shana Alexander, "Blood on the Playground," *Newsweek*, September 18, 1972, 35.

73. On May 8, Palestinian hijackers had commandeered a plane to Israel's Lod airport in Tel Aviv. They were eventually overtaken by Israeli soldiers disguised as mechanics; two were killed and two were captured. On May 30, three members of the Japanese guerrilla organization, the Red Army, armed with machine guns and grenades, had massacred twenty-eight and injured seventy-two when they opened fire at the Tel Aviv airport.

74. Marc Gunther, *House That Roone Built*, 8–11.

75. Howard K. Smith commentary, *ABC News*, September 6, 1972.

76. *ABC News* September 6, 1972; "McGovern Blames Egypt, Lebanon," *Atlanta Constitution*, September 7, 1972, A20. Others who drew the connection between Munich and Vietnam included Stephen Rosenfeld, "Terror as a Tactic of Many Aspects," *New York Times*, September 8, 1972, A22; Nicholas von Hoffman, "Munich: A History of Terror Written in Blood," *Washington Post*, September 8, 1972, B1; David Broder, "Munich and Vietnam," *Washington Post*, September 10, 1972, B7.

77. See my discussion in chapter 3. Jerry Sanders makes this argument in *Peddlers of Crisis*, 191–276.

78. *CBS Evening News*, September 8, 1972; "Israeli Retaliation," *Washington Post*, September 12, 1972, A20; "Retribution and Justice," *New York Times*, September 11, 1972, 30; " 'Eliminate This Scourge': Israel Begins Drive against Terrorism," *Atlanta Constitution*, September 11, 1972, B5. William Raspberry criticized the Israeli raid from a liberal perspective, "Arab-Israel Grievance," *Washington Post*, September 13, 1972, A15. The editors of the *National Review* criticized it from the Right, "Political Olympics," September 29, 1972, 1047–1048.

79. For summaries of these events, see Steve Posner, *Israel Undercover;* Edgar O'Ballance, *Language of Violence;* and Michael Bar-zohar and Eitan Haber, *Quest for the Red Prince.* Some numbers also from Terrance Smith, "With Life at Stake, How Can Terrorists Be Dealt With?" *New York Times*, July 11, 1976, Week in Review, 1.

80. On the PLO in this period, see Manuel Hassassian, "Policy and Attitude Changes in the PLO"; Shaul Mishal, *PLO under Arafat*, 15–23, 36–48; and Baruch Kimmerling and Joel S. Migdal, *Palestinians*, 220–225. Claire Sterling's right-wing popular book *The Terror Network* includes a summary of Palestinian actions in Europe in the early 1970s (113–130).

81. Edgar O'Ballance, *Language of Violence*, 239–258. See also "Raiders Free 106 Hostages," *Atlanta Journal-Constitution*, July 4, 1976, A1; Drama in Hijacking of Jet to Uganda," *New York Times*, July 1, 1976, 1.

82. "Hijacking Rescue Lifts Israeli Spirit," *New York Times*, July 7, 1976, 1; "The Fallout from Entebbe," *Newsweek*, July 19, 1976, 41; quote from "How the Israelis Pulled It Off," *Newsweek*, July 19, 1976, 46.

83. "Israel's Skill and Daring," *Nation*, July 17, 1976, 37; James Burnham, "Reflections on Entebbe," *National Review*, August 6, 1976, 834. Similarly, support was expressed by the African American paper the *New York Amsterdam*

News ("A Right to Be Wrong," July 10, 1976, A-4); and by the conservative *U.S. News and World Report* (" 'Israeli Raid in Uganda Was Justified': Interview with Adrian Fisher," July 9, 1976, 30).

84. "Rescue by Israel Acclaimed by US at Debate in UN," *New York Times*, July 13, 1976; also "Vindication for the Israelis," *Time*, July 26, 1976, 39.

85. *CBS Evening News*, July 7, 1976, Marvin Kalb reporting.

86. *CBS Evening News*, July 5, 1976, Marvin Kalb reporting.

87. "Israel Rescue Brings Tributes, Tears of Joy," *New York Times*, July 5, 1976, 2.

88. "How the Israelis Pulled It Off," *Newsweek*, July 19, 1976, 42ff.; "Israelis Go 2,500 Miles to Rescue Hostages," *New York Times*, July 11, 1976, Week in Review p. 1; "Rescue at Entebbe: How the Israelis Did It," *Reader's Digest*, October 1976, 122–128; Philip Ross, "The Illustrated Story of the Great Israeli Rescue," *New York*, August 2, 1976. Also *CBS Evening News*, July 8, 1976.

89. William Stevenson, *Ninety Minutes at Entebbe*; Ira Peck, *Raid at Entebbe*.

90. For discussion of the race to make movies about the event, see "Entebbe Derby," *Time*, July 26, 1976; "Hot Property," *Newsweek*, July 26, 1976, 67; and "The Unmaking of Entebbe," *Newsweek*, November 8, 1976, 42.

91. James Burnham, "Reflections on Entebbe," *National Review*, August 6, 1976, 834.

92. "Israel Points the Way," *Aviation Week and Space Technology*, July 12, 1976, 7. And the *Atlanta Journal–Constitution* editorialized: "Israel's flagrant violation of Uganda's sovereignty was a deeply satisfying performance for all of us who still hope that the nice guys of this world do not necessarily always finish last." July, 7, 1976, A4.

93. Tom Wicker, "Talking Tough on Terrorism," *New York Times*, July 20, 1976, editorial page, 31.

94. The guerrillas captured eighty-five students; in the rescue attempt, twenty-six students were killed, and more than sixty wounded. *New York Times*, May 15, 1974, May 16, 1974.

95. The *Mayaguez* incident is discussed briefly by David C. Martin and John Wolcott, *Best Laid Plans*, 36.

96. "When U.S. Rescue Mission Fizzled," *U.S. News and World Report*, July 19, 1976, 32.

97. Quoted in Jerry Sanders, *Peddlers of Crisis*, 162.

98. Ad for *Black Sunday*, in the *New York Times*, April 3, 1977.

99. As Stanley Kauffmann noted in the *New Republic*, April 9, 1977: "The thrills of football and imminent bombs are sardonically juxtaposed"; cited in Ernest Parmentier, ed., *Film Facts*, 52.

100. On the popularity of football in the 1970s, see William Oscar Johnson, "How Many Messages for This Medium?" *Sports Illustrated*, February 19, 1979, 38.

101. Kevin Phillips, "The Hype That Roared," 55. On the rise of the new Right, see Michael Kazin, *The Populist Persuasion*, 221–260.

102. David Snowball, *Rhetoric of the Moral Majority*, 16; on the multiple origin stories of the organization, see 50–53. See also James Reichley, "Evangelical and Fundamentalist Revolt."

103. Jerry Strober and Ruth Tomczak, *Jerry Falwell*, 167.

104. Wolf Blitzer, *Between Washington and Jerusalem*, 193; Grace Halsell, *Prophecy and Politics*, 75.

105. Jerry Falwell, ed., *Fundamentalist Phenomenon*, 215. Falwell had said this in print earlier as well, in the first issue of the *Moral Majority Report* (January 1980); see David Snowball, *Rhetoric of the Moral Majority*, 108.

106. Irving Kristol, "Political Dilemma of American Jews," 25. Kristol's intellectual background is discussed in Sidney Blumenthal, *Rise of the Counter-Establishment*, 148–157. Paul Boyer discusses Kristol's article, and a similar one by Nathan Perlmutter, in *When Time Shall Be No More*, 205–206.

107. James Reichley, "Evangelical and Fundamentalist Revolt," 79.

108. William Martin, *With God on Our Side*, 209.

109. Wolf Blitzer, *Between Washington and Jerusalem*, 193. On Reagan, see Paul Boyer, ed., *Reagan as President*, and Robert Dallek, *Ronald Reagan*.

110. Ibid., 73. Blitzer was the Washington correspondent for the *Jerusalem Post* for fifteen years starting in the mid-1970s. He joined CNN in 1990.

5. IRAN, ISLAM, AND THE TERRORIST THREAT

1. Robert J. Donovan and Ray Scherer, *Unsilent Revolution*, 146.

2. Ibid., 142. The hostage crisis was undoubtedly outstripped in intensity of coverage by the Gulf War in 1990–1991, but the daily coverage of that battle went on for only about six weeks. The sustained, near-daily reporting for more than a year of the hostage crisis was unique. See also Hamid Naficy "Mediating the Other."

3. Edward Herman and Gary O'Sullivan, *Terrorism Industry*, 44. See also Marc Celmer, *Terrorism, U.S. Strategy, and Reagan Policies*.

4. See, for example, Nancy Armstrong and Len Tennenhouse, *Imaginary Puritan*.

5. Following Habermas, the debate over the public sphere has provided some of the most useful theorization of this distinction. See Nancy Fraser, "Rethinking the Public Sphere"; Miriam Hansen, "Early Cinema, Late Cinema"; Robert Westbrook, " 'I Want a Girl, Just Like the Girl.' "

6. This list is derived from Richard Weekes, ed., *Muslim Peoples*, vol. 2, appendix 1: "Muslim Nationalities of the World," 882–911.

7. See especially Noam Chomsky, *Culture of Terrorism*; Edward Said and Christopher Hitchens, eds., *Blaming the Victims*; Edward Herman and Gary O'Sullivan, *Terrorism Industry*; Edward Herman, *Real Terror Network*; and Walter Laquer, *Age of Terrorism*.

8. Hamid Naficy ("Mediating the Other") uses the concept of "mediawork" to explain the power of these images. See also Carl Conetta, "Terror: Seen and Unseen," *Defense and Disarmament News*, July–August 1986, 1; and Bethami Dobkin, *Tales of Terror*.

9. *The Iran Crisis*, November 8, 1979. Tapes of the broadcast of "America Held Hostage" and later *Nightline* were obtained from the Vanderbilt University Television News Archives.

10. Iraq also did not participate in the embargo, despite Saddam Hussein's anti-American stance, for reasons that had primarily to do with its rivalry with Saudi Arabia and the other conservative oil-producing states. Daniel Yergin, *The Prize*, 607–614.

11. Gary Sick, *All Fall Down*, 16.

12. Ibid., 17; Thomas McCormick, *America's Half-Century*, 207–208; Richard Cottam, *Iran and the United States*, 144–154.

13. Richard Cottam, *Iran and the United States*, 3.

14. Robin Wright, *In the Name of God*, 79–95; Gary Sick, *All Fall Down*, describes these negotiations in some detail on pages 222–227, 263–282, 298–328, 363–392.

15. Gary Sick, *All Fall Down*, 230.

16. Richard Cottam, *Iran and the United States*, 211.

17. Marc Gunther, *The House That Roone Built*, 99.

18. Robert J. Donovan and Ray Scherer, *Unsilent Revolution*, 141.

19. *Los Angeles Times* columnist H. Rosenberg, quoted by Hamid Naficy, "Mediating the Other," 80.

20. Quoted in Robert J. Donovan and Ray Scherer, *Unsilent Revolution*, 144.

21. Marc Gunther, *The House That Roone Built*, 104.

22. Hamid Naficy, "Mediating the Other," 78.

23. Gary Sick, *All Fall Down*, 258–259.

24. ABC, *Nightline*, March 24, 1980.

25. Tad Tuleja, "Closing the Yellow Circle," and George Marsical, "In the Wake of the Gulf War," have traced the evolution of the yellow ribbon as a symbol, from the Civil War, when it was a somewhat bawdy signifier that a particular girl was "cavalry goods," to its appearance as a sign of chaste loyalty in the John Ford drama about the cavalry, *She Wore a Yellow Ribbon* (1949). The 1973 pop hit by Tony Orlando and Dawn, "Tie a Yellow Ribbon (Round the Old Oak Tree)" was about a convict returning home; the song resurfaced as a hit in 1979, when it became something of an anthem of the U.S. response to the Iranian hostage situation.

26. The best analysis of the news coverage and its limitations is Edward Said, *Covering Islam*.

27. *CBS Evening News*, February 14, 1980.

28. David C. Martin and John Walcott, *Best Laid Plans*, 7–8.

29. CBS reported that one former CIA official who sometimes publicly identified U.S. agents had his passport revoked, even though he had vowed not to identify any intelligence agents until after the hostages were released; *CBS Evening News*, December 21, 1979. On Carter's response: *ABC World News Tonight*, December 24, 1979; Gary Sick, *All Fall Down*, 273.

30. *ABC World News Tonight*, November 9, 1979.

31. *CBS Evening News*, November 17, 1979.

32. *ABC World News Tonight*, November 18, 1979. U.S. officials quoted by James Coates, *Chicago Tribune*, November 22, 1979, as recounted by Edward Said, *Covering Islam*, 99.

33. Said discusses several of these in *Covering Islam*, 78–87.

34. ABC News Special Report, *The Iran Crisis: America Held Hostage*, December 21, 1979.

35. David C. Martin and John Walcott, *Best Laid Plans*, 6–42.

36. Richard Harwood, "Series of Mishaps Defeated Rescue in Iran," *Washington Post*, April 26, 1980, A1; "Tragedy in the Desert: Rescue That Failed," *U.S. News and World Report*, May 5, 1980, 6ff.; Alan Mayer et al., "A Mission Comes to Grief in Iran," *Newsweek*, May 5, 1980, 24ff. A special commission was formed to investigate the failure; after it released its report in August 1980, a new flurry of articles appeared. For example: Richard Burt, "Military Report Says Hostage Raid on Teheran Could Have Succeeded," *New York Times*, August 24, 1980; George C. Wilson, "Over-secretive Planning Seen as Downfall of Raid," *Washington Post*, August 24, 1980, A1.

37. *ABC World News Tonight* and *CBS Evening News*, April 24, 25, 26, and 27, 1980.

38. David C. Martin and John Walcott, *Best Laid Plans*, 29.

39. *CBS Evening News*, August 7, 1980.

40. *ABC World News Tonight*, August 7, 1980.

41. These are mentioned by both Edward Said, *Covering Islam*, 117, and Hamid Naficy, "Mediating the Other," 81–82.

42. Hamid Naficy, "Mediating the Other," 82. Lou Albano et al., *Complete Idiot's Guide to Pro Wrestling*, describes the characters of the Iron Sheik in the early 1980s, including his famous 1984 bout with Hogan, 158–160.

43. Robin Wright, *In the Name of God*, 82–88; Richard Cottam, *Iran and the United States*, 222–224.

44. "Lost in the Terrorist Theater," *Harper's*, October 1984, 43.

45. Charles Krauthammer, "Partners in Crime," in *How the West Can Win*, ed. Benjamin Netanyahu, 111–113.

46. Edward Herman and Gary O'Sullivan, *Terrorism Industry*, 104–106; Bethami Dobkin, *Tales of Terror*, 95.

47. *Washington Post*, June 25, 1984. The press coverage for both conferences is discussed in Edward Herman and Gary O'Sullivan, *Terrorism Industry*, 198–201.

48. Dennis DeConcini on the front page of the *Los Angeles Times Book Review*, July 20, 1986; Robert McFarlane on the cover of the *Washington Post Book World*, May 18, 1986. The book was also reviewed positively by John Gross in the *New York Times*, April 25, 1986; by Merle Rubin in the *Christian Science Monitor*, May 2, 1986, B1ff., and then again in the same paper by Robin Wright, August 1, 1986, B8; and by Shaul Bakhash in the *New York Review of Books*, August 14, 1986, 12–14.

49. Edward Said, "The Essential Terrorist," *Nation*, June 14, 1986, 828–833; quotation on 832. Walter Laquer, writing in the *New Republic*, October 6, 1986,

42–44, was less than enthusiastic, and Marvin Zonis's review in the *New York Times Book Review*, May 18, 1986, 7, was critical.

50. From the back cover text of the Avon Books edition, April 1987.

51. Paul Johnson, "The Cancer of Terrorism," in *How the West Can Win*, ed. Benjamin Netanyahu, 31–40; quotation on 31.

52. George P. Shultz, "The Challenge to the Democracies," in *How the West Can Win*, ed. Benjamin Netanyahu, 16–24; quotation on 18.

53. Bernard Lewis, "Islamic Terrorism?" in *How the West Can Win*, ed. Benjamin Netanyahu, 65–69; quotations on 66, 78. Edward Said talks about this kind of essentialist argument in *Covering Islam*, 75–88.

54. P. J. Vatikiotis, "The Spread of Islamic Terrorism," in *How the West Can Win*, ed. Benjamin Netanyahu, 77–84; quotation on 82.

55. Jeane J. Kirkpatrick, "The Totalitarian Confusion," in *How the West Can Win*, ed. Benjamin Netanyahu, 56–60; quotation on 57.

56. The *Harper's* version of the journalists' symposium differs slightly from the version published in *How the West Can Win*. In the book, several participants were allowed to expand their extemporaneous comments into separate essays, while the liberal commentators were removed altogether. My discussion draws primarily on the *Harper's* version.

57. Besancon was a columnist for *L'Express;* O'Sullivan wrote for the *London Daily Telegraph.* Daniel Schorr went on later to join National Public Radio.

58. Ted Koppel, "Terrorism and the Media: A Discussion," *Harper's*, October 1984, 47. Koppel's comments were not included as an essay in *How the West Can Win*.

59. This comment by Schorr appears in the *Harper's* version of the conference symposium, October 1984, 53, but it was edited out of the version printed in *How the West Can Win*.

60. Both Woodward and Schorr were on President Nixon's list of media enemies in the early 1970s, which is perhaps the most straightforward testament to their liberal credentials.

61. Charles Krauthammer, "Partners in Crime," in *How the West Can Win*, ed. Benjamin Netanyahu, 111–112.

62. The phrase is another of Krauthammer's quotable aphorisms. His suggestion was that the media voluntarily refuse to cover hijackings and hostage takings. "Partners in Crime," in *How the West Can Win*, ed. Benjamin Netanyahu, 111–113; quotation on 112.

63. "Terrorism and the Media: A Discussion," *Harper's*, October 1984, 50.

64. Ibid., 54.

65. Walter Laquer, "Missing the Target" (review of *How the West Can Win*), *The New Republic*, October 6, 1986, 42–44; quote on 42.

66. James Bamford, "Bankrolling International Murder and Extortion, review of *The Financing of Terror*, by James Adams," *Washington Post Book World*, February 8, 1987.

67. Edward Said, *Orientalism*, 6. The academic and semiacademic books on terrorism in this period number in the hundreds. By the time of the publication

of *How the West Can Win*, the list included Ovid Demaris, *Brothers in Blood* (1977); Walter Laquer, *Terrorism* (1977); and Claire Sterling, *Terror Network* (1981), among others.

The watershed year in the production of intellectual discourse about terrorism was probably 1986, which, in addition to Netanyahu's collection, also saw the publication of at least a half dozen other "major" books on terrorism and an associated spate of reviews and surveys of the field, including Steven Anzovin, ed., *Terrorism*; Uri Ra'anan, *Hydras of Carnage*; Ray S. Cline and Yonah Alexander, *Terrorism as State-Sponsored Covert Warfare*; Gayle Rivers, *The Specialist*; Lawrence Freeman et al., eds., *Terrorism and International Order*; and Neil Livingstone and Terrell Arnold, *Fighting Back*. Note also the publication of a long, get-tough article by Conor Cruise O'Brien, "Thinking about Terrorism," *Atlantic*, June 1986.

For a discussion of the experts and think tanks that became the main sources of advice and knowledge about terrorism, see Edward Herman and Gary O'-Sullivan, *Terrorism Industry*.

68. Inside cover advertising copy, 1986 paperback edition, of Ken Follett's *On the Wings of Eagles*. On the TV movie, Tom Shales, " 'Eagles' to the Rescue on NBC," *Washington Post*, May 17, 1986, C1ff.

69. The top-grossing films of the 1980s, in terms of box office receipts, were: *E.T.* ($187 million); *The Return of the Jedi* ($162 million); *Terminator 2* ($112 million); *Back to the Future* ($96 million); *Ghost* ($95 million); *Tootsie* ($95 million); and *Raiders of the Lost Ark* ($90.4 million). Susan Jeffords, *Hard Bodies*, 197 n. 16, source not cited.

70. Other hostage-rescue films in this period included *Commando* (1985), *Death before Dishonor* (1987), *Hostage* (1987), *Let's Get Harry* (1986), *Navy Seals* (1990), and *Omega Syndrome* (1987), among others. I would also argue that *Aliens* (1986) is essentially a hostage-rescue film.

71. Vincent Canby, "Don't Mess with Us Celluloid Tigers," *New York Times*, February 23, 1986, sec. 2, p. 19ff.

72. The construction and valorization of muscular masculinity is also a common trope in the action films, and indeed several studies have analyzed action films as the site of reconstituted masculinity and/or reconstructed imperial adventurism. See, for example, Yvonne Tasker, *Spectacular Bodies*; Elizabeth Traube, *Dreaming Identities*; and Susan Jeffords, *Hard Bodies*.

73. Interview with ADC staff member, March 4, 1996.

74. Bethami Dobkin describes the event briefly in *Tales of Terror*, 16.

75. For an analysis of 1980s action films that does argue for the centrality of Iran, see Fredric Jameson, *Geopolitical Aesthetic*.

76. Vincent Canby, "Delta Force," *New York Times*, February 14, 1986, C14ff. See also Paul Attanasio, "Hijack Chutzpah: Norris in 'Delta Force,' " *Washington Post*, February 14, 1986, D3; Roger Ebert, "The Delta Force," *Chicago Sun-Times*, February 14, 1986.

77. Two other films about Entebbe were produced in 1977: *Raid on Entebbe*, and *Victory at Entebbe*. For a historical account of the raid, see Yeshayahu Ben-Porat, Eitan Haber, and Zeev Schiff, *Entebbe Rescue*.

78. Marita Golden, "Her Husband's Captive," *New York Times*, December 27, 1987; Maude McDaniel, "Repression in Iran," *Washington Post Book World*, September 21, 1987.

79. Carol Stocker, "Mother's Iran Ordeal Draws Fire at Home," *Boston Globe*, January 24, 1991.

80. Betty Mahmoody, *Not without My Daughter*. Further references given within the text.

81. Richard Cottam, *Iran and the United States*, 232–242; Robin Wright, *In the Name of God*, 108–153.

82. Anne McClintock, *Imperial Leather*, 170.

83. Ibid., 209–231.

84. Sander Gilman, *Jew's Body*; Albert Lindemann, *Esau's Tears*.

85. Nina Easton, "Movies' Mideast Myopia: U.S. Activists and Academics Fear the Negative Stereotypes Depicted in Films Will Lead to More Hostility toward Muslims," *Los Angeles Times*, January 10, 1991. The paperback was number two on the list for February 10, 1991, and it remained in the top ten until May 19, 1991; from *New York Times*, paperback best-sellers list for each date. On sales, see Dona Munker, "Driven to Extremes," *New York Times*, September 27, 1992.

6. MILITARY MULTICULTURALISM
IN THE GULF WAR AND AFTER

1. Both the "police action" in Korea (1950–1953) and the undeclared war in Vietnam (1963–1973) were larger in terms of number of troops engaged. But the intensity of the conflict with Iraq, and the fact that so much happened so quickly, meant that the concentration of U.S. troops and matériel present at any one time is unrivaled in the postwar period.

2. "While the world waited, Saddam Hussein systematically raped, pillaged, and plundered a tiny nation no threat to his own." George Bush, "The Liberation of Kuwait has Begun" (speech from the Oval Office, January 16, 1991), reprinted in *The Gulf War Reader*, ed. Micah Sifry and Christopher Cerf, 311–314.

3. George Bush, "In Defense of Saudi Arabia" (speech of August 8, 1990, announcing the deployment of troops to Saudi Arabia), reprinted in *The Gulf War Reader*, ed. Micah Sifry and Christopher Cerf, 197–199.

4. Peter Steinfels, "Armageddon: Book on Middle East Feeds Hunger for Meaning in Chaos," *St. Louis Post-Dispatch*, February 16, 1991, 10A; Charles Solomon, "Paperbacks: Armageddon, Oil, and the Middle East Crisis," *Los Angeles Times Book Review*, March 10, 1991, 10.

5. Greenpeace provided the higher estimate. The lower numbers can be found in John Heidenrich, "The Gulf War: How Many Iraqis Died?" Official estimates also vary: the Defense Intelligence Agency estimated one hundred thousand Iraqis dead, plus or minus 50 percent (!). Margot Norris suggests the confusion is strategic in "Only the Guns Have Eyes."

6. Allied casualties altogether were 343 dead.

7. Nancy Gibbs, "Land That They Love," *Time*, February 11, 1991, 52–53; Dana Cloud, "Operation Desert Comfort."

8. Quoted by Michelle Kendrick, "Kicking the Vietnam Syndrome."

9. Elsa Walsh and Paul Valentine, "Thousands at D.C. Rally Decry U.S. Bombings," *Washington Post*, January 20, 1991, A27.

10. One example of this kind of Left analysis was Marcy Darnovsky, L. A. Kauffman, and Billy Robinson, "What Will This War Mean?" reprinted in *The Gulf War Reader*, ed. Micah Sifry and Christopher Cerf, 480–491.

11. On the history of media obeisance during wartime, see H. Bruce Franklin, "From Realism to Virtual Reality."

12. On CNN, see Holly Cowan Shulman, "The International Media and the Persian Gulf War," and Mimi White, "Site Unseen."

13. Tom Engelhardt, "The Gulf War as Total Television," 85.

14. Susan Jeffords discusses the public familiarity with weapons systems in "The Patriot System, Or, Managerial Heroism." See also Douglas Kellner, *Persian Gulf TV War.*

15. For an analysis of the pool reporting system and its restrictions, see Robert Fisk, "Free to Report What We're Told," and James Bennet, "How the Media Missed the Story."

16. Susan Jeffords, "Bringing the Death-World Home." It later became clear that the information and images provided by the military were themselves sometimes suspect. For example, the Bush administration's claim that in September 1990 more than 250,000 Iraqi soldiers were massed in Kuwait and perhaps preparing to strike Iraq later proved to be either a serious misreading of the satellite data or a deliberate deception: Peter Zimmerman, "Experts Look Again at Wartime Satellite Photos," *St. Petersburg Times*, September 15, 1991, 1Aff.

17. Mimi White, "Site Unseen," 128–134.

18. Tom Engelhardt, "The Gulf War as Total Television," 83.

19. On the yellow ribbons, George Mariscal, "In the Wake of the Gulf War."

20. Janice Castro, "All Wired and Wary: American Consumers React to War and Hard Times," *Time*, February 4, 1991, 58–59; Lewis Lord, "The War's Other Front," *U.S. News and World Report*, February 4, 1991, 54–55; Tom Engelhardt, "The Gulf War as Total Television," 92; Jim Castonguay, "Gulf War TV Super Bowl," p. 5 of 11. For a partial list of T-shirts available, see "Frightening Commodities of the Gulf War (and More!)" at http://www.spyproducts .com/books2.html.

21. Benedict Anderson, *Imagined Communities*, 9–46.

22. Evan Carton, "The Self Besieged," 42.

23. Jean Baudrillard, "The Reality Gulf," *Guardian*, January 11, 1991, cited in Christopher Norris, *Uncritical Theory*, 11–12.

24. Christopher Norris, *Uncritical Theory*, 25–26.

25. Daniel Hallin, "Images of the Vietnam and the Persian Gulf Wars in U.S. Television."

26. In February 1991, just before the start of the ground war, an ABC news poll indicated that 85 percent of whites and 48 percent of blacks in the United

States supported the war, according to a report in the *Washington Post*, February 8, 1991.

27. Tom Engelhardt, "The Gulf War as Total Television," 85.

28. AP wire story, "Freed Hostages Headed Home," *Los Angeles Times*, December 10, 1990, P2; Dana Priest, "Saddam Orders the Release of All Hostages," *Washington Post*, December 7, 1990, A1.

29. Anthony Lake, "Confronting Backlash States."

30. Robyn Wiegman, "Missiles and Melodrama," 171.

31. John Mueller argues against any particular impact of visuality on U.S. public opinion in *Policy and Opinion in the Gulf War*, 134–137.

32. Jonathan Crary, in *Techniques of the Observer*, makes the most sustained argument for this understanding of nineteenth-century visual culture. See my Introduction, this volume, 16–19.

33. Robyn Wiegman, "Missiles and Melodrama," 171–172.

34. George Will, "Literary Politics," *Newsweek*, April 22, 1991, 72. Christopher Newfield also discusses Will's column in "What Was Political Correctness?"

35. Evan Carton, "The Self Besieged." Examples of p.c. articles include Jerry Adler, Peter Prescott, and Patrick Houston, "Taking Offense," *Newsweek*, December 24, 1990; Irving Howe, "The Value of the Canon: What's Wrong with P.C.," *New Republic*, February 18, 1991, 40; Richard Bernstein, "The Rising Hegemony of the Politically Correct," *New York Times*, October 28, 1990, E1; Charles Krauthammer, "An Insidious Rejuvenation of the Old Left," *Los Angeles Times*, 24 December 1990, B5. Also published in 1990 and 1991: Roger Kimball's *Tenured Radicals* and Dinesh D'Souza's *Illiberal Education*.

36. John Leo's columns in *U.S. News and World Report* provide an excellent example of the conflation of various "threats" of political correctness, immigration, and multiculturalism. See, for example, "PC Follies: The Year in Review," *U.S. News and World Report*, January 27, 1992, 22; and "A Political Correctness Roundup," *U.S. News and World Report*, June 22, 1992, 29.

37. "The Victims' Revolution" was *Newsweek*; "The Thought Police" was the *Atlantic*. Both cited by Evan Carton, "The Self Besieged," 40.

38. William A. Henry III, "Upside Down in the Groves of Academe," *Time*, April 1, 1991, 66.

39. The coordination between conservative organizations on this issue is chronicled in Jean Stefancic and Richard Delgado, *No Mercy*, 109–136.

40. "We the American ... Foreign Born," report by the U.S. Bureau of the Census, September 1993, and "Current Population Reports: The Foreign-Born Population: 1994," both available at http://www.uscensus.gov.

41. Louis Menand makes this argument about the campus as social microcosm in "What Are Universities For? The Real Crisis on Campus Is One of Identity," *Harper's*, December 1991, 47–56. Jochen Schulte-Sasse and Linda Schulte-Sasse connect the campus crisis with the Gulf War in "War, Otherness, and Illusionary Identifications with the State."

42. Fred Siegel, "The Cult of Multiculturalism," *New Republic*, February 18, 1991, 40.

43. George Will, "Literary Politics," *Newsweek*, April 22, 1991, 72.

44. Gerald Graff discusses one example of this kind of contextualization, the work of Renaissance scholar Stephen Greenblatt, in "The Nonpolitics of PC."

45. William A. Henry III, "Upside Down in the Groves of Academe," *Time*, April 1, 1991, 67; Jerry Adler et al., "Taking Offense," *Newsweek*, December 24, 1990. See also Jeff Grabmeier, "Clashing over Political Correctness," *USA Today* magazine, November 1992, 60–61.

46. Michael Kinsley, "Hysteria over 'Political Correctness,'" *Washington Post*, May 3, 1991, A25. See also Gerald Graff, "The Nonpolitics of PC," and Meg Greenfield, "Mainstream Mania," *Newsweek*, September 30, 1991, 68.

47. Christopher Newfield, "What Was Political Correctness?" 320.

48. Rosa Ehrenreich, "What Campus Radicals? The P.C. Undergrad Is a Useful Specter," *Harpers*, December 1991, 57–61.

49. Marc Cooper, "Dum da Dum-dum: LA Beware, the Mother of All Police Departments Is Here to Serve and Protect," *Village Voice*, April 16, 1991, quoted by Abouali Farmanfarmaian, "Sexuality in the Gulf," 12

50. Oscar Campomanes, "The American Soldier in Love and War" (paper presented at the annual meeting of the Organization of American Historians, Chicago, April 2–5, 1992). The paper developed out of chapter 3 of "American Orientalism at the Turn of the Century and Filipino Postcoloniality" (Ph.D. diss., Brown University, forthcoming). See also Benedict Anderson, *Imagined Communities*, 9–10.

51. For a discussion of the role of the reserves, see Carl Conetta and Charles Knight, *Reasonable Force*.

52. "Women Warriors: Sharing the Danger," *Newsweek*, September 10, 1990; *People*, September 10, 1990. Douglas Kellner discusses both cover stories in *Persian Gulf TV War*, 75–76.

53. American Women in Uniform, Desert Storm at http://userpages.aug .com/captbarb/femvetsds.html.

54. Nancy Gibbs, "Life on the Line," *Time*, February 25, 1991, 36–38; Ellen Goodman, "Desert Storm Is Busting Military's Glass Ceiling," *Los Angeles Times*, April 23, 1991; Alain L. Sanders, "When Dad and Mom Go to War," *Time*, February 18, 1991, 69; Elaine Donnelly, "What Did You Do in the Gulf, Mommy?" *National Review*, November 18, 1991, 41–44.

55. ABC News poll, cited in Lynne Duke, "Emerging Black Anti-war Movement Rooted in Domestic Issues," *Washington Post*, February 8, 1991, A27ff. In a poll of *Ebony* readers in January 1991, 66.9 percent reported serious reservations about the deployment of U.S. troops in the Persian Gulf. Venise Berry and Kim Karloff, "Perspectives on the Persian Gulf War in Popular Black Magazines," 251. Black support for the war is also discussed in an editorial by Juan Williams, "Race and War in the Persian Gulf ... Why Are Black Leaders Trying to Divide Blacks from the American Mainstream?" *Washington Post*, January 20, 1991. Williams decries black leaders' opposition to the war and says

that most blacks initially supported the war. Williams's essay prompted a barrage of letters; see *Washington Post*, February 2, 1991.

56. Only one member of the Congressional Black Caucus voted to support President Bush's call for arms in the Persian Gulf. Venise Berry and Kim Karloff, "Perspectives on the Persian Gulf War in Popular Black Magazines," 250, 255.

57. "Blacks: Too Much of the Burden?" *Time*, February 4, 1991, 43; "This Time, Better Deal for Black Servicemen?" *New York Times*, February 18, 1991. (The specific reference is to the experience of African American veterans of Vietnam, who said they were subject to the racist behavior of white commanders and colleagues.) Also David Treadwell, "Some Black Veterans Find Yellow Ribbon Bittersweet," *Los Angeles Times*, March 16, 1991, A1ff.; and Charisse Jones, "Blacks and the Army: Why Join?" *Los Angeles Times*, January 8, 1991, A1ff.

58. Lynne Duke, "For Soldiers, Duty Checks Racial Bias," *Washington Post*, May 19, 1991, A1.

59. Jim Castonguay, "The Gulf War TV Super Bowl," p. 7 of 11. This description draws on Castonguay's extensive analysis.

60. This assessment is offered by Joe Klein, "Can Colin Powell Save America?" *Newsweek*, October 10, 1994. At the time of his retirement from the military in 1993, Powell's approval rating in a Gallup poll topped 70 percent, as reported in Edwin Diamond, Maryann Thumser, and Virginia Trioli, "Covering Powell: Is Hero Worship ... Replacing Investigative Reporting?" *National Journal*, December 4, 1993, 2902–2903.

61. Although Powell initially preferred a "containment" approach to Iraq rather than a counterattack, he went on to become fully supportive of the military operation. See Bob Woodward, *The Commanders*, 38–42.

62. Powell quoted by Dan Balz and Rich Atkinson, "Powell Vows to Isolate Iraqi Army and 'Kill It,'" *Washington Post*, January 24, 1991, A1ff.

63. Charles Lane, "The Legend of Colin Powell," *New Republic*, April 17, 1995, 20–32.

64. Colin Powell, *My American Journey*, 604.

65. Powell speaking to House Armed Service Committee, quoted in Sam Fulwood III, "To Blacks: Powell Is a Hero and a Source of Controversy," *Los Angeles Times*, February 17, 1991, A8ff.

66. Statistics cited in Sam Fulwood III, "Black Activists Urge Bush to Declare Cease-Fire," *Los Angles Times*, February 16, 1991, A3.

67. On the "poverty draft," see Charisse Jones, "Blacks and the Army: Why Join?" *Los Angeles Times*, January 8, 1991; and Lynne Davis, "Emerging Black Anti-war Movement," *Washington Post*, February 8, 1991, A27ff. On opportunities in the military, see Leon Wynter, "Gulf War Should Boost Status of Military Blacks," *Wall Street Journal*, March 15, 1991, B1.

68. See Laura Randolph, "The Untold Story of Black Women in the Gulf War," *Ebony*, September 1991, 100–107.

69. Juan Williams, "Race and War in the Persian Gulf ... Why Are Black Leaders Trying to Divide Blacks from the American Mainstream?" *Washington Post*, January 20, 1991; Clarence Page, "The Military and Black Amer-

ica," *Wall Street Journal*, April 18, 1991, A16. The criterion for this relative privilege was, and is, acquiescence and loyalty to the institution. On Powell's role in suppressing a black-led insurrection with U.S. military units in South Korea, see Charles Lane, "The Legend of Colin Powell," *New Republic*, April 17, 1995, 28–29.

70. National Press Club president Clayton Boyce, quoted in *Washington Post*, September 30, 1933, B1ff.

71. John Ranelagh, "America's Black Eisenhower: Colin Powell, Architect of Victory," *National Review*, April 1, 1991, 26ff.

72. Richard Berke, "Waiting for the Candidate Who Can Change Everything," *New York Times*, November 5, 1995.

73. David Corn, "The Untouchable," *Nation*, October 4, 1993, 344.

74. Lynn Davis, "For Soldiers, Duty Checks Racial Bias," *Washington Post*, May 19, 1991, A1ff.

75. Abouali Farmanfarmaian, "Sexuality in the Gulf," 21.

76. Robyn Wiegman makes this argument in "Missiles and Melodrama." Another very useful discussion of the power of the images of military equipment and high-tech is Margot Norris, "Only the Guns Have Eyes." Nancy Armstrong compares the representation of "the family" in the Gulf War and in the "war on drugs" in "Fatal Abstraction: The Death and Sinister Afterlife of the American Family."

77. Gay-oriented newspapers reported that, in practice, many gay and lesbian soldiers were being ordered to ship out to the Gulf, even after coming out to their commanders. Rick Harding, "Commanders Quietly Ignore Anti-gay Rule to Build Gulf Forces," *Advocate*, February 26, 1991, 20–21. The final Clinton policy on gays in the military—"don't ask, don't tell"—was enacted in early 1993 after a protracted political battle.

78. Eric Schmitt, "Colin Powell, Who Led US Military into New Era, Resigns," *New York Times*, October 1, 1993, A12; Eric Schmitt, "The Top Soldier Is Torn between Two Loyalties," *New York Times*, February 6, 1993, A1.

79. Nancy Gibbs, "Walking a Tightrope," and "Arab-Americans: The Perils of Hyphenation," both in the *Economist*, January 26, 1991, 23–24; "They're Americans Too," *Sports Illustrated*, February 4, 1991, 9; Tahar Ben Jelloun, "I Am an Arab, I Am Suspect," *Nation*, April 15, 1991, 482–485. See also Therese Saliba, "Military Presences and Absences: Arab Women and the Persian Gulf War."

80. See James Abourezk, *Advise and Dissent*, 254, for his remarkably brief discussion of the founding of ADC.

81. Etienne Balibar, "Racism and Nationalism," discusses the connections of both racism and nationalism with the language of family and inheritance.

82. Internet Movie Data Base; business data for *The Siege* at http://us.imdb.com/Business; *Entertainment Weekly*, box office listings, December 18, 1998, 55.

83. "Four for Four," *Time*, March 14, 1994; Mary Anne Weaver, "The Trail of the Sheikh," *New Yorker*, April 12, 1993, 71–89.

84. Shalhoub had a long list of credits, including appearances in *Primary Colors* (1998), *Men in Black* (1997), and *Barton Fink* (1991), as well as numerous television appearances.

CONCLUSION

1. Michael Ignatieff, "The Burden," *New York Times Magazine*, January 5, 2003, 23–27ff. Ignatieff was Professor of the Practice of Human Rights and Director of the Carr Center for Human Rights Policy at Harvard. See also his *The Lesser Evil*.

2. Ignatieff, "The Burden," 54.

3. Susan Sontag, "Regarding the Torture of Others," *New York Times*, May 23, 2004.

4. Sontag, *On Photography* (New York: Farrar, Straus, and Giroux, 1977), 17–20. She draws on Benjamin, "The Work of Art in the Age of Mechanical Reproduction."

5. Sontag, *On Photography*, 23–24; 109.

6. I am drawing here on Roland Barthes's *Mythologies*, and specifically his wonderful analysis in "Myth Today" of the process of "turning history into nature."

7. The photo was taken by Thomas E. Franklin of northern New Jersey's *The Record*. It is posted at the "Ground Zero Spirit" site at http://www .groundzerospirit.org/about.html. On how the image was shot and its subsequent circulation as a cultural icon, see Rick Hampton, "The photo no one will forget," *USA Today*, November 27, 2001, at http://www.usatoday.com/news/ sept11/2001/12/27/usatcov-unforgettable.htm.

8. The scholarly literature on the meanings of September 11 is already vast, and I cannot do it justice here. In addition to the specific articles and books I cite elsewhere, several key texts are: Slovoj Zizek, *Welcome to the Desert of the Real;* Joanne Meyerowitz, ed. *History and September 11;* Craig Calhoun, Paul Price and Ashley Trimmer, eds., *Understanding September 11*.

9. Warren Hoge, "After the Attacks: West: Outpouring of Grief and Sympathy for Americans Is Seen Throughout Europe and Elsewhere," *New York Times*, September 14, 2001, at Lexis-Nexis Academic Universe. Jean-Marie Colomgani, "We Are All Americans," *Le Monde*, September 12, 2001 at World Press Review, http://www.worldpress.org/1101we_are_all_americans.htm. "Attacks Draw Mixed Response in Middle East," CNN.com/World, September 12, 2001 http://edition.cnn.com/2001/WORLD/europe/09/12/mideast.reaction/.

10. Warren Hoge, "After the Attacks: West: Outpouring of Grief and Sympathy for Americans Is Seen Throughout Europe and Elsewhere."

11. Ariel Dorfman, "Americans Must Now Feel What the Rest of Us Have Known," *The Independent*, October 3, 2001, at http://www.independent.co.uk/ story.jsp?story = 97282.

12. Suha Ma'ayeh, "Candlelight Vigil Draws Hundreds in Memory of Victims of Attacks on US," *Jordan Times*, September 18, 2001, at http://www .jordanembassyus.org/09182001003.htm.

13. On the Palestinian reaction: Charles Radin, "Leaders Deplore, But People Rejoice," *Boston Globe*, September 14, 2001, in Lexis-Nexis Academic Universe. In terms of Israelis and Palestinians killed, sources with very different ideological perspectives offer the same general numbers. On the conservative Israeli International Policy Institute for Counterterrorism, see Don Radlauer, "The 'al-Aqsa Intifada'—An Engineered Tragedy," at http://www.ict.org.il/ articles/articledet.cfm?articleid = 440. Palestinian deaths are tracked at Palestine Monitor, http://www.palestinemonitor.org/factsheet/Palestinian_killed_ fact_sheet.htm. Also useful are the entries at the Free Dictionary: "Terrorism Against Israel," at http://encyclopedia.thefreedictionary.com/Terrorism %20against%20Israel, and "Palestinians Killed by Israelis," http://encyclopedia .thefreedictionary.com/Terrorism%20against%20Israel%20in%202001.

14. Stephen J. Dubner, "Looking for Heroes—And Finding Them," *New York Times*, October 6, 2001. See also "Heroes Amid the Horror," *New York Times*, September 15, 2001; Dennis Smith, "A Firefighter's Story," *New York Times*, September 14, 2001; Michelle O'Donnell, "Just Regular Guys in the Urban Wild, Until the Bell Rings," *New York Times*, September 23, 2001. All available at ProQuest Newspapers.

15. Peggy Noonan, "Welcome Back, Duke," *OpinionJournal*, October 12, 2001, at http://www.opinionjournal.com/columnists/pnoonan/?id = 95001309.

16. Michiko Kakutani, "The Trivial Assumes Symbolism of Tragedy," *New York Times*, September 23, 2001, at ProQuest Newspapers.

17. The sociologist Robert Putnam reports on his survey in "Bowling Together," *The American Prospect*, February 2002, at http://www.prospect.org/ web/page.ww?section = root&name = ViewPrint&articleId = 6114.

18. Patricia Leigh Brown, "Heavy Lifting Required: The Return of Manly Men," *New York Times*, October 28, 2001, at ProQuest Newspapers; Peggy Noonan, "Welcome Back, Duke: From the Ashes of Sept. 11 Arise the Manly Virtues," *OpinionJournal*, October 12, 2001, at http://www.opinionjournal.com/ columnists/pnoonan/?id = 95001309.

19. Several commentators noted the difference between the flag and yellow ribbons. See Daniel Henninger, "Wonder Land: America Hasn't Declined; It's Rising Higher," *Wall Street Journal*, September 21, 2001; "Flag Waving," *Christian Century*, January 30–February 6, 2002. Both available at ProQuest Newspapers.

20. See the impressive photo essay on the flag in Mary Dudziak, *September 11 in History* and Peter Elliott, *Homefront: American Flags from Across the United States*.

21. Toby Keith, "Courtesy of the Red, White, and Blue," on *Shock'n Y'all*, Tokeco Tunes (BMI), 2002. Darryl Worley, "Have You Forgotten?" on *Have You Forgotten?* SKG Music, 2003.

22. Blane Harden, "Flag Fever: The Paradox of Patriotism," *New York Times*, September 30, 2001, at ProQuest Newspapers; Elizabeth O'Leary, *To Die For: The Paradox of American Patriotism.*

23. Sharon H. Rackow, "How the USA Patriot Act Will Permit Governmental Infringement upon the Privacy of Americans"; Christopher L. Eisgruber and Lawrence G. Sager, "Civil Liberties in the Dragons' Domain." See also Ruti G. Teitel, "Empire's Law: Foreign Relations by Presidential Fiat."

24. Leti Volpp, "The Citizen and the Terrorist." Felicia R. Lee, "Flag-Waving: Reading between the Stripes," *New York Times*, September 30, 2001, at ProQuest Newspapers. See also Moustafa Bayoumi, "Letter to a G-Man."

25. Caryle Murphy, "For Muslims, Benevolence Prevails over Backlash," *Washington Post*, October 6, 2001, at Lexis-Nexis Academic Universe; Bo Dart, "Kindness Honored in Wake of Attacks," *Atlanta Journal-Constitution*, December 5, 2001, at Lexis-Nexis Academic Universe.

26. "Ashcroft: Critics of New Terror Measures Undermine Effort," *CNN News*, December 6, 2001, at www.cnn.com/2001/US/12/06/inv.ashcroft .hearing.

27. Michael Denning, *Culture in the Age of Three Worlds.* Also see Arjun Appadurai, "Disjuncture and Difference in the Global Cultural Economy," and Antoinette Burton, ed., *After the Imperial Turn.*

28. "Fighting Terror / The President Speaks," *Boston Globe*, October 12, 2001, A28.

29. "Ashcroft: Critics of New Terror Measures Undermine Effort," December 6, 2001, at www.cnn.com/2001/US/12/06/inv.ashcroft.hearing.

30. Karl von Clausewitz, *On War.*

31. President George W. Bush, "Address to a Joint Session of Congress and the American People," September 20, 2001, at www.whitehouse.gov/news/ releases/2001/09/20010920–8.html; "Remarks by the President in a Photo Opportunity with the National Security Team," September 12, 2001, at http:// www.whitehouse.gov/news/releases/2001/09/20010912–4.html.

32. Evand Abrahamian, "The US Media, Huntington, and September 11," 536. See also Douglas Kellner, *Terror Wars.*

33. Amal Amireh's "Between Complicity and Subversion" offers a nuanced reading of the uses of women's bodies in Palestinian nationalist narratives. For an American example, see Linda Kerber, *Women of the Republic.*

34. Ahmed Rashid, *Taliban;* Larry Goodson, *Afghanistan's Endless War.* See also Rone Tempest, "Training Camp of Another Kind," *Los Angeles Times*, October 15, 2001, A1. Kathleen Richter, "Revolutionary Afghan Women," *Z Magazine*, November 2000, at www.zmag.org/zmag/articles/nov00richter .htm.

35. See Sonia Shah, "Unveiling the Taleban."

36. Valentine Moghadam, "Afghan Women and Transnational Feminism."

37. Noy Thrupkaew, "What Do Afghan Women Want?" *American Prospect* 13:15, August 26, 2002, at prospect.org/V13/15/thrupkaew-n.html. See also

Janelle Brown, "Eve Ensler: Afghanistan Is Everywhere," *Salon*, November 26, 2001, at www.archive.salon.com/people/feature/2001/11/ensler.htm.

38. There is a great deal of scholarship on this history; see, as one strong example, Anne McClintock, *Imperial Leather*. On feminist debates about imperial moves within contemporary feminism, see Bonnie Smith, *Global Feminisms* and Chandra Talpade Mohanty, *Feminism Without Borders*.

39. See Shahnaz Khan, "Between Here and There"; Loretta Kensinger, "Plugged in Praxis." I discuss the larger issue of U.S. feminists' engagement with Middle Eastern and African women's issues in "Suffering Sisters: American Feminists and the Problem of Female Genital Surgeries," in *Americanism: Essays on the History of an Ideal*, ed. Michael Kazin and Joseph McCartin.

40. "Radio Address by Mrs. Bush to the Nation," White House press release, November 17, 2001 at www.whitehouse.gov/news/releases/2001/11/20011117.html.

41. Samuel Huntington, *The Clash of Civilizations and the Remaking of World Order*. In the 1970s, Huntington had been director of security planning for the National Security Council in the Carter administration and a founder of *Foreign Policy*; when he published *Clash of Civilizations*, he was a University Professor at Harvard and chairman of the Harvard Academy for International and Area Studies.

42. See, for example, Fouad Ajami, "The Summoning," *Foreign Affairs* 72, no. 4 (1993), 2–9, which is a discussion of the article version; and Roy Mottahedeh, "The Clash of Civilizations: An Islamicist's Critique," *Harvard Middle Eastern and Islamic Review* 2 (1996), 1–26.

43. "A&A: A Head-On Collision of Alien Cultures?" *New York Times*, October 20, 2001. Samuel Huntington, "The Age of Muslim Wars," *Newsweek*, December 17, 2001. Robert Kaplan, "Looking the World in the Eye," *Atlantic Monthly*, 288, no. 5 (December 2001). All are at Academic Search Premier. See also Stanley Kurtz, "The Future of History," *Policy Review*, June/July 2002, 113, at ProQuest Research Library Plus; Ervand Abrahamian, "The US Media, Huntington, and September 11."

44. Robert A Kittle, "Islam vs. the West; Perilous Rift; Islamic Awakening Pursues an Anti-Western Future," *San Diego Union Tribune*, July 28, 2002 at Lexis-Nexis Academic Universe.

45. Fareed Zakaria, "The Politics of Rage: Why Do They Hate Us?" *Newsweek*, October 15, 2001, available at http://www.fareedzakaria.com/articles/newsweek/101501_why.html.

46. Mark O'Keefe, "Falwell Calls Prophet Muhammad a 'Terrorist'," Newhouse News Service, October 3, 2002; Bob Simon reporting, "Zion's Christian Soldiers," *60 Minutes*, October 6, 2002; Julie Duin, "Summit Criticizes Anti-Islam Remarks, but Evangelicals Differ with Their Leaders," *Washington Times*, May 8, 2003; all at Lexis-Nexis Academic Universe. James Beverley, "Is Islam a Religion of Peace?" *Christianity Today*, January 7, 2002, 32ff.

47. Poll by BeliefNet and the Ethics and Public Policy Center, fall 2002, re-

sults released April 7, 2003 and posted at beliefnet.com/124/story_12447
.html.

48. "Huntington Opposes Invasion," *Dawn* (Pakistani newspaper), August
9, 2003, at http://www.dawn.com/2002/08/09/int2.htm.

49. Woodward, *Plan of Attack,* 197–200. While the National Intelligence
Estimate made in fall 2002 stated unambiguously that "Baghdad has chemical
and biological weapons," the body of the report qualified that statement considerably, and offered relatively little evidence for the broad assertions it made.

50. Text from the Office of the White House Press Secretary, "President
Says Saddam Hussein Must Leave Iraq Within 48 Hours," March 17, 2003, at
http://www.whitehouse.gov/news/releases/2003/03/20030317–7.html.

51. "The 9/11 Commission Report: Final Report of the National Commission on Terrorist Attacks upon the United States," 66; 334–336. Woodward,
Plan of Attack, 25–26. Poll results at Stephen Kull, "Misperceptions, the Media, and the Iraq War," 2.

52. "President Says Saddam Hussein Must Leave Iraq Within 48 Hours,"
March 17, 2003, at http://www.whitehouse.gov/news/releases/2003/03/
20030317–7.html.

53. "The President's State of the Union Address," January 29, 2002, at
http://www.whitehouse.gov/news/releases/2002/01/20020129–11.html.

54. Remarks by the President at 2002 Graduation Exercise of the United
States Military Academy, June 2, 2002, at http://www.whitehouse.gov/news/
releases/2002/06/20020601–3.html.

55. Carl Conetta, "What Colin Powell Showed Us."

56. James Mann, *Rise of the Vulcans,* 26–31. Elizabeth Drew argues for the
intellectual influence of another University of Chicago professor, Albert
Wohlstetter, who was a theorist of the need for nuclear warfighting (rather
than nuclear deterrence)." "The Neocons in Power," *New York Review of Books*
50:10, June 12, 2003, at www.nybooks.com/articles/16378.

57. "Remarks by the President at 2002 Graduation Exercise of the United
States Military Academy," June 2, 2002, at http://www.whitehouse.gov/news/
releases/2002/06/20020601–3.html; "President Bush Discusses Freedom in
Iraq and Middle East," White House Office of the Press Secretary, November
6, 2003, at http://www.whitehouse.gov/news/releases/2003/11/20031106–2
.html. For an excellent critique of the overall theory of spreading democracy by
fiat, see Marina Ottaway et al., "Democratic Mirage in the Middle East."

58. On sweets and flowers, see George Packer, "Dreaming of Democracy,"
New York Times Magazine, March 2, 2003, 44ff.

59. In addition to other discussions of neoconservative ideology already
cited, see Jack Beatty, "History's Fools," *The Atlantic,* May 19, 2004, at http://
www.theatlantic.com/doc/prem/200405u/pp2004–05–19; David Ignatius, "A
War of Choice and One Who Chose It," *Washington Post,* November 2, 2003;
Bruce Murphy, "Neoconservative Clout Seen in US Iraq Policy," *Milwaukee
Journal Sentinel,* April 5, 2003, both at Lexis-Nexis Academic Universe. Robert
Leiber has argued that many of the examinations of neoconservatism are

conspiratorial in their outlook and guilty of "conspicuous manifestations of anti-Semitism," in "The Neoconservative Conspiracy Theory: Pure Myth," *Chronicle of Higher Education,* May 2, 2003, at http://chronicle.com/free/v49/ i34/34b01401.htm. While his essay overall is a poorly argued broadside against any attempt to even use the term "neoconservative," he is right to argue that it is inaccurate to argue that neoconservatives are primarily Jewish or to assume that their pro-Israeli policy positions are derived from specifically Jewish concerns not shared by other Americans.

60. Fukuyama, *End of History and the Last Man.*

61. "The National Security Strategy of the United States of America," September 2002, posted at http://www.comw.org/qdr/fulltext/nss2002.pdf.

62. David Armstrong, "Dick Cheney's Song of America," *Harper's,* October 2002, at http://www.thirdworldtraveler.com/American_Empire/Cheney's_Song _America.html. Also Carl Kaysen, John D. Steinbruner, and Martin Malin, "US National Security Policy: In Search of a Balance."

63. Seymour Hersh, "The Gray Zone," *New Yorker,* May 24, 2004, at http:// www.newyorker.com/fact/content/?040524fa_fact. Rafael Patai, *The Arab Mind;* Ann Marlowe, "Sex, Violence, and "the Arab Mind," Salon.com, June 8, 2001 at http://archive.salon.com/books/feature/2001/06/08/arab_mind/index_np .html.

64. Jay Nordlinger, "Star-in-Waiting: Meet George W.'s Foreign-Policy Czarina: Condoleezza Rice," *National Review,* August 30, 1999 at Academic Search Premier.

65. Elisabeth Bumiller and Douglas Jehl, "Bush Tunes In and Sees Iraqis in Celebrations," *New York Times,* April 10, 2003 at ProQuest Newspapers. Martha Brant, "A Crashing End: Baghdad Is Overtaken and the Memorable Pictures Are a Triumph for the Psychological War," *Newsweek* Web exclusive, April 9, 2003 at http://www.msnbc.msn.com/id/3068385/site/newsweek. Television news joined in the enthusiasm. On ABC, the half-hour evening newscast of April 9, 2003 replayed the image of the statue falling three times. CNN also led with the story and aired the scene repeatedly.

66. Andrew Newman, "A Nation at War: Symbols; Atop Statue, Marine Thrills Army of Fans Back Home," *New York Times,* April 11, 2003, at http:// query.nytimes.com/search/restricted/article?res = F50F13F93C5F0C728DDD AD0894DB404482.

67. "US Flag on Iraqi Monument Causes Concern," Canadian Television Network, April 9, 2003, reprinted by CommonDreams.org, at http://www .commondreams.org/headlines03/0409–07.htm. Peter Ford, "US Show of Force Galls Arab World," *Christian Science Monitor,* April 11, 2003, at Lexis-Nexis Academic Universe.

68. David Zucchino, "Army Stage Managed Fall of Hussein Statue," *Los Angeles Times,* July 3, 2004, at http://www.latimes.com/news/nationworld/ iraq/complete/la-na-statue3jul03,0,3295615.story?coll = la-iraq-complete. As far as I can tell, no other major media outlet in the United States picked up on this story, though it was widely posted on Internet sites of all stripes.

69. A useful discussion of the coverage is Robert Jensen, "The Images They Choose, and Choose to Ignore," at CommonDreams.org, at http://www.commondreams.org/views03/0409–12.htm.

70. Carl Conetta, "Disappearing the Dead: Iraq, Afghanistan, and the Idea of a 'New Warfare.'"

71. USAF Col. Sam Gardiner (ret.), *Truth from These Podia: Summary of a Study of Strategic Influence, Perceptions Management, Strategic Information Warfare, and Strategic Psychological Operations in Gulf II* at htttp://www.comw.org/warreport/fulltext/0310gardiner.pdf.

72. Bruce Cunningham, "Re-thinking Objectivity," *Columbia Journalism Review* 42, no. 2 (July/August 2003), 24ff, at Lexis-Nexis Academic Universe.

73. The embedding process was positively assessed by several scholars who study the media, largely because they saw it as so much better than the first Gulf War. Michael Pfau et al., "Embedding Journalists in Military Combat Units: Impact on Newspaper Story Frames and Tone," *Journalism and Mass Communication Quarterly* 81, no. 1 (spring 2004), 74ff. at Lexis-Nexis Academic Universe. See also Mark Jurkowitz, "Experts Say Media Access to Troops Helped More Than Hurt," *Boston Globe*, April 22, 2003, Lexis-Nexis Academic Universe.

74. Quoted by Brendan McLane, "Reporting from the Sandstorm: An Appraisal of Embedding," *Parameters* (US Army War College), 34, no. 1 (spring 2004), 77ff, at Lexis-Nexis Academic Universe.

75. David Zucchino, "The War, Up Close and Very Personal," *Los Angeles Times*, May 3, 2003, at Lexis-Nexis Academic Universe; and Robert Jensen, "Embedded Media Give Up Independence," *Boston Globe*, April 7, 2003, op ed, at Lexis-Nexis Academic Universe.

76. Geert Linneback, "Counteract Drawbacks of 'Embedded' Reporters," *USA Today*, March 31, 2003, at Lexis-Nexis Academic Universe.

77. Many outlets noted this phenomenon, among others *The Economist*. See "United States: A Step Forward; The Televisual War," *The Economist*, March 29, 2003, 366, no. 8317; at Lexis-Nexis Academic Universe.

78. "Saddam Interview Airs in Iraq," February 27, 2003, CBS News, at http://www.cbsnews.com/stories/2003/02/21/iraq/main541427.shtml. The full text and video of the interview are accessible from this site.

79. Quoted in Brent Cunningham, "Rethinking Objectivity," *Columbia Journalism Review* 42, no. 2 (July/August 2003), 24ff, at Lexis-Nexis Academic Universe.

80. "Strong Opposition to Media Cross-Ownership Emerges: Public Wants Neutrality *and* Pro-American Point of View," Pew Research Center for the People and the Press, July 13, 2002, at http://people-press.org/reports/display.php3?ReportID = 188. A more recent Pew report suggests an intensification of the trend. Pew Research Center for the People and the Press, "News Audiences Increasingly Politicized," June 8, 2004, at http://people-press.org/reports/display.php3?PageID = 833. Mark Jurkowitz, "Experts Say Media Access to Troops Helped More Than Hurt," *Boston Globe*, April 22, 2003, E1.

81. John Kampfner, "Saving Private Lynch Story 'Flawed'," *BBC News,* May 15, 2003, at http://news.bbc.co.uk/1/hi/programmes/correspondent/3028585 .stm. The documentary, *War Spin,* was broadcast on May 18, 2003. Richard Cohen, "On Not Admitting Our Mistakes," *Washington Post* editorial, May 23, 2003, at Lexis-Nexis Academic Universe. The denunciations of this manipulation were legion. They included both U.S. commentators like Robert Scheer, "Saving Pvt. Lynch, Take 2," *Milwaukee Journal Sentinel,* May 22, 2003, at Lexis-Nexis Academic Universe and also international outrage: "America Lynches Truth," *Weekend Australian* editorial, May 24, 2003, at Lexis-Nexis Academic Universe. Lynch herself debunked accounts of her heroism in Rick Bragg, *I Am a Soldier, Too: The Jessica Lynch Story.* See also my editorial "Saving Private Lynch," *New York Times,* April 6, 2003, A13.

82. Seymour Hersh, "Chain of Command," *New Yorker,* May 17, 2004, at http://www.newyorker.com/fact/content/?040517fa_fact2. Hersh's remarkable series of reports on Abu Ghraib also includes Hersh, "The Gray Zone," *New Yorker,* May 24, 2004, at http://newyorker.com/fact/content/?040524fa_ fact, and "Torture at Abu Ghraib," May 10, 2004, at http://www.newyorker .com/fact/content/?040510fa_fact. Several of the photographs are available at http://www.antiwar.com/news/?articleid = 2444.

83. Susan Sontag, "Regarding the Torture of Others," *New York Times Magazine,* May 23, 2004, at Lexis-Nexis Academic Universe.

84. Both stories are quoted by BBC News.com, "Media Fury at Abuse of Iraqis," May 1, 2004, at http://news.bbc.co.uk/1/hi/world/middle_east/3676495 .stm.

85. Bush quoted in Mike Allen and Dan Balz, "On Arab TV, President Says U.S. Is 'Appalled'; Bush Stops Short of Apology in Interviews," *Washington Post,* May 6, 2004. Powell's similar statement quoted by Robin Wright, "Top U.S. Officials Apologize to Arabs for Prisoner Abuse," *Washington Post,* May 5, 2004. On the courts-martial, see Peter Hermann, "Soldier Gets Year in Prison in Iraq Abuses," *Baltimore Sun,* May 20, 2004. All at Lexis-Nexis Academic Universe.

86. *Al-Sharq al-Awsat* newspaper, reprinted in the *Iraqi Press Monitor 73,* May 10, 2004. Published by the Institute for War and Peace Reporting. Daily Press monitors are at http://www.iwpr.net/index.pl?iraq_ipm_index.html.

87. Anthony Lewis, "Making Torture Legal," *New York Review of Books,* July 15, 2004, 4ff.

88. Quoted by Lewis, 4. See also Jess Bravin, "Pentagon Report Set Framework for Use of Torture," *Wall Streeet Journal,* June 7, 2004, A1. Full text of that memo at http://news.findlaw.com/wp/docs/torture/30603wgrpt.html. Other memos relevant to U.S. interrogation methods are at http://news.corporate .findlaw.com/hdocs/docs/dod/62204index.html.

89. Human Rights Watch, "The Road to Abu Ghraib," June 2004, at http://hrw.org/reports/2004/usa0604/.

90. Seymour Hersh, "The Gray Zone," *New Yorker,* May 24, 2004, at http://www.newyorker.com/fact/content/?040524fa_fact; Douglas Jehl and Eric

Schmitt, "In Abuse, A Portrayal of Ill-Prepared, Overwhelmed GIs," *New York Times,* May 9, 2004 at Lexis-Nexis Academic Universe. The "Taguba Report" is available at http://news.findlaw.com/hdocs/docs/iraq/tagubarpt.html.

91. See Alan Elsner, *Gates of Injustice.*

92. Mark Danner, "The Logic of Torture," *New York Review of Books,* June 24, 2004, 70ff, quoted p. 72. Kate Zernike and David Rohde, "Forced Nudity of Iraqi Prisoners Is Seen as Pervasive Pattern, Not Isolated Incidents," *New York Times,* June 8, 2004; Vikram Dodd, "Torture by the Book: The Pattern of Abuse of Iraqi Prisoners Follows Established CIA Interrogation Techniques," *Guardian* (London), May 6, 2004, both at Lexis-Nexis Academic Universe.

93. On lynching as a leisure activity, see Hazel Carby, "On the Threshhold of Woman's Era." See also "Without Sanctuary," an online exhibit of lynching photographs and postcards, at http://www.musarium.com/without sanctuary/main.html. Several commentators on Abu Ghraib have noted the connection to lynching photos; see for example Luc Sante, "Tourists and Torturers," *New York Times* editorial, May 11, 2004, at Lexis-Nexis Academic Universe.

94. Etienne Balibar, "Is There a Neo-Racism?" 22.

95. See Douglas Little, *American Orientalism.*

Bibliography

Abourezk, James. *Advise and Dissent: Memoirs of South Dakota and the U.S. Senate*. Chicago: Lawrence Hill Books, 1989.

Abraham, Sameer Y. "Detroit's Arab-American Community: A Survey of Diversity and Commonality." In *Arabs in the New World: Studies in Arab American Communities*, edited by S. Abraham and N. Abraham, 84–108.

Abraham, Sameer, and Nabeel Abraham, eds. *The Arab World and Arab-Americans: Understanding a Neglected Minority*. Detroit: Center for Urban Studies, Wayne State University, 1991.

———. *Arabs in the New World: Studies in Arab American Communities*. Detroit: Wayne State University Press, 1983.

Acheson, Dean. *Present at the Creation: My Years at the State Department*. New York: Norton, 1969.

Albano, Captain Lou. *The Complete Idiot's Guide to Pro Wrestling*. New York: Alpha Books, 1999.

Alloula, Malek. *The Colonial Harem*. Trans. Myrna Godzich and Wlad Godzich. Minneapolis: University of Minnesota Press, 1986.

Ammerman, Nancy. *Bible Believers: Fundamentalists in the Modern World*. New Brunswick, N.J.: Rutgers University Press, 1987.

———. "North American Protestant Fundamentalism." In *Media, Culture, and the Religious Right*, edited by Linda Kintz and Julia Lesage, 55–114.

Anderson, Benedict. *Imagined Communities: Reflections on the Origins and Spread of Nationalism*. New York: Verso, 1991.

Anderson, Jack, with J. Boyd. *Fiasco*. New York: Times Books, 1983.

Anzovin, Steven, ed. *Terrorism*. New York: H. W. Wilson, 1986.

Appadurai, Arjun. *Modernity at Large: Cultural Dimensions of Globalization*. Minneapolis: University of Minnesota Press, 1996.

Appiah, Kwame Anthony. *In My Father's House: Africa in the Philosophy of Culture*. New York: Oxford University Press, 1992.

Armstrong, Nancy. *Desire and Domestic Fiction: A Political History of the Novel*. New York: Oxford University Press, 1987.

———. "Fatal Abstraction: The Death and Sinister Afterlife of the American Family." In *Body Politics: Disease, Desire, and the Family*, edited by Michael Ryan and Avery Gordon, 18–31. Boulder, Colo.: Westview Press, 1994.

Armstrong, Nancy, and Len Tennenhouse. *The Imaginary Puritan: Literature, Intellectual Labor, and the Origins of Personal Life*. Berkeley and Los Angeles: University of California Press, 1992.

Ashley, Richard. "Foreign Policy as Political Performance." *International Studies Notes*, no. 13 (1987).

Avishai, Bernard. *The Tragedy of Zionism: Revolution and Democracy in the Land of Israel*. New York: Farrar, Straus and Giroux, 1985.

Babington, Bruce, and Peter William Evans. *Biblical Epics: Sacred Narrative in the Hollywood Cinema*. Manchester: Manchester University Press, 1993.

Baldwin, James. *The Fire Next Time*. New York: Dell, 1977.

———. *Notes of a Native Son*. New York: Bantam, 1964.

———. *The Price of a Ticket: Collected Nonfiction, 1948–1985*. New York: St. Martin's/Marek, 1985.

Balibar, Etienne. "Is There a 'Neo-Racism'?" In *Race, Nation, Class: Ambiguous Identities*, by Etienne Balibar and Immanuel Wallerstein, 17–28.

———. "Racism and Nationalism." In *Race, Nation, Class: Ambiguous Identities*, by Etienne Balibar and Immanuel Wallerstein, 37–68.

Balibar, Etienne, and Immanuel Wallerstein. *Race, Nation, Class: Ambiguous Identities*. New York: Verso, 1991.

Balmer, Randall. *Mine Eyes Have Seen the Glory: A Journey into the Evangelical Subculture in America*. New York: Oxford University Press, 1989.

Baraka, Amiri (LeRoi Jones). *The Autobiography of LeRoi Jones/Amiri Baraka*. New York: Freundlich Books, 1984.

———. *A Black Mass*. In *Four Black Revolutionary Plays*.

———. *Blues People: Negro Music in White America*. New York: Morrow, 1963.

———. *Four Black Revolutionary Plays*. New York: Bobbs-Merrill, 1969.

———. *Home: Social Essays*. New York: Morrow, 1966.

———. *It's Nation Time*. Chicago: Third World Press, 1970.

———. *Raise, Race, Rays, Raze: Essays since 1965*. New York: Random House, 1971.

———. *Selected Poetry of Amiri Baraka/LeRoi Jones*. New York: William Morrow, 1979.

Baraka, Amiri, and Larry Neal, eds. *Black Fire: An Anthology of Afro-American Writing*. New York: William Morrow, 1968.

Barber, Benjamin. *Jihad v. McWorld: How Globalism and Tribalism Are Reshaping the World*. New York: Ballantine, 1996.

Barber, Lucy. "On to Washington: National Political Demonstrations in the American Capital, 1894–1963." Ph.D. diss., Brown University, 1996.

Barkun, Michael. "The Language of Apocalypse: Premillennialists and Nuclear War." In *The God Pumpers: Religion in the Electronic Age,* edited by Marshall Fishwick and Ray E. Browne, 159–173. Bowling Green, Ohio: Bowling Green State University Popular Press, 1987.

Bar-Zohar, Michael, and Eitan Haber. *The Quest for the Red Prince.* New York: William Morrow, 1983.

Bederman, Gail. *Manliness and Civilization: A Cultural History of Gender and Race in the United States.* Chicago: University of Chicago Press, 1995.

Behdad, Ali. *Belated Travelers: Orientalism in the Age of Colonial Dissolution.* Durham, N.C.: Duke University Press, 1994.

Beinin, Joel, and Zachary Lockman. *Workers on the Nile: Nationalism, Communism, Islam, and the Egyptian Working Class, 1882–1954.* Princeton, N.J.: Princeton University Press, 1987.

Belkaoui, Janice Monti. "Images of Arabs and Israelis in the Prestige Press, 1966–74." *Journalism Quarterly* 55 (1978): 732–738.

Bell, Derrick. *Race, Racism, and American Law.* Boston: Little, Brown, 1992.

Belton, John. *Widescreen Cinema.* Cambridge, Mass.: Harvard University Press, 1992.

Benjamin, Walter. "The Work of Art in the Age of Mechanical Reproduction." In *Illuminations.* New York: Harcourt, Brace and World, 1968.

Benn Michaels, Walter. "Anti-imperial Americanism." In *Cultures of United States Imperialism,* edited by Amy Kaplan and Donald Pease, 3–21.

Bennet, James. "How the Media Missed the Story." In *The Gulf War Reader,* edited by Micah Sifry and Christopher Serf, 355–367.

Ben-Porat, Yeshayahu, Eitan Haber, and Zeev Schiff. *Entebbe Rescue.* New York: Delacorte, 1977.

Benson, Susan Porter. *Counter Cultures: Saleswomen, Managers, and Customers in American Department Stores, 1890–1940.* Chicago: University of Illinois Press, 1988.

Berenstein, Robin. *Attack of the Leading Ladies: Gender, Sexuality, and Spectatorship in the Classic Horror Cinema.* New York: Columbia University Press, 1996.

Berger, John. *Ways of Seeing.* New York: Penguin, 1977.

Berger, Morroe. "The Black Muslims." *Horizons,* winter 1964, 49–64.

Berlant, Lauren. *The Queen of America Goes to Washington: Essays on Sex and Citizenship.* Durham, N.C.: Duke University Press, 1997.

Bernal, Martin. *Black Athena: The Afro-Asiatic Roots of Classical Civilization.* New Brunswick, N.J.: Rutgers University Press, 1987.

Bernstein, Matthew, and Gaylyn Studlar, eds. *Visions of the East: Orientalism in Film.* New Brunswick, N.J.: Rutgers University Press, 1997.

Berry, Venise, and Kim Karloff. "Perspectives on the Persian Gulf War in Popular Black Magazines." In *Seeing through the Media,* edited by Susan Jeffords and Lauren Rabinovitz, 249–262.

Bhabha, Homi K. "DissemiNation: Time, Narrative, and the Margins of the Modern Nation." In *Nation and Narration,* edited by Homi K. Bhabha, 291–321.

———, ed. *Nation and Narration.* New York: Routledge, 1990.

Black Public Sphere Collective, ed. *The Black Public Sphere.* Chicago: University of Chicago Press, 1995.

Blitzer, Wolf. *Between Washington and Jerusalem: A Reporter's Notebook.* New York: Oxford University Press, 1985.

Bluestone, Barry, and Bennett Harrison. *The Great U-Turn.* New York: Basic Books, 1988.

Blumenthal, Sidney. *The Rise of the Counter-Establishment: From Conservative Ideology to Political Power.* New York: Harper and Row, 1988.

Bourdieu, Pierre. *The Field of Cultural Production: Essays on Art and Literature.* Edited and introduced by Randal Johnson. New York: Columbia University Press, 1993.

Bowie, Robert. "Eisenhower, Dulles, and the Suez Crisis." In *Suez 1956,* edited by William Roger Louis and Roger Owen, 189–214.

Boyarin, Jonathan. "Reading Exodus into History." *New Literary History* 23, no. 3 (1992): 523–554.

Boyer, Paul. *When Time Shall Be No More: Prophecy Belief in Modern American Culture.* Cambridge, Mass.: Harvard University Press, 1992.

———, ed. *Reagan as President: Contemporary Views of the Man, His Politics, and His Policies.* New York: Ivan R. Dee, 1992.

Boyer, Paul, et al. *The Enduring Vision: A History of the American People.* Vol. 2. New York: Heath, 1996.

Bracey, John, Jr., August Meier, and Elliot Rudwick, eds. *Black Nationalism in America.* Indianapolis: Bobbs-Merrill, 1970.

Branch, Taylor. *Parting the Waters: America in the King Years, 1954–63.* New York: Simon and Schuster, 1988.

Bratlinger, Patrick. *Rule of Darkness: British Literature and Imperialism, 1830–1914.* Ithaca, N.Y.: Cornell University Press, 1988.

Breines, Paul. *Tough Jews: Political Fantasies and the Moral Dilemma of American Jewry.* New York: Basic Books, 1990.

Brennan, Timothy. " 'PC' and the Decline of the American Empire." *Social Policy,* summer 1991, 16–29.

Brouwer, Steve, Paul Gifford, and Susan Rose. *Exporting the American Gospel: Global Christian Fundamentalism.* New York: Routledge, 1996.

Brunson, James. "Ancient Egyptians: The Dark Red Face Myth." In *Egypt Revisited,* edited by Ivan Van Sertima, 53–55.

Buell, Fredrick. "Nationalist Postnationalism: Globalist Discourse in Contemporary American Culture." *American Quarterly* 50, no. 3 (1998): 548–591.

Buhle, Mari Jo. *Feminism and Its Discontents: A Century of Struggle with Psychoanalysis.* Cambridge, Mass.: Harvard University Press, 1998.

———. *Women and American Socialism, 1870–1920.* Urbana: University of Illinois Press, 1981.

Bullins, Ed. "A Short Statement on Street Theatre." *Drama Review* 12, no. 4 (summer 1968): 93.

———, ed. *New Plays from the Black Theatre.* New York: Bantam, 1969.

Burger, Peter. *Theory of the Avant-Garde.* Minneapolis: University of Minnesota Press, 1984.

Campbell, David. *Writing Security: United States Foreign Policy and the Politics of Identity.* Minneapolis: University of Minnesota Press, 1998.

Campomanes, Oscar. "American Orientalism at the Turn of the Century and Filipino Postcoloniality." Ph.D. diss., Brown University, forthcoming.

Carmichael [Kwame Ture], Stokely, and Charles Hamilton. *Black Power: The Politics of Liberation.* New York: Vintage, 1992.

Carrott, Richard. *The Egyptian Revival: Its Sources, Monuments, and Meaning, 1808–1958.* Berkeley and Los Angeles: University of California Press, 1978.

Carson, Clayborne. "Blacks and Jews in the Civil Rights Movement: The Case of SNCC." In *Bridges and Boundaries: African Americans and American Jews,* edited by Jack Salzman, 36–49.

———. *In Struggle: SNCC and the 1960s.* Cambridge, Mass.: Harvard University Press, 1981.

Carter, Howard. *Wonderful Things: The Discovery of Tutankhamun's Tomb.* New York: Metropolitan Museum of Art, 1976.

Carter, Howard, with A. C. Mace. *The Tomb of Tut Ank Amen.* 3 vols. New York: Cooper Square Press, 1922–1933.

Carton, Evan. "The Self Besieged: American Identity on Campus and in the Gulf." *Tikkun* 6, no. 4 (1991): 40–47.

Castonguay, Jim. "The Gulf War TV Super Bowl." *Bad Subjects,* no. 35 (1997). At http://eserver.org/bs/35/castonguay.html; 11 pp.

Celik, Zeynep. *Displaying the Orient: Architecture of Islam at Nineteenth-Century World's Fairs.* Berkeley and Los Angeles: University of California Press, 1992.

Celmer, Marc. *Terrorism, U.S. Strategy, and Reagan Policies.* Westport, Conn.: Greenwood Press, 1987.

Chauncey, George. *Gay New York: Gender, Urban Culture, and the Making of the Gay Male World, 1890–1940.* New York: Basic Books, 1994.

Chomsky, Noam. *The Culture of Terrorism.* Boston: South End Press, 1988.

Christison, Kathleen. "The Arab in Recent Popular Fiction." *Middle East Journal* 41, no. 3 (1987).

Clark, John Henrik, and Josef Ben-Jochannan. "Early Egypt: A Different Perspective." *Journal of African Civilizations* 1, no. 1 (1979): 6–14.

Clegg, Leland. "Black Rulers of the Golden Age." In *Egypt Revisited,* edited by Ivan Van Sertima, 239–260.

Clifford, James. *The Predicament of Culture: Twentieth-Century Ethnography, Literature, and Art.* Cambridge, Mass.: Harvard University Press, 1988.

Cline, Ray S., and Yonah Alexander. *Terrorism as State-Sponsored Covert Warfare.* Fairfax, Va.: Hero Books, 1986.

Cloud, Dana. "Operation Desert Comfort." In *Seeing through the Media,* edited by Susan Jeffords and Lauren Rabinovitz, 155–170.

Cohen, Michael J. *Truman and Israel.* Berkeley and Los Angeles: University of California Press, 1990.

Cohen, Naomi. *American Jews and the Zionist Idea.* New York: Ktav Publishing House, 1975.

Cohen, Ronny H. "Tut and the '20s: The 'Egyptian Look.' " *Art in America* 67, no. 2 (1979): 87.

Cone, James. *Black Theology and Black Power.* New York: Seabury, 1969.

Conetta, Carl, and Charles Knight. *Reasonable Force: Adapting the US Army and Marine Corps to the New Era.* PDA Briefing Report 3. Cambridge, Mass.: Project on Defense Alternatives, 1992.

Conrad, Joseph. *Heart of Darkness.* New York: Penguin, 1973.

Coombes, Annie E. *Reinventing Africa: Museums, Material Culture, and Popular Imagination in Late Victorian and Edwardian England.* New Haven, Conn.: Yale University Press, 1994.

Corber, Robert. *Homosexuality in Cold War America: Resistance and the Crisis of Masculinity.* Durham, N.C.: Duke University Press, 1997.

Cottam, Richard. *Iran and the United States: A Cold War Case Study.* Pittsburgh: University of Pittsburgh Press, 1988.

Crary, Jonathan. "Modernizing Vision." In *Viewing Positions: Ways of Seeing Film,* edited by Linda Williams, 23–35.

———. *Techniques of the Observer.* Cambridge, Mass.: MIT Press, 1990.

Cruse, Harold. *The Crisis of the Negro Intellectual: A Historical Analysis of the Failure of Black Leadership.* Foreword by Bazel Allen and Ernest Wilson III. New York: Quill, 1984 [1967].

Curl, James Stevens. *Egyptomania: The Egyptian Revival, a Recurring Theme in the History of Taste.* Manchester: Manchester University Press, 1994.

Dallek, Robert. *Ronald Reagan: The Politics of Symbolism.* Cambridge, Mass.: Harvard University Press, 1999.

Davis, John. *The Landscape of Belief: Encountering the Holy Land in Nineteenth-Century American Art and Culture.* Princeton, N.J.: Princeton University Press, 1996.

Dawley, Alan. *Struggles for Justice: Social Responsibility and the Liberal State.* Cambridge, Mass.: Harvard University Press, 1991.

Decker, Jeff, ed. *Black Arts Movement.* Dictionary of Literary Biography Documentary Series, vol. 8. Detroit: Gale, 1991.

Deleuze, Giles. *Cinema 1: The Movement-Image.* Minneapolis: University of Minnesota Press, 1986.

Demaris, Ovid. *Brothers in Blood: The International Terrorist Network.* New York: Scribner, 1977.

Diawara, Manthia. "Malcolm X and the Black Public Sphere." In *The Black Public Sphere,* edited by Black Public Sphere Collective, 39–52.

Diner, Hasia. *In the Almost Promised Land: American Jews and Blacks, 1915–1935.* Baltimore: Johns Hopkins University Press, 1995.

Dinnerstein, Leonard. *Antisemitism in America.* New York: Oxford University Press, 1994.

Diop, Cheikh Anta. *The African Origin of Civilization: Myth or Reality?* Translated by Mercer Cook. New York: L Hill, 1974.

Dobkin, Bethami. *Tales of Terror: Television News and the Construction of the Terrorist Threat.* New York: Praeger, 1992.

Donovan, Robert J., and Ray Scherer. *Unsilent Revolution: Television News and American Public Life, 1948–1991.* New York: Woodrow Wilson International Center for Scholars and Cambridge University Press, 1992.

Donzelot, Jacques. *The Policing of Families.* New York: Pantheon, 1979.

Doyle, Michael W. *Empires.* Ithaca, N.Y.: Cornell University Press, 1986.

D'Souza, Dinesh. *Illiberal Education: The Politics of Race and Sex on Campus.* New York: Free Press, 1991.

Du Bois, Shirley Graham. "Egypt Is Africa." *The Black Scholar,* May 1970, 20–39.

Du Bois, W. E. B. *The Creative Writings of W. E. B. Du Bois.* Ed. Herbert Aptheker. White Plains, N.Y.: Kraus-Thompson, 1985.

———. *The Negro.* Introduction by George Shepperson. New York: Oxford University Press, 1970.

Dudziak, Mary. "Desegregation as a Cold War Imperative." *Stanford Law Review* 41 (November 1988): 61–120.

———. "Josephine Baker, Racial Protest, and the Cold War." *Journal of American History* 81 (September 1994): 543–570.

Elshtain, Jean. *Public Man, Private Woman: Women in Social and Political Thought.* Princeton, N.J.: Princeton University Press, 1993.

Engelhardt, Tom. "The Gulf War as Total Television." In *Seeing through the Media,* edited by Susan Jeffords and Lauren Rabinovitz, 81–96.

Essien-Udom, E. U. *Black Nationalism: A Search for an Identity in America.* New York: Dell, 1964.

Ettema, Michael J. "History Museums and the Culture of Materialism." In *Past Meets Present: Essays about Historic Interpretation and Public Audiences,* edited by Jo Blatti. Washington, D.C.: Smithsonian Institution Press, 1987.

Etzold, Thomas, and John Lewis Gaddis, eds. *Containment: Documents on American Policy and Strategy.* New York: Columbia University Press, 1978.

Evanzz, Karl. *The Messenger: The Rise and Fall of Elijah Muhammed.* New York: Pantheon, 1999.

Fagan, Brian. *The Rape of the Nile: Tomb Robbers, Tourists, and Archaeologists in Egypt.* Wakefield, R.I.: Moyer Bell, 1992.

Falwell, Jerry, ed., with Ed Dobson and Ed Hindson. *The Fundamentalist Phenomenon.* Garden City, N.Y.: Doubleday-Galilee, 1981.

Fanon, Frantz. *The Wretched of the Earth.* 1961. New York: Grove Press, 1968.

Farmanfarmaian, Abouali. "Sexuality in the Gulf: Did You Measure Up?" *Genders*, no. 13 (1992): 1–27.

Feldstein, Ruth. "'I Wanted the Whole World to See': Race, Gender, and Constructions of Motherhood in the Death of Emmett Till." In *Not June Cleaver: Women and Gender in Postwar America, 1945–1960*, edited by Joanne Meyerowitz, 263–303.

———. *Motherhood in Black and White: Race and Sex in American Liberalism, 1930–1965*. Ithaca, N.Y.: Cornell University Press, 2000.

Fishman, Hertzel. *American Protestantism and a Jewish State*. Detroit: Wayne State University Press, 1973.

Fisk, Robert. "Free to Report What We're Told." In *The Gulf War Reader*, edited by Micah Sifry and Christopher Serf, 376–380.

Fitzgerald, Frances. "A Disciplined, Charging Army." *New Yorker*, May 18, 1981, 53ff.

Flapan, Simha. *The Birth of Israel: Myths and Realities*. New York: Pantheon, 1987.

Follet, Ken. *On the Wings of Eagles*. New York: New American Library, 1986.

Foran, John. "Discursive Subversions: *Time* Magazine, the CIA Overthrow of Mussaddiq, and the Installation of the Shah." In *Cold War Constructions: The Political Culture of United States Imperialism, 1945–1966*, edited by Christopher Appy. Boston: University of Massachusetts Press, 2000.

Foster, Hal. "The 'Primitive' Unconscious of Modern Art." *October*, no. 34 (fall 1985): 45–70.

Frankel, Jonathan. *Prophecy and Politics: Socialism, Nationalism, and the Russian Jews, 1862–1917*. New York: Cambridge University Press, 1981.

Franklin, H. Bruce. "From Realism to Virtual Reality." In *Seeing through the Media*, edited by Susan Jeffords and Lauren Rabinovitz, 25–44.

Fraser, Nancy. "Rethinking the Public Sphere: A Contribution to the Critique of Actually Existing Democracy." In *The Phantom Public Sphere*, edited by Bruce Robbins, 1–32.

———. *Unruly Practices: Power, Discourse, and Gender in Contemporary Social Theory*. Minneapolis: University of Minnesota Press, 1989.

Freeman, Lawrence, et al., eds. *Terrorism and International Order*. New York: Routledge and Kegan Paul, 1986.

Friedman, Murray. *What Went Wrong: The Creation and Collapse of the Black-Jewish Alliance*. New York: Free Press, 1995.

Gaddis, John Lewis. *Strategies of Containment: A Critical Appraisal of Postwar American National Security Policy*. New York: Oxford University Press, 1982.

———. "The Strategy of Containment." In *American Cold War Strategy: Interpreting NSC 68*, edited by Ernest May, 140–146.

Ganin, Zvi. *Truman, American Jewry, and Israel, 1945–1948*. New York: Holmes and Meir, 1979.

Gardell, Mattias. *In the Name of Elijah Muhammad: Louis Farrakkan and the Nation of Islam*. Durham, N.C.: Duke University Press, 1996.

Garrow, David. *Bearing the Cross: Martin Luther King, Jr., and the Southern Christian Leadership Conference.* New York: Vintage, 1988.

Gates, Henry Louis. *The Signifying Monkey: A Theory of Afro-American Literary Criticism.* New York: Oxford University Press, 1988.

Gates, Henry Louis, and Nellie McKay, eds. *The Norton Anthology of African American Literature.* New York: Norton, 1996.

Gayle, Addison, Jr. "Cultural Strangulation: Black Literature and the White Aesthetic." In *The Black Aesthetic,* edited by Addison Gayle Jr., 39–46.

——, ed. *The Black Aesthetic.* New York: Anchor Books, 1971.

Gendzier, Irene. *Frantz Fanon: A Critical Study.* New York: Vintage, 1974.

Georgakas, Dan, and Miriam Rosen, eds. *The Arab Image in American Film and Television.* Washington, D.C.: American-Arab Anti-Discrimination Committee, n.d.

Gerhard, Jane. *Desiring Revolutions: Second-Wave Feminism and the Rewriting of American Sexual Thought, 1920–1982.* New York: Columbia University Press, 2001.

Ghareeb, Edmund, ed. *Split Vision: The Portrayal of Arabs in the American Media.* Washington, D.C.: American-Arab Affairs Council, 1983.

Gilbert, Katherine, ed. *Treasures of Tutankhamun.* New York: Metropolitan Museum of Art and Ballantine, 1978.

Gilman, Sander. *The Jew's Body.* New York: Routledge, 1991.

Gilman, Sander, and Steven Katz, eds. *Anti-Semitism in Times of Crisis.* New York: New York University Press, 1991.

Gilroy, Paul. *The Black Atlantic.* Cambridge, Mass.: Harvard University Press, 1993.

Ginzberg, Lori. *Women and the Work of Benevolence: Morality, Politics, and Class in the Nineteenth-Century United States.* New Haven, Conn.: Yale University Press, 1990.

Goldman, Peter. *The Death and Life of Malcolm X.* Urbana: University of Illinois Press, 1979.

Gomery, Douglas. *Shared Pleasures: A History of Movie Presentation in the United States.* Madison: University of Wisconsin Press, 1992.

Gordan, Avery, and Christopher Newfield, eds. *Mapping Multiculturalism.* Minneapolis: University of Minnesota Press, 1996.

Gould, Steven Jay. *The Mismeasure of Man.* New York: Norton, 1981.

Graff, Gerald. "The Nonpolitics of PC." *Tikkun* 6, no. 4 (1991): 50–52.

Graham-Brown, Sarah. *Images of Women: Portrayal of Women and Photography in the Middle East, 1860–1950.* New York: Columbia University Press, 1988.

Groussard, Serge. *The Blood of Israel: The Massacre of the Israeli Athletes, the Olympics, 1972.* New York: William Morrow, 1975.

Gunther, Marc. *The House That Roone Built: The Inside Story of ABC News.* Boston: Little, Brown, 1994.

Hahn, Peter. *The United States, Great Britain, and Egypt, 1945–1956: Strategy and Diplomacy in the Early Cold War.* Chapel Hill: University of North Carolina Press, 1991.

Haley, Alex. *Alex Haley: The Playboy Interviews.* Edited by Murray Fisher. New York: Ballantine, 1993.

Hallin, Daniel. "Images of the Vietnam and the Persian Gulf Wars in U.S. Television." In *Seeing through the Media,* edited by Susan Jeffords and Lauren Rabinovitz, 45–58.

Halsell, Grace. *Prophecy and Politics: Militant Evangelists on the Road to Nuclear War.* Westport, Conn.: Lawrence Hill, 1986.

Hampton, Henry, and Steve Fayer. *Voices of Freedom: An Oral History of the Civil Rights Movement from the 1950s through the 1980s.* New York: Bantam, 1990.

Hansen, Miriam. *Babel and Babylon: Spectatorship in American Silent Film.* Cambridge, Mass.: Harvard University Press, 1991.

———. "Early Cinema, Late Cinema: Permutations of the Public Sphere." *Screen* 34, no. 3 (1993): 197–210.

Hanson, Patricia, and Alan Gevinson, eds. *The American Film Institute Catalog of Motion Pictures Produced in the United States.* Berkeley and Los Angeles: University of California Press, 1988.

Harper, Phillip Brian. *Are We Not Men? Masculine Anxiety and the Problem of African American Identity.* New York: Oxford University Press, 1996.

Harvey, David. *The Condition of Postmodernity.* London: Basil Blackwell, 1989.

Hassassian, Manuel S. "Policy and Attitude Changes in the Palestine Liberation Organization, 1965–1994: A Democracy in the Making." In *The PLO and Israel: From Armed Conflict to Political Solution, 1964–1994,* edited by Avraham Sela and Moshe Ma'oz, 73–96. New York: St. Martin's Press, 1997.

Hauser, Thomas. *Muhammad Ali: His Life and Times.* New York: Simon and Schuster, 1991.

Haynes, Joyce, ed. *Nubia: Ancient Kingdoms of Africa.* Boston: Museum of Fine Arts, 1992.

Heidenrich, John. "The Gulf War: How Many Iraqis Died?" *Foreign Policy* 90 (spring 1993): 108–126.

Henry, Carl F., ed. *Prophecy in the Making.* Carol Stream, Ill.: Creation House, 1971.

Herberg, William. *Protestant, Catholic, Jew: An Essay in American Religious Sociology.* Garden City, N.Y.: Doubleday, 1956.

Herman, Edward S. *The Real Terror Network.* Boston: South End Press, 1982.

Herman, Edward S., and Gary O'Sullivan. *The Terrorism Industry: The Experts and Institutions That Shape Our View of Terror.* New York: Pantheon, 1989.

Hertzberg, Arthur. "Israel and American Jewry." *Commentary,* August 1967, 69–73.

Hertzberg, Hendrik. "Why the War Was Immoral." In *Vietnam: Ten Years After,* edited by Robert E. Long, 113–119. New York: H. W. Wilson, 1986.

Higashi, Sumiko. *Cecil B. DeMille and American Culture: The Silent Era.* Berkeley and Los Angeles: University of California Press, 1994.

Higham, Charles. *Cecil B. DeMille.* New York: Scribner, 1973.

Hilliard, Charles. *The Cross, the Sword, and the Dollar*. New York: North River Press, 1951.

Himmelfarb, Milton. "In the Light of Israel's Victory." *Commentary*, October 1967, 53–61.

Hincha, Richard. "Selling CinemaScope: 1953–1956." *Velvet Light Trap*, summer 1985, 44–53.

Hobsbawm, Eric. *The Age of Empire, 1875–1914*. New York: Vintage, 1987.

Hodson, Joel C. *Lawrence of Arabia and American Culture: The Making of a Transatlantic Legend*. Westport, Conn.: Greenwood Press, 1995.

Hoganson, Kristen. *Fighting for American Manhood: How Gender Politics Provoked the Spanish-American and Philippine-American Wars*. New Haven, Conn.: Yale University Press, 1998.

Hooper-Greenhill, Eilean. *Museums and the Shaping of Knowledge*. New York: Routledge, 1992.

Horne, Gerald. "Who Lost the Cold War? Africans and African Americans." *Diplomatic History* 20, no. 4 (1996): 613–626.

Horowitz, Morton. "The History of the Public/Private Distinction." *University of Pennsylvania Law Review*, no. 30 (1982): 1423–1428.

Horsfield, Peter. *Religious Television: The American Experience*. New York: Longman, 1984.

Horsman, Reginald. *Race and Manifest Destiny: The Origins of American Racial Anglo-Saxonism*. Cambridge, Mass.: Harvard University Press, 1981.

Hoving, Thomas. *Making the Mummies Dance: Inside the Metropolitan Museum of Art*. New York: Simon and Schuster, 1993.

———. *Tutankhamun: The Untold Story*. New York: Simon and Schuster, 1978.

Hunter, James D. *American Evangelicalism: Conservative Religion and the Quandary of Modernity*. New Brunswick, N.J.: Rutgers University Press, 1983.

———. "The Evangelical Worldview since 1890." In *Piety and Politics: Evangelicals and Fundamentalists Confront the World*, edited by Richard Neuhaus and Michael Cromartie, 19–53.

Hunter, Jane. *The Gospel of Gentility: American Women Missionaries in Turn-of-the-Century China*. New Haven, Conn.: Yale University Press, 1984.

Huntington, Samuel. "The Clash of Civilizations?" *Foreign Affairs* 72, no. 3 (summer 1993): 22–49.

———. *The Clash of Civilizations and the Remaking of World Order*. New York: Simon and Schuster, 1996.

Hurewitz, J. C. "The Historical Context [of Suez]." In *Suez 1956*, edited by William Roger Louis and Roger Owens, 19–30.

Hurston, Zora Neale. *Mules and Men*. Introduction by Robert Hemenway. Bloomington: Indiana University Press, 1978.

Hutchison, William. *Errand to the World: American Protestant Thought and Foreign Missions*. Chicago: University of Chicago Press, 1987.

Huyssen, Andreas. *After the Great Divide: Modernism, Mass Culture, Postmodernism*. Bloomington: Indiana University Press, 1986.

Izod, John. *Hollywood and the Box Office, 1895–1986.* New York: Columbia University Press, 1988.

Jackson, William. *Withdrawal from Empire: A Military View.* New York: St. Martin's Press, 1986.

Jacobson, Matthew Frye. *Barbarian Virtues: The United States Encounters Foreign Peoples at Home and Abroad, 1876–1917.* New York: Hill and Wang, 2000.

———. *Whiteness of a Different Color: European Immigrants and the Alchemy of Race.* Cambridge, Mass.: Harvard University Press, 1998.

James, George G. M. *Stolen Legacy: The Greeks Were Not the Author of Greek Philosophy, but the People of North Africa, Commonly Called the Egyptians.* New York: Philosophical Society, 1954.

Jameson, Fredric. *The Geopolitical Aesthetic: Cinema and Space in the World System.* Bloomington: Indiana University Press, 1992.

———. "Modernism and Imperialism." In *Nationalism, Colonialism, and Literature,* by Terry Eagleton, Fredric Jameson, and Edward Said, 43–68. Minneapolis: University of Minnesota Press, 1990.

———. *The Political Unconscious: Narrative as a Socially Symbolic Act.* Ithaca, N.Y.: Cornell University Press, 1981.

———. *Postmodernism: Or, the Cultural Logic of Late Capitalism.* Durham, N.C.: Duke University Press, 1991.

Jeffords, Susan. "Afterword: Bringing the Death-World Home." In *Seeing through the Media,* edited by Susan Jeffords and Lauren Rabinovitz, 301–306.

———. *Hard Bodies: Hollywood Masculinity in the Reagan Era.* New Brunswick, N.J.: Rutgers University Press, 1994.

———. "The Patriot System, or, Managerial Heroism." In *Cultures of United States Imperialism,* edited by Amy Kaplan and Donald Pease, 535–556.

Jeffords, Susan, and Lauren Rabinovitz, eds. *Seeing through the Media: The Persian Gulf War.* New Brunswick, N.J.: Rutgers University Press, 1994.

Johnson, Eithne. "The Emergence of Christian Video and the Cultivation of Videovangelism." In *Media, Culture, and the Religious Right,* edited by Linda Kintz and Julie Lesage, 191–210.

Johnson, James Weldon. *God's Trombones: Seven Negro Sermons in Verse.* New York: Viking, 1944.

Kabbani, Rana. *Europe's Myths of Orient.* Bloomington: Indiana University Press, 1986.

Kamalipour, Yahya, ed. *The U.S. Media and the Middle East.* Westport, Conn.: Greenwood Press, 1995.

Kaplan, Amy. "Left Alone with America: The Absence of Empire in the Study of American Culture." In *Cultures of United States Imperialism,* edited by Amy Kaplan and Donald Pease, 3–21.

———. "Romancing the Empire: The Embodiment of American Masculinity in the Popular Historical Novel of the 1890s." *American Literary History* 2, no. 4 (1990): 659–690.

Kaplan, Amy, and Donald Pease, eds. *Cultures of United States Imperialism.* Durham, N.C.: Duke University Press, 1993.

Kasson, John. *Amusing the Million: Coney Island at the Turn of the Century.* New York: Hill and Wang, 1978.

Kaufman, Jonathan. *Broken Alliance: The Turbulent Times between Blacks and Jews in America.* New York: Scribner, 1988.

Kazin, Michael. *The Populist Persuasion: An American History.* Ithaca: Cornell University Press, 1995.

Kellner, Douglas. *The Persian Gulf TV War.* Boulder, Colo.: Westview Press, 1992.

Kendrick, Michelle. "Kicking the Vietnam Syndrome: CNN's and CBS's Video Narratives of the Persian Gulf War." In *Seeing through the Media,* edited by Susan Jeffords and Lauren Rabinovitz, 59–76.

Keppel, Ben. *The Work of Democracy: Ralph Bunche, Kenneth Clark, Lorraine Hansberry, and the Cultural Politics of Race.* Cambridge, Mass.: Harvard University Press, 1995.

Kevles, Daniel. *In the Name of Eugenics: Genetics and the Uses of Human Heredity.* New York: Knopf, 1985.

Kimball, Roger. *Tenured Radicals: How Politics Has Corrupted Higher Education.* New York: Harper and Row, 1970.

Kimmerling, Baruch, and Joel S. Migdal. *Pulestinians: The Making of a People.* New York: Free Press, 1993.

King, Martin Luther, Jr. *Stride toward Freedom: The Montgomery Story.* San Francisco: HarperCollins, 1958.

———. *A Testament of Hope: The Essential Writings and Speeches of Martin Luther King, Jr.* Edited by James Washington. San Francisco: HarperSanFrancisco, 1986.

Kintz, Linda, and Julie Lesage, eds. *Media, Culture, and the Religious Right.* Minneapolis: University of Minnesota Press, 1998.

Kolsky, Thomas A. *Jews against Zionism: The American Council for Judaism, 1942–1948.* Philadelphia: Temple University Press, 1990.

Kristol, Irving. "The Political Dilemma of American Jews." *Commentary,* July 1984, 23–29.

Kuklick, Bruce. *Puritans in Babylon: The Ancient Near East and American Intellectual Life, 1880–1930.* Princeton, N.J.: Princeton University Press, 1996.

Kunz, Diane. "Economic Diplomacy of the Suez Crisis." In *Suez 1956,* edited by William Roger Louis and Roger Owen, 215–232.

LaFeber, Walter. *America, Russia, and the Cold War, 1945–1984.* New York: Knopf, 1985.

———. *The American Age: United States Foreign Policy at Home and Abroad since 1750.* 2d ed. New York: Norton, 1994.

———, ed. *The Origins of the Cold War, 1941–1947: A Historical Problem with Interpretations and Documents.* New York: Wiley, 1971.

LaHaye, Tim. *The Coming Peace in the Middle East.* Grand Rapids, Mich.: Zondervan, 1984.

Lake, Anthony. "Confronting Backlash States." *Foreign Affairs* 73, no. 2 (spring 1994): 45.

Lant, Antonia. "The Curse of the Pharaoh, or How Cinema Contracted Egyptomania." In *Visions of the East: Orientalism in Film*, edited by Matthew Bernstein and Gaylyn Studlar, 69–98.

Laquer, Walter. *The Age of Terrorism*. Boston: Little, Brown, 1987.

———. *Terrorism*. Boston: Little, Brown, 1977.

Laquer, Walter, and Barry Rubin, eds. *The Israeli-Arab Reader: A Documentary History of the Middle East Conflict*. New York: Penguin, 1984.

Laville, Helen, and Scott Lucas. "The American Way: Edith Sampson, the NAACP, and African American Identity in the Cold War." *Diplomatic History* 20, no. 4 (1996): 565–590.

Lazarus, Neil. *Nationalism and Cultural Practice in the Postcolonial World*. New York: Cambridge University Press, 1999.

Leach, William. *Land of Desire: Merchants, Power, and the Rise of a New American Culture*. New York: Pantheon, 1993.

Le Carré, John. *The Little Drummer Girl*. New York: Bantam, 1984.

Lee, Robert. *Orientals: Asian Americans in Popular Culture*. Philadelphia: Temple University Press, 1999.

Leffler, Melvyn. *A Preponderance of Power: National Security, the Truman Administration, and the Cold War*. Stanford, Calif.: Stanford University Press, 1992.

Lenczowski, George. *American Presidents and the Middle East*. Durham, N.C.: Duke University Press, 1990.

Levine, Lawrence. *Black Culture and Black Consciousness: Afro-American Folk Thought from Slavery to Freedom*. New York: Oxford University Press, 1977.

Levy, Walter. "Oil and the Decline of the West." *Foreign Affairs* 58, no. 5 (summer 1980): 999–1015.

———. "The Years That the Locust Hath Eaten: Oil Policy and OPEC Development Prospects." *Foreign Affairs* 57 (winter 1978/79): 288.

Lewontin, Richard, Steven Rose, and Leon J. Kamin. *Not in Our Genes: Biology, Ideology, and Human Nature*. New York: Pantheon, 1984.

Lieb, Michael. *Children of Ezekiel: Aliens, UFOs, the Crisis of Race, and the Advent of the End Time*. Durham, N.C.: Duke University Press, 1998.

Lieber, Robert. *The Oil Decade: Conflict and Cooperation in the West*. New York: Praeger, 1983.

Liebman, Robert. "Making of the New Christian Right." In *The New Christian Right: Mobilization and Legitimization*, edited by Robert Liebman and Robert Wuthnow.

Liebman, Robert, and Robert Wuthnow, eds. *The New Christian Right: Mobilization and Legitimization*. New York: Aldine, 1983.

Lincoln, C. Eric. *The Black Muslims in America*. Grand Rapids, Mich.: Eerdmans, 1993.

Lindemann, Albert. *Esau's Tears: Modern Anti-Semitism and the Rise of the Jews*. New York: Cambridge University Press, 1997.

Lindsey, Hal, with C. C. Carlson. *The Late Great Planet Earth*. Grand Rapids, Mich.: Zondervan, 1970.

Lipsitz, George. *Dangerous Crossroads: Popular Music, Postmodernism, and the Poetics of Place.* New York: Verso, 1994.

———. *Rainbow at Midnight: Labor and Culture in the 1940s.* Urbana: University of Illinois Press, 1994.

Livingston, James. *Pragmatism and the Political Economy of Cultural Revolution, 1850–1940.* Chapel Hill: University of North Carolina Press, 1994.

Livingstone, Neil, and Terrell Arnold. *Fighting Back: Winning the War against Terrorism.* Lexington, Mass.: Lexington Books, 1986.

Lomax, Louis. *When the Word Is Given: A Report of Elijah Muhammad, Malcolm X, and the Black Muslim World.* New York: Signet, 1963.

Lott, Eric. *Love and Theft: Blackface Minstrelsy and the American Working Class.* New York: Oxford University Press, 1993.

———. "White Like Me: Racial Cross-Dressing and the Construction of American Whiteness." In *Cultures of United States Imperialism,* edited by Amy Kaplan and Donald Pease, 474–498.

Louis, William Roger. *The British Empire in the Middle East, 1945–1951: Arab Nationalism, the United States, and Postwar Imperialism.* New York: Oxford University Press, 1985.

Louis, William Roger, and Roger Owen, eds. *Suez 1956: The Crisis and Its Consequences.* Oxford: Clarendon Press, 1989.

Loveland, Anne. *American Evangelicals and the U.S. Military, 1942–1993.* Baton Rouge: Louisiana State University Press, 1996.

Lowe, Lisa. *Critical Terrains: French and British Orientalisms.* Ithaca, N.Y.: Cornell University Press, 1991.

———. *Immigrant Acts: On Asian American Cultural Politics.* Durham, N.C.: Duke University Press, 1996.

Luce, Henry R. *The American Century.* New York: Farrar and Rinehart, 1941.

Lynch, Hollis. *Edward Wilmont Blyden: Pan-Negro Patriot, 1832–1912.* New York: Oxford University Press, 1967.

Mahmoody, Betty, with William Hoffer. *Not Without My Daughter.* New York: St. Martin's, 1987.

Malcolm X. *Malcolm X Speaks: Selected Speeches and Statements.* Edited by George Breitman. New York: Grove Weidenfeld, 1965.

———. *Malcolm X: Speeches at Harvard.* Edited by Archie Epps. New York: Paragon House, 1992.

Malcolm X with Alex Haley. *The Autobiography of Malcolm X.* 1964. New York: Ballantine, 1992.

Maltby, Richard. *Hollywood Cinema: An Introduction.* Oxford: Blackwell, 1995.

Mariscal, George. "In the Wake of the Gulf War: Untying the Yellow Ribbon." *Cultural Critique,* no. 19 (1991): 97–117.

Marr, Timothy. "Imagining Ishmael: Studies in Islamic Orientalism in America from Puritans to Melville." Ph.D. diss., University of Michigan, 1998.

Marsden, George. *Fundamentalism and American Culture: The Shaping of Twentieth-Century Evangelism, 1870–1925.* New York: Oxford University Press, 1980.

Mart, Michelle. " 'Tough Guys' and American Cold War Policy: Images of Israel, 1945–1960." *Diplomatic History*, no. 20 (1996): 357–380.

Martin, David C., and John Walcott. *Best Laid Plans: The Inside Story of America's War against Terrorism.* New York: Harper and Row, 1988.

Martin, Reginald. *Ishmael Reed and the New Black Aesthetic Critics.* New York: St. Martin's, 1988.

Martin, Waldo, Jr. " 'Nation Time!': Black Nationalism, the Third World, and Jews." In *Struggles in the Promised Land,* edited by Jack Salzman and Cornel West, 341–355.

Martin, William. "Waiting for the End." *Atlantic Monthly,* June 1982, 31–37.

———. *With God on Our Side: The Rise of the Religious Right in America.* New York: Broadway Books, 1996.

Marty, Martin, and Scott Appleby, eds. *Fundamentalism and the State.* Chicago: University of Chicago Press, 1993.

Marvin X, and Faruk X. "Islam and Black Art: An Interview with LeRoi Jones." In *Dictionary of Literary Biography: Black Arts Movement,* edited by Jeff Decker, 122–129. Dictionary of Literary Biography Documentary Series. Detroit: Gale, 1984.

Marx, Karl. "The Eighteenth Brumiere of Louis Bonaparte." In *The Marx-Engels Reader,* edited by Robert Tucker, 594–617. 2d ed. New York: Norton, 1978.

Massad, Joseph. "Palestinians and the Limits of Racialized Discourse." *Social Text,* no. 34 (1993): 94–114.

May, Elaine Tyler. *Homeward Bound: American Families in the Cold War Era.* New York: Basic Books, 1988.

May, Ernest. "NSC 68: The Theory and Politics of Strategy." In *American Cold War Strategy: Interpreting NSC 68,* edited by Ernest May, 1–20.

———, ed. *American Cold War Strategy: Interpreting NSC 68.* Boston: Bedford Books of St. Martin's Press, 1993.

McCall, Thomas, and Zola Levitt. *The Coming Russian Invasion of Israel.* Chicago: Moody Press, 1974.

McClintock, Anne. *Imperial Leather: Race, Gender, and Sexuality in the Colonial Contest.* New York: Routledge, 1995.

McCloud, Aminah Beverly. *African American Islam.* New York: Routledge, 1995.

McCormick, Thomas. *America's Half-Century: United States Foreign Policy in the Cold War.* Baltimore: Johns Hopkins University Press, 1989.

McDowell, Edwin. "Publishers: A Matter of Faith." *New York Times Book Review,* April 6, 1980, 8.

Mercer, Kobena. "1968: Periodizing Politics and Identity." In *Cultural Studies,* edited by Lawrence Grossberg, Cary Nelson, and Paula Treichler, 424–437. New York: Routledge, 1992.

Merkley, Paul. *The Politics of Christian Zionism, 1891–1948.* London: Frank Cass, 1998.

Metz, Christian. "Story/Discourse (A Note on Two Kinds of Voyeurism)." In *The Imaginary Signifier: Psychoanalysis and the Cinema,* 91–98. Bloomington: Indiana University Press, 1982.

Meyerowitz, Joanne, ed. *Not June Cleaver: Women and Gender in Postwar America, 1945–1960.* Philadelphia: Temple University Press, 1994.

Michalak, Laurence. *Cruel and Unusual: Negative Images of Arabs in Popular Culture.* Washington, D.C.: American-Arab Anti-Discrimination Committee, n.d.

Miller, Angela. "The Panorama, the Cinema, and the Emergence of the Spectacular." *Wide Angle,* no. 18 (1996): 34–69.

Miller, Christopher. *Blank Darkness: Africanist Discourse in French.* Chicago: University of Chicago Press, 1985.

Miller, James A. "Amiri Baraka." In *The Beats: Literary Bohemians in Postwar America,* edited by Ann Charters, 3–24. Dictionary of Literary Biography, 16, pt. 1. Detroit: Gayle, 1983.

Miller, Stuart Creighton. *"Benevolent Assimilation": The American Conquest of the Philippines, 1899–1903.* New Haven, Conn.: Yale University Press, 1982.

Mishal, Shaul. *The PLO under Arafat: Between Gun and Olive Branch.* New Haven, Conn.: Yale University Press, 1986.

Mitchell, Timothy. *Colonising Egypt.* New York: Cambridge University Press, 1988.

———. "Middle East Studies." In *The Politics of Knowledge: Area Studies and the Disciplines,* edited by David Szanton. In preparation.

Mitchell, W. J. T. "Holy Landscape: Israel, Palestine, and the American Wilderness." *Critical Inquiry,* no. 26 (2000): 193–223.

Monaco, James, ed. *Encyclopedia of Film.* New York: Perigee Books, 1991.

Moses, Wilson J. *Black Messiahs and Uncle Toms: Social and Literary Manipulations of a Religious Myth.* University Park: Pennsylvania State University Press, 1982.

———. *The Golden Age of Black Nationalism, 1850–1925.* Hamden, Conn.: Archon Books, 1978.

———. *Wings of Ethiopia: Studies in African-American Life and Letters.* Ames: Iowa State University Press, 1990.

Moughrabi, Fouad. "The Arab Basic Personality: A Critical Survey of the Literature." *International Journal of Middle East Studies* 9 (1978): 99–112.

Mueller, John. *Policy and Opinion in the Gulf War.* Chicago: University of Chicago Press, 1994.

Muhammad, Elijah. *Message to the Blackman in America.* No. 2. Chicago: Muhammad Mosque of Islam, 1965.

Mulvey, Laura. "Visual Pleasure and Narrative Cinema." In *Narrative, Apparatus, Ideology,* edited by Philip Rosen, 198–209.

Nadel, Alan. "God's Law and the Wide Screen: *The Ten Commandments* as Cold War Epic." *Publications of the Modern Language Association of America (PMLA)* 108, no. 3 (1993): 415–430.

Naficy, Hamid. *The Making of Exile Cultures: Iranian Television in Los Angeles.* Minneapolis: University of Minnesota Press, 1993.

———. "Mediating the Other." In *The U.S. Media and the Middle East,* edited by Yahya Kamalipour, 73–90.

Neal, Larry. "The Black Arts Movement." In *Visions of a Liberated Future: Black Arts Movement Writings*, 62–78. New York: Thunder's Mouth Press, 1989.

———. "Malcolm and the Conscience of Black America." *The Liberator* 6, no. 2 (February 1966): 10–11.

Neale, Stephen. *Genre*. London: British Film Institute, 1980.

Neff, Donald. *Warriors at Suez: Eisenhower Takes America into the Middle East*. New York: Simon and Schuster, 1981.

———. *Warriors for Jerusalem: The Six Days That Changed the Middle East in 1967*. Brattleboro, Vt.: Amana Books, 1988.

Nelson, John Wiley. "The Apocalyptic Vision in American Culture." In *The Apocalyptic Vision in America*, edited by Lois P. Zamora, 154–182. Bowling Green, Ohio: Bowling Green University Press, 1982.

Netanyahu, Benjamin, ed. *Terrorism: How the West Can Win*. New York: Farrar, Straus and Giroux, 1986.

Neuhaus, Richard. "What the Fundamentalists Want." In *Piety and Politics: Evangelicals and Fundamentalists Confront the World*, edited by Richard Neuhaus and Michael Cromartie, 3–18.

Neuhaus, Richard, and Michael Cromartie, eds. *Piety and Politics: Evangelicals and Fundamentalists Confront the World*. Washington, D.C.: Ethics and Public Policy Center, 1987.

Newfield, Christopher. "What Was Political Correctness? Race, the Right, and Managerial Democracy in the Humanities." *Critical Inquiry* 19 (1993): 308–336.

Niebuhr, Reinhold. *The Irony of American History*. New York: Scribner, 1952.

———. *The World Crisis and American Responsibility: Nine Essays*. New York: Association Press, 1958.

Noerdlinger, Henry. *Moses and Egypt: The Documentation to the Motion Picture "The Ten Commandments."* Introduction by Cecil B. DeMille. Los Angeles: University of Southern California Press, 1956.

Norris, Christopher. *Uncritical Theory: Postmodernism, Intellectuals, and the Gulf War*. Amherst: University of Massachusetts Press, 1992.

Norris, Margot. "Only the Guns Have Eyes: Military Censorship and the Body Count." In *Seeing through the Media*, edited by Susan Jeffords and Lauren Rabinovitz, 285–300.

O'Ballance, Edgar. *Language of Violence: The Blood Politics of Terrorism*. Novato, Calif.: Presidio, 1979.

Ockenga, Harold John. "Fulfilled and Unfulfilled Prophecy." In *Prophecy in the Making*, edited by Carl Henry, 291–331.

Omi, Michael, and Howard Winant. *Racial Formation in the United States: From the 1960s to 1990s*. 2d ed. New York: Routledge, 1994.

Orfalea, Gregory. *Before the Flames: A Quest for the History of Arab Americans*. Austin: University of Texas Press, 1988.

Painter, David S. *Oil and the American Century: The Political Economy of U.S. Foreign Policy, 1941–1954*. Baltimore: Johns Hopkins University Press, 1986.

Patterson, James. *America in the Twentieth Century: A History.* 3d ed. New York: Harcourt Brace Jovanovich.

Pauly, Thomas H. "The Way to Salvation: The Hollywood Blockbuster of the 1950s." *Prospects: An Annual Journal of American Cultural Studies* 5 (1980): 467–487.

Peck, Ira. *Raid at Entebbe.* New York: Scholastic, 1977.

Perry, Bruce. *Malcolm: The Life of a Man Who Changed Black America.* New York: Station Hill, 1991.

Peterson, J. E., ed. *The Politics of Middle Eastern Oil.* Washington, D.C.: Middle East Institute, 1983.

Pfeil, Fred. *Another Tale to Tell: Politics and Narrative in Postmodern Culture.* London: Verso, 1990.

Phillips, Kevin. "The Hype That Roared." *Politics Today,* May/June 1979, 54–58.

Plummer, Brenda Gayle. *Rising Wind: Black Americans and U.S. Foreign Policy.* Chapel Hill: University of North Carolina Press, 1996.

Poiger, Uta. *Jazz, Rock, and Rebels: Cold War Politics and American Culture in a Divided Germany.* Berkeley and Los Angeles: University of California Press, 2000.

Pollock, John. *Billy Graham, Evangelist to the World: An Authorized Biography of the Decisive Years.* San Francisco: Harper and Row, 1979.

Posner, Steve. *Israel Undercover: Secret Warfare and Hidden Diplomacy in the Middle East.* Syracuse, N.Y.: Syracuse University Press, 1987.

Pouissant, Alvin. "An Overview of Fanon's Significance to the American Civil Rights Movement." In *International Tribute to Frantz Fanon: Record of the Special Meeting of the United Nations Special Committee against Apartheid, 3 November 1978.* New York: United Nations Centre against Apartheid, 1979.

Powell, Colin, with Joseph E. Persico. *My American Journey.* New York: Random House, 1995.

Pratt, David. "Widescreen Box Office Performance to 1959." *Velvet Light Trap,* summer 1985, 65–66.

Pratt, Mary Louise. *Imperial Eyes: Travel Writing and Transculturalism.* New York: Routledge, 1992.

Quandt, William. *Decade of Decisions: American Policy toward the Arab-Israeli Conflict, 1967–1976.* Berkeley and Los Angeles: University of California Press, 1977.

Ra'anan, Uri. *Hydras of Carnage: International Linkages of Terrorism.* Lexington, Mass.: Lexington Books, 1986.

Raboteau, Albert. *Slave Religion: The "Invisible Institution" in the Antebellum South.* New York: Oxford University Press, 1978.

Rafael, Vincente. "The Cultures of Area Studies in the United States." *Social Text,* winter 1994, 91–111.

———. "White Love: Surveillance and Nationalist Resistance in U.S. Colonization of the Philippines." In *Cultures of United States Imperialism,* edited by Amy Kaplan and Donald Pease, 3–21.

Raider, Mark. *The Emergence of American Zionism*. New York: New York University Press, 1998.

Raines, Howard. *My Soul Is Rested*. New York: Penguin, 1983.

Randall, Dudley, and Margaret G. Burroughs, eds. *For Malcolm: Poems on the Life and Death of Malcolm X*. Detroit: Broadside Press, 1969.

Rausch, David. *Zionism within Early American Fundamentalism: A Convergence of Two Traditions*. New York: Edwin Mellen Press, 1979.

Reed, Ishmael. *Mumbo Jumbo*. 1972. New York: Simon and Schuster, 1996.

Reichley, James. "The Evangelical and Fundamentalist Revolt." In *Piety and Politics: Evangelicals and Fundamentalists Confront the World*, edited by Richard Neuhaus and Michael Cromartie, 69–97.

Reid, Roddey. *Families in Jeopardy: Regulating the Social Body in France, 1750–1910*. Stanford, Calif.: Stanford University Press, 1993.

Ribuffo, Leo P. "God and Contemporary Politics." *Journal of American History* 79 (March 1993): 1515ff.

———. *The Old Christian Right: The Protestant Far Right from the Depression to the Cold War*. Philadelphia: Temple University Press, 1983.

Ridderbos, Herman. "The Future of Israel." In *Prophecy in the Making*, edited by Carl F. Henry, 315–323.

Rivers, Gayle. *The Specialist: Revelations of a Counterterrorist*. New York: Stein and Day, 1985.

Robbins, Bruce. *Feeling Global: Internationalism in Distress*. New York: New York University Press, 1999.

———, ed. *The Phantom Public Sphere*. Minneapolis: University of Minnesota Press, 1993.

Rogers, J. A. *The World's Great Men of Color*. 1946. New York: Collier Books, 1972.

Rogin, Michael. *Blackface, White Noise: Jewish Immigrants in the Hollywood Melting Pot*. Berkeley and Los Angeles: University of California Press, 1996.

Rosen, Philip. "Making a Nation in Sembene's *Ceddo*." *Quarterly Review of Film and Video* 13 (1991): 147–172.

———. "Securing the Historical: Historiography and the Classic Cinema." In *Cinema Histories and Cinema Practices*, edited by Philip Rosen and Patricia Mellencamp, 17–34. New York: University Press of America, 1984.

———, ed. *Narrative, Apparatus, Ideology*. New York: Columbia University Press, 1986.

Rosenberg, Emily. *Spreading the American Dream: American Economic and Cultural Expansion, 1890–1945*. New York: Hill and Wang, 1982.

Rubin, Gary. "African Americans and Israel." In *Struggles in the Promised Land*, edited by Jack Salzman and Cornel West, 357–370.

Ryan, Mary. *Women in Public: Between Banners and Ballots, 1825–1880*. Baltimore: Johns Hopkins University Press, 1990.

Sabbagh, Suha. *Sex, Lies, and Stereotypes: The Image of Arabs in American Popular Fiction*. Washington, D.C.: American-Arab Anti-Discrimination Committee Report, n.d.

Said, Edward. *Covering Islam*. New York: Pantheon, 1981.

———. *Culture and Imperialism*. New York: Knopf, 1993.

———. "Michael Walzer's *Exodus and Revolution:* A Canaanite Reading." In *Blaming the Victims: Spurious Scholarship and the Palestinian Question*, edited by Edward Said and Christopher Hitchens.

———. *Orientalism*. New York: Vintage, 1979.

Said, Edward, and Christopher Hitchens, eds. *Blaming the Victims: Spurious Scholarship and the Palestinian Question*. New York: Verso, 1988.

Saldívar, José David. *Border Matters: Remapping American Culture Studies*. Berkeley and Los Angeles: University of California Press, 1997.

Saliba, John. "Religious Dimensions of the UFO Phenomenon." In *The Gods Have Landed: New Religions from Other Worlds*, edited by James R. Lewis, 65–84. Albany: State University of New York Press, 1995.

Saliba, Theresa. "Military Presences and Absences: Arab Women and the Persian Gulf War." In *Seeing through the Media*, edited by Susan Jeffords and Lauren Rabinovitz, 263–284.

Salzman, Jack, ed. *Bridges and Boundaries: African Americans and American Jews*. Exhibition catalog. New York: George Braziller in association with the Jewish Museum, New York, 1992.

Salzman, Jack, and Cornel West, eds. *Struggles in the Promised Land*. New York: Oxford University Press, 1997.

Sanders, Jerry. *Peddlers of Crisis: The Committee on the Present Danger and the Politics of Containment*. Boston: South End Press, 1983.

Saxton, Alexander. *Rise and Fall of the White Republic: Class Politics and Mass Culture in Nineteenth-Century America*. New York: Verso, 1990.

Schulte-Sasse, Jochen, and Linda Schulte-Sasse. "War, Otherness, and Illusionary Identifications with the State." *Cultural Critique*, no. 19 (1991): 67–95.

Scott, Joyce Hope. "From Foreground to Margin: Female Configuration and Masculine Self-Representation in Black Nationalist Fiction." In *Nationalisms and Sexualities*, edited by Andrew Parker, 296–312. New York: Routledge, 1992.

Scott-Gibson, Herbert. *Tutankhamun and the African Heritage: A View of Society in the Time of the Boy King*. New York: Metropolitan Museum of Art, 1978.

Shaheen, Jack. "The Hollywood Arab (1984–86)." *Journal of Popular Film and Television* 14, no. 4 (1987).

———. *The TV Arab*. Bowling Green, Ohio: Bowling Green State University Press, 1984.

Shapiro, Michael. "Moral Geographies and the Ethics of Post-Sovereignty." *Public Culture* 6, no. 3 (1994): 479–502.

Shohat, Ella. "Imagining Terra Incognita: The Disciplinary Gaze of Empire." *Public Culture* 3, no. 2 (spring 1991): 41–70.

Shulman, Holly Cowan. "The International Media and the Persian Gulf War: The Importance of the Flow of News." In *Seeing through the Media*, edited by Susan Jeffords and Lauren Rabinovitz, 107–120.

Sick, Gary. *All Fall Down: America's Tragic Encounter with Iran*. New York: Penguin, 1986.

Sifry, Micah, and Christopher Cerf, eds. *The Gulf War Reader: History, Documents, Opinions.* New York: Random House, 1991.

Silberman, Charles. *A Certain People: American Jews and Their Lives Today.* New York: Summit Books, 1985.

Simon, Merrill. *Jerry Falwell and the Jews.* Middle Village, N.Y.: Jonathan David, 1984.

Singh, Nikhil Pal. "Culture Wars: Recoding Empire in an Age of Democracy." *American Quarterly* 50, no. 3 (1998): 471–522.

Sklar, Martin. *The Corporate Reconstruction of American Capitalism, 1890–1916: The Market, the Law, and Politics.* New York: Cambridge University Press, 1988.

Sklar, Robert. *Movie-Made America: A Cultural History of American Movies.* New York: Vintage, 1976.

Smith, David Lionel. "The Black Arts Movement and Its Critics." *American Literary History* 3, no. 1 (1991): 93–110.

———. "Chicago Poets, OBAC, and the Black Arts Movement." In *The Black Columbiad: Defining Moments in African American Literature and Culture,* edited by Werner Sollars and Maria Diedrich, 253–264. Cambridge, Mass.: Harvard University Press, 1994.

Smith, Wilbur. *Israeli-Arab Conflict and the Bible.* Glendale, Calif.: G. L. Regal Books, 1967.

———. "Signs of the Second Advent of Christ." In *Prophecy in the Making,* edited by Carl Henry, 187–215.

Snowball, David. *Continuity and Change in the Rhetoric of the Moral Majority.* New York: Praeger, 1991.

Sobchack, Vivian. " 'Surge and Splendor': A Phenomenology of the Hollywood Historical Epic." *Representations,* no. 29 (1990): 24–49.

Soja, Edward. *Postmodern Geographies: The Reassertion of Space in Critical Theory.* New York: Verso, 1999.

Sollors, Werner. *Amiri Baraka/LeRoi Jones: The Quest for a "Populist Modernism."* New York: Columbia University Press, 1978.

Spady, James. "Cheik Anta Diop and Freddie Thomas: Two Philosophical Perspectives on Pristine Black History." *Journal of African Civilizations* 1, no. 1 (1979): 15–28.

Spanier, John. *American Foreign Policy since World War II.* 7th ed. New York: Holt, Rinehart and Winston, 1977.

Spector, Ronald. *After Tet: The Bloodiest Year in Vietnam.* New York: Free Press, 1993.

Stanton, William. *The Leopard's Spots: Scientific Attitudes toward Race in America, 1815–1959.* Chicago: University of Chicago Press, 1960.

Stefancic, Jean, and Richard Delgado. *No Mercy: How Conservative Think Tanks and Foundations Changed America's Social Agenda.* Philadelphia: Temple University Press, 1996.

Steinberg, Cobbett. *Film Facts.* New York: Facts on File, 1980.

Sterling, Claire. *The Terror Network: The Secret War of International Terrorism.* New York: Holt, Rinehart, and Winston, 1981.

Stevenson, William. *Ninety Minutes at Entebbe*. New York: Bantam, 1976.

Stork, Joe. *Middle East Oil and the Energy Crisis*. New York: Monthly Review Press, 1975.

Strober, Jerry, and Ruth Tomczak. *Jerry Falwell: Aflame for God*. Nashville, Tenn.: Thomas Nelson, 1979.

Strozier, Charles. *Apocalypse: On the Psychology of Fundamentalism in America*. Boston: Beacon Press, 1994.

Studlar, Gaylyn. "Out-Salomeing Salome: Dance, the New Woman, and Fan Magazine Orientalism." In *Visions of the East: Orientalism in Film*, edited by Matthew Bernstein and Gaylyn Studlar, 99–129.

———. *This Mad Masquerade: Stardom and Masculinity in the Jazz Age*. New York: Columbia University Press, 1996.

Suleiman, Michael. *The Arabs in the Mind of America*. Brattleboro, Vt.: Amana Books, 1988.

Takaki, Ronald. *Strangers from a Different Shore: A History of Asian Americans*. Boston: Little, Brown, 1989.

Tasker, Yvonne. *Spectacular Bodies: Gender, Genre, and the Action Cinema*. New York: Routledge, 1993.

Tawil, Ezra. "The Frontier Romance, the Problem of Slavery, and the Making of Race." Ph.D. diss., Brown University, 2000.

Taylor, Alan R. *The Superpowers and the Middle East*. Syracuse, N.Y.: Syracuse University Press, 1991.

Theisen, Lee Scott. " 'My God, Did I Set All of This in Motion?' General Lew Wallace and *Ben-Hur*." *Journal of Popular Culture* 18 (fall 1984): 33–41.

Tinnin, David, with Dag Christensen. *The Hit Team*. Boston: Little, Brown, 1976.

Tivnan, Edward. *The Lobby: Jewish Political Power and American Foreign Policy*. New York: Simon and Schuster, 1987.

Torgovnick, Marianna. *Gone Primitive: Savage Intellects, Modern Lives*. Chicago: University of Chicago Press, 1990.

Traube, Elizabeth. *Dreaming Identities: Class, Gender, and Generation in 1980s Hollywood Movies*. Boulder, Colo.: Westview Press, 1992.

Tucker, Robert W. "The American Outlook: Change and Continuity." In *Retreat from Empire? The First Nixon Administration*, edited by Robert Osgood and others, 29–78. Baltimore: Johns Hopkins University Press, 1973.

Tuleja, Tad. "Closing the Yellow Circle: Yellow Ribbons and the Redemption of the Past." *Journal of American Culture* 17, no. 1 (1994): 23–30.

Turner, Richard. *Islam in the African-American Experience*. Bloomington: Indiana University Press, 1997.

Twain, Mark. *The Innocents Abroad, or The New Pilgrims' Progress*. 1869. Pleasantville, N.Y.: Reader's Digest, 1990.

UNESCO. *The Peopling of Ancient Egypt and the Deciphering of Meriotic Script*. Ghent: UNESCO, 1978.

Uris, Leon. *Exodus*. New York: Bantam, 1959.

Van Deburg, William. *A New Day in Babylon: The Black Power Movement and American Culture, 1965–1975*. Chicago: University of Chicago Press, 1992.

Van Impe, Jack, with Roger F. Campbell. *Israel's Final Holocaust*. Nashville, Tenn.: Thomas Nelson, 1979.

Van Sertima, Ivan. "Introduction: Black Dynasties and Rulers." In *Egypt Revisited*, edited by Ivan Van Sertima, 85–89. New Brunswick, N.J.: Transaction, 1989.

Vitalis, Robert. *When Capitalists Collide: Business Conflict and the End of Empire in Egypt*. Berkeley and Los Angeles: University of California Press, 1995.

Vogel, Lester. *To See a Promised Land: Americans and the Holy Land in the Nineteenth Century*. University Park: Penn State University Press, 1993.

Voll, John. *Islam: Continuity and Change in the Modern World*. Syracuse, N.Y.: Syracuse University Press, 1994.

Von Eschen, Penny. "Challenging Cold War Habits: African Americans, Race, and Foreign Policy." *Diplomatic History* 20, no. 4 (1996): 627–638.

———. *Race against Empire: Black Americans and Anticolonialism, 1937–1957*. Ithaca, N.Y.: Cornell University Press, 1997.

Wald, Gayle. *Crossing the Line: Racial Passing in Twentieth-Century U.S. Literature and Culture*. Durham, N.C.: Duke University Press, 2000.

Walker, Alice. *In Search of Our Mothers' Gardens*. San Diego: Harcourt Brace Jovanovich, 1983.

Wallace, Lew. *Ben-Hur: A Tale of the Christ*. New York: Harper and Brothers, 1900.

Walvoord, John F. *Armageddon, Oil, and the Middle East Crisis: What the Bible Says about the Future of the Middle East and the End of Western Civilization*. Grand Rapids, Mich.: Zondervan, 1990.

———. "The Future of Israel." In *Prophecy in the Making*, edited by Carl Henry, 327–343.

———. *Israel in Prophecy*. Grand Rapids, Mich.: Zondervan, 1962.

Walvoord, John F., and John E. Walvoord. *Armageddon, Oil, and the Middle East Crisis: What the Bible Says about the Future of the Middle East and the End of Western Civilization*. Grand Rapids, Mich.: Zondervan, 1976.

Walzer, Michael. *Exodus and Revolution*. New York: Basic Books, 1985.

Waterbury, John. *The Egypt of Nasser and Sadat*. Princeton, N.J.: Princeton University Press, 1983.

Weekes, Richard, ed. *Muslim Peoples: A World Ethnographic Survey*. Vol. 2. 2d ed. Westport, Conn.: Greenwood Press, 1984.

Weisbord, Robert, and Richard Kazarian Jr. *Israel in the Black American Perspective*. Westport, Conn.: Greenwood Press, 1985.

West, Cornel. "On Black-Jewish Relations." In *Blacks and Jews: Alliances and Arguments*, edited by Paul Berman. New York: Dell, 1995.

Westbrook, Robert. " 'I Want a Girl, Just Like the Girl That Married Harry James': American Women and the Problem of Political Obligation in World War II." *American Quarterly* 42, no. 4 (1990): 587–614.

White, E. Francis. "Africa on My Mind: Gender, Counterdiscourse, and African American Nationalism." In *Words of Fire*, edited by Beverly Guy-Sheftall, 504–524. New York: New Press, 1995.

White, Mimi. "Site Unseen: An Analysis of CNN's *War in the Gulf.*" In *Seeing through the Media,* edited by Susan Jeffords and Lauren Rabinovitz, 121–142.

White, Richard. *"It's Your Misfortune and None of My Own": A History of the American West.* Norman: University of Oklahoma Press, 1991.

Whitfield, Steven. *The Culture of the Cold War.* Baltimore: Johns Hopkins University Press, 1991.

Wiegman, Robyn. "Missiles and Melodrama (Masculinity and the Televisual War)." In *Seeing through the Media,* edited by Susan Jeffords and Lauren Rabinovitz, 171–188.

Wilburn, Gary. "The Doomsday Chic." *Christianity Today,* January 27, 1978.

Williams, Juan. *Eyes on the Prize: American's Civil Rights Years, 1954–1965.* New York: Viking Penguin, 1987.

Williams, Linda. *Hardcore: Power, Pleasure, and the "Frenzy of the Visible."* Berkeley and Los Angeles: University of California Press, 1989.

———, ed. *Viewing Positions: Ways of Seeing Film.* New Brunswick, N.J.: Rutgers University Press, 1994.

Williams, Mance. *Black Theatre in the 1960s and 1970s: A Historical-Critical Analysis of the Movement.* Westport, Conn.: Greenwood Press, 1985.

Williams, William Appleman. *Empire as a Way of Life: An Essay on the Causes and Character of America's Present Predicament, along with a Few Thoughts about an Alternative.* New York: Oxford University Press, 1980.

———. *The Tragedy of American Diplomacy.* 2d ed. New York: Dell, 1972.

Willis, Ellen. "The Myth of the Powerful Jew, with Prologue." In *Blacks and Jews: Alliances and Arguments,* edited by Paul Berman. New York: Delacorte Press, 1994.

Wilmore, Gayraud S. *Black Religion and Black Radicalism.* Garden City, N.Y.: Doubleday, 1972.

Wilson, John. *Signs and Wonders Upon Pharaoh: A History of American Egyptology.* Chicago: University of Chicago Press, 1964.

Wolf, Stacy. *A Problem Like Maria? Gender and Sexuality in the American Musical.* Ann Arbor: University of Michigan Press, 2002.

Wood, Joe, ed. *Malcolm X: In Our Own Image.* New York: St. Martin's Press, 1992.

Wood, Michael. *America in the Movies, or "Santa Maria It Had Slipped My Mind."* New York: Columbia University Press, 1989.

Woodard, Komozi. *A Nation within a Nation: Amiri Baraka (LeRoi Jones) and Black Power Politics.* Chapel Hill: University of North Carolina Press, 1999.

Woodward, Bob. *The Commanders.* New York: Simon and Schuster, 1991.

Wright, Richard. *The Color Curtain: A Report on the Bandung Conference.* 1956. Jackson: University of Mississippi Press, 1994.

Wright, Robin. *In the Name of God: The Khomeini Decade.* New York: Touchstone, 1989.

Wuthnow, Robert. *After Heaven: Spirituality in America since the 1950s.* Berkeley and Los Angeles: University of California Press, 1998.

———. "The Political Rebirth of American Evangelicals." In *The New Christian Right: Mobilization and Legitimization,* edited by Robert Liebman and Robert Wuthnow, 168–187.

———. "The Social Significance of Religious Television." In *Religious Television: Controversies and Conclusions,* edited by Robert Abelman and Stewart Hoover, 87–98. Norwood, N.J.: Ablex, 1990.

Yergin, Daniel. *The Prize: The Epic Quest for Oil, Money, and Power.* New York: Simon and Schuster, 1991.

———. *Shattered Peace: The Origins of the Cold War and the National Security State.* Boston: Houghton Mifflin, 1977.

Yoshihara, Mari. "Women's Asia: American Women and the Gendering of American Orientalism, 1870–WWII." Ph.D. diss., Brown University, 1997.

Young, Robert. *Colonial Desire: Hybridity in Theory, Culture, and Race.* New York: Routledge, 1995.

Zeadey, Baha, and Faith Zeadey, eds. *Arabs in America: Myths and Realities.* Wilmette, Ill.: Medina University Press International, 1975.

SUPPLEMENTAL BIBLIOGRAPHY FOR THE 2005 EDITION

9/11 Commission, *The 9/11 Commission Report: Final Report of the National Commission on Terrorist Attacks upon the United States* (New York: W.W. Norton, 2004).

Abrahamian, Ervand. "The US Media, Huntington, and September 11." *Third World Quarterly* 24, no. 3 (2003): 529–544.

Ajami, Fouad. "The Summoning." *Foreign Affairs* 72, no. 4 (1993): 2–9.

Amireh, Amal. "Between Complicity and Subversion: Body Politics in Palestinian National Narrative." In *Palestine/America,* edited by Mohammed Bamyeh, 747–774.

Anderson, Benedict. *Imagined Communities: On the Origin and Spread of Nationalism.* New York: Verso, 1991.

Appadurai, Arjun. *Modernity at Large.* Minneapolis: University of Minnesota Press, 1996.

Appy, Christian G., ed. *Cold War Constructions: The Political Culture of United States Imperialism, 1945–1966.* Amherst: University of Massachusetts Press, 2000.

Bamyeh, Mohammed, ed. *Palestine/America,* special issue of *South Atlantic Quarterly.* Durham: Duke University Press, 2003.

Barthes, Roland. *Mythologies.* New York: Hill and Wang, 1972.

Bayoumi, Moustafa. "Letter to a G-Man." In *After the World Trade Center: Rethinking New York City,* edited by Michael Sorkin, 131–142.

Bederman, Gail. *Manliness and Civilization: A Cultural History of Gender and Race in the United States, 1880–1917.* Chicago: University of Chicago Press, 1995.

Bragg, Rick. *I Am A Soldier, Too: The Jessica Lynch Story.* New York: Knopf, 2003.

Briggs, Laura. *Reproducing Empire: Race, Sex, Science, and U.S. Imperialism in Puerto Rico.* Berkeley: University of California Press, 2002.

Burton, Antoinette, ed. *After the Imperial Turn: Thinking With and Through the Nation.* Durham: Duke University Press, 2003.

Butler, Judith. "Is Kinship Always Heterosexual?" *Differences* 13, no. 1, (spring 2002). *Project Muse.* George Washington University Library.

Calhoun, Craig, Paul Price, and Ashely Trimmer, eds. *Understanding September 11.* New York: W.W. Norton, 2002.

Carby, Hazel. " 'On the Threshold of Woman's Era': Lynching, Sexuality, and Empire in Black Feminist Theory." *Critical Inquiry* 12, no. 1 (1985): 262–277.

Clausewitz, Carl von. *On War.* New York: Dorset Press, 1968.

Coll, Steve. *Ghost Wars: The Secret History of the CIA, Afghanistan, and bin Laden, From the Soviet Invasion to September 10, 2001.* New York: Penguin Press, 2004.

Conetta, Carl. "Disappearing the Dead: Iraq, Afghanistan, and the Idea of a 'New Warfare.' " Project on Defense Alternatives Research Monograph #9, February 2004. http://www.comw.org/pda/0402rm9.html.

——. "Strange Victory: A Critical Appraisal of Operation Enduring Freedom and the Afghanistan War." Project on Defense Alternatives Research Monograph #6, January 2002. http://www.comw.org/pda/0201strangevic.html.

——. "What Colin Powell Showed Us: The End of Arms Control and the Normalization of War." Project on Defense Alternatives Briefing Report #14, May 5, 2003. http://www.comw.org/pda/0305br14.html.

Cunningham, Brent. "Re-thinking Objectivity," *Columbia Journalism Review* 42, no. 2, (July/August 2003). Lexis-Nexis Academic Universe. George Washington University Library.

Davis, Angela Y. *Women, Race, and Class.* New York: Vintage Books, 1981.

Denning, Michael. *Culture in the Age of Three Worlds.* New York: Verso, 2004.

Dower, John. *War Without Mercy: Race and Power in the Pacific War.* New York: Pantheon, 1987.

Dudziak, Mary. *September 11 in History: A Watershed Moment?* Durham: Duke University Press, 2000.

Elliott, Peter. *Homefront: American Flags from Across the United States.* Chicago: University of Chicago Press, 2002.

El-Nawawy, Mohammed, and Adel Iskandar. *Al Jazeera: How the Free Arab News Network Scooped the World and Changed the Middle East.* Westview Press, 2002.

Elsner, Alan. *Gates of Injustice: The Crisis in America's Prisons.* New York: Financial Times/Prentice Hall, 2004.

Enloe, Cynthia. *Bananas, Beaches and Bases: Making Feminist Sense of International Politics.* Berkeley: University of California Press, 1990.

Gardiner, Sam, USAF Col. (ret.). *Truth from These Podia: Summary of a Study of Strategic Influence, Perceptions Management, Strategic Information Warfare, and Strategic Psychological Operations in Gulf II.* http://www.comw.org/warreport/fulltext/0310gardiner.pdf.

Goodson, Larry P. *Afghanistan's Endless War: State Failure, Regional Politics, and the Rise of the Taliban.* Seattle: University of Washington Press, 2001.

Hahn, Stephen. *A Nation under Our Feet: Black Political Struggles in the Rural South from Slavery to the Great Migration.* Cambridge: Belknap Press of Harvard University Press, 2003.

Hardt, Michael, and Antonio Negri. *Empire.* Cambridge: Harvard University Press, 2000.

Ignatieff, Michael. *The Lesser Evil: Political Ethics in an Age of Terror.* Princeton: Princeton University Press, 2004.

———. "The Burden," *New York Times Magazine,* Jan. 5, 2003. 23–25ff.

Iriye, Akira. *Cultural Internationalism and World Order.* Baltimore: Johns Hopkins University Press, 2001.

Jacobson, Matthew Frye. *Barbarian Virtues: The United States Encounters Foreign Peoples at Home and Abroad, 1876–1917.* New York: Hill and Wang, 2000.

Jesperson, Christopher. *American Images of China, 1931–1949.* Stanford: Stanford University Press, 1996.

Kaplan, Amy. *The Anarchy of Empire in the Making of U.S. Culture.* Cambridge: Harvard University Press, 2002.

Kaysen, Carl, John D. Steinbruner, and Martin Malin. "US National Security Policy: In Search of a Balance." In *War with Iraq: Causes, Consequences, and Alternatives.* Cambridge, Mass.: American Academy of Arts and Sciences, 2002. http://www.amacad.org/publications/monographs/War_with_Iraq.pdf.

Kazin, Michael, and Joseph McCartin, eds. *Americanism: Essays on the History of an Ideal.* Chapel Hill: University of North Carolina Press, forthcoming.

Kellner, Douglas. *From 9/11 to Terror War: The Dangers of the Bush Legacy.* Lanham, Md.: Rowman & Littlefield, 2003.

Kensinger, Loretta. "Plugged in Praxis: Critical Reflections on US Feminism, Internet Activism, and Solidarity with Women in Afghanistan." *Journal of International Women's Studies,* 5, no. 1 (November 2003): 1ff.

Kerber, Linda. *Women of the Republic: Intellect and Ideology in Revolutionary America.* Chapel Hill: University of North Carolina Press, 1997.

Khalidi, Rashid. *Resurrecting Empire: Western Footprints and America's Perilous Path in the Middle East.* Boston: Beacon Press, 2004.

Khan, Shahnaz. "Between Here and There: Feminist Solidarity and Afghan Women." *Genders* 23 (2001). http://www.genders.org/g33/g33_kahn.html.

Klein, Christina. *Cold War Orientalism: Asia in the Middlebrow Imagination, 1945–1961.* Berkeley: University of California Press, 2003.

Kull, Steven. "Misperceptions, the Media, and the Iraq War." *The PIPA/ Knowledge Networks Poll* (October 2003). http://www.pipa.org/Online Reports/Iraq/Media_10_02_03_Report.pdf.

Kurtz, Stanley. "The Future of 'History.' " *Policy Review* 113 (June/July 2002). ProQuest Research Library. George Washington University Library.

Layoun, Mary. *Wedded to the Land? Gender, Boundaries, and Nationalism in Crisis.* Durham: Duke University Press, 2000.

Little, Douglas. *American Orientalism: The United States and the Middle East Since 1945*. Chapel Hill: University of North Carolina Press, 2002.

Lloyd, David, and Lisa Lowe, eds. *The Politics of Culture in the Shadow of Capital: Worlds Aligned*. Durham: Duke University Press, 1997.

Mann, James. *Rise of the Vulcans: The History of Bush's War Cabinet*. New York: Viking, 2004.

McClintock, Anne. *Imperial Leather: Race, Gender, and Sexuality in the Colonial Conquest*. New York: Routledge, 1995.

McLane, Brendan. "Reporting from the Sandstorm: An Appraisal of Embedding." *Parameters: US Army War College* 34, no. 1 (spring 2004). Lexis-Nexis Academic Universe.

Meyerowitz, Joanne, ed. *History and September 11*. Philadelphia: Temple University Press, 2002.

Moghadam, Valentine. "Afghan Women and Transnational Feminism." *Middle East Women's Studies Review* 3, no. 4 (fall 2001): 1ff.

Mohanty, Chandra Talpade. *Feminism Without Borders: Decolonizing Theory, Practicing Solidarity*. Durham: Duke University Press, 2003.

Mottahedeh, Roy. "The Clash of Civilizations: An Islamicist's Critique." *Harvard Middle Eastern and Islamic Review* 2 (1996): 1–26.

"News Audiences Increasingly Politicized." Pew Research Center for the People and the Press, June 8, 2004. http://peoplepress.org/reports/display.php3?PageID = 833.

O'Leary, Elizabeth. *To Die For: The Paradox of American Patriotism*. Princeton: Princeton University Press, 1999.

Ottaway, Marina, et al. "Democratic Mirage in the Middle East." Carnegie Endowment for International Peace Policy Brief, #20, October 2002. http://www.ceip.org/files/Publications/Democracy_PB20.asp?from = pubdate.

Pfau, Michael, et al. "Embedding Journalists in Military Combat Units: Impact on Newspaper Story Frames and Tone." *Journalism and Mass Communication Quarterly* 81, no. 1 (spring 2004). Lexis-Nexis Academic Universe.

Rackow, Sharon H. "How the USA Patriot Act Will Permit Governmental Infringement upon the Privacy of Americans in the Name of 'Intelligence' Investigations." *University of Pennsylvania Law Review* 150 (May 2002). Academic Search Premier.

Rashid, Ahmed. *Taliban: Militant Islam, Oil, and Fundamentalism in Central Asia*. New Haven, Conn.: Yale University Press, 2001.

Renda, Mary A. *Taking Haiti: Military Occupation and the Culture of U.S. Imperialism, 1915–1940*. Chapel Hill : University of North Carolina Press, 2001.

Rotter, Andrew John. *Comrades at Odds: The United States and India, 1947–1964*. Ithaca: Cornell University Press, 2000.

Shah, Sonia. "Unveiling the Taleban: Dress Codes Are Not the Issue, New Study Finds." July 10, 2001. ZNet Commentaries. http://www.zmag.org/sustainers/content/2001–07/10shah.htm.

Smith, Bonnie. *Global Feminisms: A Survey of Issues and Controversies.* New York: Routledge, 2000.

Sontag, Susan. *On Photography.* New York: Farrar, Straus, and Giroux, 1977.

Sorkin, Michael. *After the World Trade Center: Rethinking New York City.* New York: Routledge, 2002.

Stoler, Ann Laura. *Carnal Knowledge and Imperial Power: Race and the Intimate in Colonial Rule.* Berkeley: University of California Press, 2002.

Streeby, Shelby. *American Sensations: Class, Empire, and the Production of Popular Culture.* Berkeley: University of California Press, 2002.

Wexler, Laura. *Tender Violence: Domestic Visions in an Age of U.S. Imperialism.* Chapel Hill: University of North Carolina Press, 2000.

Woodward, Bob. *Plan of Attack.* New York: Simon & Schuster, 2004.

Yoshihara, Mari. *Embracing the East: White Women and American Orientalism.* Oxford: Oxford University Press, 2003.

Zizek, Slavoj. *Welcome to the Desert of the Real: Five Essays on September 11 and Related Dates.* New York: Verso, 2002.

Filmography

Aliens. Dir. James Cameron. 20th Century Fox, 1986.

Ben-Hur. Dir. William Wyler. Metro-Goldwyn-Mayer, 1959.

Black Sunday. Dir. John Frankenheimer. Paramount, 1977.

Delta Force. Dir. Menahem Golan. Golan-Globus, 1986.

Die Hard. Dir. John McTiernan. 20th Century Fox, 1988.

Exodus. Dir. Otto Preminger. United Artists, 1960.

Garden of Allah. Dir. Colin Campbell. Selig Polyscope Company, 1916.

Garden of Allah. Dir. Rex Ingram. Metro-Goldwyn-Mayer, 1927.

His Land. Dir. James Collier. Billy Graham Ministries, 1970, and distributed on video by World Wide Pictures, 1983. Library of Congress collection.

Iron Eagle. Dir. Sidney Furie. TriStar Pictures, 1986.

Land of the Pharaohs. Dir. Howard Hawks. Continental Company and Warner Bros., 1955.

The Late, Great Planet Earth. Dir. Robert Amram. Pacific International, 1979.

Navy Seals. Dir. Lewis Teague. Orion Pictures, 1990.

Not without My Daughter. Dir Brian Gilbert. Pathe Entertainment and Ufland, 1991.

Quo Vadis. Dir. Mervyn LeRoy. Metro-Goldwyn-Mayer, 1951.

Raid on Entebbe. Dir. Irvin Kershner. 20th Century Fox Television and NBC, 1977.

The Robe. Dir. Henry Koster. 20th Century Fox, 1953.

Samson and Delilah. Dir. Cecil B. DeMille. Paramount, 1949.

The Sheik. Dir. George Melford. Famous Players–Lasky, 1921.

The Siege. Dir. Edward Zwick. 20th Century Fox, 1998.

The Ten Commandments. Dir. Cecil B. DeMille. Paramount, 1956.

True Lies. Dir. James Cameron. 20th Century Fox, Lightstorm Entertainment, and Universal Pictures, 1994.

Victory at Entebbe. Dir. Marvin J. Chomsky. David L. Wolper Productions and ABC, 1976.

Index